SPEAKING OF RADIO

Jack Benny and Chuck Schaden, September 3, 1970

SPEAKING
OF RADIO

Chuck Schaden's conversations
with the Stars of the
Golden Age of Radio

NOSTALGIA
DIGEST
PRESS

Published by Nostalgia Digest Press
Post Office Box 421
Morton Grove, Illinois 60053
Telephone and Fax (847) 965-7763
www.nostalgiadigest.com

Printed in the United States of America
First printing, October, 2003
Cover design and illustration by Joel Bogart

Library of Congress Control Number 2003094989

ISBN: 0-9743180-0-0

To Ellen
...the wind beneath my wings...

Contents

Alphabetical Listing of Interviews

A Foreword on Looking Back

When I was 10 years old, living in Oklahoma, my father turned our kitchen into a concert hall. Using the dining table as a stage, he built our first radio.

It was just a bunch of wires coiled around what must have been two oatmeal boxes, but it worked. One wire was called a cat whisker. Dad touched this wire to a piece of crystal, moved it around, and music came out through earphones he put in a glass bowl on the table. With the bowl as amplifier, everyone in our kitchen could enjoy the music.

The wire picked up voices, too. There was not much as far as variety of programs went, but this would change.

Little did I think, while we listened to some stranger's voice in our kitchen, that one day my own voice would be heard in homes everywhere.

While most listeners stayed home by their radios, others came out in all sorts of weather to watch *First Nighter,* my signature show with Barbara Luddy, broadcast before a live audience. Barbara wore beautiful formal gowns and I worked in my tux with top hat, gloves and a walking stick inlaid with rhino tusk that belonged to my great-grandfather. We alternated billing for this show: *First Nighter* starring Barbara Luddy and Les Tremayne one week, then *First Nighter* starring Les Tremayne and Barbara Luddy the following week.

There was never a more appreciative audience than the family who gathered in front of their talking furniture and listened to favorite shows. Some, who had no electricity, depended on batteries for their entertainment. People who lived a distance from friends suddenly had new friends who came into their homes at a set time each day to share troubles and solve problems as you listened with sympathy.

Radio enabled people to experience an assortment of exciting events, all within the safety and comfort of their own homes. New ideas were brought into lives as all over the world, many daily activities were regulated by what time a certain show aired.

The sound men, who supplied footsteps, horses galloping, autos starting, doors opening, doors closing, and other miscellaneous background, helped create the setting, but you, the listener, had the ability to make a location and character into whatever you wanted.

A young man who sang as well as spoke in a mature tone helped sell *The Romance of Helen Trent.* He successfully played the part of a 40-year-old architect until the sponsor's representative came to Chicago and discovered their leading man was a 20-year-old actor. "Too young for the part." So I was replaced and went on to other shows.

The people on radio were real to their listeners. When a group of ladies representing a number of women's clubs visited our *Betty and Bob* show, they were shocked to learn Betty and I were not married. "We're just acting," I tried to explain, but they weren't too happy about that. And when our baby on the show, little Bobby, was introduced and turned out to be a young lady, they threatened to boycott the sponsor. That's how *real* radio was to the audience.

I've found that radio audiences never forget you. When Chuck Schaden announced on the air, during his *Those Were The Days* radio program, that I was about to celebrate my 90th birthday, hundreds of cards and letters arrived. I felt so much love in every envelope. Is it any wonder that these people remain special in my memories?

Thanks for those memories and thanks for listening.

– Les Tremayne
1995 Radio Hall of Fame Inductee

Introduction

I grew up listening to radio. I was seven years old and sitting on the living room floor in front of my family's Zenith console radio listening to *The Shadow* when the program was interrupted by a news bulletin about the bombing of Pearl Harbor.

In the years that followed – those glorious *radio years* of the Forties – I raced home after school to listen to *Captain Midnight* and get his daily message to members of the Secret Squadron, which I would quickly translate on my Ovaltine Secret Decoder.

During radio's prime-time 1940s I always listened to *Fibber McGee and Molly,* the *Great Gildersleeve* and *The Aldrich Family.* My Dad and I enjoyed *Mr. District Attorney, Lights Out* and *Truth or Consequences.* My Mother sat on the living room sofa mending socks while we all listened to *First Nighter* (from the "little theater off Times Square), *Kate Smith* and *Our Miss Brooks.*

Even my younger brother Kenny sat still long enough at the end of the decade to laugh with us at the antics of David and Ricky Nelson (to whom we were often compared) on *The Adventures of Ozzie and Harriet.*

And our whole family never missed the great Sunday comedy shows: *Jack Benny, Phil Harris-Alice Faye* and *Charlie McCarthy.* What a line-up!

These and so many other wonderful radio shows brought great pleasure to our lives and, for me, they actually helped *shape* my life.

In 1970, long after the untimely demise of radio due to the onslaught of television, I began hosting a Saturday afternoon program of vintage radio rebroadcasts called *Those Were The Days.* The program began on WLTD, a small daytime station in Evanston, Illinois. Five years later it moved to WNIB, Chicago, where it stayed for 25 years. In 2001, after the sale of WNIB, I switched to WDCB, the public radio station at the College of DuPage in suburban Chicago.

Aside from the pleasure of planning and broadcasting *Those Were The Days,* my greatest joy has been meeting a great many of the stars of the Golden Age of Radio – performers and behind-the-scenes people – who actually created and brought to life all the wonderful programs I listened to on the air as a youngster.

Never in my wildest dreams did I think I would get to sit across from Jack Benny and talk with him about his radio days. But that happened in 1970 when he came to Chicago for a personal appearance and we met backstage for a short visit. I had been on the radio for less than six months and here I was talking with the biggest radio star of them all!

Many other radio personalities visited the Chicago area over the years, some performing at various theatrical venues in the city and suburbs. Because of my broadcast, I was able to meet and talk with a lot of them: Eve Arden, Kate Smith, Alice Faye, Don Wilson, Don Ameche, Mercedes McCambridge and others. These were the people I had heard on my radio in the Forties! And now I was actually holding a microphone between us and we were speaking of radio.

Encouraged by the response of *Those Were The Days* listeners to my interviews, I started taking regular trips to the West Coast to record more conversations with the folks who had entertained us so royally during radio's glory days. On one visit I met Jim Jordan, radio's *Fibber McGee,* in his home, where we had a long chat about his career and he told me how the "hall closet" gag was developed! (Jim and I became friends and we even had the opportunity to work together on a nostalgic seven-part 1974 radio series called *Fibber McGee and the Good Old Days of Radio.*)

On another visit, I actually attended a luncheon meeting of "The Bridge-Is-Up-Club" of former Chicago actors in Southern California. At that one meeting I met Les Tremayne, Bret Morrison and Ed Prentiss – the stars of three of my favorite shows: *First Nighter, The Shadow* and *Captain Midnight.*

Later, my wife Ellen, who shares my appreciation for radio and who is so much a part of all this, accompanied me on these trips. She served as navigator as we drove the freeways in Los Angeles, traveling to meet the radio people in Beverly Hills, Hollywood and other places in and out of the San Fernando Valley. She also operated the tape recorder, kept an eye on the stopwatch and gave me a signal if we were running out of tape. She shared my delight as we sat with broadcasters who welcomed us for conversations about their radio careers.

We visited Arch Oboler, who talked about his *Lights Out* mysteries in his comfortably-cluttered home in Studio City, filled with small and large ceramic likenesses of hippos. We rang the doorbell at the Mandeville Canyon home of Dennis Day, who answered the door himself and led us through his antique-filled house to a cozy den, where he regaled us with stories about Jack Benny.

One warm summer day we drove to Palm Springs to talk with Mary Lee Robb (Marjorie on *The Great Gildersleeve*) in her beautiful Palm Desert home. It was a double-header trip for us, because that same day I also talked with Phil Harris in his nearby country club hideaway.

Harriet Nelson recalled her career for us as we viewed the Pacific Ocean through the picture window in her living room and gave us her son David's phone number so we could arrange to chat with him, too.

Many of the people I spoke with seemed pleased and eager to help me find other radio stars to interview. Les Tremayne generously found many interview subjects for me through his membership in the Pacific Pioneer Broadcasters. After talking with Howard Duff on the deck of his Malibu Beach house, he got out his address book and gave me the telephone numbers of Lurene Tuttle (his co-star on *Sam Spade*) and his Armed Forces Radio pal Elliott Lewis. This enabled me to set up a conversation with Lurene in her West Hollywood apartment and to visit Elliott in his office on the Paramount Pictures lot. *On the Paramount Pictures lot!* "I'll leave your name at the gate," he said. This was a particular thrill for Ellen and me. We drove up to that legendary Paramount gate, told the guard our name and waited for a few seconds while he checked his list. "Yes, Mr. Schaden, Mr. Lewis is expecting you. Just drive straight ahead and park anywhere there's a space. He's in the Cecil B. DeMille Building. Go right up." Wow! What a special day!

Truth be told, every day that included meeting and talking with someone from the Golden Age of Radio was a very special day for me. The "radio folk," as Jim Jordan called his broadcast colleagues, were friendly and cordial as we chatted about their "good old days." They were generous with their time and seemed flattered to learn that people were still interested in the work they had done on the air so many years ago. Often, at the conclusion of our time together, I had a chance to tell these people – whom I admired so much – what their work meant to me and all of their fans and how much we appreciated their contribution to the radio days. Just about every one of them expressed appreciation for that thought and added that those days were the best of times.

It's been a pleasure to put *Speaking of Radio* together for you, and I hope you'll enjoy these conversations with the stars of the Golden Age of Radio.

– *Chuck Schaden*

Acknowledgments

It should be noted, of course, that this book is the result of the collaboration of friends, so many good friends, who helped this project from start to finish.

First of all, the taped interviews had to be transcribed to paper and that's not an easy task. Repeated listening was required in order to "translate" spoken words that ran together. For the printed page, unfinished thoughts that were not actually spoken but implied had to be completed – few of us speak in complete sentences when we're simply reminiscing (*especially* when we're reminiscing) and recalling events from times past. Rising to the task, however, were Rosemary and Wally Cwik, Kathy Garofalo, Janet Hoshaw, Gardner Kissack, Koni Shaughnessy and Larry Youngberg, each of whom spent countless hours at tape recorder and type-writer (and computer) doing an outstanding job.

Ken Alexander read every transcribed word and checked for proper punctuation, seldom evident in spoken conversation, but so necessary to the printed page. He was tireless in the effort to preserve the actual words and personality of the interviewees. The goal was to let the reader "hear" the subject speaking of radio while reading his words, and Ken helped considerably. A stickler for style, he also provided needed input in the selection of the book's settled-upon editorial format. His help has been invaluable.

Nowhere in the pages of history could I have found a better collaborator than Ellen Schaden, who has been a part of this project since before either of us knew it was going to be a project. Her support and encouragement of my interest in old time radio began, I think, with the first reels of tape that came to our apartment during the early years of our marriage and continue to this day. She didn't know what she was getting into, but she has been such a huge part of everything that it is absolutely true that I could not have done it without her. For this book (and our *Nostalgia Digest* magazine) her suggestions, advice and computer skills have been monumental and substantial. We worked together on the book's graphic design and her input and common sense have guided us throughout the experience. She is the perfect mate and helpmate.

Jim Randstrom has been the perfect computer consultant. When we have tried everything to restore frozen or unreadable files, Jim has come to the rescue time and again and saved us from disasters of titanic proportions. And though he's occasionally spent long hours in our office at our computer, he has often saved our day with simple (to him) instructions over the telephone. Without Jim this book might be handwritten on parchment.

I'd like to express thanks to John Dunning, whose *On The Air Encyclopedia of Old-Time Radio* (Oxford University Press) helped us to verify and clarify certain statements and dates mentioned throughout the book. Thanks also go to Thomas A. DeLong, author of *Radio Stars, An Illustrated Biographical Dictionary of 953 Performers, 1920 through 1960* (McFarland) and to Jay Hickerson, whose *Necrology of Radio Personalities* compilation provided additional confirmation of various dates used throughout this book.

Most of the photographs in *Speaking of Radio* are from the *Nostalgia Digest* collection, but we are grateful to Photofest of New York for providing additional photos, which are identified throughout the book. Don Pointer took the photo on the back cover.

Joel Bogart created the cover design and illustration. His many talents have been intertwined with old-time radio for more than a quarter-century and his work here gives this book a good beginning.

Towards the end of the editorial process, I asked a few people to give the completed manuscript one last read-through. That task was accepted by Ken Alexander (again searching, searching for grammatical boo-boos, style violations and typographical errors), Karl Pearson, Rev. Kevin Shanley and Koni Shaughnessy. This proved to be a good idea and their last-minute corrections and comments were most helpful.

Finally, I would like to thank all the radio personalities who spoke with us.

You will never be forgotten.

– C. S.

Jim Jordan

 Jim Jordan starred as Fibber McGee on radio for some 25 years during the Golden Age of Broadcasting. We met on July 3, 1973 at his home on Tower Road in Beverly Hills, California. I remarked that he came from Peoria, Illinois, and asked if that was where he met Marian Driscoll, who became his wife and co-star on the **Fibber McGee and Molly** *program.*

We met in Peoria and we were married there in 1918. I started in the business in 1917, in vaudeville, and I went to Chicago to start. Then I came home to wait for the draft, in April of 1918. We were married in August, because the head of the draft board lived next door and he told us that the war was winding down and I wouldn't be called. So we got married on August 31st and we went to St. Louis and spent a little honeymoon with a sister who lived there. We were there about five days when I got the summons. Uncle Sam needed me then, so I went right into the service.

I went to France. I was in France inside of about six weeks. The war did end then, on November 11th. I had been in a hospital with dysentery. We started a show there, an Army show, and I worked in the show about five months. We came home in July.

Did you and Marian first work together after you came out of the service?

We worked together, yes, but I stayed out of [show] business for about a year after that, trying to do other things in Peoria. I did something new about every month. I worked at all kinds of jobs. We got going again, in the business, in about 1921. We went to Chicago, and this is where we formed the little concert company that we had for about three years after that – before radio came along to us.

What was your first radio job?

Well, in those days, you didn't speak of it as a radio *job,* because radio didn't pay anybody any money. All you did was go in and perform. You could walk in off the street, into any radio station, and they were glad to have you. If you had a ukulele under your arm, you could go to work. For nothing. We finally got a little job on a station called WIBO on the north side of Chicago, on Broadway near Devon. We got paid there. We did a show once a week on Friday night for which we were paid $10. That was our first pay.

Did you write the show yourselves? What was the nature of it?

Nobody talked except the announcer. We sang. We sang together. We did duets. That's what we did in vaudeville, too. After we fooled around with WIBO for quite a while, and other stations, we also worked for a song publisher. We got $35 a week from a publisher for going around to all the stations in town plugging their songs. But the whole thing added up to about $75 a week less than what we needed to live! So, by the end of a year of this, we had to go back in vaudeville again.

We went back in about 1926, I guess it was, and we worked for about a year. We were playing a theater in Danville, Illinois, at Hallowe'en time in 1927, and we were on the bill with Tim and Irene Ryan. Tim said if we would go to New York, he would get us the Lowe [Vaudeville] Time, which would be a good year's work in vaudeville in those days. It would keep you going for about a year, a great thing if we could do it! So we made a deal to meet him in New York on a certain date. When we got back to Chicago, we went to dinner one night at a restaurant called Brentano's – I think it was on South Wabash Avenue near Jackson. There we ran into a fellow, Howard Newmiller, who was a pianist. He was from Peoria and he'd been with the Oriole Terrace Orchestra – Ted Fio Rito and Danny Russo – and he had gone to work for a radio station called WENR. He said "If you'll come over there, I think I can get you a job there." So we went over the next day and got a job, and that's where we stayed in radio. That was in October in 1927, and from that day until Marian's illness in 1960 we were on the radio constantly – always.

That was your first job?

That was our first real, professional radio job, you might say. They were going to use us three days a week at the radio station. We made a deal with Western Vaudeville where they would use us one day, or two, or three, around Chicago. We could bill ourselves as "radio stars," you see, which increased your value a lot, even then. So that's what we did. That's how we started.

What was The Smith Family?

They had a kind of a stock company group working at this radio station. Everybody sort of doubled. And the station organized this family radio show. It was a "talk" show – we were beginning to talk a little by that time, very little. So we did the show. It was formed out of all the people working at the station. There were about seven or eight of us in it, and that's where *The Smith Family* started. I think it started about 1928; I'm not sure of the date. It might have been a little earlier than that.*

The Smith Family became a very hot item. It was a very popular show, because it was one of the first "talk" of that type. *Amos 'n' Andy* had been on before that, as *Sam 'n' Henry,* but there wasn't very much of that type of talking being done on radio in those days.

Was The Smith Family *a situation kind of a thing?*

Oh, yes! It was a very funny situation. It was about a contractor and his wife, named Smith. It was an Irish-type family, and he had become influential; he made some money. He had a wife and two daughters. One daughter went with a Jewish violinist and the other one went with an Irish prizefighter. I was the Irish prizefighter and Marian was the Irish mother, the wife of Smith. Her name was Nora Smith. That was the deal, and it made for a lot of nice comedy. It was real good.

In 1931, WENR was sold to NBC. We didn't want to go to NBC, because we were playing theaters, and by this time we were making six, seven, eight hundred dollars a week. We could go play theaters on the weekend. One night would pay you well [because of] what *The Smith Family* had done for us, principally, and what we were doing for ourselves. We kept doing other shows at the same time. We did a little show called *Luke and Mirandy.* And Luke was, well, he was Fibber McGee, really.

He was?

Fibber McGee was Luke. It's the same Luke that was later in the *Smackout.* Same guy. Luke eventually became McGee.

Mirandy was Molly?

Yes.

The Smith Family *was just a couple times a week?*

Once a week. It was a half-hour show.

Now, Smackout –

---

* According to radio historians Tom Price and John Dunning, *The Smith Family* was broadcast June 9, 1929-April 3, 1932.

That was a daily program.

And in it, you were the proprietor of a –

– grocery store. At a little crossroads. There was nothing there except the store. This old guy ran the store. Marian and Jim Jordan were his friends and they had a lot of other friends. We had 10 or 11 people in the cast. We did all of them.

You did all of the characters?

Oh, yeah, nobody else – we did everything! I produced the show, directed it, performed in it, the whole works! Nobody in the studio but an announcer.

What was the significance of the name, Smackout?

Among other things we were doin' on WENR, we worked on a farm program with a man named Farmer Rusk, who did farm advisory work via radio. They put us on there to entertain a little bit through this, you know, sing some songs. And he had been at the University of Missouri, and a few miles out of Columbia, Missouri, there was a little crossroads. This old guy had a store and the students of the University somehow or another went into this place and they'd say, "I'm looking for a hoe handle," or something, and he'd say "I'm sorry, I'm just smack outa hoe handles. I'll have one here for you tomorrow." He did this so much that the kids hung a sign out in front of the store reading "Smackout." That's where we picked up the name, *Smackout.*

When did you meet Don Quinn?

While we were at WENR, in 1929 or 1930. In *The Smith Family* there was [an actress] named Thora Martins. She was the daughter who was in love with the prizefighter, who was me. Thora Martins had been in *The Student Prince* and her girlfriend dated Don Quinn and she brought him over to the station and introduced him to us.

Had he been doing some writing for The Smith Family?

No, he hadn't written anything in radio. He was a commercial artist. It was 1930, after the crash, and he went *kaplop*, with the agency that he had. This was a very clever artist. He wanted to write, and so he started writing stuff for us, and it just evolved from there.

Where did you use the things he wrote?

We didn't use them! He wrote, and we didn't have the opportunity to use them. We were doing this *Luke and Mirandy* at WENR and, in 1931, WENR was sold to NBC. We didn't want to go on NBC because of the theater thing, and they would not allow us to announce the date. They wouldn't allow us to come on the radio at 5:00 in the evening, or 6:00, and say that we were going to be in Barrington at the theater tonight at eight. NBC wouldn't allow that kind of business, so we didn't want to go there. We went to the Chicago Daily News, WMAQ.

During the switch, this is when we said we would have Don write the show, and we had this name *Smackout* in the back of our mind to use, 'cause we never did use it at WENR. We used it when we went over and started at WMAQ. That's when he started writing for us.

Amos 'n' Andy wrote their own material, and they were on WMAQ, a Columbia station. They were broadcasting on a Columbia station over WMAQ in the Chicago area, and over the rest of the country NBC was picking it up. That was a kind of a novel deal, too. But they wrote their own material. When we went to WMAQ we said we'd have to have a writer, and we wanted to bring in Don Quinn. But they had the feeling that if you didn't write it yourself, you didn't deserve to do it.

They were spoiled with Freeman Gosden and Charles Correll!

That's right. They ruined the whole thing! So we let a fellow there write it for a while, but he had a lot of other jobs to do. He couldn't go on writing it, so we said we'd just take it over ourselves. We just didn't tell anybody where the material was coming from; we just provided it. We were there about six months when WMAQ was sold to NBC. We were stuck then; we had to go. We went with NBC at that time, and that was in 1931. We did *Smackout* until after we started *Fibber McGee and Molly,* in 1935.

You were still doing Smackout *when* Fibber McGee *started?*

Right.

At that time, when NBC took over WMAQ from the Daily News, that was the end of your vaudeville days, right?

That's right. We couldn't play dates, because you just couldn't go out and play a date without people knowing. The tie-in was to announce it on the air and then go do it.

Which theaters were you playing in the Chicago area?

We played mostly in the rural areas, because that's where radio had its pull. Prior to that we'd been on Western Vaudeville, and played some theaters in Chicago. I don't know what they were. Small-time theaters, Western three-a-day theaters.

When you first started Fibber McGee and Molly, *and you were still doing*

Smackout, weren't you involved a little bit with Kaltenmeyer's Kindergarten?

We were also doing *Kaltenmeyer's Kindergarten* at WENR. We couldn't do the *Smith Family* any more, because it was broken up. There was a fellow named Bruce Kamman, who had this *Kaltenmeyer's* show, and NBC put us in there. We did that show for a while. That was once a week on a Saturday. That was a good radio show, too, a half-hour show.

You were Mickey Donovan, and Marian was Gertie Glump.

That's right.

Were those similar to Fibber McGee and Molly *characters, or were they totally different?*

No, Mickey Donovan was *The Smith Family* prizefighter; a tough little kid. And Giggling Gertie, that was kind of part of Teeny, which Marian had done; that's what that was.

A great many people fondly remember Kaltenmeyer's Kindergarten.

It was a great radio show. And that again was done by people who did other things on the show. Bruce Kamman was a producer and a director. He was also a musician, by the way, a trumpet player. We had a Jewish kid – I can't remember his name – he was done by Johnny Wolff, who was a fine trumpet player. The Italian kid was Don Mangano, who was a clarinet player. Marian was, of course, a musician. There were some others who were not musicians, but the principal people in the thing were people who were doing other things. They were musicians. Yes, it was a great show, written by the fellow who had written *Luke and Mirandy* for us, and he wrote *The Smith Family*, too. His name was Harry Lawrence. He wrote *Kaltenmeyer's Kindergarten.*

When were the names Fibber McGee and Molly *first used?*

Well, when we did *The Smith Family,* and Marian was Nora Smith, she used the same voice that later became Molly. All you had on radio was the voice, you see, and we said we would not use that voice ever again until the right thing came along. Now, we did *Smackout*, we did *Kaltenmeyer's,* and we did all these things, but we never used that voice. We kept it away. We said when the right opportunity comes, we'll use it. And we also had the name: Molly. We said, we will call her Molly when we do it. And the opportunity came in 1935 when we had the opportunity to do an audition for the Johnson Company. They had never heard Molly McGee, but they had heard Nora Smith, and they had heard Luke Gray.

Is that how the audition came about, because they had heard Luke and Nora?

Yes. They had heard us, not Nora, on *Smackout*. That was on every day. Henrietta Johnson – who was Mrs. Jack Louis, and her maiden name was Johnson of the Johnson Company – had been listening to us at home all this time for months. She finally got her husband to listen, and he had the agency with the Johnson account. That's how it came about.

And they obviously liked the audition.

Yes, they did, and they wanted us. They had had other shows on NBC, but they didn't want NBC to know that they wanted us. We didn't know this either, till a long time later [when] they told us. They just wanted to have NBC present some things to them, because if they went to NBC and said that they wanted us, that would have been one deal, but if NBC sold it to them, that would be another type of a deal. You understand what I mean?

Dollars and cents were involved!

Sure! So they went to NBC and said "We want to listen to some shows." They listened to about 20 shows, but they never heard us. NBC never presented us. They didn't picture us as doing a half-hour evening show. We were daytime radio, 15-minute show. They didn't realize that we were doing a half-hour show, in fact two, on NBC at that time. Not that we were doing all of it. We were not only on *Kaltenmeyer's Kindergarten*; we were also on a show called *Saturday Night Jamboree*. They never did hear us, so finally we put an audition together and we went over to the McClurg Building. We didn't say anything to NBC about it at all, and neither did the Johnson Company. And we went over, and did the audition, and they virtually bought it right there, right then. It wasn't *Fibber McGee*, it was Marian and Jim Jordan. After they agreed that we would get together and make some kind of a deal, we went back and told NBC.

And NBC said, "Why didn't we know about this?"

Well, they had their chance, but they didn't think about us in that light.

What happened after this? You put a "Marian and Jim Jordan" show together –

– yes, then we sold it! They bought it. It was in the fall of 1934. In the process of getting it all together, and taking our time, 'cause it was going to go on in April, we had meetings with the Johnson Company [about] how we will do this, and what we will do, all down the line. And one time, in one of these meetings – of course Don was writing our stuff then – Jack Louis, who was head of the agency and Henrietta Johnson's husband, said "It's too bad [we can't use] Luke Gray," who was on *Smackout*. He was an awful liar, that's what he was. He told tall tales. He was in every war that was ever fought. And he told these stories to this little girl who would come into the grocery store. We kind of followed through into this new show with that. And one day, at one of those meetings, Jack Louis said, "You know, it would be kind of nice if we had a name that reflected this character." We had debated whether to use our own name or to put another name handle on the people that were going to do this show. "It would be nice if we had a name that was kind of significant of a liar," which he was. And so nobody said anything.

The next meeting we had, which was the next day or the day after, we all walked into the agency office, and sat down at the desk. Don Quinn walked in and he had a little slip of paper about six inches long and an inch wide. He had been an artist, so he had just printed on there, "FIBBER McGEE." He just passed it around and that was it.

Everybody bought that right off the bat?

Sure! Then we tacked on the name Molly, which we had had in our mind all this time. That's how it was born.

Molly had a rather thick Irish brogue in some of the early programs, as compared with the shows from the middle Forties and early Fifties.

Might have changed a little bit.

A softening of the Irish brogue?

I think maybe so. She started out doing Molly McGee much like she had done Nora Smith. I don't know, though, even in the end, when she'd really get mad, you see, she'd go back into this real broad Irish.

The character of Molly McGee on the radio program was one who loved and respected Fibber, but she kind of knew Fibber's shortcomings and had to kind of tap him on the wrist every once in a while.

That's right. She was much more lovable than Nora Smith had been. Nora Smith had been the Irish mother.

Fibber was a little harsh in the beginning, wasn't he?

Well, we found, doing *Fibber McGee and Molly,* that he could tell a lie on *Smackout* that would last 15 minutes. The whole thing would be one lie. I have some of the scripts back there; you should read some of them. They're precious, even now. But we didn't have time to do that on *Fibber McGee and Molly.* We had to move faster, you see, so that's why we changed that around a little. When we were doing 10 or 12 voices, you had nothing but the voice to go on, and you did a great deal of making your character by the level of your voice, by the pitch.

In the original Fibber McGee and Molly *programs for Johnson's Wax you did a great many voices, the two of you, didn't you?*

I didn't do any. Marian did more. The only one I did, I think, was Mort Toops.

Mort Toops was Willie Toops' father! Didn't you play Uncle Dennis at one time?

No, no. There never was an Uncle Dennis. He was an offstage character that was never heard. He was just somebody that we talked about. It was great as long as we did that. Many years later, we decided to bring him on, to do him. And that ended it. The appeal of it was gone. We dropped it after that.

That would be like introducing Sweetie Face, eh? Wallace Wimple's wife?

Yes. You'd spoil it if you had her on. You wouldn't think of having her on. That's what Uncle Dennis was. There would only be two or three lines' mention of him, and it was always very funny, because everybody knew that he was a drunk and a bum, and so that made it easy. We'd be doing the show, and all of a sudden there'd be a terrible rumble of footsteps, and you could hear him going up the steps, you know, and falling back, and we'd just wait until it was all done and there'd be a door slam and we'd say, "Uncle Dennis is home early tonight."

Was 79 Wistful Vista the address of Fibber McGee and Molly *right from the very beginning?*

No, not at the beginning. We didn't have an address and we didn't have a house in the beginning. We started selling a wax product called CarNu, and we traveled around in a car for about a year.

What kind of a car was it?

Oh, a broken-down jalopy. We'd drive into filling stations, and that would lead into the CarNu commercial. We made a deal with them in the beginning. We said we didn't care what money we got, we didn't care. We only cared for one thing: they leave us on for 26 weeks, don't stop us after 13. Which they did. They told us afterwards if they hadn't promised that, they probably would have dropped us after the first 13 weeks, because it was summertime to begin with, so we didn't bother them very much! When they decided to renew us after the 26 weeks, they decided to put us into a house, to make our home the crux of the whole thing. So, how will we get this house? Fibber didn't have any money. Somebody conceived the idea of our entering a raffle of a real estate subdivision. We won it. We won the house in a raffle, that's how we got it. The name of the town that was having this raffle, this place was called "Wistful Vista." "Wistful" is sad, "vista" is view, so Wistful Vista was the place that had a sad view. That's what it was. That's where Wistful Vista came from, and then we named our house the same as the town, 79 Wistful Vista.

And that's where so many of the citizens of Wistful Vista came to visit you each Tuesday night. Were you on Tuesdays in the very beginning?

No, we were on Monday in the very beginning. And we later switched to Tuesday.

You stayed on Tuesday night for the whole span of half-hour shows.

Oh, yes. That's right. Well, we started on Tuesday – I don't know when we moved – I think we started on Tuesday night and moved to Monday to get away from *Burns and Allen,* because we were opposite them. We didn't figure that was good for us. We moved to Monday night, and then *Lux* came in there, so we moved back to Tuesday.

So Burns and Allen *was easier competition than* The Lux Radio Theatre?

Well, we weren't opposite them after that. We followed each other, I think.

In the beginning you didn't have a doorbell at your house, at 79 Wistful Vista. You used to have people just –

– knock on the door. We got a doorbell put in, finally.

There were some great characters on the show, and most of them were played by Bill Thompson! How did he get involved with your program? Was he an actor in Chicago?

Yes, he was just starting, and he had done a few things on NBC and we'd heard about him. We auditioned him and put him on the show. All these people that later became running characters on the show started on the show just doing one thing one night. They were just radio actors that were – we didn't just make a deal with somebody to hire them for a year. We'd hire them to do a character, and if it went well, we'd have them do another week, and then later make them a permanent fixture if they had the time to do it.

Bill Thompson did Wallace Wimple and Horatio K. Boomer, who was kind of a W. C. Fields character.

Yes, he was.

Why did he stop doing that after a while? Was there any special reason, or was it that the character was not well-received by the audience? Because he kept some of the other characters, but not Boomer. Nick Depopoulous, too –

Well, he dropped that, too. You see, the time came when you didn't do the Greek or the Jew or the Swede or the black or the white. It had to go.

So those characters were victims of the ethnic picture.

That's right.

Bill Thompson was not the first man to play the Old Timer.

Cliff Arquette did the Old Timer. There was another guy did the Old Timer before Cliff Arquette.

Oh, really?

Um-hmm.

Do you remember the name?

Yeah. Jim Jordan.

Jim Jord– oh, you were the first Old Timer!

Yeah, that's right! I didn't do the same voice that those fellows did. They didn't take the voice, but the character was pretty much Luke Gray, you know. As much Luke Gray as McGee was, probably a little more. But his voice was the same. I'd pitch him way up, you know, cause he was a little bit older. As I say, we had to use voice levels to create those different characters. I didn't do it very much on the show, and when Bill did it, why, we made it a fixture.

Harold Peary was involved –

I can't think of all the things that Hal did before he did Gildersleeve. I think he did Gildersleeve pretty soon after he started doing the show.

You moved to Hollywood, to California, for the broadcasts in 1939.

That's correct. We came in '37, we worked here for 10 weeks and we made a picture for Paramount, and we went back to Chicago until '39.

It was called This Way, Please, *from 1937.* Heavenly Days *was based on a catch-saying of Molly's.*

That's right. The others, *Look Who's Laughing* and *Here We Go Again,* we made those with Edgar Bergen and Charlie McCarthy. *Heavenly Days* we did alone; that was the last picture we made. We did some shorts and so on.

You brought in Gale Gordon as Mayor La Trivia and Arthur Q. Bryan as Doc Gamble after Hal Peary as Gildersleeve left Fibber McGee and Molly *to go on to his own show,* The Great Gildersleeve.

Well, I recall this very well, because this show, that I'm going to tell about, to me, was the funniest damn radio show I ever heard. I don't know whether anybody else would think so or not. But Molly had an old boyfriend, named Otis Cadwallader. Did you ever hear that name?

Oh, sure.

Well, that's Gale Gordon. He came to Wistful Vista to visit and we had him for dinner. We had nothing, and I went to Gildersleeve, who lived next door. He was always involved with us at this time. We wanted to impress this guy. I didn't want him to know that I didn't have anything. So Gildersleeve and I talked and I asked him if he would be our butler for the night and he said he would. So he put on his tuxedo and he came over and acted as our butler. And when he was standing behind the dining room table – I'll never forget this – McGee, to show you what a rat he really was, couldn't resist telling Cadwallader what a rat he had living next door.

In front of Gildersleeve!

And Gildersleeve just stood there. He didn't say a word. But to me, that was a very funny picture, a very funny scene.

And that, of course, is from the radio show, and you can picture it! You could always picture these things, because that's what radio is.

You betcha. This is something that's very important. We learned that a long time ago with *The Smith Family.* You painted a picture, just the same as if you were doing a motion picture, or doing it on the stage for people to see. You painted that picture so that people could see what they were laughing at. That was the trick. We had an expression that we used, "I don't get the picture." If you don't make a picture, you're not going anywhere. This is the way we thought about it, anyway. That was a funny picture. I'll never forget a line in that show. I don't know why I remember this show so well. It was just, to me, it was just the best *Fibber McGee.* I remember another line in there. Molly said, "Shall we have coffee in the library?" after we got finished, and McGee says, "It's too late, they close at 7:00." That was a funny show.* But there Hal Peary and Gale Gordon

---

* Original broadcast date December 26, 1939.

were in that show together. So he was on doing other things before Hal left.

Hal was on his own for the Gildersleeve *program, and there was another person there who went on to his own show: Marlin Hurt, as Beulah. Beulah was your maid in the story for a while.*

That's right. He was great, too.

Marlin Hurt was a white man playing a black woman.

Yes. He worked in a trio, a singing trio, for years, called Tom, Dick and Harry. He was a wonderful guy. He had the ability to do this black woman, who was just very funny.

Molly did a number of characters on the program. She was Teeny, or Sis.

That's right, yeah. McGee always called Teeny "Sis." She was the same little girl.

Molly would go up the stairs – I can picture McGee's living room today – and McGee would be downstairs, and the doorbell would ring, and "Hi, mister!"

Usually, that way. Sometimes they'd be on together, but that was more work, and didn't mean that much. Still, we would often have them on together.

Teeny used to talk about Willie Toops and the bicycle that he had. Marian also played Mrs. Wearybottom.

Now, that was Mirandy, from *Luke and Mirandy.* 'Course, all the characters that we ever did – I think this applies to most performers – they take them from live people that they know. That's where Mirandy came from.

There was a character in Chicago who didn't make the trip to Hollywood with you. He was played by Hugh Studebaker.

Silly Watson. He was a butler for McGee. He never got any money; McGee never paid him anything. It was a little bit incongruous. There was a lot of fantasy about *Fibber McGee and Molly* all the way down the line! He was wonderful, he was great!

McGee never had a visible means of support yet he had a butler and a maid, and the butler was never paid, and the maid didn't last, and he always had some kind of get-rich-quick scheme.

That's right! [And] there was only one thing downtown in Wistful Vista.

That was 14th and Oak. Everything happened on the corner of 14th and Oak. The railroad station was there, the post office was there, a great big high rise building was there. Anything that we wanted: the park, City Hall, it was always on the corner of 14th and Oak. That was a pretty crowded place! Well, that's fantasy, you see.

And everything happened around a little light theme. The genius behind that, of course, was Don Quinn.

That's right. All the story lines came out of a meeting. Not that Don didn't bring them in, but we would hash them over. Sometimes other people would bring in an idea that would become a story. We always had a couple of them ahead, more or less. He would develop them. It seems to me people are beginning to realize what a great writer he was. I was over at Walt Disney Studios yesterday, talking with some people, and one of these fellows said to me, "Don Quinn. He was one of the great writers, wasn't he?" We hear that now more than we did 20 years ago, which is as it should be. Several times we would give up on a show on Monday noon. It's all on paper, ready to go and it wasn't just coming off. I can remember him saying, "Well, I'll start here, and I'll take it home and re-write it tonight." Monday night! And we'd do it Tuesday. We had a lot of things that were pat that we could do, that would take time. Sure-fire, like the closet, and this, and that, and the other thing. But very few writers can do that.

What about that closet, as long as you brought it up?

That also came from *The Smith Family.*

It did? The full closet, with all the –

No. In *The Smith Family*, as I told you, these people became affluent. They got dough. And they had a davenport. They were "lace curtain Irish" people but they had a davenport. And this davenport had a spring in one certain seat that would squeal when you sat on it. If you wanted to embarrass anybody, you'd say, "Sit here." They called it the horsehair sofa, which were in vogue years ago. That became the Smith family's horsehair sofa, and when anybody would say, "Sit here," the audience would know what's coming, and they'd laugh.

When we started the *McGee* show, we said we'd find something like that. We called it a running gag, a gag that you could throw in anyplace. We tried several things. I remember one was a shade that flew up, and that was no good. We tried other things, and we kind of gave up on it. In one show, to show how slovenly these people were, McGee went to the closet and opened it up, and it was so full, it had so much stuff in it, that it couldn't hold it and it all fell out. And we said, well, gee, let's try that again. That's where it came from. That's where the closet came from. But the idea for that sort of thing came from the sofa way back on *The Smith Family.*

I'm glad we asked!

Many of the ideas that we had for that sort of thing came from the theatre. When we were young and doing things on radio, we would think of something we had seen when we were kids on the vaudeville stage to bring in. That's show biz!

Show biz helped the commercials on their way for Johnson's Wax. Was it Don Quinn's idea to get the commercial integrated into the show?

Yes. This was Don's forte. You bet! I think we were the first ones to do that. I think that was the thing that made the show as much as anything.

Was it the custom of the time to have two breaks in the show? You had Billy Mills and the orchestra, and the King's Men, each with a spot in there. At one time it was Donald Novis and even Ted Weems and the orchestra in there for a while. Was it just to break the action? To add variety?

That's right. There was a lot of discussion. Oh, I know lots of people thought that we didn't need an orchestra, that we shouldn't use it, but we thought we should. It gave it a tempo, it made it important in the beginning, to have the orchestra, we thought. I'm sure we were right.

There were some great shows, over the years. We lost Molly in 1961, and then there were no more new Fibber and Molly *performances on the radio.*

No. There couldn't be.

The sounds from 79 Wistful Vista have continued to create pictures in our memories. I can't tell you what a thrill it's been for me to have this chance to chat with you. I'd like to say thanks to you and to Marian, too, for providing the best there was – the best there is – on good old radio.

Thanks. That's nice to hear.

Jim Jordan was born November 16, 1896 and was 76 at the time of our conversation. He died April 1, 1988 at the age of 91.

Phil Leslie

Phil Leslie spent a great many years writing scripts for **Fibber McGee and Molly** *and other radio and television shows. On December 13, 1973 we met at a recording studio in Hollywood, California, to chat about his long and successful career. I asked him when he started writing for the McGee show.*

 Ninteen forty-three, Chuck, and wrote until 1956.

That was when Fibber McGee and Molly *went off the air.*

Yes. Actually, I worked with Don Quinn, of course, through those early years, and we did the half-hour show until 1954, I believe. Then we went to a quarter-hour, five times a week until 1956, which is when we finally went off the air.

And then Fibber and Molly *were heard on* Monitor *on NBC?*

Yes, *Monitor*. I didn't write for them on *Monitor*. At that point it was time for me to get into television. The fun was all gone out of radio, and most of the money, for the writers, anyhow.

If you were writing Fibber McGee and Molly *for radio in the Fifties, you were probably one of the last original radio writers.*

I stayed in there just as long as I could, Chuck. I didn't want to leave radio because it was a lot of fun, and I wasn't eager to get into television because it didn't look like it was going to be as much fun. As a writer, I was particularly fortunate on the *Fibber* show, because we had a thing there, with Don Quinn as the writer who had founded the show with Marian and Jim back in the middle Thirties. And then when I joined Don in '43, I kind of fell heir to the same respect from the actors, and so forth. We had a thing there where there was a minimum of interference with the script from anybody. The writers wrote it, Marian and Jim read it, and that was largely it. And I knew that when I went into television, everybody [would have] had their hand in it, because it was that much bigger. There were cameramen and lights, and film editors and so forth. And I was right. Television was never quite as much fun for me as radio was.

What was your first writing job in radio?

My first writing assignment, that brought me from St. Louis, Missouri, out to Hollywood, was with *Al Pearce and His Gang*. It was 1939, and it was pretty exciting stuff. I was married, had three little kids, was working as a theater manager – assistant manager – in theaters, and as a bookkeeper in the theater office. I was putting in a pretty good schedule at 40 hours a week on one job, 40 hours a week on the other, trying to support the wife and the kids. I had a chance to try some jokes for Al Pearce. I did and Pearce sent me a wire from New York, where he had gone for a four-week rest. He offered me a chance to join the show there, and said that if he thought I could cut it, he'd bring me to the Coast with him. So that's what happened. I got out here and got my family out here. Then Al Pearce went off the air shortly thereafter, and there was quite a little dry spell.

You were without a job?

I went to work at Lockheed [Aircraft] as a timekeeper. This was in late 1939 and early '40, and I left Lockheed in '41, just to get more chance to write, to get a job where I'd have more time for writing. Finally, running around and ringing doorbells and calling on ad agencies and so forth, [I] eventually got a crack at writing with Don Quinn for *Fibber McGee and Molly*. That was in March of 1943.

From the time you were bumped off the Al Pearce show, when Pearce was bumped, you were just trying to do whatever you could do?

It was a dull time. I managed to sell one story for a short two-reel comedy to Columbia Pictures. I got $150 for it, brought it home in cash and spread it all over the dining room table. That was a very exciting moment, because I probably hadn't made $150 in the preceding two or three months.

What was that two-reel comedy?

I remember the title. It was a bowling story called *For Whom the Belles Bowl*, which was the way they named those two-reelers in those days. They took up a well-known title and switched it around and I've forgotten who played in it.

Nobody much. I couldn't write the screenplay. I didn't know enough about it to be allowed to do that. I got $150 for the story, and that was big stuff!

You started with Fibber McGee and Molly *after the show had been on the air for...*

Seven years, at least. Seven or eight years.*

Don Quinn created that show, and he was the sole writer on it up to that time.

No. Don had been the sole writer for much of the time, but in the previous couple of years, before I came with him, he had had assistants. The show came out here in 1939, out here on the Coast. It had been in Chicago before that. Don had had a couple of assistants. One of them had gone into the Army, in about '43 I guess, and Don was looking for somebody else, and that was when fortune fell in my lap. But in Chicago, Paul Henning had written with Don on the show for not too long a time, for a season maybe. Paul created the *Beverly Hillbillies,* and he did a lot of *The Bob Cummings Show,* a lot of big television stuff out here. But then, Don had been by himself for a few months in '43, after his then assistant Bill Dench had gone into the Army.

I had met Don briefly at a Writers Guild dinner or something a year or so before but made no impression on him, apparently. My agent asked him to listen to a couple of shows that I was writing at that time, by late '42. I had gotten a chance to write a show called *Major Hoople,* and also, at the same time, got a chance to write for Victor Borge on *The Kraft Music Hall.* So suddenly, from absolute famine I was working two shows a week! One show and part of another show. Don liked the fact that I could do stories, which he always had trouble with.

Create the idea, the gag?

Yes, do the plot. *Fibber and Molly* didn't require much of a plot, but it needed a story with a finish of some kind to hang the door knocks on. I started the first few weeks, just bringing Don story ideas, sitting in. I began to write a little bit for him, and then, after a few months, my routine was that I would write the whole show, and we would get together out at the Jordans' house, Fibber and Molly's house, on Saturday afternoon. We would all read the script – read it aloud. Don would read all the parts. He'd read the Old Timer, and read Doc Gamble, and Mayor LaTrivia, and Wallace Wimple. Marian and Jim would read their own roles and I would sit and sweat – wondering how good it was. Then Don would rewrite it over the weekend on Saturday night and Sunday, as much as he thought it needed, which was a lot in the beginning. Then Monday, we'd do a reading, and Don would make cuts and polishes. Tuesday we'd rehearse all day and do the show. Well, after about a year and a half, Don felt that I was writing

---

* Mr. Leslie's first *Fibber McGee* script was broadcast March 9, 1943.

well enough for the show that we could break it in half – in two. So we'd get the story set with Marian and Jim on a Tuesday afternoon. Before we did tonight's show we'd get next week's story set. They'd agree on it. Then Don and I would break it in half, in two. And I would write the first half and he would write the second half. The next week we would do it the other way around. Then on Sunday, or later on Monday, Don and I would get together – put the show together, and we'd go into rehearsal later.

You must have worked very well together for each of you to do a half of the show.

Well, it was just a fine chemistry. Don was a wonderful, wonderful man. Don's gone now, been gone for seven or eight years. He was a great comedy mind. Comedy dialogue just flowed out of him, just a beautiful, quick, comedy mind, and he was an awfully nice man. Everybody loved Don. And he liked me and I was just as eager to please. Oh, boy! I was overwhelmed by this opportunity. I was very anxious to do well, and I worked hard. It just worked out that I began to write enough like him. Marian and Jim were so great to write for, because they had all these wonderful, little things that they did, and they were great people to work with. This made my whole life.

I can imagine. They made our lives too, doing all those things.

That was the fun of it!

How did you develop a story for Fibber McGee?

I've often tried to figure how I would get the beginning of a story. You get it mainly by just knocking your head against the wall. You try to think of every possible thing you can, and sometimes ideas come out of news stories that you've read.

The first story I ever did – Don had hired me, and I was to come in on Tuesday with some story ideas. I sat in our little house over on Las Palmas just sweating blood, because I was overwhelmed by the opportunity, and nothing was happening much. I had a few ideas. I didn't care too much for them. I was having a cup of coffee late at night in the kitchen, and I picked up a bottle of cream to put some in the coffee. It said on the bottle, "Adair Dairy Farms invites you to visit our dairy." It just struck me that that would be a funny notion for Fibber and Molly to take up that invitation off the milk bottle and go visit the dairy. The finish I had for the show was that that had been on the milk bottle for 20 years, and nobody had ever come to see them. Arthur Q. Bryan, who had played Major Hoople, that I had been writing – they hired him to play the president of the dairy. He just broke down and cried when they came, because all these years, nobody had ever come to see the dairy. That was how the first idea came to me.

I remember another one. We saw a picture, in *Life* or *Time* perhaps, of a woman who tried to get on a bus with an armful of packages at Christmas rush or something, and the bus driver closed the door in her face because the bus was full. She got furious and went around quickly and stood in front of the bus and wouldn't let it move until they let her on. It developed into the thing between the woman and the bus driver that went on for about an hour. Well, we just borrowed that and used it for Fibber. He went out and stood in front of the bus, and we rallied the merchants with him, and people on both sides. The merchants brought a chair out for him to sit on, and they were bringing him ice cream. He was loving it. The finish was typical. When you get to know the characters well, you know how to react to things and exactly what Fibber would do in a situation. He did the very logical thing for him. He made a big thing out of not being allowed on the bus, and it took all afternoon while they fought back and forth. They called the mayor and everybody to come and try to settle the argument. When the driver finally agreed to let Fibber on the bus, he discovered that it wasn't his bus after all, which was typically Fibber. It was the wrong bus. He said, "Get that thing out of here, Bud. I've been waiting here long enough."

Arthur Q. Bryan, who played Major Hoople, *based on the comic strip –*

Yes, Gene Ahern's comic strip, *Our Boarding House.*

– was that Arthur Q. Bryan's first appearance on the McGee *show?*

I think it was. I remember when I turned in that dairy idea, Don was so pleased. Of course, so was I. I called him on the phone at night – midnight – and gave him the idea because Don was always up very late at night. He said, very simply, "I think you're going to make me very happy." Well, of course, this made me just ecstatic. I remember, Monday, when we read it – we didn't have to hire an actor for the role for the first day of reading – somebody said, "I wonder who could play the president of the dairy." I said, "Gee, I've been working with a guy who I think would be great, Arthur Q. Bryan." Well, everybody knew Arthur and agreed. It was just one of those things. They might have hired somebody else, but I just happened to mention Arthur's name, out of my head, I thought of it. He did that, and then he began to do a few other roles, and eventually, Don created Doctor Gamble for him, and of course Doc Gamble was a wonderful character. They used to have great fun with him!

Which of the characters on Fibber McGee and Molly *did you have a hand in creating?*

I can't remember that any of them were specifically mine. We would have a character in to do a bit, and just get a notion to use him again, and then they sort of grew. While I was writing with Don, Doc Gamble was created, and Mayor LaTrivia began. Gale Gordon, who is doing *Lucy* now, and has done so many wonderful things. Such a beautiful voice, great sense of timing and a wonderful actor. As I remember, Gale had never played any comedy. He has a beautiful, fine dramatic voice, and he had done *Lux* [*Radio Theatre*] and a lot of dramatic stuff. It's my recollection, and I think this is right, that Cecil Underwood, who was then our producer, decided to cast Gale in some pompous businessman role that later led us to do Mayor LaTrivia when we heard Gale work. That was the first time Gale had played comedy. Of course, he's played virtually nothing but comedy since.

When did Beulah appear with Fibber and Molly? *Was that before or after you joined the show?*

It was during my tenure there. It was a good while after. I can't remember the dates, I'm not sure, but Marlin Hurt did Beulah for two years with us, I guess. Then spun off his own *Beulah* show. Then he and his agent Ken Dillon, who was also my agent, came up with the idea that Marlin was ready to do his own show, and he would play Marlin Hurt and Beulah, who was his colored housekeeper. He played a couple of other characters like Bill, who was Beulah's boyfriend. I wrote the pilot for it. It was in as a summer replacement.

Was it a replacement for Fibber and Molly?

No, it wasn't. I've forgotten now. It went on CBS, I believe, that first summer. But it was a summer replacement for somebody and went in with a 13-week buy. They liked it so well, they kept it. I can't even remember the sponsor at this point. I wrote it that summer, then I went back to work with *Fibber and Molly*. Various writers did it then. Then Marlin died at quite a young age, in the midst of the *Beulah* success. They recast it and put it into television.

Did you write it for TV?

No, never did.

Marlin Hurt was a male playing Beulah, *a female.*

Marlin, a big, good-looking man from DuQuoin, Illinois, was a fine actor. We developed a line for him, a couple of catch phrases. Beulah used to say, "Love that man!" when Fibber would do a joke of some kind. That was his almost "Tain't funny" but not quite that formula. She would give him that big, squealing laugh. Marlin had a wonderful song that he had brought from DuQuoin, Illinois. He remembered colored section hands singing it as they worked on the railroad, which became the theme song for his own radio show. I can't sing it at all, but the words were, "I've got the world in a jug, Lord. I've got the stopper in my hand." It was beautiful, the way he sang it. That became his theme.

Were you on loan from the Fibber McGee and Molly *show to do something with a couple of other shows? What was that situation?*

No, I did summertime shows, a few. Let's see, there was a time you may be talking about when Don and I did *The Roy Rogers Show* one summer. Roy and Dale Evans and Gabby Hayes. Don had a young brother who did some writing on it during that period. I wrote it on through that summer and partly into the fall. I believe while I was doing *Fibber and Molly* I was doing part of *The Roy Rogers Show* also. It gets a little dim at this point.

We always remember the McGees' hall closet. That started, I think, before you joined the show.

It started in Chicago, yes, before I ever knew the show.*

That gag really wasn't used every week.

No. In the beginning it was used more frequently. Toward the end we felt like we were beginning to wear it out. It's kind of an odd thing now. That's one of the things you still hear often. That and "Tain't funny, McGee" you read or hear. You hear references to that, "It looks like Fibber McGee's closet."

I remember, in the middle Forties, my wife and my four children and I went to Canada for a summertime trip. We were packed to the gills. We had three daughters and a son. The girls took such things as formal clothes for teatime or tea dances at the Empress Hotel, Victoria. We had all our fishing gear and summertime clothing. So the car was just packed and jammed. Every time anyone would open the trunk, like going through customs, they would invariably say, "This looks like Fibber McGee's closet." I heard that phrase three weeks ago!

The closet was a wonderful effect. It was a great visual effect for the audience in the studio. The soundman was Monty Fraser for a great many years that I worked. The last time I saw Monty he was head of sound effects at NBC out in the Valley, in Burbank. Monty had a stair-step arrangement with all kinds of junk piled on it. I couldn't identify the stuff now, but it follows a specific pattern. Monty had developed the sound exactly. The end of it was always a little dinner bell that he would rattle, and then drop. Tinkle and drop, because that was the cue for Fibber to say, "I gotta straighten out that closet one of these days," then the roars of laughter that came with it!

The Fibber McGee and Molly *show was great for running gags. People often think about the* Jack Benny *show with running gags – the vault, and the Maxwell, and his stinginess and that, but* Fibber McGee and Molly *had some beautiful running gags. The Uncle Dennis thing. And weren't they always after a fish?*

Old Muley! Old Muley was the big bass in Dugan's Lake, and we'd do a fishing show about once a year. Fibber was always after Old Muley. We did shows in which he had invented his own lure. One particularly that I remember was the show in which he invited everybody to go fishing with him: Doc Gamble,

---

* The first use of the closet gag was in Hollywood on March 5, 1940.

Wallace Wimple, Mayor LaTrivia, Harlow Wilcox, everybody. It was a beautiful day, maybe opening day of the fishing season. They had all tried to get out of it, because they said, "You lie so much. You're no fun to go with. You exaggerate everything terribly." He said, "I only stretch the truth an inch." They all agreed that if he told any kind of a lie, they would throw him in the lake. On that basis, they went fishing. Now, this story idea came out of a magazine article I had read from Phillip Wiley. He gave a prize every year to the hard luck fisherman in a Florida fishing derby that somebody else ran, a big-money fishing derby. They'd all bring their hard luck stories in, and I read this story, which gave me the idea. They all went with Fibber to Dugan's Lake on the promise that if he lied – stretched the truth at all – they would throw him in the lake.

Now, Fibber went out around the bend looking for Old Muley, walked around the shoreline and out through the woods, and he caught this great bass. He was 12 pounds or something, and he landed him. He was all by himself. He brought Old Muley in and he was having a fit because he finally got him. "Boy, wait'll the other guys see this." He hung him up on a tree limb to take a picture of him, so that he'd be sure to have this for posterity. The Old Timer came galloping through the brush. Bill Thompson played the Old Timer, and he came galloping through the brush, all out of breath and excited, and delighted to see Fibber there, and he said, "Big news! A lion escaped from the circus in town." Everybody was looking for the lion that had escaped from the circus. Fibber was going to pose beside Old Muley, the great, record-breaking bass, and have his picture taken. Just as they were about to do this, there was a crashing in the underbrush and the lion comes through the brush. Fibber and the Old Timer back off, of course, and the lion eats the fish. They stand there watching in horror as the lion eats the fish.

Now the Old Timer runs back into town to tell them where their lion is. Fibber runs back down to the dock to tell them that he caught Old Muley. He told them he was going to catch the big bass, and he caught the big bass. He came in all excited with this story, and they all said, "Oh, great. Yeah, wonderful. Where is it?"

Jim just looked out at the audience in the studio and they started to laugh before he ever got to say anything, because what he had to turn around and say to these guys was, "A lion ate it." There was just a roar from the audience because they knew the situation. And of course, nobody believed him and into the lake he went. The show ended with, "uh one, uh two, uh three," and Fibber doing a big fade, "No-oo!" *Splash!* It was a funny, funny show!

Isn't it interesting how a show like that stands out in your memory?

This has been 20-odd years ago, 25, maybe. But you get an idea that you just know is going to play. It just played beautifully.

Jim Jordan told me once about a specific Fibber McGee and Molly *show that he remembered as being maybe the funniest one of all. I think it was in the early part of the series, when Otis Cadwallader was paying a visit to town. He was*

Molly's ex-boyfriend –

Old sweetheart, yeah!

– and they wanted to put on the ritz for him.

They got [neighbor] Gildersleeve [who] agreed to be their butler, and Fibber just took shameless advantage of him. He just treated him like dirt on the theory that Gildy would not give him away, which he didn't. It was a funny show! It was before my time.

There were a lot of funny McGee *shows. Did you have fun writing them?*

Lots of fun, Chuck. I don't know how to describe it. It was just wonderful. Don was such a joy to work with, Marian and Jim were wonderful to work with. We were surrounded with talent – Gale Gordon [as] Mayor LaTrivia, Bill Thompson doing the Old Timer, Wallace Wimple, Horatio K. Boomer. When we had roles for them we would call in Cliff Arquette, and lots of the fine actors that went from show to show.

Isabel Randolph was in there, too.

Isabel Randolph did Mrs. Uppington. She was just great. It was really a joy. I have often said that I have been so blessed to have worked all my life and made a good living in the midst of having so much fun doing it. My father was a banker. He enjoyed his work, but if my dad got a laugh once a week that was unusual in the banking business. And the laughs were very small. I know lots of guys who work for a living and hate their work, but they do it honestly and willingly because this is how they live. To be able to make a good living and do something that is as much fun is just great. I felt awfully blessed, and I don't forget to say so.

I know the feeling! You did a lot of other things on radio and into television, too. Didn't you write for The Charlotte Greenwood Show?

Yes, I did *The Charlotte Greenwood Show* one summer in my early summer vacations from *Fibber* when I was trying to make some money. I did summer shows and the *Fibber* credit was a good one. I had the pick of a few shows. I did *The Charlotte Greenwood Show* one summer. I did *Glamour Manor* with Cliff Arquette. *Glamour Manor* was a kind of beat-up *Hollywood Hotel*. It was played pretty wild. And, as I told you, I did *The Beulah Show* the one summer. I did a show called *Johnny Mercer's Music Shop* one time at CBS. It was a summer replacement. I did briefly a summer show with The King's Men which replaced *Fibber and Molly*. Gee, there must have been others.

At the end of the McGee *series, in the mid-Fifties, that's when you moved into writing for television. What was the first exposure to that?*

Nineteen fifty-six. The rest of that year I did very little. I was kind of tired and I was looking for the right thing to do in television, a little scared of it maybe. The first thing I ever did was a script for *Leave It to Beaver,* which had been on a year, I guess. Harold Ackerman – who is a fine producer and has a great big background in radio and in television – gave me an assignment to do a script for *Leave It to Beaver,* and about the same month, the following month or so I did one for Harry for *Bachelor Father* [with] John Forsythe.

Then Ackerman went over to Screen Gems and was going to produce *The Donna Reed Show.* He had a pilot script written and decided they were going to offer it to ABC. They decided they would shoot the pilot film, and they would like to take four more scripts with it to show the network: "Here's a film and here's the next four scripts." So, Harry asked me to write one of them, and three other writers did three other scripts. When they got the scripts in and got ready to shoot the pilot, Ackerman decided to shoot my script as the pilot. I didn't even know this until after it had been shot. He decided to shoot mine instead of the original pilot script. It turned out to be a beautiful break for me, because my Writers Guild had only recently established the fact that the man who writes the script for the pilot film that sells the series shall be entitled to a weekly royalty for each episode of the show.

Oh, great!

I had quite a little flurry about it, because the writer who had done the pilot had been assured that if it was sold he would get royalties. I felt like it was a little heavy-handed, and I was taking it away from him. We finally, at my suggestion, worked out a compromise in which we would split the royalties. I don't know [but] I had the feeling that the producers were stuck to pay the other writer the entire royalty contractually, and that they were going to have to pay it to him anyhow. I don't know, but in any case, I had a royalty on that show, a half-royalty which amounted to, like, $57 an episode. I think they did 260 episodes. I think that's right, some enormous sum.

It went on for a long time.

About nine years! Then each episode reran five times. It was my third script. It turned out to be just delightful. I'd like to have it still going!

You did a lot of writing for a great many other TV shows.

I did a couple. I started over at Screen Gems a little after *The Donna Reed Show.* I started over there doing *Dennis the Menace.* I did about three years of *Dennis the Menace,* 40, 45 shows, I guess. I did the first 10 and they decided they would like to get them out of me faster. It took several writers, of course, to do each season, so each writer would do 10 or 15, and there would be three of four writers, groups of writers. They asked me if I would team with somebody so we could put out the scripts faster. Keith Fowler had written with me for the last couple of years of *Fibber McGee and Molly,* and was a very good friend, a very capable, fine writer. So Keith came in with me. I had done 10, I guess, by myself, and we did 33, I believe, together.

We also did a pilot for *Gidget* at Screen Gems. We got it finished and were casting and getting ready to shoot and Columbia Pictures decided they weren't going to let us do *Gidget* on television. They were going to make some more movies. Then, a few years later, they decided to do *Gidget* on television after all, but you never go back to the original writers, you know. That whole project's gone, so they started all over. Keith and I did a couple of *Beverly Hillbillies* together, and we did a couple of *Petticoat Junctions.* I don't know, several other things. Then after that, I did a dozen or so *Lucys.* A couple alone and a couple with George Balzer, who was also a very fine writer. George wrote for 25 years with Jack Benny, one of Benny's fine writers.

Did you ever write for any of the standup comics on radio or TV?

Never had. I've always felt that was sort of out of my field. That sort of show like… well, all of the standup comic shows and things like Bob Hope, every writer trying to get into radio had a crack at Bob Hope. I did monologue jokes for Bob on a kind of an off-and-on basis one season. I'd get three of four pages of jokes together and take them out to Bob at Paramount, and then I'd go to his Sunday preview, where he'd use everybody's jokes. He'd do an hour and a half show on Sundays in front of an audience.

His radio show? He would do a preview?

He'd do a Sunday night preview. Tickets and everything in the studio. He'd run an hour, an hour and a half, because he'd have all the material from everybody. Bob would just check off the reactions to the jokes that he got. Then when he went on Tuesday night, that show was boiled down by the audience reaction to what he wanted to send out on the air. I did do monologue jokes there for a while. It was just kind of a "Bring me a bunch of jokes and I'll give you some money" basis. Every now and then I would get a check for $50 from Bob. But I always thought standup comedy just wasn't my field. You'd go into a meeting with 10 writers and sit around a table throwing jokes. I was just overwhelmed. I don't do jokes that fast and I don't do gags that way.

You build a situation.

It's character comedy, I think. I like to think that they're jokes, and if you laugh, they're jokes. But to sit and compete with other writers is just not my dish. I was just overwhelmed by the fast gagmen who really can flip them off the top of their heads. I have little to say. I just have to sit and shut up.

Did many of the radio comedians do what Bob Hope did? A preview, a full-fledged preview with all the material?

I don't remember that. I can't really answer that. Now, it seems to me that Red Skelton used to do a preview, but I'm not sure, Chuck. It seems to me it was such a good format that it must have been used by other people. It's a great way to take three times as much material as you need when you're big enough to use the studio, because it's expensive having the studio and getting the audience together and everything. But when you're important enough that the network will give you that in those days in radio, it seems a good format and I'm sure other shows did do it.

There's a crisis on a script situation on radio, and one that I heard of on television. I've never been able to ask the writers of The Lone Ranger *what the scene was when Earle Graser died in an auto accident, and Brace Beemer took over. I would imagine there had to be a lot of excitement going on at a time like that.*

You betcha.

I think you had a hand in a situation similar to that on the Dennis the Menace *TV program. Joe Kearns, who was a very well-known radio actor, was Mr. Wilson on that show. And then he died during the course of it.*

In the middle of filming, we got terrible news one morning, terrible in all directions, because we all loved Joe. Joe had had a massive cerebral hemorrhage and was unconscious in the hospital. In a couple of days, Joe died. Now, from a purely practical standpoint, aside from all our shock at losing Joe, whom we were all fond of, we had perhaps five or six scripts written and ready to shoot. I think we were in the second day of shooting one of them. There were other writers involved. Keith and I were writing – we were under contract to do 15 a year at that point. Bill Colley and Peggy Chandler, who had written the pilot for Dennis, were writing a block and there were some other writers involved. We all sat down together with the producer in a kind of panic and to decide, "What do we do?"

Fortunately, there was always a buffer. There were four or five shows on film, and edited and ready to go. So we had a little leeway. What we finally decided to do, all of us in conference, was that you can't say Mr. Wilson died. It's a comedy show. You just don't go out and just say, "Sorry, folks." We decided that Mr. Wilson had been suddenly called east on business, that he didn't want to leave his wife alone, and his brother had agreed to come and sort of look after the house while Mr. Wilson was gone. Now, that was a little touchy situation too, but we decided we could live with it. We decided his brother would be a writer doing magazine pieces and stuff, and we decided that if we could get Gale Gordon to do it, we would be very fortunate.

Well, Gale did do it. I don't think he ever liked it too well but he did it well for a couple of seasons. We just never explained that Mr. Wilson wouldn't be back. For the first couple of weeks or so, Mrs. Wilson had a message from him. He was still detained back there, hoped everything was all right at home. Then we just began to let it go. But these are the things that happen to you. It was really panic.

In the early days, you felt that you had to explain every single thing you did. You thought that the people believed you so hard, which they did at first maybe, that you had to explain everything.

You've had an illustrious career as a writer in both radio and television. Which did you prefer?

Well, I guess I've given that away. Radio was a charmed life for me. Even compared with other writers in radio, Don and I had the very best of it. I had the best years of radio, I guess, because I was in there – radio had just begun to get really big when I came in, in 1943. It had been going well for a good while. Then I saw it on out till the end, so I had the best of it, I think.

Phil Leslie was born in 1909 and was 64 at the time of our conversation. He died September 23, 1988 at the age of 79.

Kate Smith

1999 RADIO HALL OF FAME. *Kate Smith had a career that began on the stage in 1927 and continued with success on records, in radio, motion pictures and television. She was starring at the Mill Run Theatre in suburban Chicago when, on November 11, 1975 I had an opportunity to talk with her about her show business life and her first professional appearance.*

I made my first professional appearance in New York City. I had just entered pre-med school at George Washington University. I was going to be a doctor – that's what my family wanted me to be – and I got a call. A theatrical scout had been around Washington. I didn't know anything about it, of course, but he had heard me perform as an amateur and he was getting ready to go into a big Broadway show called *Honeymoon Lane*. He heard me sing and so he contacted my father and asked if there was a possibility of my coming to New York and trying out for the show. He said that he definitely had a part for me and, after hearing me sing, he wanted me in the show.

Well, I had to plead with my father, because he did not want me to leave medical school and just go flying off someplace and not know what was going to happen. So, my mother went to New York with me and I appeared in the show and the show was a tremendous success. And that, incidentally, was the first time that I ever came to Chicago. When we finished our New York run, which was a year and a half, then we went on the road for a year and we were here nine months, in Chicago, with that show. That was my visit in about 1929. We also went to Philadelphia and we went to the various big cities and it ran for a year on the road and then it disbanded and I went home.

About six months later I got a call from George White, [who] wanted me in another big Broadway show. My father said, "I don't know whether you should go or not." I said, "Well, look, Dad. I'll try this one. If it becomes too long, I'll stop." Well, it was while I was in that show – while it was in New York – that I met Ted

Collins, God rest his soul. He was in charge of all the recordings for Columbia Records. He wanted me to make records for them. He made an appointment with me and we had a long talk and I started making records for him. Then, in 1931, he took some of my records to Mr. William Paley, who was the president of the CBS network. He owned it – had just bought it – and was a young man at the time. After he heard my records he said, "I'll put that young lady on anytime you want her to go on the radio." And that's how it all started.

Mr. Collins asked me if I had a manager. I said, "No, I don't" and he knew it. I didn't have an agent and so he said, "How about me managing your affairs?" I said, "It's all right with me." So he became my manager. Then we set up the time to go on [the air], May 1, 1931 at 7:00, three nights a week, against *Amos 'n' Andy,* who were on NBC at the time. And that's how I got into radio!

Were you known as "The Songbird of the South" before radio?

Yes. That was a title that I took when I first came to New York. They gave it to me in the show and I've never been able to get away from it. To me, it's corny now, but it has stuck to me, Chuck.

Well, you're from the South.

Yes. I was born in Virginia and raised and schooled in Washington, D.C.

Let's back up to 1931 when you first went on CBS opposite Amos 'n' Andy. *Everybody was listening to them. That must have been a challenge for you.*

Yes, it was a challenge, but I was so young then, Chuck, that nothing was a challenge for me. You know how fresh kids are! I always had great confidence in myself in what I had been doing because I had started young, singing around Washington as an amateur. So I knew the public and I had seen the response to my efforts as a youngster and I thought, well, I must have something people like, if they enjoy it. I always had the feeling that I had a good rapport with the audience and the response was very beautiful.

I had thousands of fan letters after I started in radio and I knew then that I was gonna go, that I was established. I was very happy and I've always had a deep concern about my audiences. I have always kept my shows top-rank.

I know you had great confidence when you were pitted against Amos 'n' Andy, *but weren't you just a little bit nervous about it all?*

No, sir! No, sir! Not at all, Chuck. I had confidence in myself and that's what's needed, no matter who your competition is, no matter what field it's in. If you have the confidence – self-confidence – and you know you are giving your best, and your best is being accepted, there's nothing to worry about. This applies in every field of endeavor in life. If you falter in your own belief, then you're not going to make it. I don't care whether you're an executive in business or the President of the United States. No matter what, you've got to have self-confidence and believe in yourself. This way you can prove your worth.

What kind of confidence did CBS have in you? Did they give you a one-year contract, or what?

They gave me carte blanche. I could do what I wanted to do and they were happy about it. After a month, they put me on five times a week instead of three times a week because they were making great inroads into the opposition network. Within a couple of months I had a wonderful sponsor and, for the whole time that I remained in radio I was never without a sponsor, a big sponsor, a well-paying sponsor. When I had my television show, I was on five days a week, every day, for seven years with a TV hour. And I was never without a sponsor. As a matter of fact, I can truthfully say, because it was told to me by the top echelon of the network, NBC for television, we had a waiting list of over 80 sponsors, always wanting to buy 15 minutes of time on our show. And we were in the position where we were earning for the network three and one half million dollars every 39 weeks!

That's confidence! Who was your first sponsor on radio?

That's easy! The Congress Cigar Company, in Philadelphia. And they sold tobacco and cigars. And I had La Palina Cigars. And that was funny because here I was... I don't smoke! I never smoked, never even tried.

Not a cigar, especially!

Certainly not a cigar, but not a cigarette either. But here I was, my very first sponsor being a cigar company. I just couldn't believe it. But anyhow, it was very successful. I was on with them for three years. And then I went with A&P. I had A&P coffee, all of their coffee: Eight O'Clock, Red Circle, Bokar... I think that was the three of them. And I was on with A&P for about six years and then I got an automobile sponsor – Hudson was the name of the car that I sold. And then after that – I was with them for a couple of years – and then I went with General Foods for 24 years. That was a magnificent association. It was just beautiful, beautiful. And, needless to say, Chuck, you know what they had me selling? Food!

Food!

Cakes, Calumet, Swans Down, the jellies and jams, and Grape-Nuts, and coffee, Jell-O. I sold everything for them, but mainly cakes. I could always sell food, Chuck! I guess it was my fat – me looking so fat and happy [laughs] – and I've always been able to sell food!

When you started with your 15-minute radio show, was it a live show?

Oh, yes, yes. And then when I got the night radio show, I had to go on twice a night in New York. I had to go on from 8 to 9 for New York. Then I had to wait at the theater and go on from [11 till midnight] so they'd get it on the Pacific Coast from 8 to 9. So we had to do it twice a night, and they were all live. And so were all the television shows until just the last. When mistakes were made, they went out on the air just as they were done.

That adds to the rapport between the performer and the audience, I think. It shows nobody's perfect.

That's right. And this is the way I used to love it. Now they do get a perfect show by taping it, because they can do it over and over if they have to, as many times as they have to, to get it perfect.

Well, you had some perfect live shows. When you were doing that one hour a night, repeating for the West Coast, that's when you made the top 10 radio shows in the country –

Consistently.

– and you brought so much quality entertainment to the radio audience.

That was our purpose. We wanted to give the very best that we could get. We got top names of every division of the entertainment industry. We got the top names in motion pictures, in the theatre, the dramatics, vaudeville, radio, every type of entertainment. We went to the entire field to bring the best to our audiences. And we had the best.

And not only did you bring established stars, but you made some stars. Radio firsts.

Yes, we did. We made quite a few. We made Abbott and Costello, we made Henny Youngman. We had Henry Aldrich and we started Charlie Ruggles in a series for radio. We created *It Pays to Be Ignorant* – Tom Howard, George Shelton, Lulu McConnell and Harry McNaughton. Oh, I could give you a big list. I'm very, very happy about that.

I read that, as a warm-up announcer for one of your series, you had a young fellow –

– Bert Parks! He was out there every evening, warming up the audience. Bert Parks was with us for years.

Your manager then, Ted Collins, was with you from the very beginning.

Nineteen thirty. We formed our own company in 1931 and we were together until he had a massive heart attack in 1964. And we had been together [for 33 years] as business partners and artist and manager.

Ted shared a lot of radio with you.

Right. He was my announcer and producer for all of my shows – radio and television – and we were also in a lot of sports enterprises together. I've been a great sports enthusiast and so was he. A lot of people don't realize it, but we owned, in the National Football League, the New York Yanks [for] seven years. Now, we also had, in the Fifties, the championship Celtics basketball team.

I have two questions yet to ask.

Go ahead.

When was the first time you sang "God Bless America"?

November 11, 1938, on Armistice Day, which is now known as Veterans' Day.

And how many times have you sung it?

Now, that I can't answer. That I could never answer. I wouldn't even offer an estimate, I've done it so much.

What about your theme song, "When The Moon Comes Over the Mountain"?

I wrote the lyrics for that. I'm kind of an amateur poetry writer and have been practically all my life. And so I wrote this poem down in the Blue Ridge Mountains and then when we decided to go on the air, Ted had Harry Wood write the melody to it. And that's how we happened [to write] a very simple little thing that everybody can sing.

A beautiful melody for a beautiful lady. You always signed off your radio programs with –

"Thanks for listening and good-bye, folks."

Kate Smith was born May 1, 1907 and was 68 at the time of our conversation. She died June 17, 1986 at the age of 79.

Ralph
Edwards

1995 RADIO HALL OF FAME. *Ralph Edwards gained fame in radio as the host of* **Truth or Consequences** *and, later,* **This Is Your Life.** *A telephone call to his office in Beverly Hills, California, on October 7, 1971 brought us together. He said that he was a Colorado farm boy who studied to be an English teacher.*

I was born on a farm, 13 miles east of Sterling, Colorado, the county seat of Logan County, and nearer to a town called Merino, named after the Merino sheep that used to be there. It used to be called Fort Buffalo, because of the buffalo that were there. We had a little farm near the South Platte River, on which I was born. Then we got a homestead, another two-and-a-half miles out into the dry lands of northeastern Colorado, and we lived on that for five years. You had to live on it for five years, until you proved it up, and then it became yours. I think we sold it for about $500 when we all left to go to California.

Once in California, you got started script writing at quite an early age, didn't you?

That's very true. I had always been interested in writing, even on the farm. I used to make up plays. We'd go around to the neighboring farms, little pals of mine, and we'd put on shows. Then, when I got into the first grade there Miss Effie, who was my teacher in Merino, would put me in charge of making up the plays for the mothers when they'd come to visit the first grade. This whetted my enthusiasm. When I got to California, when I was 12 years of age, I continued this and even wrote the school play for the grammar school for [many] successive years, [even] after I had gone on to high school and then into the University of California. I worked my way through the University of California writing various series for local radio there.

Did you write a dramatic show called Alvin and Betty?

Yes. I was still in Oakland High School when I wrote that. It was a 15-minute show a day. The premise of it was married life. It was a treatise on married life. Now, what's a 15-year-old guy gonna know about married life? But at any rate, I wrote it. Carl Botino was Alvin and he gave me my first paycheck of $1 a script. I was announcer and wrote it and did all the sound effects. We even had a contest to name a goat! I had a goat [on the show] you know, *baa-baaa!* I even did the sound effects! So I'd ask the listeners if they would write in and tell us what the goat – it was a black goat – should be named. Colleen Moore, who was playing in *The Church Mouse* at the Fulton Theatre, was the judge and she chose the name, "Anthracite." So that's where you might say the genesis of the "Hush" contest, the "Walking Man" contest, "Miss Hush" and all those great contests that raised so much money for charity came from. When I graduated from the University of California, I went from the station in which I'd worked all during my days at the University in Berkley, KROW and KTAB, which later became the call letters KSFO. I went from there over to KFRC in San Francisco, which was a CBS outlet at that time, and, gee, I heard those guys say, "This is the Columbia Broadcasting System" and then I'd have to open the microphone and give the call letters. I thought, "Well, I can do what they're doing back there and maybe I'll get up enough nerve and go back there sometime."

About that time, I got a card from Sam Taylor, who was the editor of our humor magazine at Cal. I was knee-deep in little theater work on the stage there at Cal, and he'd seen me. When he went back to New York, he wrote saying, "If you can get back here, I'll get you a walk-on in a Broadway play." Well, I got a ride back to that big city of New York. But when I got there, of course, the show didn't even run! It died aborning. But I was in New York. Then I lined up with the boys and girls at the stage entrance [looking for work] and I thought, "Well, this is going a little slow." So I thought I'd go to what I know, which is radio. And I went over and auditioned all around and I finally got on as an announcer at CBS.

It took two years. I had more shows than any commercial announcer in radio. I don't know if anybody's come up to that number yet. It was 45 shows a week, but I was getting $45 a week as just my sustaining salary at the CBS station. So the radio announcers and producers formed a union called AGRAP – the American Guild of Radio Announcers and Producers – and they cited me as a case. "Look," they said, "this kid has all these shows and look what he's getting paid." And I said, "Now, look, leave me alone. I starved in this city and I know what it is, and I'm happy as I am. I don't want to get mixed up in any union thing." And they said, "No, go ahead and do it." Well, AGRAP went on for a while and I actually lost money. Sure, they would pay me for the number of hours I worked on a show, but they would take that out of my sustaining salaries. So, I'd end up with about $43 or $42 at the end of a week. But then, when AFRA [the American Federation of Radio Artists] came in, then they had this big thing that you got X-amount of dollars a show, I forget what it was, and with my 45 shows, why, wow! Bonanza, you know!

I announced *Life Can Be Beautiful, Against the Storm, Road of Life, The O'Neills, Vic and Sade, The Emily Post Show,* the *Tony Wons* show. Then [later] I gave them all up and an announcer by the name of Art Stark inherited them all. They made the announcers listen to all these things that I said [on the air] and they copied my way of doing it. I had a kind of throw-away thing: "Now look, girls, you don't have to listen if you don't want to. If you don't want to have the smoothest, most beautiful hands in town, well, the heck with it. Turn me off, will you!" In other words, I just chatted with them and developed kind of a style. This is when Godfrey was just starting to come out of Washington. And so, the style hit and I got a lot of shows off it, but they made these poor guys try to imitate me when I went off. Art Stark came the closest to it and so he took over.

But I did *Life Can Be Beautiful* for a great many years. And *Vic and Sade.* It came out of Chicago, but I announced them in New York. But I've never to this day – and I never will now, of course – I've never seen Vic and Sade. I met Rush, the boy, you know, Billy Idelson. I met him at a restaurant out here one time during the war. I walked up to him and said, "I'm Ralph Edwards" and he said "I'm Billy Idelson." And I said, "Can you imagine? We were on the show together two years and never saw each other, because you were in Chicago." I announced from New York, because I was doing most of the Procter and Gamble shows.

Did you have anything to do with the Major Bowes' Amateur Hour?

Yes. I was the announcer of that for four years. A lot of funny things happened to me on that show. I had the hiccups one time, the very first show that I was on, and I was living in one room overlooking Grant's Tomb on 125th Street and Riverside Drive in New York. I had a towel in the broken window. I had just come off poverty row there. And so, by the time I got down to the show, I was excited and hiccupping and I said, "Does anybody (hic) know (hic) how to stop (hic) hiccups?" And a guy said, "Well, go around to the soda fountain, just around the corner, and get yourself a glass of water." I said, "(hic) Okay, now, I'll be right back. I promise you." So I went and I said, "Listen, can you give me a glass of water?" So the fellow, instead of pouring water, put on the fizz water. He turned it the other way, you know, like he was making an ice cream soda. So, I drank this thing. Now, I've really got a tornado going in me. "Now (hic) you're (hic) killing (hic) me!" I go back and say to the producer, Paul LaPorte, "(hic) Okay, I'm all (hic) set!" He says, "You can't go on with the hiccups!" and I said, "I'll (hic) just go ahead." I walked up on the stage. All the people who were connected with the show – the producer, the director, and so on – used to sit in the front row, and I sat there, too. And the major sat up at his table with the gong and the hammer that he hit it with. The producer gives the signal from the control booth and I'm thinking (hic) now, how am I (hic) gonna get over these hiccups? The major hits the gong and I say, "Four great cars – Plymouth, Dodge, DeSoto and Chrysler, bring you *Major Bowes and His Original Amateur Hour...*" I went right on, Chuck, and I never had a hiccup the rest of the show.

Beautiful!

Well, you know, nerves will sometimes get you. But I don't know. I've been in the business so long I go to sleep on pianos. During *Life Can Be Beautiful*, can you believe? I had so many shows, 'cause at night I would do the *Ben Bernie* show, *Your Hit Parade, The Phil Baker Show, Ninety-Nine Men and a Girl,* just a whole mess of them, with repeats if you please! You know, we would do two shows then, because there was no such thing as tape or recording. And I was pooped out, so, during my daytime shows, I would go to sleep and I'd tell Bill Meter, the organist, "If I'm not awake before Chi Chi and Papa David have stopped hitting each other, you wake me up." And I would go to sleep on that piano and I still can control myself, pretty much that way. You have to, in this business. No more hiccups.

Did you do a local New York show for the automat?

Yes. The Horn and Hardart Cafeterias, where you put in a nickel, at that time, and you get the pie or sandwich and everything else. They had *The Horn and Hardart Children's Hour.* Paul Douglas, the actor, then an announcer, had done the show for six years. I took over for him and when I gave it up for *Truth or Consequences,* Ed Herlihy took it over. Ed had the show for 20 years, I think.

You mentioned Truth or Consequences, *that great brain child of yours. It was a new concept in radio quiz programs. How did you get the idea for it?*

The idea sprang from some of the games we used to play on the farm in Colorado, called "Heavy, Heavy Hangs Over Thy Head" or "Fine or Super Fine." You'd take an object from one of the people playing and you'd hold it over the person's head, the person who was "it." You'd be behind them and they couldn't see what it was. If they guessed it was "superfine" it was a girl's object, then okay, they wouldn't have to pay the consequences. But if it were in reality, in fact, a male object like a jackknife or a slingshot, or whatever you'd have on the farm, and they hadn't said "fine," then they had not told the truth, so they'd have to pay the consequence, which was usually to kiss the girl, or do some crazy little thing.

But when I got to having so many shows that I started seeing box tops in front of my eyes, I thought about having a show where I only had to work once a week, instead of all that time. So I got to thinking that quiz shows were the trend at the time, but I thought, well, one quiz show is enough. Can you imagine that? There must be fifty thousand now! But, I thought, let's get a different slant. Let's do the old penalty angle and the consequence. So I just jazzed it up more and made it more adaptable to pranks and stunts and that sort of thing. Of course, as time went on, we put in nostalgia, or the heart into it, and *This Is Your Life* sprang from that.

It's amazing how you had so many visual stunts in the days of radio.

Yes. I remember the first review from *Variety.* It said, "When television comes, *Truth or Consequences* has to be the number one show because it is so visual." Well, there's a thing about that – two things.

One is, if you honestly do the things... if you say, "All right, we're going to blindfold you, Mr. Jones. We're going to take you all around New York, and you're gonna have to guess where you end up. We'll tune you in, wherever you end up." And then you do just that, and you put a lot of sound effects to it, and he's on his way, and you hear river boats and all that kind of stuff, and then he ends up on the stage of the Winter Garden Theatre where, say, Olson and Johnson were playing in *Helzapoppin,* and he's still blindfolded. He guesses that he was on one of the big ocean liners, because of the sound effects, and we took off the blindfold and there he is on the stage in front of 1500 people. And, of course, they blast out and laugh!

Or, you're at the Amphitheatre in Chicago playing a food show down there at the Stockyards, and you send the guy out with a baby buggy and his friend dressed as a little baby. And the guy starts to talk and the passer-by says, "How cute is the baby!" and the baby takes a cigar out and says, "Yeah? Do you want a whiff of my cigar?" Now, actually doing that is the license to do it, although it is visual. Radio really came alive with that.

The second thing is that your imagination built it even beyond what it might have been. We might have said, "All right, it's George Washington's birthday. Now, Mr. Jones, we want you to climb this tree and we want you to sing 'Old MacDonald Had A Farm' in four choruses. If you can finish those four choruses before Mr. Smith, over here, chops down the cherry tree, you'll win $100. If you don't, you'll fall right into this tub of water." Okay, now the listening audience has a picture of a tree, a tub of water, a guy chopping, and you hear the *chop-chop.* Even though the tree wasn't the biggest tree in the world, or the tub of water the deepest tub, or the man the greatest singer, or the ax the biggest ax your imagination – whatever you wanted to make of the act – was okay. It was successful, I think, because you could take it beyond the realm of reality and put it into your creative thoughts and make of it whatever you wanted to.

Once again, the imagination of the listener helped to build the magic of radio.

You know it, Chuck! This is what, in a way, is lacking in television. Unless you have a supernatural or some kind of a foggy scrim to your project on television, whatever play you are doing, there is no great imagination. It's spelled out. It's like the movies. It's a different type of story-telling. You are right. Radio made you think.

You changed the name of a town on your tenth anniversary, didn't you?

Yes. Truth or Consequences, New Mexico now exists... the former Hot

Springs, New Mexico, a county seat of Sierra County, halfway between Albuquerque and El Paso on Highway 85, a nice big four-lane freeway all the way. And Elephant Butte Lake is there, the second largest body of impounded water in the United States of America. How's that for selling that city?

Wow!

Really, I don't get a cent out of it, so don't think poorly of me.

Why did Hot Springs, New Mexico, agree to change its name to Truth or Consequences, New Mexico?

For our tenth anniversary of *Truth or Consequences*, we were trying to think of something that would shake the people up in America, something that would make them aware of the fact that *Truth or Consequences* was still going strong. And so I had the writers and I bring in thoughts on what we might do. Al Simon was an idea man for me then and he came up with the idea of changing the name of some town or city to "Truth or Consequences." So we sent out feelers to Chambers of Commerce and we heard from three different cities who agreed to do it. And one, the most promising, was this county seat of Sierra County, Hot Springs, New Mexico. So I sent Ed Bailey, my producer, down to talk to them and the result was that we did just that. The city voted to change the name. They've voted three times since then, to maintain it, to retain it, and now it is permanently Truth or Consequences, New Mexico.

So Truth or Consequences *will always be on the map of the United States.*

Yes, it has been for 20 years. Rand McNally put it on, the post office, letterheads, the newspapers, the Truth or Consequences *Herald,* and so on down the line.

What about some of the great contests from the show? "The Walking Man" and so forth.

Well, it may be interesting to you, Chuck, to know that the reason these contests started was my building a backfire to something that I had started and was sorry I started it.

Way back in '41, I brought a young lady out of the audience. I chose her in the warm-up, as we do to select our contestants, and she was a struggling secretary and we said, "You're going to be Cinderella and go to the ball!" And we gave her a gown and a mink coat and shoes and hairdo. And then I said, "This is from I. J. Fox, the mink coat; this is a Saks Fifth Avenue dress; these are I. Miller Shoes; this is a Charles of the Ritz hairdo." And I didn't get them free for doing that, I just wanted the audience to know these were quality goods. We brought her back at the end of the show and she looked beautiful. I said, "Here's your Prince

Charming." It was before the war, but the Armory was aboard up there and a National Guardsman, a lieutenant, took her to the ball. As she went out, I said, "Oh, by the way, the dress and the mink coat and everything else, the handbag and the money, are yours to keep." Well, the listeners thought that was real great.

And then other packagers of shows and producers thought it was great, too. But you see, they didn't take the heart, they just stole the bones or something. But they got to the point, finally, around 1945 or 1946 and they said, "Right, Grant is buried in Grant's Tomb. You have won a Cadillac sedan!" So it was just terrible. The giveaway craze got to be nonsense. I thought, well, yes, inadvertently we started this, so how do we stop it? So, one night on *Truth or Consequences* in 1945 I said, "Well, I'm sorry you haven't told the truth, but if you can tell me who 'Mr. Hush' is, you will win" – it was a big satire and I thought I was satirizing this whole giveaway thing – "you will win a Cadillac sedan, a house and lot and a mink coat." And man, that shook them up. Next week I added three more fantastic things: a yacht, a year's supply of nylon hose, which in post-war was very difficult to get, and things like that.

Well, they started flying in from Boston, New Orleans and they'd raise their greedy little hands and I thought, now what've I done? I've got all these people here, getting this loot for nothing. When they guess off "Mr. Hush" I'll make it work for some good. Which has been the theme of *Truth or Consequences* all through the 32 years of existence, Chuck, to turn the big things into something good.

At any rate, they guessed "Mr. Hush" as Jack Dempsey. Then we started "Mrs. Hush" and that was Clara Bow. And I didn't tell them who it was, but I said, "Now, you folks who didn't get a chance, you listeners, with 'Mr. Hush,' you have a chance with 'Mrs. Hush.' Just send in, in 25 words or less, why we should all support the March of Dimes and try to end the polio epidemic. Include, if you please, a donation." Well, in those contests we raised over three million dollars for the March of Dimes. In the "Miss Hush" contest, who was Martha Graham, the dancer, we raised $1,639,000 and put the American Heart Association in business coast-to-coast, as a volunteer agency.

It was the most powerful thing in rating-getting, attention-getting, next to the FDR fireside speeches and the Joe Louis heavyweight fights. The "Hush" contests, the "Walking Man" and "Miss Hush" and all those, commanded, next to those two broadcasts, the highest ratings ever run up in radio in those days, Chuck.

How many of the Truth or Consequences *shows incorporated the* This Is Your Life-*type feature?*

Well, the original *This Is Your Life* was done on *Truth or Consequences* in 1946. And there was one before that in 1945 that had the flavor, and really was the seed that sprung into *This Is Your Life.* Instead of having the subject on stage, we tuned him in by remote control in Hawaii and took him to his home town, in North Dakota or somewhere like that, and went into the drug store and talked to the druggist, went into the church and talked to the minister, then to the school and talked to the teacher, and they talked two-way communication from his sick bed in the naval hospital somewhere. I would guess, maybe, we have done, oh, a hundred acts that are on the *This Is Your Life* theme on *Truth or Consequences*.

In 1948, on radio, This Is Your Life *made it as a program on its own.*

That's right. I had Harry Von Zell in it first, trying to sell the show with him in it. But *Truth or Consequences* was so hot and strong a show then, they wanted me in it and finally I said, "Okay, I'll do it." Then we sold it. But, it became increasingly difficult to be a devil on Saturday night and an angel on Wednesday. So I turned *Truth or Consequences,* the master of ceremonies chores, over to Jack Bailey first and then, of course, to Bob Barker. He is just fantastic.

You did about two years on radio before you translated This Is Your Life *to television.*

Yes, I did. We did some marvelous radio shows. People still talk about them.

Ralph Edwards was born June 13, 1913. He was 58 at the time of our conversation.

Eve
Arden

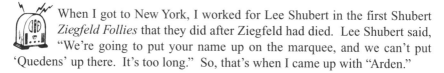

Eve Arden created the role of Connie Brooks for the popular radio series **Our Miss Brooks.** *We met on January 31, 1975 backstage at the Drury Lane Theatre in Evergreen Park, Illinois, where she was appearing in the play* **Under Papa's Picture.** *I observed that her real name is Eunice Quedens.*

When I got to New York, I worked for Lee Shubert in the first Shubert *Ziegfeld Follies* that they did after Ziegfeld had died. Lee Shubert said, "We're going to put your name up on the marquee, and we can't put 'Quedens' up there. It's too long." So, that's when I came up with "Arden."

Did you just pull it out of the air?

More or less, yes, I did. I was waiting to go in and see him and he had given me a deadline on a name. I was reading a book and the heroine was Eve. I had a package of Elizabeth Arden cosmetics in my hand. I tried it out on him and he liked it. That was it.

Perhaps if you had used a different cosmetic your name today could be Lady Esther!

Right! [laughs]

Well, how did you get from Mill Valley, California, where you were born, to the Ziegfeld Follies?

I went to San Francisco first, and I worked for the Henry Duffy Stock Company there. It was a marvelous kind of super-stock, where you rehearsed for four weeks and played eight to 12 weeks, depending on how popular the play was. It was great training. Then I joined a little band box repertoire company. There were just four of us in the company.

That meant a lot of long parts, because I played all the leads, and they were divided among four people. From there, I did a revue at the Pasadena Playhouse. We took it into Hollywood, and that's where Mr. Shubert saw me and signed me for the *Follies*. So that got me to New York.

You were in the Follies *and a couple of other shows, too, before you went back to California?*

Yes, I did the Theatre Guild Revue called *Parade* and then I did another *Follies*. Then I came out to California. My mother had passed away. I came out and suddenly I got a picture to do. So I stayed and did some pictures. And then I went back and did another show – two shows, as a matter of fact. Came back and did some more pictures, and then I went back and did *Let's Face It*. I sort of commuted in those days. I love the theatre. I was a comedienne, and I did numbers and sketches and things like that in revues that were great fun. I sang and danced.

Your first major screen role was in Stage Door.

Well, that was the first one, and then I did *Voice of the Turtle*.

You even worked with the Marx Brothers!

Yes. *A Day at the Circus,* practically the only picture that ever impressed our son! [laughs] That pulled me up a few notches!

You were in the movies with Warner Brothers and for RKO, too.

Oh, I worked for all the studios: MGM, RKO, Paramount.

You and Lucille Ball were somewhat typecast as the businesswoman, or the secretary.

Yes, secretary and best friend of the heroine, who never got the man!

Ted Sennett wrote a book called Lunatics and Lovers *about those screwball comedies of the Thirties and Forties, and you were very evident in many of those. Describing the roles that you played in those films, he said you "would walk onto the screen, dispense acid like wine to the fools you were obliged to tolerate and then make a nice exit." I think that really did sum up your screen roles.*

Well, maybe that covered a few of them, but I never thought that I was so acid, you know. They called me brittle, which annoyed me, because I was always really the gal with the good heart who saved the heroine and patched up all her troubles, and took care of everybody. But I did make a flip remark now and then.

Well, those flip remarks really were very well remembered, and kind of became the trademark for Eve Arden. Mildred Pierce *was one of your finest screen appearances.*

Yes, so they tell me. I was so amazed, because you make a picture – or you did in those days – and if you're not the lead, you work maybe two weeks in a row. Then I used to go to Palm Springs for two or three weeks during the making of the picture – which always distressed the cameraman, 'cause I came back eight shades darker. Then you would work a week or two more. So you had really very little concept of what you had done in a picture. I could never bear to see them after. It destroyed me. So I gave it up. But then I read in the paper that I had been nominated for an Oscar in *Mildred Pierce.* So I felt I had to go and see what the heck I had done. I went and the theater was very crowded. I went and sat in the second row down front. There were no other seats. After 10 minutes I left. I never saw it again until it was on TV, as an old picture. I enjoyed it, but I wasn't that mad about it. I think *Voice of the Turtle* was one of the best things I had done.

You moved from film with ease into radio, working with Ken Murray for a while and Jack Haley.

I did those things when I was working in the theatre in New York. Then I came out on the Coast with another one of those. Then I did a show with Danny Kaye on radio. Then finally along came *Miss Brooks.*

How did Our Miss Brooks *come along?*

Well, they had made a couple of recordings with a couple of other actresses – I believe Joan Blondell was one. They didn't feel she was right, and Shirley Booth was one. So they asked me to do it and I held very little hope for it. But they said they wanted to put it on as a summer replacement. I said, "Well, then you're going to have to do it right fast, 'cause I'm going to New York." So we taped all of them very fast. I got to New York and at the end of my stay there, Frank Stanton, the president of CBS, said, "Congratulations. You're the number one show on the air," which astounded me! So then we went into fall production. It was on radio five years, one of which overlapped the four years on television.

There's something very interesting about the transition from radio to television. With one exception, every member of the Our Miss Brooks *radio broadcast moved into television.*

And the only one who didn't, as you know, was Jeff Chandler. The reason for that was that Jeff had suddenly become a big motion picture star. He really wanted to do it with us, but he just physically didn't look the part. I mean, when you looked at Jeff, you didn't believe he was the shy, bumbling Mr. Boynton. Vocally, he did it. So Bob Rockwell was the perfect replacement for him on television.

They didn't want to take Dick Crenna into TV. They asked me to make tests with some boys. And I said, "What for?" They said, "For Walter Denton." I said, "You're crazy. People know Dick." They said, "He's too old." But I said, "He doesn't look it. He doesn't sound it. They'll love him." They pressured me to make the tests. So I said, "I'll do it if you make a test of Dick, too." There was no question after that.

Then they came to me part way through the series and said, "We're going to make a big change. Just keep you and Gale Gordon as Mr. Conklin, and that's all. We're going to send you to Hollywood, and it's..." I said, "It's not going to work. I bet I have my people back in three months." And I did. It was a shame, but that spoiled it.

They changed from a public school to a private school, and from a high school to a grammar school.

It never recovered from that. That was really the reason we went off the air.

When the Our Miss Brooks *series ended, you came back shortly thereafter with* The Eve Arden Show.

Yes. We made a good pilot, which sold immediately. Then they came to me and said, "Well, we're on now, but you can't have the same producer, director or writer." I said, "How can you do that?" They said, "Oh, we'll put 15 writers on it." Well, you put 15 people in a little screening room, and have them look at one thing. They all come up with a totally different idea. So it just didn't homogenize, you know.

That didn't click too well, but you were a big hit with Kaye Ballard in The Mothers-In-Law.

Yes, and then they dropped that.

You never got away from making movies.

Yes, my life seems to go in spurts, but mostly we love the theatre. At one time my husband Brooks West and I took our four children on summer stock tour. It gave them a wonderful vacation and allowed us to be with them in a kind of different role than we were at home, where we were always having to say, "Did you do your homework? Did you make your bed? Did you do this? Well, do it." We would tour in a station wagon with a nurse and a dog. We would talk with them, and they would see the countryside with us. We would be by a mountain lake one time, and by the seashore another. So it was a good way of life for us for quite a few years. Then we took them to Europe for a year and a half. That was a wonderful period.

I was flipping through an old TV Guide *and there was something in there about the animals on your ranch being named after movie stars.*

Oh, yes. That was, of course, quite a few years ago, when the children were young. We had three cows. They were named Marilyn Monroe, dear Marilyn – her namesake died from eating baling wire; Elizabeth Taylor – that was a black angus with a white face, looked like Liz, we thought, and Jane Russell. We had the Gabor sisters, who were our sheep. And, Mama Gabor, who promptly gave birth to triplets. We had all the animals named for different people. It was fun!

Names are somewhat significant to you, because your first two daughters are Connie and Liza.

Liza is the eldest, Connie, then Duncan and Douglas are the boys.

Connie was Connie Brooks! Didn't you choose that name for the series?

People always asked if *Our Miss Brooks* was named after my husband, Brooks West. But Brooks and I hadn't met until I had been on radio for almost four years.

You actually met when you were in a play together?

Yes, toured in summer stock the first year. But when they were giving Miss Brooks a first name, I had just adopted a little girl and named her Connie. So I said, "How about calling her Connie Brooks?" That's when it hit. Liza has never forgiven me, because I had named a little business that I had, after her first. Then the business went defunct. In the second show I did, I was named for Liza, but she lost out on *Miss Brooks.*

Well, we haven't lost out! We thank you very much for so many good things that you've done over the years.

Well, thank you. I must say it is very pleasant when people come up to say they enjoy *Miss Brooks* more than anything that I've done. They always mention that. It's nice to hear.

Eve Arden was born April 30, 1912 and was 62 at the time of our conversation. She died November 12, 1990 at the age of 78.

Harold Peary

Harold Peary starred on radio as Throckmorton P. Gildersleeve in* Fibber McGee and Molly *and* The Great Gildersleeve. *Mr. Peary had a long career before the microphones, and on April 28, 1971 I called him at his California home to chat about his work on the air. Commenting on his very distinctive voice, I was surprised to learn that he created many different voices over the years.

I do a lot of characters. In the old days in Chicago I used to do seven voices on *The Tom Mix Ralston Straight Shooters* show, which a lot of people don't know about. That was way back in '37, '38, '39. I did Sheriff Mike Shaw and I did an Englishman, and I did Henry Akins, the town banker, and I did Hawk Barrett, who was a villain, and I did Hawk Barrett's brother named Shotgun Barrett in the same voice except that he had a lisp, and then of course I did Lee Lou, the Chinese cook. I did the Indian Chief, also. Then, when I left in '39 to come [to Hollywood] with *Fibber McGee and Molly,* there were four or five fellows who took over the parts, including a chap by the name of Forrest Lewis, who did very well in several characters, including one called Wash.

Another actor who played Mike Shaw on the Tom Mix *show was a fellow by the name of Waterman.*

Yes, Willard Waterman. Well, as a matter of fact, when I left they had to find about three people to succeed me in various characters on that show and another one. Willard Waterman had a voice similar to mine and later on, of course, when I left the *Gildersleeve* show because of an impasse with the sponsor, he played Gildersleeve. And he also did the ill-fated television version, which was a bad series and they dumped it.

Why would you say that the television series didn't make it?

Well, I don't know exactly, except that Willard Waterman was a very tall man and it is very difficult for a tall man to do comedy. I mean, a real tall man. When he said "Leeeeroy" it looked like he was going to kill the kid, you know. See, Gildersleeve, in my opinion, was not a tall man. He was a little man who thought he was a big man. That was the character. But that had nothing to do with Willard. We were very good friends and I thought he did a very good job on the radio show; I just think he was miscast on the television show.

Was there any possibility or opportunity for you to do the television show?

Not really. I was approached on it once, but I wouldn't consider doing it unless I owned it. I did not own the name Gildersleeve. That was the difficulty. That was the reason I left. It was owned first by Johnson's Wax, who owned the *Fibber McGee* show and then it was owned by Kraft, who bought it from Johnson and then evidently Kraft sold it to NBC. I don't really know what happened there. I only know that I didn't own it and they wouldn't sell it to me, so I wouldn't play it. In those days what you did for just salary went out the window, taxwise.

And you had no residual benefits from it, either?

No, no protection at all, except that I was paying a heavy tax and I had other interests and so I decided not to do it.

That was a sad day for the fans of Hal Peary.

Well, it was for me and for a great many people who wrote me thousands of letters asking me why I had done such a thing. They thought I had sold out for a lot of money and, as one person said, "left us in the lurch." That wasn't the condition at all. I didn't want to go into details in the press. We were all friends and it was just one of those things.

When exactly did you exit from the Great Gildersleeve *character?*

Ninteen fifty-one. I played it for exactly 11 seasons, from '41 to '51. I started the character on *Fibber McGee* in 1937 and then I played it until 1941.*

You were with Fibber McGee and Molly *some time before you actually created a character known as Throckmorton P. Gildersleeve.*

Yes, that's right. I did several things. One of them – the first one I did, I believe – was an Italian father and that's how I happened to get on the show. There was somebody in the orchestra who used to play the part and he was snowbound or

---

* Radio historians agree that Mr. Peary appeared as Throckmorton P. Gildersleeve on *Fibber McGee and Molly* from September 26, 1939 through June 24, 1941. He starred as *The Great Gildersleeve* from August 31, 1941 through June 14, 1950.

something in Wisconsin and he couldn't make it. I had worked with Marian and Jim Jordan on *Kaltenmeyer's Kindergarten,* the show they used to do even after they did *Fibber McGee.* They loved doing it. And I did this Italian father and then I stayed on the show and did a number of parts: Gooey Fooey, a laundry man; George Fiditch, kind of an insurance salesman, and I did a character called Perry, the Portuguese Piccolo player in Ted Weems' band. Perry Como was still in the band, on the *Fibber McGee* show. And I did other characters. I took over the part that an actor by the name of Tom Post had played, the mayor of the town. His name was Mayor Applebee and McGee called him Mayor Applepuss.

McGee would!

Yeah! And I have some tapes which I had completely forgotten about: I played George Gildersleeve first, then Harry Gildersleeve.

I heard one program where you are Homer Gildersleeve.

Yeah! Don Quinn loved the name Gildersleeve, so he tried out several things. I did an old Englishman on the show when McGee was going on a safari.

I have another show where you were an interior decorator and an Italian wrestler!

Yes, I remember that. We had a lot of fun on the show. Actually, Gildersleeve wasn't born until – I had played the voice – but he wasn't born until Molly became quite ill and she was off the show for a few months. And then they kind of pumped up all the smaller parts like myself and things that Bill Thompson did and suddenly we were very important to the show. Well, they gave the Gildersleeve character an opportunity and I threw in that laugh one night, that I had never used on the show, and that was it!

As Throckmorton Gildersleeve, you were always rivals with Fibber and there were always fights and arguments.

See, after they called the character Throckmorton, then I moved in next door. You remember, I was his neighbor. And I even had a wife on the show, but she was never heard, she was only talked about. Molly occasionally said, "Oh, there's Mrs. Gildersleeve." That was about it. So, when I made the transition to my own show and became a bachelor, why, I don't think I had even one letter asking "what happened to your wife?"

I guess Don Quinn did this with a number of characters on the show. Sweetie Face [the wife of Wallace Wimple] never appeared.

Right. Sweetie Face was just somebody who was talked about. Something that Bill Thompson did and he, of course, created many other characters: Nick

Depopoulous, and [Horatio K.] Boomer, and "that ain't the way I heard it, Johnny" [the Old Timer].

There was somewhat of a difference between the Gildersleeve character on the Fibber McGee *show and the warmer character that you created for* The Great Gildersleeve.

Yes. I was an antagonist to McGee on his show, which is what Gale Gordon became when I left. Mayor LaTrivia. McGee had to have somebody he could fight all the time. So, when I decided to do my own show, then I warmed up the character a little bit, even changed the [laugh] attitude, you know, so that he became a warmer person and because he had a family to raise. And it wasn't too difficult to do, because all I had to do was lighten up the voice a little bit and make the laugh more human. We were just lucky. I just happened to hit the air at the right time and made it.

It was a wonderful show and we remember it well. We are delighted to have had this chance to reminisce with you.

I am delighted you called. Thank you very much.

Thank you, Mr. Gildersleeve... eh, er, Mr. Peary!

Harold Peary was born July 25, 1905 and was 65 at the time of this conversation. He died March 30, 1985 at the age of 79.

Willard
Waterman

Willard Waterman starred as **The Great Gildersleeve** *and appeared on many radio shows in a long broadcast career which began in Chicago. We met in his Van Nuys, California, home on March 17, 1984 and I asked when he first came to Chicago.*

Ninteen thirty-five. Came from the University of Wisconsin. They asked me to leave because I didn't have time to attend classes! I was too busy in the theatre and in the radio station, WHA, which was the first educational radio station in the country, actually. And it's a very powerful one now, I understand.

Then you were just out of school in '35. Was your first professional job in radio in Chicago?

I had done some professional work in Madison. I guess you'd call it "insulting" professional work. I made about $2.50 a program or something like that. I worked with a trio in Madison. We had a morning devotional service on WIBA, when I was in high school, actually, and I'd do that from 7 to 7:30 in the morning and then go over to Central High and my high school classes.

So you were, as they say, bitten by the show business bug pretty early?

Fairly early, yes. As a matter of fact, all through high school I prepped for an engineering course – architectural engineering – and planned to be in the Engineering School at the University of Wisconsin. And the summer between graduating from high school and matriculating, I guess the word is, to the University of Wisconsin, I got interested in a [theatrical] company playing in Madison. We played *The Drunkard* for about six months in a hotel, and I got involved with other local dramatics, and finally decided, by the time I went to University, to change to the speech and drama major. I guess I've never looked back much. The engineering went down the drain, sort of.

I think your contribution to the entertainment world is perhaps more than it might have been if you had contributed to the engineering world.

I hope so. I've tried to build a few bridges in the entertainment world, which I might've done as an architect, I don't know!

That's a good way to put it. Now, what was your first radio job in Chicago?

My first radio job was in a show called *Chandu, the Magician.* The show was just beginning to go on the air. I auditioned for about three weeks for *Chandu,* and it got down to between myself and Howard Hoffman, and finally they [chose] one cast around me and one around him, and we each did the [audition] show. We wired to New York, to the sponsors, and they chose his cast, with him. So I was, of course, crushed at my first big opportunity. At least I thought so anyway, and I thought my life had ended, but before the first show went on there was a call from Blair Walliser, who was producing the show, to do a part on the first program. I got to the studio and looked at the script, and here it's this lawyer, and it's every line throughout the whole script and I thought, "Oh boy, this is good, I'm gonna have a part on this show" and I turned to the last page and the lawyer died at the hand of the Red Ghost of Rangoon!

So, at the start of the series, I think the first three or four, I guess I was noted for dying. The first three or four shows I got in in Chicago were dying performances – an aviator who crashed, and there were four or five on *Helen Trent,* and I don't remember exactly the others – and I began to be known as being able to do a fine swan song!

It must've been pretty exciting though, to be up for the lead in a series right out of the box, more or less.

It was. It was terribly exciting. When it didn't work, I was crushed. I have learned over the years that you don't let adversity bother you much, because if that one doesn't work, another one will. You win some, you lose some. You play the law of averages in our business.

What role did you have, in the beginning, as a continuing role where you were an established character on a series?

Well, I did a lot of them on soap operas. In fact, on *Guiding Light* Betty Lou Gerson and I did the two leads for a long spell and then, actually, after they moved *Guiding Light* to the Coast here, we both happened to be out here and they brought the characters back into the show, so we did *Guiding Light* for two or three years out here, before it went off, before it went back to New York.

You played a role on the Tom Mix *radio series in Chicago.*

Oh, yes, I played a couple roles. Long Bow Billy was one, and I played Diamonds, who was the heavy. It's an interesting thing. Hal Peary played a heavy on *Mix* called Hog Barrett and I played this one called Diamonds. I was a 350-pound character, and I ate chocolates, loved chocolates. "Tom, pass me the chocolates up there. Tom, there ain't room in this town for both you and me; one of us has got to go..." And I also played Long Bow Billy [who] was an old friend of Tom. That was one of the things in radio which doesn't apply to television: You could play anything you could sound. We all did many different characters on the same show a lot of times.

That was your value to the producer or the director, that you could double or triple sometimes?

We were more hireable because they knew we could do a couple of different characters. I played a doctor on *Road of Life* who talked [with] a very aspirate voice. I'm doing it very badly now, but I haven't done it in a long time. So you learn to do tricks with your voice.

Did you feel that by doing two or three voices in a show that you were thinning down the pay that you were getting? Would they hire you to do three or four voices?

Well, at times in the beginning that was true; and then when AFRA,* the forerunner of AFTRA, came in there was a provision on doubling. You could do one voice and if you did more than that, you got another fee. In later years that changed so that you got a fee for whatever you did.

Everybody I've spoken with about the radio days in Chicago has told me about the dash from the Merchandise Mart to the Tribune Tower or the Wrigley Building. Were you part of that "Bridge is Up" group?

That's right. We all did that. Yeah, "The Bridge is Up." I belonged to that group out here when it was formed. We had lunch every Wednesday noon, quite often anyway. At one time, I was on three networks, within 45 minutes. I did a show on CBS called *Bachelor's Children* and it happened inadvertently. Somebody didn't see the name in the script, and so I wasn't called, and at the last minute they called me and said, "Hey, you're in today." That was on, I don't remember the date or time, 10:45 or something like that, and then the program on WGN-Mutual was on from 11:00 to 11:15 and then the one on NBC called *Thunder in the Air* was on from 11:15 to 11:30. So, all of a sudden I turned up in all three of 'em the same day. I did the show on CBS, *Bachelor's Children,* ran across the street to the

---

* AFRA, the American Federation of Radio Artists, the forerunner of AFTRA, the American Federation of Television and Radio Artists.

Tribune Tower, and up in the elevator, which I had "greased" the man. And then I had a cab waiting for me down in the lower level [of Michigan Avenue] under the Tribune Tower, and I dashed down when the commercial came on, into the cab, across Kinzie Street, which doesn't take the bridge into consideration, so you don't have to worry about that. In *Thunder in the Air* I was supposed to be in the first three or four minutes, and then another scene, so they reversed the two scenes and I had about three minutes plus the commercials – the commercials on the other end – to make the show. I had the elevator waiting for me and ran me up and I went in the studio and picked up the script. I don't know how many other times that was done, but I was on three networks in 45 minutes!

Cabs were speeding in the other direction...

...doing the same thing! Very true! Yeah, we all did that, working in the soaps, because there were a lot of conflicts.

You were free-lancing all of this time, is that right?

Yes. Well, I was under contract on *Guiding Light* and most of us free-lanced.

Most of the actors for radio at that period of time could get whatever jobs they wanted. They were not on the NBC staff, for example.

Well, I was. Not the very beginning, but soon after I got to Chicago. I was signed to an NBC contract, which actually didn't mean much. All it meant was that you were free-lancing at NBC, 'cause you had to be called by the NBC producers for whatever show they were doing, and you couldn't work across town. I won't go into it, but I finally got into a little contretemps with NBC and I walked out on my contract – not without notice – so I could free-lance all over town. But, actually, we were doing the same thing and people who were signed to NBC were free-lancing only at NBC, that's all. The contract had no salary involved. [You were paid for] just whatever you did.

Were other Chicago stations doing original drama?

Well, WGN was, but that was the Mutual Network. There was WCFL, the Blue Network of NBC; WMAQ, the Red Network, and WBBM was the CBS station. We used to do some drama down on WIND. Actually, they were religious dramas of some kind. We'd read them every Sunday morning.

So you could easily work seven days a week with all of this?

I used to average 40 shows a week.

Forty shows a week? In other words, if you were in Guiding Light, *that would be five shows.*

And for the other 35 I worked mostly, erratically, of course, but from 7:00 in the morning until 10, 11:00 at night with *First Nighter, Grand Hotel, Fifth Row Center,* a lot of the evening shows.

You worked a lot for First Nighter, *didn't you?*

I was sort of in the resident company, you'd call it. Les Tremayne and Olan [Soulé] and Barbara [Luddy] of course, but I did *First Nighter* before any of them, with Don Ameche and June Meredith, [and] later, when Joe Ainley was producing and directing, I was in it every week. For instance, they had the Christmas show, a show that we did every Christmas, and I played every part in it over the years except Mary!

And if she had been sick one year, you might have been called...

I might have tried that, I don't know! But it was a great company. Marvin Miller, of course, was around then, and playing in the company, and Harry Elders, and Herb Butterfield. We were together almost every week. Very unusual that there wasn't a part, some kind of a part, in it for all of us.

You had to put on a show for the studio audience as much as for the listening audience, didn't you?

Well, in those days in Chicago, if there was a studio audience, it was a "dress" show. We all kept dinner jackets. I used to have a room, four or five of us, actually, over at the Croydon Hotel and when we'd get down to any show after 6:00, we all had to dash and get into our dinner jackets. They had very appreciative audiences all the time, in the studios at CBS, WBBM and the Wrigley Building, and, of course, the Merchandise Mart. All of the dramatic studios had an audience provision.

The major network show on WGN and Mutual was the prestigious Chicago Theatre of the Air *and you must have worked that a lot.*

Oh, yes, there again it was sort of a stock company. Bret Morrison, and Bobby Ellis, and Fran Carlon and Muriel Bremner and, there were a great many of us that worked that every week. We did the dramatic roles. Marion Claire, a soprano, and all of the great tenors from the Met came in, a different one every week, to do the male singing lead.

We talked about doing shows in front of a studio audience. Were the performers on the radio shows apt to sign autographs for the members of the studio audience?

Yes, quite often, after the show, they'd catch us on the way out and we'd sign some autographs.

It was very nice to be able to see a radio show, because all the listener ever had was his imagination.

That's true. In radio you built your own sets and created your own characters. I guess sometimes it was maybe a little bit disappointing for an audience to see what the voice, that they had been hearing, looked like. Other times they were pleased with what they saw. But, the one thing that was the main attraction in every audience show, was the sound effects man, because they just loved to see what he was doing, the *clop-clop* of the coconut shells for the horses' hooves, and opening a door and all that sort of thing. You know, all the sound effect equipment was then done live. In later days it was done on record and on tape.

In a romantic scene, especially in a light comedy, maybe the leading players would embrace and kiss, and often there would be a little ripple of laughter from the audience because somebody was, what, kissing the back of their hand?

Yeah. That's right. [*SMOOCH!*]

I point out that you're kissing the back of your hand and not me!

Or your lovely wife!

Yes! Those were nice days, doing all of that. Now, you had 40 shows a week running like mad from 7:00 in the morning maybe till 10:00 at night. Did you ever say, "This is ridiculous, doing all this stuff"? Was it worth it?

Well, you got a little bit jaded, sometimes, yes. We used to take what we called a 12-hour vacation. You'd pick an evening when you were through fairly early and didn't have a show until perhaps noon the next day, and you'd imbibe a little heavily and the next morning you were usually a little hung over but, boy, were you relaxed! It did the trick!

Twelve-hour getaway! I think it was probably in the middle Forties, and you were still in Chicago...

Yes, I left Chicago in '46.

...you had the lead in a series called Those Websters.

That's right. That's what I came to California with – *Those Websters.* We did it for two years out here after we came out in '46. I played Father Webster and I'd done that for, I think, three years in Chicago.

Now, Those Websters *was a program that replaced another show called* That Brewster Boy.

That's right.

I don't know this whole story behind this, but I had heard there was some problem, either with the sponsor or with the producers or something on That Brewster Boy *and they just switched the whole thing around and made it* Those Websters.

I don't really know all of the details involved, but it became *Those Websters* after there was some sort of an uproar in the writing or production department, I don't know the exact details of that.

But it had a healthy run for about five years, and you stayed with it the entire time.

Yes. Well, it was like coming out here with a piece of cake under my arm, because I came out here with the show. We did the show one Sunday in Chicago, and the next Sunday out here in Los Angeles. I didn't have to go around and knock on doors here. I could meet people socially in the business, and they'd say, "What do you do?" and I'd say, "Well, I play Dad Webster on *Those Websters,*" "Well, uh, how would you like to do my show?" and I'd say, "I'll be happy to," and so it was a real great entrée out here.

What were some of the things that you did out here?

Well, the first one I did was *Screen Guild Theatre* and then later I did a lot of *Lux Theatres,* and then *The Guiding Light;* I picked that up out here again, after some succession, and I think I did a lot of *Amos 'n' Andy* shows with Correll and Gosden. I did Joan Davis' boss on her radio show for a number of years and I did *Lux Radio Theatre* quite often.

The Lux *show was probably the premier hour-long show on radio as far as the great public was concerned, and that took longer to rehearse than most of the routine half-hour shows, certainly more than a soap opera.*

Oh, yes, soap opera was an hour rehearsal and 15-minute show. *Lux* was practically a whole week's production. I don't know that it was necessary; it certainly wasn't necessary for the radio people – the people that worked in radio all the time – because we walked from one show to the other with no problem. Some of the picture people were very uncomfortable and they had to be, sort of, lulled into a sense of security. So they had plenty of rehearsal, they didn't stint on rehearsal at all, and over a period of three or four days, as a general rule.

You kind of set the stage for appearing in The Great Gildersleeve *with your role in* Those Websters, *didn't you? I mean, you got the acknowledgement of your posi-*

tion on the show, you handled the lead, in a light comedy.

Yes, that's true. Well, I hadn't even thought of it in that way, but I guess it could be somewhat true. Actually, the strange thing that happened was that Hal Peary, who was playing Gildersleeve, started it on *Fibber*, and had played it from 1941 till 1950. That was the time that CBS was raiding all of the NBC talent, and so Hal's agent signed him to CBS and then Kraft decided they did not want to change networks, and so they had to recast Gildy. Hal and I had a voice similarity, and it finally came down to the fact that Frank Pittman, who was the producer, felt that I could do it without having to do an imitation, and it worked out very nicely.

It was a difficult decision, because the producers weren't quite sure whether they wanted to try to keep the voice somewhat the same or whether they wanted a completely different voice. I wasn't sure whether I wanted to do it because – I took a career chance, I guess – if I had failed with it I'd have been out on my ear, probably. So we finally did a reading with the writers, and the character was so well written that I found that I could play it. My voice is a little bit deeper than Hal's, but the voice quality was there and I didn't have to make any conscious effort to do any imitation or anything like that. One rather strange thing that a lot of people don't understand, don't know, is that the laugh, the Gildersleeve laugh, the "He he he he," laugh, was really Hal's, and he used it as Gildersleeve. When I came into the picture, I decided I didn't want to use it, because he used to do a character called Professor Rollo on a show we did in Chicago called *Thank You, Stoogio* with Bernardine Flynn. And so I never did the laugh. I laughed, but not *that* laugh. I used to do what they called the Gildersleeve "social chuckle: Heh heh heh heh." But I didn't do the laugh. To this day if I'm introduced to somebody they say, "Oh, you were Gildersleeve. Let me hear you laugh," 'cause it was so well ingrained in the character.

Did you find it difficult to follow Hal Peary in that role?

No, I didn't because, as I say, the writing was so beautifully done. John Elliotte and Andy White and Paul West were writing the show, wrote it so wonderfully that I just played the character. Hal and I had been friends and still continue to be friends. I've seen him through the years a lot and we get along very well. I think Hal may have been a little resentful at the time but I don't think, for the long range, that he was.

Didn't you each play Sheriff Mike Shaw on the Tom Mix *show?*

No. I never did play Mike Shaw, the Sheriff. That was played by Leo Curley, and never by anybody else to my knowledge.

I think Hal Peary said that he played Shaw once or twice.

He may have, I don't know. As I say, the only character that I know for sure that he played was Hog Barrett.

You used to pick up for him occasionally in Chicago, didn't you, when one or the other of you was not able to make a role and it was a continuing thing or something like that?

No, we never replaced each other in a role like that. We played in the same show many times, and when we went in for rehearsal, he and I would get together and say, "You wanna go high and I'll go low?" or "You do a dialect and I won't," something so that we got away from the similarity.

Did the general public realize that there was a change of lead actors in The Great Gildersleeve *back at that time?*

I think many of them did not know. The billing was different, but in those days people didn't pay all that much attention to billing. The voice had enough similarity that a lot of people, for a long time, didn't know there was a change. I guess some people still don't know. The name Gildersleeve is bigger than the name Peary or Waterman and neither one of us have that personal identification.

You certainly do have a personal identification with the role of The Great Gildersleeve.

A lot of people still say, "Oh, that was Hal Peary." And as I say, we both did it for nine years.

I can't imagine that Hal Peary would've thought in 1950, when you took it over, that it was going to last for that many more years.

I had no idea at the time how long it would last. I think it was really a shame that Hal maybe got a little short shrift from his agent because they thought they could deliver the show to CBS, and they signed him to the contract. So now, he was under contract to CBS and they had to produce a show for him, so they started a show called *Honest Harold,* and I think it was unfortunate. What they tried to do was pattern the show after the *Gildersleeve* show and of course *Gildersleeve* was still on, on NBC, so it didn't work. It was too bad, because Hal was a very, very versatile actor. He could do many, many, many voices, many, many things, and it would've been far better for him, I believe, had he developed another character, and a new show around it.

You did the radio Gildersleeve *right to the very end of radio.*

For two years before the end of the era, we did it as a five-a-week, 15-minute show and it was very, very popular at that time. And then, after Kraft dropped it, we went back to a half-hour format, and we were, I think, the last audience show in Hollywood.

By that time you were only doing one show, not two shows, one for the East Coast and West Coast.

By that time, it was on tape. I mean we did the East Coast show [live] and the second one was on tape, but that took a long time to happen, because Kraft had a very adverse feeling about tape; they didn't like tape. Actually, the way we got to taping, under Kraft's supervision anyway, was [that] I had to have an appendectomy, and so I recorded, at that time, the first scene and last scene for what was to be the next show, and I did the show one Wednesday, went in Thursday morning to the hospital and had my operation. In actuality, I could've done the show the next week, but they did this to protect themselves, and then later, when they found out that it didn't change the show any, we were able to go to tape.

So the other actors did the show live, but they inserted your recording.

They did the show, inserted my record opening and the record close.

So you were written out of the body of the show?

I stayed home, listened to the show, it was a lot of fun. I enjoyed it!

You took The Great Gildersleeve *from radio into television, didn't you?*

Yes, I did the television series, which only was one season, 39 films. Unfortunately, it was not on the network; it was in syndication and due to some circumstances, it just didn't go beyond the one season. It probably isn't known, but Hal and I both did audition for it, and then they decided I looked more like Gildersleeve. When they were trying to decide about going to television, we did, actually we did, I think, three pilots before it went on the air, but we both had a crack at it, anyway.

And he didn't seem to be the type! He created the role!

Well, I don't know. He created it, but then again it's one of those things where in radio you could play anything that you could sound.

That's right. As Leroy, Walter Tetley, couldn't take the role to television.

No, and that's the greatest misfortune in the world. Matter of fact, I think that may have been one of the factors that [worked] against the television series, because that relationship between Gildy and Leroy just wasn't there.

You had a child actor playing Leroy on TV.

Yes, and that was the point. He was an *actor*, he seemed to be an *actor,* and with Walter, you never had any indication that he was an actor at all.

How old was Walter Tetley at that time? He, of course, was a grown man at that time.

He started in *Gildersleeve* in the very beginning and before that he had been on the NBC *Children's Hour* [also known as *Coast-to-Coast on a Bus*].

He worked with Fred Allen in the old Town Hall Tonight *in the Thirties.*

That's right. Well, his voice never changed and he, I guess, would've been what you want to call one of the little people. His family gave him growth shots when he was younger, and he grew to, I guess he was about five-foot-four inches, five-foot-five inches, something like that, but his voice never changed and he never had any beard.

He was so bright!

Oh, nobody read lines like Walter! He was just all boy, and Leroy was really the boy down the block. He was great, but unfortunately he couldn't be used in the television series.

When you were doing Gildersleeve *on radio, as the lead in a major network series, were you also doing other roles on radio, supporting roles?*

In the very beginning I was under contract to Kraft for *Gildersleeve* exclusively, and I didn't do anything else. But then in later years, after Kraft dropped the show, why, I did other things, too. But I did a lot of other things before I did *Gildersleeve,* between '46 and '50.

When you went into television you started doing a number of things.

Yes, well, I had done some before that, but after the *Gildersleeve* series, why, I did other things. I'd done some picture work, motion picture work, after the time I came out here. I did a film with Bing Crosby in 1947 called *Riding High,* the first picture I did. Then I went on to a number of other films.

You did some work on the stage as well.

Yes, that came later. I did a lot of stage work early, and when I was here, I'd usually go down to La Jolla, in the summer, and do summer stock down there. Then, in 1962, I auditioned for [the role of] J. B. Bigley in *How to Succeed in Business Without Really Trying,* out here on the Coast. Cy Feuer, the producer, was out here and I read for him and then I went back to New York and auditioned again, and got the part and I did that for two years in the national company. It was the Rudy Vallee part in *How to Succeed,* on stage. Then in 1966 I was back in New York doing *Succeed,* out at Paper Mill Playhouse, and I got a chance to audition for [the role of] Babcock in *Mame.* I won that audition and in 1966 I went back and we opened on Broadway with Angela Lansbury and played it for two years with her. Then we came out to the Coast and did the Civic Light Opera Circuit, San Francisco and Los Angeles. I went back into the Broadway company with Janis Page and then Jane Morgan and then finally it wound up with Ann Miller, so I had four years of that on Broadway. I had gone into New York expecting to come back here and when that ended in 1970, it wasn't all that much going on out here, so I just stayed on in New York, did a revival of *Pajama Game,* which was a lot of fun, and I did a lot of commercials.

Which role were you in Pajama Game, *were you Hinesy?*

No, no, no. I was the boss of... whew!

Oh, I know, yeah, the one who wouldn't give in for the seven-and-a-half cents!

Yeah, that's right. Can't say the name!

I can't think of it either!

Vice of getting old!

You're not getting old, you're getting better!

Oh, that's what they say, we hope!

Have you had any musical training or background to be able to appear in these musicals?

Well, actually in *Mame,* I did not have a number, I didn't sing. And in *Pajama Game,* I didn't sing. But in *Succeed,* I did. I had two numbers and I had taken some voice back in college, actually, and had done a lot of singing in church and –

Old man Hassler!

Hassler! That's right! Thank you!

Your role in Pajama Game!

You've got the memory! Yeah, Hassler!
So I had done a lot of singing, not solo work particularly, but a lot of work, glee club, and so I had some semblance of a voice, enough to get by, for musical

comedy doesn't take a lot of voice, really.

Well, to do it on Broadway takes a lot of talent.

Well, if you can get by with it, it's all right.

Radio, television, movies, the stage, you seem to have done it all. Which do you prefer?

Well, it's strange, I really prefer stage. As I say, I didn't get involved in it until later in my career, I guess, but the satisfaction of walking on stage and having that live audience out there, and not only that but the fact that you do it every night to a different audience and you get a different reaction! You get a chance to play with a character and if something doesn't work tonight, well, you do something different so it does work tomorrow night, and you really enjoy it. I enjoy being on stage very much.

Next on the agenda for you?

I don't know. I'm available, I guess it's what you'd say.

Do you want to work? Do you want to do some things?

Oh, yes! Oh, yeah! I want to do things. I want to do things that I want to do. If something comes along that I like, I'd be very happy to do it.

I want to thank you for all of your contributions to the entertainment world. You've done a wonderful job entertaining the public. You've made a lasting contribution and on their behalf we thank you.

Thank you, Chuck, thank you very much. It's always a great pleasure to hear that and it gives you a warm feeling to know that you have been able to entertain people over the years, and I'm thankful for that.

Willard Waterman was born August 29, 1914 and was 69 at the time of our conversation. He died February 2, 1995 at the age of 80.

Lillian Randolph

Lillian Randolph appeared on radio as the **Great Gildersleeve's** *housekeeper, Birdie Lee Coggins, during the entire 16-year run of the series. On August 9, 1976 I visited her in her Los Angeles, California, home while she was waiting for a call to report to a film studio to appear in a segment of an upcoming television miniseries. I asked her how she got her start in show business.*

 Well, let's see. I might as well start [with] the first time I appeared in public. I think I was four years old, in my father's little Methodist Church in Sewickley, Pennsylvania. That's about 12 miles from Pittsburgh. There's where I sang my first song. My sister Amanda, who [later] played the mother-in-law on *Amos 'n' Andy,* played the piano for me. She was a little older than I. We had a very, very nice little thing that we did in our father's church, just that way. We continued to appear in public, everywhere.

And then your first professional engagement?

My first professional engagement was in Chester Park in Cincinnati, and I sang there with a band. I was quite young. I was frightened about making the audition, and my sister made it for me. We looked so much alike. She had gotten another job, so she said, "Now, you go take the job, and they won't know the difference between you and I." And I went there and he [the bandleader] didn't know! I stayed there for a couple of summer seasons.

Did he continue to call you Amanda or did she audition under "Lillian"?

He didn't call me anything. He just listened to the band. We'd go there in the evening, get up on the bandstand and do our little number and come away. I can't remember his name. It's so long ago, but it was a nice job, I know.

Were you doing many other singing engagements after that?

Yes, I continued to sing. Then in Cleveland I started in radio, on WTAM. My first announcer on that was a man by the name of Red Barber. I started working there and I was asked to come over [to Detroit] to WXYZ and WJR to audition with a group. Fortunately, I was the only one in the group that showed. Mr. – oh, my goodness, I must not forget his name – Trendle, George Trendle. Mr. Trendle wanted me to do a skit, a Negro comedy skit. He got a comedian by the name of Billy Mitchell, and I was taught – this sounds ridiculous but it's the truth – I was taught Negro dialect by a Caucasian by the name of James Jewell. He was one of the originators of *The Lone Ranger*. He's out of Chicago. One of the nicest men I've ever met in my life. I owe everything I've ever done in radio to Mr. Jewell, who I think now, they've told me, has passed on.

Yes, he passed away a little better than a year ago [on August 5, 1975].

Is that so? A wonderful man. I worked there and the whole time Mr. Jewell was training me, Mr. Trendle paid me $30 a week. That was a lot of money during those days. Then he put us to work. We did a little show called *Lulu and Leander.* I had to do about five different voices and so did Billy, but that's the way they were doing things in those days. I got very anxious to get to the Coast. Young and ambitious! So out here I came [and] my first show out here was with Al Jolson on radio. This was *The Lux Radio Theatre.* A gentleman by the name of Dick Ryan, who has passed away too, got the job for me. I just went from one agency to another. They would call me anytime whenever they'd want a Negro maid or cook or anything like that.

So, you were doing more acting now than singing?

Yes, but when the acting would get slow, I'd go back to singing. I worked for a man in Hollywood, on Hollywood Boulevard, by the name of Larry Potter, who had a supper club. While I was doing this radio work, I used to work for him at night. If I got a picture call, why, I'd run and do that. I worked as an extra then. I had never had the good fortune of getting a character part. So one job led to another and from that I got with Joe Penner, who used to say, "You wanna buy a duck?" And Al Pearce, who was a salesman…

"Nobody home, I hope, I hope, hope."

Yeah! [laughing] "Nobody home, I hope, I hope, I hope!"

What did you do on those shows?

I generally did the part of the maid or housekeeper. Each producer that I would work with – I would learn something from him. I'd just keep going. I'd watch everybody and take in everything I saw and pile it up in the back of my mind that I could use that sometime. Finally, I got *The Great Gildersleeve* show.

This was at the beginning of Gildersleeve, *right when it started?*

Oh, yes, but prior to that, I had done several *Amos 'n' Andy* shows in 1937. But I wasn't working regularly on that. The *Gildersleeve* show was a regular show I started in 1941. And that didn't close until [1957].

That was a long haul and you were on it for the full run of the show?

For the full length of time. Now, the first Gildersleeve that you had was a man by the name of Hal Peary, and he was with us nine years. We had the Kraft Foods Company out of Chicago. The agency that handled the show was Needham, Louis and Brorby. Well, then I thought of doing the *Gildersleeve* show, and they would let me run over and do the *Amos 'n' Andy* show whenever I was called. Then, Hattie McDaniel was doing the *Beulah* show and she got sick. She asked me to take her place. I continued doing the *Beulah* show for about five years. And I was doing all three of them at the same time.

All three!

Now, the *Gildersleeve* show was the regular show. That was really my bread and butter. I was Birdie on *The Great Gildersleeve.*

In my mind, you were as much a star on that show as Hal Peary or Willard Waterman or any of them. You were on every show.

Every show. I didn't miss one. I've never been as happy in my life with a group of people as I was with those folks.

How did you get the part of Birdie?

There was an audition out for this character. I heard of the audition. I was over at MGM singing with a group of people – the background music for a picture. At the time I was to be at NBC to audition, we would be singing there at MGM. So, I told the kids to cover for me; I was going to slip out. I pointed my car so that I wouldn't have any trouble scooting away from there. Fortunately, just at the time I was to leave – the length of time it would take me to drive from MGM to NBC – we got a break, a coffee break. I slipped out and got into my car and I shot over to NBC and ran all the way inside. When I ran into the place, I slid all the way across the floor. The men in the control booth laughed and I laughed, too. There were loads of women in there waiting for it. Some had already auditioned. I auditioned and they said, "That's the gal we want."

I think they loved your laugh, too!

Maybe so! But, however, I got the job. Oh, they were the nicest people. Mr. Cecil Underwood was the producer. Harold Peary was great to work with. Great. A fine man. He stayed there, I guess, until he got tired and then Willard Waterman took it over. He was there nine years. But, I stayed right straight along.

If you don't mind giving us a little Birdie's eye view of the situation, how much rehearsal did that particular show take? When you finished one broadcast, what did it take to get the next Gildersleeve *broadcast on? It started on Sundays, I believe.*

Yes, but we would go there, perhaps, Friday and work with the show. Sometimes different parts would have to be changed. We worked not too many hours. By the way, we were sitting on that stage when Pearl Harbor was bombed.

Oh, you were!

And we were sitting there when the President's voice came over declaring war. After that, we couldn't travel at night with any lights on our cars.

It certainly had to have put a damper on your spirits, at the beginning of that rehearsal period.

It was quite a frightening thing. We didn't realize the enormity of this thing until maybe weeks later. We didn't know what was going to happen, and why it was happening. But, there is where we were when it happened.

The Gildersleeve *show gave you plenty of opportunities to sing, didn't it?*

Yes, on Easter I would sing and at Christmastime I would sing. There was a beautiful little song I would sing on Christmas. It was an old song from the Seventeenth Century. It was about the Christ Child – the baby. On Easter I would sing "Were You There When They Crucified My Lord?"

On one of the shows, there was a story line that stands out in my memory about the possibility that Birdie was going to leave the Gildersleeve household. She was going to go home and, just before leaving, was auditioning for a role in the Summerfield music festival or something...

Yes. Yes.

I think you sang "Going Home." It was beautiful.

Yes, it was something like that. You know, I'd almost forgotten that. Yes, I remember doing that.

There was so much warmth in that show. It's interesting, because the Gildersleeve character created on the Fibber McGee and Molly *show was a harsh, abrasive kind of a guy, always fighting with McGee, but when this series began, he took on a whole different kind of a character. It had warmth and it was nicer.*

Well, he was himself. He was just a fine man.

You were one of the characters on the show that always got one up on Gildersleeve. You were one step ahead of him, weren't you?

Well, there was no wife or mother. This was a home where he had a niece and a nephew, Marjorie and Leroy. I was the housekeeper and had been around them, supposedly, for many, many years. I was more or less like a mother to them. I'd quarrel with him if he didn't pick up things. So, we just enjoyed it. It was a lovely, lovely family thing. I was happy doing it.

Did The Beulah Show *continue after* Gildersleeve *went off?*

No, no. It folded. Let me tell you about *The Beulah Show.* There were several Beulahs. Ethel Waters did Beulah out of New York. Then Hattie [McDaniel] did it out here, and another woman, a character woman who's passed away, Louise Beavers, she did a part of it. After that, why, I continued on. The show was a good show, but it wasn't a show that I was attached to like I was to *The Great Gildersleeve* show.

You had created the character of Birdie, and I don't think anyone else could have played it.

Yes. That was my line [of work] and I liked it. So, now what I do is quite a bit of picture work.

When I talked with you before we had a chance to get together, you said you were waiting for a call from a picture that you were going to go into this week or next. What is that?

It's a picture called *Roots.* There are 12 episodes in it. I'm in one of the episodes, number five. Before you leave today, I'll show you the script. I'm in that. This is a different type of movie than any that I've already done, because I think each one of these, as much as I understand about it, each one is a different story. I think they intend to make a serial out of it.

It's for television.

I think it is. There's quite a number of name actors and actresses in it.

What kind of role will you have?

It's a slave picture, and I have the part of – what do they call me? Sara. I'm an old slave and there's a young woman – she's a widow – and I'm trying to get her interested in another young man because I think that she should have a husband.

You've been doing lots of picture work over the years?

Yes, I've done quite a number of pictures.

Did you ever do any voice work for any of the animated cartoons on TV or in the movies?

Yes. You know *Tom and Jerry*? Well, remember the legs with the striped stockings, and the big feet of the cook and that's all you could see?

Oh, yes.

It's my voice!

That was you?

My legs and my big feet! Oh, listen, the funniest thing, I saw that cartoon in Japan, with a Japanese woman doing the part. I laughed, I'm telling you. I'm sitting in the theater. It was really funny and they still show it over there. They show it around here in a lot of places.

That's a bonus now! We didn't know that you were in the cartoon. Well, you got involved in television too, in the Fifties, didn't you?

Oh, yes. But I can't remember all the things I did. I've done quite a lot of work. I just got through doing a commercial for the Wesson Oil people, which will be out soon.

You'll be on camera talking about Wesson Oil, huh?

Yes, I fried some chicken and it was very crispy and nice. That's what you'll be seeing me on TV next.

They kept you in the kitchen a lot, from Kraft Mayonnaise to Wesson Oil.

I don't mind it at all. It's work, and I'm an actress, so what difference does it make what type character I play?

You have worked almost all of the time from the point where you first got interested in this area.

Yes, I have had quite a bit of work. Some work that I have [been offered] lately, I have turned down. If it was a character that was in a picture where there was a lot of pornography, I didn't want any part of it. Because I'm an old fuddy-duddy, I don't go for that.

Well, it's nice that you have that kind of integrity, too.

Yes. I'm a Christian. My life isn't like that. None of my family are like that. So I don't care for that sort of thing. I wouldn't want my children or the members of my church to see me in a picture of that kind. Do you think that's silly?

No, I think that's wonderful.

Well, that's me whether it's silly or not. I'm not going to do it.

You've done some great things and we appreciate you taking a few moments to spend some time to share your career with us today.

I like to see young people go ahead doing things and being progressive in all their work. To think, now, here you are, out here, talking to me in Los Angeles, and you live in Chicago. Isn't that nice?

It's nice for us.

I think that's very nice, and I appreciate you coming over.

Thank you for all the great hours of entertainment you've given us.

Well, let's hope to God that I can continue to do it.

Lillian Randolph was born December 14, 1898 and was 77 at the time of our conversation. She died September 12, 1980 at the age of 81.

Mary Lee Robb

Mary Lee Robb appeared for many years as Marjorie Forrester, the niece of Throckmorton P. Gildersleeve, on **The Great Gildersleeve** *program. We met on June 15, 1988 at her home in Palm Desert, California. I told her that she was an important part of those shows.*

Those were wonderful days. They were just absolutely wonderful days.

You were the only member of the Gildersleeve household who grew during the course of the show. Your character got older, you got married, you had a family.

At the time I wasn't so happy about it, frankly. I didn't want to see her get married. I was a little afraid that the character would go off into the sunset, and that was that. But it was amazing! They really did go on for a long time. When we did the marriage – Richard Crenna, who played my husband, Bronco – we "dressed" it. It was the first time that we ever did anything like it. We dressed the wedding. What we mean by "dressed the wedding" is, they got me a wedding dress. We did it all on the show and it was done in costume, and very rarely did you do anything like that, in front of a studio audience. So, of course, they all adored it, the flowers and everything. It was very cute. It was a cute idea.

Later, when Bronco and Marjorie had children, you didn't simulate that in front of a studio audience!

Oh, no, no! That would have been going just a little bit too far, I'm afraid.

Too much for art's sake.

Right! But we did have some awfully cute children. They had a big contest. Kraft was our sponsor, and there was a big "Name the Babies" contest. So we had to go through all of that. That was kind of fun, too.

How did you get the role of Marjorie?

I am, I think, the third Marjorie. Lurene Tuttle, Louise Erickson and then myself. Louise was doing a play and was doing something else that day. Something came up and she could not get back for the dress rehearsal. I was one of those little people who was in what they called the background noise. They "blah, blah, blah" with everyone talking in a scene. The time came for the rehearsal, and we were sitting there. We had everybody waiting and whether it was traffic or something like that, she couldn't get back. I said, "I'll read for it. I'll time it for you, if you want," because they had the orchestra. We had full orchestra and everything, wonderful musicians. Perry Botkin, who was the great guitarist who had been with Bing Crosby, and wonderful musicians. They were all waiting. So, we did the show. Something came up – I don't know what happened – and she couldn't get back. So, all of a sudden, I thought, "Oh, my gosh! Here I am, the little background noise suddenly being pushed into this thing." Walter Tetley, who was so wonderful, said, "Now, don't be worried." And Una Merkel, a terrific actress, was playing on the show with us at the time. They were going over it with me. All of a sudden, about five minutes before we went on, Louise came in! Something had transpired that she was now able to get there. Later, I think she went on to New York. But having done that was a great step for me. So, when the time came, I was able to get the job in the fall.

Because you had been at the post but never got off?

Yes, isn't that amazing? It was just a funny thing. After that, I did some *Burns and Allen*. I played the little girl next door. Again, Richard Crenna was my boyfriend. He was boyfriend to more women, I tell you, than anybody else around! He was terrific.

He was the perennial teen-ager on radio.

Right. There's another young man, Gil Stratton, who has been out here, who was a very fine actor and also a successful sports announcer on one of the L.A. stations. He would come in and out, but basically Dick was always [around], at least in my time on the show.

What other radio things had you done?

My first show was *Lum and Abner.* I had two lines. I said, "I do" and "Don't cry, Papa." That was my great break in radio!

You learned those lines and you never forgot them.

Oh, I'll never forget them! It's just like the first time you do anything. That was my break. They said, "Come on in, we've got a part." So, it's been most interesting. That was where I started. Then I did *The Railroad Hour* with Gordon MacRae. He was a dear, dear man. I did some of those shows and I did *Red Ryder,* which was a little cowboy series. Let's see, *This Is Your FBI.* The two series that I worked on a lot were mostly *Gildersleeve* and some with *Burns and Allen* when it was on radio. Then when *Gildersleeve* went into television, there were very few of us who were on it. I can't remember. I don't think Walter Tetley was on the TV series. Willard Waterman was on it.

Walter Tetley never did any television as any of the characters he created on radio.

No. I think it's a sad thing but when the time came for it to be on television, some of us either were a little older or just didn't fit the character. The voices weren't the way they wanted them.

You are originally from Chicago. Was it in Chicago that the acting bug bit you, as they say?

My dad was with NBC in Chicago and so I was always around show business, that part of it. I took drama at Mundelein College as a little girl. In fact, my dad was the one who discovered Mercedes McCambridge when she was at Mundelein. Wonderful actress. She was part of a group they had. Sister Mary Viola, who was head of the drama department, had a verse-speaking choir, which was very unique at that particular time. That's where he found Mercedes. I started there and we moved out here to Los Angeles in 1939. I was a little girl and grew up in Westwood. I did a lot of stuff in high school. So that was what I thought I was going to do. Eventually, my father died and I started on more of a career. I was going to college and I chose, then, to go into radio.

Did you have to pound the pavement between CBS and NBC?

You bet! You bet! I'll tell you, we really did. It was a wonderful man who gave me my first break on *Gildersleeve,* simply because I went back and forth. At that time everything was very centralized. On Vine Street you went from CBS to Mutual to NBC. And the agencies were all around there. So, it wasn't a tough thing to do. They were very pleasant and it all seemed wonderful. It was great fun! I've always been interested in show business. In fact, we'd finish *Gildersleeve* sometimes and I'd go back in and stand in line to see Crosby in those days. That was when he was still at NBC, just to see some of these great performers. I was very much stage-struck.

You mean a performer on the network had to stand in line with the rest of the people to see Bing Crosby?

Yes, I think so. I may have gotten in a little earlier, but you did stand in line. They didn't know. That was the great thing about radio, that you could have sort of an anonymous life, and it was fun. You just went in and did what you did and you could leave it and go home. You don't have that same thing today in television or the theatre. I'm sure it's a lovely situation, but there is that being able to remove that coat of the theatre and walk away from it. The people in it were so wonderful. We did a little thing for a group called SPERDVAC [Society to Preserve and Encourage Radio Drama, Variety and Comedy], and we re-created *Gildersleeve*. Shirley Mitchell was on it. It was as though time had stood still. I had not worked with them, I hadn't seen them [for a long time] and we had some situations come up that were just so much fun. It was like yesterday, like we came in that door and we were all sitting there again. It was all those years ago.

It was a very miraculous time and people were very fond of each other. We'd have picnics. Dick LeGrand – Peavey – had a wonderful boat and we'd go out and have parties on the boat. It was more like a family. I think now, in a long situation, they may get that rapport, but we had that. It was very remarkable. On a motion picture, you don't hear that. You make the picture and then you leave and maybe don't see each other for years.

When you joined the show, around 1948, Hal Peary was Gildy.

That's right.

And then, in 1950, Willard Waterman came over. What was the reaction of the listening audience to the change?

Well, Willard is a lovely man, just a very warm gentleman. It looked like the show was not going to go on, and then suddenly they called Walter and me. They said, "Would you come in? We're going to do a little testing." We started in September and that was that. It was a most unusual situation, particularly because the voices of Willard and Hal were very corresponding, if you ever noticed. A lot of times it was difficult, because their voices were very similar in many ways. In looks, Willard was a much taller, much larger man. Willard said at one time it was kind of a hindrance, because there was the same timbre in the voice. So when he came on, it was just incredible. There were a few letters from people saying, "What happened?" or "Where is he?" or "What's going on?" But it was much less than one would have thought. Maybe it was because it went off and then it went on again, and there was a little summer off. But he was very pleasant and a good actor, a very good actor, and had good timing. He had lots of experience. So, this was almost like just putting on another coat that was really quite familiar.

If you were to listen to the last Hal Peary show and the first Waterman show, there are some subtle differences between the two voices. The laugh was a little different, but for all purposes it was the same kind of character.

As it turned out, it worked well, because Willard was very good in the role, particularly for television, I think. It's different, too, because Hal originated that role. It was his role, and as you say, there is a little difference. But, for all intents and purposes, it was a very easy transition, much easier than it could have been, where people suddenly went, "Oh, no, we won't accept that at all." I think they loved the show, and everybody [in] it. The same people were still locked into the characters.

It was the first spin-off, too. I think that was the original spin-off of any show. He had come off of *Fibber McGee* and then they started that show. I can't tell you what a family feeling it was. I think many people have said that about all their own shows that they've been on. I'm sure if you talk to any of the gang from *Our Miss Brooks* or any of them, but we did have a very professional group. I thought I was very fortunate to be among these people, because the timing was great, the quality of the work, the care. When I came on it, we did two shows live. Those were the days before the tapes. One for the West Coast, as they used to say. Then, we'd go in on Monday morning and listen to [a recording of the] show from the week before. There was a lot of quality control on it. It was not haphazard that it was a good show.

They made a recording of it and you went in and listened to it?

Yes. We critiqued it to see how it went, how the timing went on the various things. What worked and didn't work. They were very, very careful. They were very critical of the work to see that it came up to that high standard.

That's why that show lasted so long.

Right. We had great sponsors. Kraft was our sponsor for all those years, to my knowledge. It was just the whole thing. It was just a nice relationship for me. I loved it. In my personal life, I was married in the Fifties. My daughter was born in July. At that time, I was pregnant, did the show and had her in July, and went back on in September. That was radio. You could do things like that.

What kind of rehearsal did you have on the Gildersleeve *show to prepare for the broadcast?*

As I say, we went in on Monday and rehearsed Monday morning. We read it over and on Wednesday we did a rehearsal. Then at 1:00 we did a dress. Then about an hour before the show, maybe a little longer, we'd go back in and do a cutting session, because by this time they could see what jokes or what humor was going to work and what wasn't. Then we went to our dressing rooms, got ready and went out and did the show. I loved it! When you think about it today!

Doing them live like that! But there's a certain magic to the liveness of it.

One time something happened and I lost it. I lost a page in my script, and I looked up. It was my week. I was doing one of those Marjories where she used to babble, blah, blah. I just thought, "I'm going to die right now." I could feel the perspiration just moving down my body. Fortunately, Dick was standing next to me – Dick Crenna – and I just started looking at his page and we went through it until I finally found where my page came in. That was the only time. I must have had nightmares over that. If ever I was going to have a nightmare, that was what it was about, that night where the pages were [lost]. There was nothing there and you're standing there talking to people.

You described earlier the show that you dressed for, the wedding between you and Bronco. How did the listening audience react to that wedding?

They were very responsive to all the things we did. Because it was a kind of a family show, they liked it. As a matter of fact, we were fortunate enough [that] *Look* magazine covered it, which was kind of unusual. For that we went to a little Episcopal church in Hollywood and simulated the whole thing, set up the pictures. So, that was kind of a thrill. I don't think it had been done much at that particular time. It's not like it was in the olden days, but nevertheless, it was a different kind of thing. It was a new way of promotion.

Some proper time after that, Marjorie and Bronco became parents and you had twins. There was a whole big to-do about that on the show, a long sequence of things.

Yes. As I said, there was a contest, "Name the Children." That went on and on and on. It was all kind of fun.

Did they finally name the children? Do you remember?

Yes, and don't ask me! I wish I could say I remember.* That was fun.

Could you tell us a little bit about some of the other people on the show? Now, you said that Dick LeGrand had a yacht.

Yes. A boat.

A boat. The last person I would think that would have a boat would be Mr. Peavey.

I know! He was very interesting, kind of an outdoor person, which one would not have thought. Lillian Randolph, who I absolutely adored, was Birdie

---

* The winning entry in the contest named the twins Ronald Lynn and Rhonda Linda.

with us. We used to have the best time. We went to her dressing room and we'd sit there and have the best time and chat. I met some very interesting people, but she was the kindest woman and just so much fun. She would tell us stories about her early days. There was a lot of that going on. We had some great, great talent on the show. Kay Starr, the singer, was one of Gildersleeve's romances. Martha Scott, lovely lady, was on for a while. Una, as I said, and of course, Shirley Mitchell. I think I was closer to the gals.

It was a gentle show.

Yes, it was.

Thank you on behalf of all those who listened and enjoyed what you did.

It was so much fun.

Mary Lee Robb was born February 15, 1930 and was 58 at the time of our conversation.

Harry
Von Zell

*Harry Von Zell's career spanned
the entire Golden Age of Radio,
and when we met at his home in
Encino, California on February 19, 1975, I referred to him as one of the most
famous radio announcers and personalities of all time. He disagreed.*

 The term "notorious" might be better! After all, a man who would boggle
the name of a now immortal President of the United States could hardly
become famous because of it, but I certainly have become notorious.

*I was going to get to that eventually, but as long as you brought it up now, you are
the author of one of the most famous bloopers of all time. When did that happen?*

Well, let's see, it had to be what – 1931, I guess. As often as this has been re-
dramatized, printed, or spoken about, I've never heard it told right. They always
have me introducing the President. We weren't even in the same city. It was on
the occasion of Hoover's birthday, and CBS had decided they wanted to make
some sort of a special tribute to him on that occasion. So they decided to devote
a full evening – two and a half, three hours – of all-star radio entertainment. They
had everybody that could make a noise do anything to participate in the program.

It began with about a seven-page review of Herbert Hoover's life, from the
time he was a small boy in elementary school already showing the qualities of
initiative and leadership, and so on. Herbert Hoover, later in high school, entrusted
with the business of managing the football team. Later, in college, he was
repeatedly president of the student body. Managed the athletic departments. I
must have mentioned, in that opening, the name of Herbert Hoover no less than
20 times.

I was very young at the time, actually still in the category of a "cub" announcer
on the Columbia Broadcasting staff, and was very nervous. It was an assignment

I never would have expected to get. It came right out of the blue, and I performed this chore at the opening of the evening in a state of trance. It was like I was standing over here listening to somebody over there say these things and, as it progressed, I began to feel – I couldn't feel relaxed – but it impressed me that whoever that was talking over there was doing a pretty good job. I went all the way through it, and got down to where I only had one last thing to say, and I relaxed. I don't think I can repeat it verbatim, but this last line was merely in the form of wishing this tribute, simple as it was in its conception, would add to his happiness and somehow convey to him the extent of our love and respect and esteem to the President on his birthday and said, of course, there's only one way we can say it, along, we hope, we are joined by the voices of all the people in the world who are receiving this program by short wave. Happy birthday to our President, Heever Heeby Hoover, er, ah, ahba Heeby, Heeby Heeby.

You see, what happened is that the tension I had been under, not just during the process of delivering this review of his life, but I had carried this tension for about three days in anticipation of the responsibility and it relaxed, and when it did, the tongue went right to the roof of my mouth and stuck there, and nothing worked. I walked out of that studio. We were on the 23rd floor of the Columbia Broadcasting System Building. Fortunately, the windows there were not operative; they were fixed windows, or I would have jumped out! I wouldn't try to break the glass for fear I would cut myself, I guess. I thought, of course, whatever career might have been a potential in my life began and ended right there in that one incident. It turned out not to be so. Evidently, that has been my chief claim to fame, notoriety or what.

Notoriety perhaps; not your claim to fame, certainly. How did you recover? What did the bosses at CBS say?

Well, everybody was very kind. [William] Paley, who was then the owner of the network, and a large party of important people, the governor of the state was there. Mayor Walker was there. I would say there were about a hundred seated in the studio. And of course, I thought, "Well, I have no job anymore."

The first one to get to me was Paley, and he said, "Son, you did a beautiful, beautiful job, and you needn't worry, because it's understandable that emotionally you could have been moved in such a way as to cause this slip of the tongue." The only answer I had to that was, "I want to kill myself." But they kept me on and good fortune just seemed to come my way, one good thing after another. I think it was perhaps because of the uproar that came out of that bloop that I became a target. All the people who were buying programs on CBS wanted me for their announcer. They thought everybody would listen to see what I would do next!

You had been in radio a few years before that.

Oh, yes. I went to New York and went with Columbia Broadcasting in 1930. I had been working in radio here on the West Coast in local stations since 1922.

That was pretty early in the radio game.

Yes. Well, I was young. It was as young as I was. I think we were about the same age.

What were the radio stations like at that time?

Well, we had KFI, which was at that time very large in its wattage power, covered a lot of territory; KHJ, which later became the Mutual Broadcasting outlet; (KFI was, of course, the National Broadcasting outlet on the West Coast); KFWB, the Warner Brothers' station, and KNX in Hollywood. They all came along in pretty rapid succession. So there was quite a field of stations. If you could perform in any way, average or perhaps a little above average, you could get work. If you were average, you usually worked for nothing. People who had the urge to sing or play or whatever they did, or recite, all flocked into those stations and offered themselves. If they were acceptable they worked. But I began to get paid. I think it was at KNX. They gave me a half-hour a week, for which I got $25.

What did you do?

I sang. Yes, I started as a singer! Then later, I became employed by a man by the name of Bill Shartles, who was known then on radio as the "new idea man." He had formed a breakfast club from our audience, and had, at that time, nearly 200,000 or 300,000 members. The only thing they had to do in order to hold a card in the breakfast club, which gave them certain buying benefits at shops and markets and so on, was to religiously use the products that we advertised.

That little local show worked on practically every station then in operation from 6:30 until 9:30 in the morning. Our group numbered about 25, 30. We had the Gump Family – Andy, Chester and whoever – a banjo trio of excellent quality. We had a girl by the name of Louise Howlett, who could sing and play the piano like nobody you ever [heard]. We had good entertainment. That grew to be very big. Then one of the stations on which we periodically appeared – he would shift around from station to station to be sure he covered every possible audience – offered me a job to work at the station permanently as an announcer, time salesman, copywriter, engineer.

I sang under two different names. I did my popular songs and sort of a call-in request program with my ukulele where I accompanied myself. I performed that under my own name. Then I assumed some name I've forgotten [and] performed as a concert soloist [with] an accompanist and violinist who played along with me. I was trained at that time so I could do either one fairly well. I'm sure I didn't fool anybody, because the voice was close enough that there had to be some connection between those two names.

People were really eager for any kind of entertainment on radio in the Twenties.

Yes. Originally we were still on the cat's whisker. The quality, the reception, was not that good, because of the static. And then later, when they improved the microphones, they came along with the carbon microphone that worked if the carbon didn't become disturbed. Then you would have to hit it with a pencil or something, because it made a noise like bacon frying. But the technological progress was very rapid. With that, the sale of radios picked up. It boomed. I think our home probably was one of the last to have a radio set, because my father never thought the thing would last more than five years. He thought it was sort of a grown-up toy that would wear itself out. He later changed his mind.

You proved it!

Well, you see, he criticized my decision to take a steady job in radio. I was, at the time, assistant paymaster of the Los Angeles and Salt Lake Railroad, and as such, was in a small office. There were only five people in that office, which meant that, the way railroads operate, if you were looking for a promotion and were in a large office, you had a long time to wait, because there were always X-number of people ahead of you when promotions came up. So he thought when I left that position to go to work at a radio station for $25 a week that I had made a mistake. He expressed his reasoning by simply saying, "It won't amount to anything. It's a toy and it'll disappear."

I had had enough experience at that time to form an opinion of my own, which was that this medium, aside from what it could do for people in outlying places where they were more or less isolated from cities, could expand their imaginations, their vision, and their lives. Even more pointedly than that, because of the obvious appeal of this medium to a listener, and to a listener here and there, [to] millions of people, it was destined to become the most powerful and the most economical advertising medium the world had ever known. That's what it did and that's what it still is.

And how! You actually got involved in an advertising agency operation for a while, didn't you?

Yes. Well, you see, the work that I had to do early was public relations, promotions, sales, everything. That taught me something. I was only with CBS, I think, about four years.

You did The March of Time *for them in that period.*

Yes. I was the original "Voice of Time." This came about through the efforts of one man. He was the man who talked me into going to New York in the first place. He was, himself, at that time, with a large advertising agency, and he said, "You're bound to get a job on the networks, and you're bound to do well." Well, anyway, he later left the advertising agency that he was with and became head of the programming department at CBS, their headquarters in New York. When *The*

March of Time came along, they wanted Ted Husing as the "Voice of Time." Ted's love was sports and he was already involved with setting up, particularly during the fall and winter months, a football schedule that would take him to cities and towns away from New York, and he didn't want to do *The March of Time*. But if they had to have him, he had made up his mind. But, Burt, this man of whom I spoke, went to them and said, "I want you to at least listen to a new, young fellow that we have on the staff. They were coming close then to releasing their first show, and were within a day or so of doing a dress rehearsal of that show. So they had me do that. Then Arthur Pryor, who was the director of *The March of Time* at that time, came out of the studio and said, "Do you want this job?" and I said, "Yes." So I became the "Voice of Time."

How long did that last?

Four years. Then Young and Rubicam, who were moving pretty rapidly into the top spot among advertising agencies for their radio production for their clients, asked me, the way they put it, "needed me" for a certain program. The only way they felt that they could get me, because that program was on the opposing network, would be to hire me away from CBS. So they did. I went over there and was in their radio department for about six or seven years. The program they needed me for was the Fred Allen program.

The program called Town Hall Tonight.

Yes, and that was a joy. I enjoyed doing that. But they had others. They had Kate Smith, they had Ed Wynn, they had *We, the People,* which was very big with the audience. This consisted of picking people out of the news, wherever they could find them, that had interesting stories to tell. That was a big show. I found myself really spread around. I was not just on one network, but I was on all networks at one time or another.

You were actually employed by Young and Rubicam.

Yes. I could service only their clients.

Which had to be Bristol Myers...

Bristol Myers had *Town Hall Tonight,* yes. Then came a situation. You will remember that the *Town Hall Tonight* hour had co-sponsors: Sal Hepatica for the smile of health, Ipana for the smile of beauty. There was a conflict in the thinking of two men. Now, those companies under Bristol Myers operated as separate entities although the parent company was, of course, Bristol Myers. The advertising head of Ipana did not feel that Fred Allen covered as much of the audience as perhaps another personality might. They knew he had a good audience because our ratings were always very high. But because of his particular style, his particular personality, his particular approach to humor, they felt he was missing a large segment of potential audience. So, there was this constant bickering back and forth. They finally decided to split the hour into two half-hours. When that decision was made, Fred backed off. He said, "It would be impossible for me to do a half-hour. I've been doing this hour." He wrote it entirely himself. He said, "I've been doing this for so long, I wouldn't know what to do in a half-hour." So, he said, "You go and get somebody and I'll go off somewhere else." They got Eddie Cantor.

Then I became Eddie Cantor's announcer. Eddie Cantor would not stay in New York during the winter, so that meant that I was migrating back and forth, back and forth, every year. I was eight or nine months in Hollywood, and three or four months in New York in the summer. New York in the summer, I never liked. I never really liked New York at all. No, I shouldn't say that. There was a lot about New York that I liked. But, for living, I still liked California. After I'd gone through that experience for several years, I was still receiving my salary from the advertising agency, but I was only servicing, really, one program, one client. I just didn't like it. I resigned two or three times and they paid no attention to me. Well, finally they gave up, and when that happened, I moved out here, came back to California as a free lance, and of course, I had Eddie Cantor, with whom I signed exclusively until Dinah Shore became so big. The demand for her on the part of a number of advertisers was constant and very big.

She was a regular on Cantor's show.

That's right, yes, for quite a number of years. Eddie finally felt that he just couldn't hold her, and he gave her a release from her contract. Now, we were on NBC and she took a show on CBS. It was only a matter of weeks until Eddie came to me and said, "Harry, Dinah wants you to do her show." So I did. Then he contracted Joan Davis, a comedienne, to work on the show. Well, it wasn't very long before she became big enough that she was wanted badly by a number of advertisers for a show of her own. So, she got a show of her own and Eddie came to me again. So then I had three shows.

This was about the time when you could see television as an industry right on the horizon. Their testing in the East was convincing, and I was concerned with this problem of perhaps making a transition from the total audio side of the electronic medium to the visual side and the camera. So I had hired an agent to see if he might find me some small parts in movies – character parts. I said, "I want nothing that has anything to do with radio, because I want to be off of that and I want to find a place in pictures, if I can, as a character actor." And he did [but] it became a problem. Twentieth Century Fox, during the summer months, had me in a picture. It was pretty good, in the nature of a supporting role, a character role. They were coming up with other things, but they couldn't shoot around me, and here I had these three radio shows a week. Well, that finally resolved itself.

Television came along. I looked at it, didn't like it. I was dumbfounded that they introduced television as a comparable operation to network radio. I couldn't see where there was a possibility of that. Television gave everything. Gave the sound. Gave the picture. Gave the voice. Gave the music. Gave everything. As a mass-production medium, around-the-clock release, I felt it just was not what the medium was meant to do.

I tried. I did a few programs locally. Did one big hour with Alvino Rey and the King Sisters, which held a big audience for a long time, until it got too expensive for the local advertiser to afford, and that dropped. I tried another little program, a late evening thing. I think we called it *The Lazy Boners*. It was a sort of relaxed, forget-it type of thing: Life is easy. Life is pleasant. People are good. I was able to get enough guest stars of stature to keep that on the air, but I didn't like doing that. I wasn't getting any satisfaction out of it, really.

I had about made up my mind that there was nothing in television for me when I got word that Bill Goodwin had left the *Burns and Allen* television show, which I watched religiously every week. I was fascinated by what they were able to do on television in contrast with what others were trying to do. When I got that news, I immediately picked up the phone and got ahold of Willy Burns, George's brother, and he didn't even ask who it was. He said, "All right, Harry, you're on the list. This is a very critical change that we have to make." Which it was. Bill had been a very important part of their cast, in addition to handling the commercials. He said, "We don't know what we're going to do. We're just going to test, and you will be tested."

There were about 20 of us, I think, who tested and when they finally got down to a decision, I ended up with the show. I will never know exactly how or why. It came down to a choice between two of us, and the other one was Bill Bannion, who had done Red Ryder in the movies. He had done some acting on radio, but not a lot. But he was not associated in the public mind with radio, and I think that when they finally got down to where they had to make a decision between the two, they picked me because people were used to hearing me sell products. They felt that I would do a better job of selling the product than Bannion would. So, I got the job and am I glad.

You did a marvelous job of it. Did you work with George and Gracie in the radio series as well as the television?

Well, I did several series with George and Gracie early, when they first went on radio. First of all, because of this business with the exclusive thing with Cantor, I couldn't at that time. Bill Goodwin became their announcer and was with them permanently, oh, for about 17 years, so he would have to be their man. During that time, Bill and his agent were convinced that he should have had a show of his own. And he should have. There were two or three times when he got the opportunity and at that time he would go to George and say, "I've got this thing," and George would say, "All right. Go." And then [George] would call me and he'd talk to Eddie. And Eddie would say, "All right. If you want him. Go ahead. He can do it." We had no conflict, sponsor-wise or anything of that sort. I had done that two or three times and that's why I think Willy said, "You're on the list." Because as close as the audience could place Bill Goodwin with Burns and Allen, there were reasons why they could associate me with them also, because I had spelled Bill Goodwin on and off when he went off on these trials for a show of his own that didn't quite work out.

That led to another problem. My association with them on television lasted about 11 years. Then with the failing health of Gracie, she had to retire. We had to finish, and I was at loose ends. We knew two years prior to the time of our conclusion with the production that we were going to finish. Of course, my agents were out scouting around and when we finished, they had three new shows, all of which had been sold and were ready to go into production and take to the air on television. Two of them had a running part, and they wanted me for it. The other one offered me so many weeks out of each year, and they wanted me for it. I asked for a script of each one, which puzzled my agent. He said, "Harry, the show is sold." I said, " I know, but I have to know what I'm going to do." I read each of the scripts, and said, "Sorry." I wouldn't have been happy. They didn't, any of them, last very long.

What were the shows?

I'm not going to tell you, because several of the people involved are still around and it was not their fault that the show failed. The production was not good, the writing was not good, at least not in my opinion, and they didn't do well. It doesn't serve any but ill purpose to say who the stars were.

You knew you weren't able to work with it.

The premise of two of the shows and the quality of the writing, I thought, was very weak. I didn't see how that could hold up. I put no blame on anybody for that, because they had good writers, experienced writers, but they were not experienced in television. They were experienced in radio and a couple of them had done some pretty good screenwriting. But they didn't have the feel, or something, for television.

You see, people go to a theater to see motion pictures. They pay money, they go in to see it. If they've picked a bad picture, that's their problem. Radio and television went into your homes. One of the things that always troubled me, [was] that so many of the advertisers who use television – so many of the people who held positions as producers or directors in radio – looked upon it always as a mass medium, which, of course, it was in that there was a mass of people out there. But in the strict and basic sense, it was the most intimate and the most socially personal medium in the world, because you were entertaining one, two or three, or four, five people of the family in their living room, or their den, or their bedroom in their own home.

An advertiser in radio would give me copy which was orating and pounding and shouting the wares. I simply couldn't do it. I said, "I will not holler at people in their own houses. You must speak to them as if you're sitting there with them in their home, and appreciate if they keep that dial tuned to where you are. You owe them a great debt of thanks for allowing you in and letting you stay." They never got it.

You were the number one announcer in radio and in television –

I wouldn't say the number one announcer. I would say, certainly for a period of years, I had to be the busiest, because Young and Rubicam's stature in the advertising field attracted more and more large advertisers. [For] those who used the networks, I was there unless there was a conflict from one network to the other: I couldn't do them both. But, I was running from studio to studio practically every night of the week.

How many shows did you have on at a single time?

Someone told me – I never counted them – that there was a period there when they counted me on 23 commercial shows in one week. And I don't know how I ever did that.

Mostly out of breath, probably!

I know that in two-and-a-half years I shed about 70 very healthy young pounds of muscle.

You worked with the major comedians on radio, being much more than an announcer, because you were always part of the show.

Well, that came out of the Fred Allen experience. I hadn't been with Fred as his announcer for more than two or three weeks before an occasion arose in which one of the cast of "The Mighty Allen Art Players" – there were four of them – got an opportunity to do a rather important role in a new Broadway play and Fred said, "All right, we can work around you while you're in rehearsal and so on. But they got to a point where the producers of that play decided they'd better take it out of town for a few weeks, maybe to Boston or someplace, and give it a trial run in a theater. Well, that posed a problem for Fred, and that came up very suddenly. So the first reading rehearsal after Fred had gotten the news that Teddy [Bergman] was not going to be available, he asked me to read his lines in the "Mighty Art Players" sketch. I did, and Fred said, "Look, would the agency mind if I hired you, paid you separately, to become one of the "Art Players?" I said, "Fine." Now, this put me in a little different category. I was a performer as well as an announcer. Then, of course, when I went with Eddie Cantor, he used me as a foil.

He used you extensively. You were really half the show with him.

I was the straight man, yes, and in whatever sketches we had, there was always a crazy little part of some kind right in there for me.

Well, there was one season for sure that I know of – it may have lasted longer than that – when you became the father of a baby named Eddie Cantor Von Zell, Junior.

Oh, that was a frightful thing! The way it started – the news came that Mickey, my wife, was with child. We were expecting and right away Eddie said, "It's got to be a boy, and I'm going to adopt it, and I'll have a son!" That was the pitch. He milked that to death on the program. It turned out to be a girl! Well, he wouldn't have any part of that. We had to pretend it was a boy. He was just beside himself with disappointment. So he hired Billy Gray, wonderful entertainer. He had that little night club over on La Seneca. It was a favorite spot for show people for years. It's kind of a naughty place, but it was good. But anyway, Billy Gray could do a baby, could cry like a baby and make little noises like a baby. So for weeks, my little girl was on radio as a boy. Well, that finally petered out because everybody knew it was a girl.

It was good fun, though! A whole Cantor show would be built around some kind of a conflict between you and him.

Yes. He ran Gracie Allen for President. Or he put her up for President when she did a guest spot on his show. Then Burns picked it up. The public and the press went for that very big. I forgot who she was running against. It had to be Roosevelt, I guess. George wrote little campaign speeches for her to give each week on the program, typical Gracie Allen speeches. She got over 25,000 write-in votes! They only had a few weeks. I think if it had run longer, the write-in votes would have been more impressive.

Cantor was on for Bristol Myers again. Sal Hepatica and Ipana.

Yes, for a while. Then he switched over to Pabst Blue Ribbon Beer. His contract with Pabst was for seven years originally, with option. It still had about three or four years to go when Eddie, who was really trying to do too much, had done the picture at Warner Brothers, and he was doing our show, and then going around to the military camps when the Second World War came along. He over-taxed himself and suffered a little setback, which prompted his doctors to say, "Eddie, at your age, and the way you expend energy, you just have to back off. We recommend that you get yourself off the air for at least six months or a year, or whatever." Eddie said, "Well, I can't do it. I have a contract." So they wrote a letter to the Pabst Company and they, of course, released him then from the conditions of the contract. He proceeded to take it easy by doing a quiz show. I think it was "The Sixty-Four Dollar Question" which he took over from Garry Moore.

It was called Take It or Leave It.

Yes, *Take It or Leave It.* That left me in the middle of the season without employment. I went back to movies. I did 10 two-reel comedy shorts – quote, unquote – for Columbia Pictures. I played myself. The plots had to do with what happens to a fellow who is a broadcaster.

What was the series called?

The series had no name. Like the Andy Clyde series and The Three Stooges, it was done by the same department that did all those. It was just the name of the show starring Harry Von Zell, and then what the sequence would be about. These two-reel shorts ran about 15, 16 minutes, I guess, in the theater. I never saw one.

You still have never seen one?

No, I've never seen one. At that time, the double main feature had gone into effect, as a result of the major studios having been divorced from their releasing units, and they had to have some wedge by which to sell the product they were turning out. In those days, a major studio would turn out anywhere from 30 to 40 what you would call "major" release pictures a year. When they found themselves in a situation where the theater management or the management of theater chains with whom they were dealing could be discerning in what they wanted, they had to [use] a little leverage.

If a big picture came out with a lot of publicity by the producing studio, all of the theater managers and managements wanted that picture. A policy evolved from that on the part of the majors that if they wanted this picture as a first-run in their neighborhood, in their theater, then they had to take this picture as a co-feature. Whether they wanted it or not, they had to pay for it. That's the way that came about. There was only one way to go.

I had these 10 two-reelers under my belt when I quit. It got to be too tough. I used that, and the agent that I employed used that, to have at least an entrance into picture companies. I think the first big one I did was with Universal: *The Saxon Charm,* a five-star picture. I had a good role in that and then I got a good one in a big picture at Fox, *For Heaven's Sake,* with Edmund Gwenn. That was another five- or six-star picture. It was a good hit picture. Then there were one, two, three, four, five following pictures, so that kept us eating.

It's good experience, because it would get you ready for the TV series.

Well, I did get something on radio during that dearth. It was an audience-participation show, *Meet the Missus,* over the Columbia Network, which I didn't like. I didn't like the idea of it. I think the reason they had me do that was that I had replaced Tom Breneman on *Breakfast in Hollywood,* which was one of the biggest shows ever for audience. They felt that that would take me into this thing.

But *Meet the Missus* was nothing like *Breakfast in Hollywood.* The little gimmicks they had were, I thought, sort of childish. I don't know why I'm saying these things now – I may want to take a job at CBS one of these days!

You said you were on Town Hall Tonight. *What did it take to put that program together in the Thirties?*

First of all, it was a Herculean task that Fred Allen took on, in that he wrote every week with a lead pencil, on yellow paper in little, tiny print, that entire show. A full hour. At that time, people who were putting on hour shows, with guest stars – a variety type show – would hire three or four writers and still have trouble getting a product ready for air sufficiently ahead of time in order to go over it and get it right. But here was Fred, week after week, turning out this full hour. It meant sitting in a dark hotel room or apartment room all the days of the week we weren't on the air, and working nights to get the thing finished.

Another thing about that show was the, well, the element of the unexpected. Fred had a little imp in him somewhere, which moved him at times to simply depart from the script altogether. He would throw things at you from left field, and you darn well better be ready to step in. In the "Mighty Allen Art" sketches there was variety. He had "the little big businessman" sketch, the "Judge Zeke Allen" sketches, the circus sketches, the "One Long Pan" Chinese detective sketches. Oh, there were a number.

On [one] particular occasion he was doing a "Judge Zeke Allen," the hillbilly judge. A murder had been commited in this little rural community and the trial was in process, Judge Zeke Allen presiding. My part in it was that of Zeb, and it was an interrupted line. He was supposed to call Zeb to the stand to say what he knew. His farm happened to be adjacent to the Widdy's farm, Widdy Brown, who was the victim of the murder. Zeb, evidently in the judge's opinion, didn't have anything to say that was worthwhile anyway, so the speech is interrupted after he'd said about four or five words. Well, we had done a complete rehearsal in the afternoon and I had said my four words and got stood down by the judge for being incompetent and irrelevant. Well, on the air show, when it came to the interruption, Fred just walked away about eight, ten paces from the microphone, and gave me the signal to just keep talking, and I did.

In the course of presenting my testimony, I brought in the Atlantic Fleet, an air squadron, a regiment of Marines, a flock of crows that lasted for miles and you couldn't see the sun because there were so many crows, a cyclone went through the property, and Fred just kept standing there. By this time the audience – we were in the large studio at NBC which held about 1,400 people – were absolutely in an uproar, and people at home knew what was being done to me. This resulted in, I still say, and I've had nobody challenge me on it, was the first time [for] the expression, "We're a little late folks, good night." I had used up, with my ad-libbing, about 11 or 12 minutes. We came that far from the end of the show, and we had to get off, so Fred just walked up to the microphone, said, "Thanks to Zeb's testimony, we're a little late, folks. We'll see you next week." Then the following week, instead of coming on with the billboard and the fanfare, and the *Town Hall Tonight* opening, we just took up the dialogue wherever we were the week before.

Fred didn't want to throw it away?

Well, it was just complete. It's another slant on the unique quality, and the depth of humor that was possessed by Fred Allen.

There came to New York a man with a highly publicized mynah bird whose name was Major Ramshaw. It had already become world famous. He had toured Europe with it. It could answer questions. You say, "How old are you, Major?" and he would say, "I'm 12 years old. How old are you?" It could sing like Caruso. It could do anything. Of course, on his "People You Didn't Expect to Meet," Fred had to have Major Ramshaw. He contacted the mynah's trainer. I can't remember his name, and, of course, he was immediately responsive. Fred offered him a good price. He said, "You'll have your bird wherever you go, and when you go people will want to have you make a personal appearance with Major Ramshaw." Well, nobody knew what was happening, because we never rehearsed the bird, of course.

Came the air show, and now comes "People You Didn't Expect to Meet," and here was Mr. So-and-So with Major Ramshaw, the famous, genius mynah bird. Fred said, "Well, Major Ramshaw, welcome to *Town Hall Tonight.* Have you ever been on radio?" Nothing. Not a whistle, not a peep, not a chirp. Nothing. It went on and on and on. The bird's trainer would say, "Speak up. Sing a little song for us." Nothing. Pretty soon Fred, assuming an attitude of embarrassed frustration, just said, "Major, you may be a bird, but if you were a chicken..." You know, things like that. Then he said, "It must be, being on the radio, maybe an audience of this size has frightened him, the orchestra sitting here, all the paraphernalia, the microphones, the major may just be nervous and not able to function right, so we'll try again next week." It went on the next week, the next week, the next week, and our ratings were just going [up, up, up].

It became obvious, to me at least. I went to Fred one day and I said, "How much did you pay this guy to bring a dumb bird?" He said, "Well, I'm paying him double." He said, "I'll keep it going until we have the biggest rating that radio could ever possibly have. Everybody will listen to hear if Major Ramshaw ever does anything." He said, "All I did was ask him if he had one who didn't do anything, that's the one I want, and I'll pay you double." The advertising manager of the Sal Hepatica company never quite gathered Fred's humor. He got more angry every week when this bird wouldn't talk. He said, "Well, this is ridiculous. We're making fools of ourselves." Finally, he put his foot down. He said, "Fred, I won't stand for it. I just won't stand for it. I want that foolish bird off of here, because we will —" Fred said, "The ratings —" "Never mind the ratings. It's embarrassing. My friends are all calling me up and saying, 'What kind of a bird is this?'" So we had to stop it.

And he never did speak?

No! Never said a word.

There was another incident with Fred Allen where a bird played an important role. Didn't he have an eagle in the studio?

Oh, yes, yes! That was a beautiful incident. It was a terrific bird. Wingspread close to eight feet. The bird perched stood about two feet, three feet tall, and had a beak, if it went to caress you, would cut your arm off. I don't remember the name of that bird. Hmm. Now my memory has played a bad trick on you and me and whoever is listening to this, because the mynah bird's name was not Major Ramshaw. That was the eagle.

The eagle was Ramshaw?

Yes. I don't remember the mynah bird's name at all.

Well, he never said a word anyway, so it doesn't matter.

He never said a word anyway, so he shall be nameless.

To heck with him!

We don't want to embarrass him. We had to rehearse the trainer, because he had dialogue to read with Fred.

The trainer of the eagle, now.

Yes. He had to have the eagle with him because Fred wanted the eagle to fly. He said, "Would he fly in the studio?" The studio was about three stories high and very large. He had room to fly. The trainer said, "Yes, on my order he will fly." He said, "The way we do that, I send him off to fly. Then I hold a piece of raw meat in my hand, and he'll circle two or three times and then he'll come and land on this gauntlet." He had a big, leather gauntlet that he wore on his wrist. "He'll come and land on there to get the meat." Fred said, "Fine. We'll have him fly." I said, "How about the people in the studio? Might they be in danger?" "No," the trainer said, "he's used to people." He said, "The only thing, we shouldn't make a lot of noise, and you must tell your audience before the show that if he swoops in his flight, and it looks like he might be swooping down to land on somebody, don't worry about it, because he won't go that near. He just likes to fly that way."

All right, we did that. But the audience couldn't keep quiet. A woman would scream and then another one would scream, and the bird got more and more – instead of making two or three circles it made about a dozen. By this time, the people who weren't scared were laughing uproariously as the trainer kept calling the bird and holding the meat up higher and getting bigger pieces of meat. Finally, it looked like it was going to come and land on the trainer's wrist, but instead it swooped up and landed on a big flat, a stage flat that we had there on the stage. Here it was, perched up, oh, about 30 feet in the air. Sitting right down here were members of the cast, including myself. Our singing guest star of the week, Tony Martin, [was] resplendent in full dress, because he was working a supper club at the time and had to be dressed for it. Fred described it to the air audience after the incident occurred, and said, "Major Ramshaw, as you will understand, in a fit of distemper and nervousness, has suddenly been moved by an act of nature." Which, incidentally, by some miracle missed our resplendent and talented guest star by about a half-inch. Yes, that was the incident of the evening.*

It's radio and Fred Allen brings mynah birds and eagles...

Yes! Here's another example of how Fred's mind worked. He had a field man, a wonderful old gentleman back from the beginning of vaudeville by the name of Harkins, Jim Harkins. It was Jim's job to comb the newspapers and newsreels, any source of public information that would enable him to recommend to Fred people who were in town or going to be in town that would be good on the "You Didn't Expect to Meet" spot. He came up with one man, and he told Fred at the time, "I don't know that this would be so much." Fred said, "Oh, yes. It'll be terrific." Jim said, "Well, don't blame me if it doesn't hit hard enough." "Don't worry about it." Now, this man turned out to be a man of the sea. He had spent his whole adult life on the water and he had, for years, been the skipper of a vessel. He recounted experiences of shipwreck, collision, storm, fog, very dramatic things. He went through the whole thing. There wasn't much funny about it, until it developed he had spent all that time running a ferry boat from New York over to New Jersey. He had never been out of the Hudson River. Yet he had lived a full life of a sea captain, and that was funny and shocking, surprising. Oh, we got a lot of mail about that! They wanted him to come on again and tell some more of his experiences. People jumping overboard, rescues, all kinds of things.

Fred Allen started a lot of things on that early Town Hall Tonight *show that really were modified and moved so easily into the various half-hour shows he did in the Forties. I think "Allen's Alley" started out with kind of a round table, didn't it?*

Yes. "Allen's Alley" was really just a series of characters that lived at a place. He tried to carry that into television.

It didn't work.

No, it didn't. See, you make these people visual and you disappoint [the audience].

---

* The trainer was Charles Knight, a falconer, and the "eagle broadcast" was March 20, 1940.

You worked for a long time with Eddie Cantor. How was Cantor as a comedian different from Fred Allen, from your point of view?

Well, Cantor was what you call a heavyweight. He literally subdued his audience with the power of his energy and his delivery. A simple line, he delivered it with an impact that was 10 times its normal weight as a line. He was very physical. I never knew when it was going to happen, or if it was going to happen. But, if we were exchanging dialogue with jokes in it which I would set up and he'd pop them off me, he would suddenly leap on me! Grab me around the neck and leap! Well, Cantor weighed about 175 pounds, and was like a piece of rock, an extemely strong man. There was a time when he jumped on Errol Flynn in the ballroom of a hotel before an audience. They both went into the laps of the audience! Errol Flynn couldn't hold him up. Of course, he had no idea he was going to get hit that hard.

He did that to get a rise from the audience? A laugh?

Yes. Sometimes he would take Dinah – and I used to feel so sorry for her, because she dressed in beautiful gowns – he would pick her up and start whirling her around his body like an adagio team. Here she would be, flying through the air! Nobody ever knew when these things were going to strike him. It was just something that he had to do.

When he worked on radio in front of the microphone, he went through all of the physical motions – the jumping up and down that he had become famous for on the stage – that little prance that he did with clapping the hands, and then prancing around. If there was a passage of music, a segue of some kind, he would literally dance away from the mike like he was putting on a regular circus perfomance. I never knew a man who was able to expend that much energy over so many years and still maintain it.

There may have been an answer to that. Eddie told me once, I don't know whether it was something he fabricated [but] it sounds logical. He had already become a star with Ziegfeld. He was very young. He became a star when he was in his teens, really. As he matured, he became a bigger star. Of course, the big thing was the eyes. In a large theater, the person in the back row could see when [Eddie] rolled his eyes. You could see them go backwards and forwards. And they popped! They were big eyes.

This is Eddie's story that he told me. A doctor contacted Eddie and said, "I don't want to intrude, but actually, as a doctor, I should bring this to your attention. I would like to examine you. It's my opinion that you have an overdeveloped, or hyperthyroid." He said, "This is the source of this energy that you have. It's also the thing that makes your eyes pop, and enables you to handle them the way you do." He said, "As you get older, that could be threatening to your health. You could lose your energy. A simple operation would, in my opinion, correct it. Of course, you'll want to get the opinion of surgeons, other doctors. I offer you this just because I'm a doctor."

Eddie was moved by it, but he said, "One thing you said, this operation, if I had it, my eyes wouldn't pop anymore?" He said, "No, they wouldn't. It would be more or less normal." He said, "Forget it. Forget it. Never mind my energy, my health. My eyes stop popping, I'm through." Now, this was the dedication of a man who – it wouldn't make any difference whether it was an audience of four or four thousand – worked with every bit of the energy and the talents that he had and, very often, at charity affairs, little church affairs, things that he wasn't even getting paid for. Yet he put on the whole show, and then went back to the dressing room.

He had a man that was with him for years. He was, I think, a Norwegian who was a masseur, and a body conditioner. After every performance, first thing, in his dressing room, he stripped down and this man would work him over, bathe him with oil, get the perspiration off him. The nearest thing to Cantor, as a physical performer, was Al Jolson, who worked like Eddie. He, too, expended needless energy, 'cause all he had to do was stand up there and sing, and go through a few motions. But he burned up energy and gave out with muscle, every word, every word he sang or uttered in dialogue or whatever.

Did you ever work with Jolson?

Yes. The first time I worked with him, Eddie had him as a guest. Not Eddie, Fred Allen. Then I did a series. We had Jolson one week, Phil Baker would be with *Beetle and Bottle* the next week. The only full series I ever did with Jolson was dropped after the first 13 weeks. He didn't have any audience. I don't remember who the sponsor was of that. It was very early. Harry Richman started a series. He only did two shows and then quit. He said, "This is not for me; I have to be seen." I think Jolson felt the same way. He said, "If they can't see me..." Of course, he was wrong. He didn't like radio too much.

You liked it, didn't you?

Yes! Loved it. Still do

Did you work with Stoopnagle and Budd?

Yes. Debuts! I introduced Stoopnagle and Budd. I introduced the Boswell Sisters to the network audience. I introduced the Mills Brothers. I don't know what else or who else. Oh! [I introduced] Kate Smith to radio. I had seen Kate Smith in a Broadway show with Fred Allen and Bert Lahr, *Flying High*. She was, at the time, about 18 or 19 years old. Tremendous woman, and yet sang like... I still say she is the greatest natural singer I've ever heard in my life. Voice and ability to use it, expression, and [she] could tap dance like Eleanor Powell.

Kate Smith?

Kate Smith! She still could if she put her mind to it. She's taken off a lot of weight. Still is a tremendous woman. I had seen her in the show, and I was just so impressed by her. Not just her dancing, which always came as a complete surprise to a first audience, but her singing. I thought, "My golly, more people should hear this than a theater audience." I spoke to Freddy Rich, who at that time was in charge of the popular music department at CBS. He went over to see the show, and the next thing I knew she was signed up by CBS. I always did the Freddie Rich *Novelty Half Hour*. It went on around 7:00 in the evening, and often on a split network. It depended on what sponsorship we got for it. But it was mainly orchestra with an occasional no-name singer, or a comedian of type. We used to use Lou Holtz on those occasionally, a fellow who was famed for his Lapidus stories. He was a Jewish comedian and he told the most wonderful Hebraic stories you ever heard.

Did you ever do any band remotes?

Oh, a lot of them, yes. And there are some more debuts. The Ozzie Nelson debut, I did on remote. Glen Gray also debuted on remote, necessarily, because they were so in demand in hotels. Ozzie was from the Glen Island Casino. Glen Gray, I think, was from the hotel on 59th Street, the San Moritz. Of course, Tommy Dorsey and then later Jimmy Dorsey. They had been staff band men at CBS, but then they broke away from that to form their own band. They were just using a house band at the time. Mark Warnow was a house band. He was the sound group, the more classic, and his brother, who became the clarinetist who became so great. He used a different name. Oh, shoot! Very good looking young fellow. Brunet, very finely molded features. Well, it doesn't matter now. It will come to my mind tomorrow, or maybe in the middle of the night.*

You did a lot of news work, too, didn't you?

Yes, I did 15 minutes of news three times a week, CBS. I think that was only local, however. Graham McNamee had been doing the voice of Pathe News, newsreel. I don't know whether he quit or they decided to make a change, but they contacted me. Then I, for a year or two, also did the Pathe News voice.

Reasonably early in your career you broadcast reports of Admiral Byrd's Antarctic expedition.

Yes. Well, that was a two years' expedition and, of course, the series lasted two years. That was a very challenging assignment in that the communications by short wave in those times were very risky and undependable, especially from the Antarctic, where most of our weather patterns form. The static that generates from there is tremendous. So the only way we could handle the situation like this was for our engineering department to make daily contacts at some time or another

---

* Mark Warnow's brother was Raymond Scott, born Harry Warnow.

when they could hear each other with clarity. They would make contact with the expedition every day and get reports what had happened that day. This would be provided to me in cryptic form.

On Monday, such and such happened, something of significance. Tuesday something else happened. They would provide me with this sort of guide sheet in the event we hit a time during the network broadcast where the static got so bad the audience couldn't hear what was coming out of the South Pole. Then I would have to say, in our daily reports, "We know that on Tuesday of this week, they had a rather dramatic incident," and I would go into it.

Coming close to the Herbert Hoover thing, but it was not a spoonerism or a blooper, they had provided me with the information that during the week they'd had a tragedy. They had a little reconnoitering plane down there that they would send out occasionally to get pictures and to check weather and what not. Upon returning to the base, it had been caught in a whirl of wind. The average wind velocity where they were bunked in underground was 80 miles an hour. That was average, so you can imagine, it would get up to 500 or 600 miles an hour when the wind really moved. It hit his plane and dumped him down, and put him through the ice. Well, right away, I asked about the pilot. He said, "Evidently he's fine, according to the reports we got. The plane is completely demolished. They won't be able to use it anymore, but the pilot got off relatively easy."

All right, came Friday night and time for the broadcast, and we went on the air with fairly good reception. I was working with earphones which were unlike the [radio] sets they had by that time, with improvements that would tend to minimize static. But on earphones, whatever static there is, it magnified. They can do nothing to cut it down, but it's worse. We'd only been on the air a few minutes trying to get clarity and it just wasn't coming through. So they pitched it to me to take over. Well, here I explain this and, here again, atmospheric conditions are such that we've had to take over from the studio. But in our daily reports, we learned that a tragedy, a real tragedy and could have been even a more frightful tragedy, occurred during the week.

About that time, I got the finger again and they pointed south. So I said, "Oh, I'm getting a signal now that we have resumed communications with Charlie down there, and I'm going to ask him to tell you about this incident that happened." I said, "Are you there, Charlie?" He said, "Yes, Harry, I hear you fine." "Well, I understand that your plane was destroyed during the week, caught in a gust of wind when it returned to base and crashed throught the ice." "Well (garbled talk)." He begins to get mixed up in the static again. I said, "How is..?" I named the pilot, and I can't name him now. "How is so and so? How is the pilot? Is he badly hurt." (More garbled talk).

I didn't hear a word he said, but when he got through, I said, "Oh, thank God. Thank God. That's wonderful. We're so happy to know that he's doing so well." Now, what a lot of people in their homes heard – they could hear what he was saying and in my earphones, I couldn't hear what he actually said – was, "Well, considering, he's going to be all right. He has multiple fractures of both legs, severe lacerations of the face and head, fractured collarbone." The man was literally broken to pieces and cut to pieces and here I was saying, "Well, thank God." The station received a lot of phone calls saying, "What is the matter with that crazy man?" They explained, "With the earphones, when the static got bad, he just couldn't hear, and he had had information indicating that the pilot was not severely injured." The next week, when we came on the air, we explained that situation.

When you were involved in all of these radio things over the many years of your career, did you ever have anything from a blooper point of view to top the Herbert Hoover thing?

No. I got the credit for some. There was a man, maybe you have heard of. His name was Paul Douglas, later became an Academy Award winning movie actor. When I left CBS he said, "I know a fellow who sounds just like Harry, and he's versatile." As a matter of fact, the fellow had auditioned for CBS with a record on which he reproduced the voices and speech patterns of Hans Kaltenborn and Lowell Thomas and me and Norman Brokenshire. But they didn't hire him. At that time, they didn't need anybody.

Well, they finally ended up hiring him. I was now working with the advertising agency. All of a sudden people started saying to me, "Harry, what's happening to you?" I started getting mail from people saying, "What do you mean, the senator died of *skepticism*. He died of septicemia." I said, "I never said these things." I finally figured out what it was. It was this other fellow who thought he was hired by the network to sound like me. He was doing me almost perfectly but when he was reading the news, "The senator died of *skepticism*," all of these things, and I was getting the blame for it. I went to him. I said, "Charlie, listen, I make enough of my own." He took it well. I said, "You are better, actually, as yourself than you could ever be as anyone else. I'm sure that CBS would have hired you whether you sounded like me or whatever, because you are, in your own right, talented. You have a beautiful voice and everything that you need." He said, "Well, I've been sort of embarrassed about it. I thought that's what they wanted me to do." So, that was the end of that.

And we've come to the end of our interesting chat with you. You've done a great job for us all these years with good entertainment.

There is no one anywhere out of whoever was listening all of those years who could have possibly derived the pleasure that I got.

Harry Von Zell was born July 11, 1906 and was 68 at the time of our conversation. He died November 21, 1981 at the age of 75.

Ed Prentiss

***Ed Prentiss was a major Chicago actor during radio's Golden Age, starring as* Captain Midnight** *and appearing in a great many dramas from the Windy City. We met on September 4, 1981 at his home in the Pacific Palisades in Southern California. I asked if he got his start in Chicago.*

 No, it was in Cedar Rapids, Iowa. I started as an announcer out there in a little 200-watt station. I finally decided to take a chance and go into Chicago and see what could happen. Fortunately, everything worked out very well for me. In those times, there were no agents. You went to the advertising agencies and the stations. You introduced yourself and if some station was having a show, why, you went in and tried to meet the director and introduce yourself. Maybe he'd call you for an audition, maybe he wouldn't. But that was the way it was in those days.

Was it hard to get an audition with a director?

No, it wasn't. I was fortunate, I guess. I didn't have any problem at all. I started right to work, right away, as soon as I got in, about the third day in Chicago. There were shows that I worked like *Guiding Light, Ma Perkins* and *Today's Children.* They were called soap operas in those days.

Being a former Chicagoan, you were and still are a member of the "Bridge Is Up Club."

Absolutely! As a matter of fact, we have luncheons out here. There is a group of us that meet and get together. We have a lot of fun, because we talk about old times and things that happened then. Lots of times that bridge was up.

Ha! But we used it as an excuse most of the time.

Most of the people in those days were free lance actors.

Definitely. Except that there were staff announcers. But there were no staff actors. If a station had a show, they called actors from all over Chicago. There was no particular group of actors that worked at any particular station. They worked all the stations.

If you were a regular character on Guiding Light, *for example, –*

I took the part of Ned Holden on *The Guiding Light* for years.

– how would you know of a job opening up on another series or another soap opera? How would you get wind of that?

Word of mouth, usually. We'd hear about it. You'd meet somebody having a martini in the Wrigley Bar or something like that. Ha! Somebody would say, "Hey, did you hear about such and such a show?" "Who's directing it?" "Where can you get in touch with him?" And that was the way a lot of it went. The advertising agencies, then the networks, controlled everything. You couldn't take a new idea to an advertising agency or sponsor unless the network agreed to put it on. That was bad, because it stopped a lot of new things. The minute the advertising agencies came into the picture, then people with ideas went to them, because they knew that, for example, that this particular advertising agency had P&G [Procter and Gamble]. How do we get to P&G with this show idea? Well, the advertising agency would do it.

When you were working on Guiding Light *did you have to do that program more than once a day for the West Coast or East Coast broadcast?*

No, it would be recorded. Those things were always recorded if you had a later time for the West.

So you were free to do other programs.

Oh, yes. You could as long as it wasn't the same time. Well, you couldn't do more than maybe a couple of things, because you had rehearsal of an hour and a half for a 15-minute show. Then your 15-minute show. So maybe, if you were fortunate, you could do one in the morning and one in the afternoon. But if you had a running part, you had to be very careful about what you took that might interfere with it.

You were involved for many years with the soap operas, but you were involved for perhaps even more years on the adventure shows, the after-school radio. You were Captain Midnight!

That's right.

I look around your home here in the Pacific Palisades and don't see any Ovaltine jars anywhere.

Ha! Well, no, that's very true. But there are a lot of wonderful memories of the *Captain Midnight* show. That came out of WGN in Chicago.

How did you land the role of Captain Midnight?

Went in and auditioned for it. I just happened to have the voice that they wanted. So it was a lot of fun, I mean it really was. [On the show itself] you had a different script every day, of course, and your sound effects. You had the same rehearsal time, about an hour and a half, and then they made a recording of the show, too. So it was no more rehearsal for me, because it was a story angle, and whatever part of the story you were in, why, that was all rehearsed the same, about an hour and a half rehearsal.

How long did you stay with Captain Midnight*?*

Well, let me see. I was with the show up until about 1951. I went to New York in 1951.

How far in advance did the scripts come out?

We never saw the scripts until we went down to rehearsal.

Were they pretty much complete at the time you got them?

Never. There was always a lot to be cut, because of time. We would read it once for time. Then most often parts of the script had to be cut and that was, of course, the director's job.

What kind of mail did you get from the audience?

Really not too much, because a lot of the kids that listened to it couldn't write. It wasn't like a soap opera, where you'd have adults listening to it. But a lot of the young people would, if we had a giveaway or an offer or something, then they'd send in.

Secret decoders and all that sort of thing. There must have been tremendous response to those things.

Oh, yes, they would write in for something like that, but just ordinary things about the show there wasn't too much of it.

Did you get much fan mail then on the soap operas?

Quite a bit of fan mail. Most of that, however, would go to the advertising agency or to the sponsor, unless it was something that directly concerned you as the actor. If it was addressed to you, you always got it.

The only shows that the actors got credit on, for example, would be like *First Nighter*, that type of show. But unless they read the papers, they didn't know who did the parts on *Ma Perkins* or *Guiding Light* or *Today's Children*. The radio columns, maybe, would mention somebody [by name].

You mentioned First Nighter. *That was a major network show from Chicago and you worked on that frequently.*

I did for a while. I did "Mr. First Nighter," who introduced the shows and what have you. Then I also did acting jobs. Les Tremayne, by the way, was a lead on *First Nighter.*

Followed by Olan Soulé.

Olan Soulé, yes, I should say so. That brings back a lot of memories.

When you did a show like that, as opposed to a soap opera or kids' adventure show, I would assume a greater amount of rehearsal time was required.

Yes, because you had an orchestra with it and you're bridging the drama with the music and the timing of all those things. I've forgotten exactly, but I think sometimes it was around two hours or two-and-a-half hours or something like that.

Mostly, again, on the same day?

Yes. We never got together to read the script without the music and sound effects.

That's how professional all of you were. You'd just pick up the script and go right in and you did it. And you needed to put on a show for the studio audience, too.

Oh, definitely. The announcer of the show would speak to the audience and he gave them a cue for applause and what have you. The fading down and the fading up of the music and all of that. Yes, everybody realized that they were really more like a stage show.

And the actors had to dress formally for the broadcast.

That's right, and we never mentioned alcohol or cigarettes in any of the scripts.

It was all good, clean, wholesome entertainment.

That's right. It was so different than some of the things that we have today. It seems as though everybody is searching today for somebody in a bad situation that they can report on. Looking for trouble! But we didn't do that then.

Soap operas, daytime dramas, were pretty melodramatic in those days and the content was supposed to mirror real life.

After they got interested in one particular show, [listeners] would really follow the sequence, 'cause they wanted to know what happened to those performers. And they got to, pretty much, believe in it. It was that type of thing and it was a relief to a lot of women who said, "Oh, boy. I can quit cleaning house now and sit down and listen to my favorite show."

Well, you could continue to do what you were doing while you were listening to those shows on radio. I remember, as a kid, racing home from school to listen to the gongs that opened Captain Midnight *and all the excitement. Captain Midnight and Chuck Ramsey were always working on a secret decoder to foil Ivan Shark!*

Oh, sure! I've still got one of them around somewhere. I don't know where it is.

Well, the one you had was always the newest one. I always had last year's decoder, so I had to go for the Ovaltine and send in for the new one.

I never worked any other kid shows while on *Midnight.* At one time, before I got the job on *Captain Midnight*, I worked on *Orphan Annie.* Oh, it was a great time and I kind of miss it.

One day I had a line on *Captain Midnight* that was, "What we need here is some good mop-up operations." The actor working with me, Mike Romano, was supposed to come in right afterwards with, "That's what I like, a man with a quick tongue." So rehearsals went swell, no problem at all. We got on the show and I got to the line and I said, "What we need here is some good mop, -op, mm-, oop..." I couldn't get off of the thing! Mike, trying to cover up my mistake, comes in with, "That's what I like, a man with a quick tongue." The guy I felt so sorry for was Pierre Andre, who was the announcer on the show. I don't know how he ever came in to finish it but he did. Ha! And then we all went over to the Wrigley Bar to listen to the second show. Oh, it was so funny.

Did you socialize much with the other radio people?

Oh, yes. Oh, yes, we always got together. There was always a party of some kind on the weekend or something like that. Everybody that you associated with, your cast, like on *Guiding Light*, we always got together as a group. Yes, there was a great camaraderie and a feeling of fun. You never heard anybody talking against anybody else or anything like that. It was always a really great time of entertainment.

When you moved to New York, did you have additional opportunities in radio at that time?

I went to New York with the idea that I had to make a move. I felt that I did. I had lot of people that I knew in advertising agencies that were there. They knew of my record and background, so I didn't have as much of a problem in moving from Chicago to New York as I might have had. I did TV on *Guiding Light* and commercials, an awful lot of voice-over commercials.

I know that many people who enjoyed Captain Midnight *and some of the other things you did for so many years, would want me to thank you for all of your efforts in those areas, because you did a good job.*

Well, thank you for being so kind as to be interested. It was a lot of fun, and something that you just don't forget.

In closing I'd like to tell you, which I don't think I mentioned, that I found out that I could write poetry. I have written about 300 poems, not for publication or anything, but this is an example of the first one I wrote:

> Please God, guide me in what I do and say
> On this important interview today.
> Give me confidence and pride in what I know.
> But if I should brag a bit, please don't let it show.

Ed Prentiss was born on September 9, 1908 and was 72 at the time of our conversation. He died March 19, 1992 at the age of 83.

Arch Oboler

Arch Oboler captured the imagination of listeners every- where as the writer of **Lights Out,** *one of the most memorable series in the history of radio. We met on August 5, 1976 in his home in Studio City, California, where he spoke of his career in radio and how it began in Chicago, in the Merchandise Mart studios of NBC.*

 I wore out dozens of pairs of pants – the seats of them only – sitting in the reception room at NBC, hoping breathlessly that I could catch the eye – or preferably the ear – of one of the network executives with one of my plays.

How did you sell your first radio play? Was it to NBC?

I was fortunate in that they were opening up Radio City in New York which, of course, was to be part of the world of the future. One of the executives of NBC remembered that one of the plays that I had been trying to interest him in was the one called "Futuristics," a tongue-in-cheek look at the world of the future. So they bought it. And they bought it for the magnificent sum of $75. I remember when they told me it was $75, I batted my big red eyes and I said, "But, I've worked four months on this play. Is that all I get – $75? And then I got one of those lectures: "You should be happy that we are permitting you..." you know.

That was a big break for you, to have a play produced on the air then, wasn't it?

It was. But it almost cut my career short, because since it was a play about the future, I had a tongue-in-cheek something to say about cigarettes. In my play I was concerned with the "last" of everything. We were having an obituary for the last horse in the future and this was an obituary for the last cigarette, as I recall.

Now, it just so happened that no one bothered to listen attentively when we were rehearsing and when that hit the air and the boys in brass heard me ribbing their major sponsors, it almost was the end of me.

But it wasn't. It was the beginning. Did you start working regularly with writing scripts for NBC at that time then, or shortly after that?

No. You know, Charles, nothing goes that easily. It was quite a bit of time later that a chap named Wyllis Cooper got ill. He had started a program called *Lights Out*. It was kind of a revolutionary program because it was an opportunity to write radio drama for radio. You see, up to that time, radio was an imitation of the theatre and motion pictures. *Lux Radio Theatre,* the *Screen Guild* [*Players*], they really were three-act plays done in the manner that one would do a play, but not look at it. And *Lights Out* – when it was offered to me – I saw an opportunity. So, I started and although it was a horror series – one out of three was a horror play and the other two were idea plays – I had fun because, you see, I started to do radio for radio... for the ear. It wasn't an imitation of anything. I took a few words, a bit of music, a sound effect – and suddenly you were transported where I wanted to take you.

You really knew how to draw a word picture. You started literally getting away with murder, then, when you were doing Lights Out.

That's well put! The first play that I did, again almost took me off the air. You know, even now, particularly among executives, they don't understand the impact of radio over motion pictures and over television. I have had a touch of both and I know, because in radio – and it's so old I hate to say it – you give of yourself, you're part of communication. I challenge the listener to remember the [television] play that moved him a week ago. But in radio, I have had listeners remind me of plays that they heard 40 years ago. I have had that experience again and again. I had one the other day. Someone said to me, "You know, when I was 10 years old, I heard a play of yours and I've never forgotten it." And he told me a story that I wrote that I had completely forgotten. It was done that long ago and it stayed there in his neurons, so to speak, because he gave of himself when he listened to that.

That was, of course, the magic of radio, because we, as listeners, could participate. We had to build the sets and do all of that at the suggestion of you, the writer, and the actors, sound effects and a little bit of music.

Yes. That's the wonder of it.

Lights Out *went on from Chicago.*

Yes, and then when I went to the [West] Coast. We had it out here and then I brought Boris Karloff back to Chicago to do his first radio. He was a charming man, such a gentleman.

He did an outstanding job for you on a Lights Out *program, a story called "Cat Wife."*

Yes! Yes! A man whose wife, because of suggestion and because she has all the latent terrors in her of a witch cat, thinks she's a cat and how he tries to hide it from the world.

I always have a marvelous picture of Karloff in Chicago. We finished a broadcast and he disappeared. I knew how shy he was and I suddenly realized that he had left – his cab was going down Michigan Avenue. I went after him and I had to run to get to him and I said, "Boris, what is it?" And he said, "Look, look" pointing over his shoulder. Well, I expected to see Dracula and a few others and a few network vice presidents after him. [But I saw] three little children running after him with autograph books. He was terrified! I solved the problem simply, you see. I intercepted the boys and I said, "Let me sign." And they said, "Who are you?" I said, "I'm Harpo Marx." And they accepted and I signed "Harpo Marx" and I took care of that.

But you don't look like Harpo Marx!

I do, indeed! At Metro, when I was working there, I had more fun. One day I met Harpo and I told him the story. And he said, "Isn't that funny? I always sign Arch Oboler!"

He spoke! When you were writing in Chicago, you were writing more than just the things for Lights Out. *You wrote for the "little theater off Times Square," didn't you?* The First Nighter Program.

Before *Lights Out,* and trying to make a living, I was writing for that program, but that wasn't really radio drama. That, again, was an approximation, an imitation. What I was writing *Lights Out* for was in the hope that, out of that, the network would let me do a series of plays on a more gratuitous time, where I could write about the world, write about human beings and conflict and happiness.

Did you get to do that?

Yes. I was in New York and getting nowhere. I had just about had enough of *Lights Out,* so I got a group of actors together. There were no greater group of radio actors in existence at that time, and up at my apartment, I got them in front of a microphone and I rented a record maker. (In those days there was no tape.) You had to scrape the grooves out of a big record, and I made a recording of a thing called "The Ugliest Man in the World."

A few days later, I brought it in to a marvelous man named Louis Tiderton, a rare kind in the network. He was head of the literary part of the network, whatever that meant, and I brought my own record player and I said, "Mr. Tiderton, I know you're a very busy man, but please bear with me. Just hear the beginning of this." Well, this was such, as they say in France, *chutzpah,* to actually bring a record and phonograph and put it on one's desk!

So I started to play it and he listened to the whole thing. He didn't say a word when I was finished. I stopped the record player. He picked the record off and he disappeared. About an hour later he came back and he sat down behind his desk. He looked at me and he said, "I have just left the general" – that meant General Sarnoff, head of NBC in those years – and he said, "You are going on the air at 8:30 on the Blue Network on a series to be called *Arch Oboler's Plays.* Good Luck." And that was it. So suddenly the ogre turned into a fairy princess with a long wand and star at the end of it. And life was beautiful.

Wow! Now, when you were working in the radio days, you had almost total control over the entire program, didn't you?

Not "almost" – I had *complete* control.

You wrote, you produced, you directed, you cast the actors –

– and I swept out the studio when I was finished!

Did you always have your script intact at the time you went on the air?

I can hear numerous actors, still in Chicago, chuckling in their beards and up their pinafores now if I say "yes," because many a time I would write it during rehearsal.

I understand that you didn't always get along well with your talent, your actors. As a matter of fact, one time you even took a punch at an actor, didn't you?

To put it very simply, I have respect for one thing only, and that is not temperament, but talent. All the rest of it is just dressing, it's nonsense. I got along beautifully with actors and actresses. Most people don't realize that the average life of any actor is seven years. Seven earning years. So, if they have trepidations and nerves and concerns...

My only episode with actors and particularly one that you talk about was with a man, now deceased, by the name of Lou Merrill, a very fine actor. But, he had all sorts of inner hates and inner turmoils. I think in this broadcast – we were doing one with, I think, Greer Garson, and he was playing opposite her – he was difficult and we had so little time. And through the microphone all over the rehearsal, he was making all kinds of scurrilous remarks to his director.

Just before we went on the air he said something. And I don't remember anything except literally seeing red. And they tell me I tore out of the control room, tore into the studio, ran up to him and, with the hardest punch I've ever thrown – and I used to fight in the ring when I was young – I hit him smack on the jaw. He outweighed me three to one. Lou shuddered and, just at that moment, I saw the red arm of the clock go up to tell me that we were on the air. The red light went on and I pointed to him... and the reflex action worked. He began to talk and he did a beautiful performance. After that we were very, very good friends. We never had any more trouble, but I don't recommend to budding directors that they break their hands, as I did!

You broke your hand?

I broke a knuckle. There are other ways, I assure you!

You set the scene yourself for so many of the stories that you told on radio. You actually were on the air and you would set the scene. Was that a style that you purposely decided to develop or did it just happen?

Well, I'm no Orson Welles. I did it because I wanted that one-to-one with the audience. That's why I introduced the plays.

Your voice is spellbinding and I think it's the quality of it that draws that one listener a little closer to the radio, to hear everything that you have to say, and they don't want to miss a syllable.

Well, I always like to have one person in mind. You know, over the years I have known the great and the near-great and the notorious... and the comedians. The best of the comedians, for example, told me that they always – say, in Las Vegas – pick out a face in the audience and play for that face. I always have a picture of someone in mind.

You have been a tremendous contributor to radio and I cannot thank you enough, not only for having this chance to sit down and chat with you, but for everything you did.

Well, I think you are being extremely kind. I can only thank you for bringing back memories of Michigan Boulevard in the wind and the Merchandise Mart around the corner in the spring. The air was full of wonderful things in those days.

Arch Oboler was born December 7, 1909 and was 66 at the time of our conversation. He died March 19, 1987 at the age of 77.

Les Tremayne

PHOTOFEST

Les Tremayne carved a great career for himself in radio, appearing for many years on the popular **First Nighter** *program and in hundreds of broadcasts during the Golden Age. We met on December 12, 1973 in Hollywood, California. I acknowledged that he was not "Mr. First Nighter" on the show, but rather the romantic leading man, and asked when he made his first appearance on that series.*

I was on the show from about 1932 on. I became the leading man in 1937 and I left the show in the middle of 1943. Prior to that, I had been the leading man for two years on Campana's other half-hour dramatic show, which was on Sunday afternoons on NBC, called *Grand Hotel*. I did that with Anne Seymour for two or three years. I left the show in 1943, but every actor needs an identification point, and for me it was *First Nighter*. It's really the luckiest, most fortunate thing I ever did in show business, and I've been in it since I was three-and-a-half years old.

Did you play on the First Nighter *totally in Chicago or did you move with it?*

It was always in Chicago when I did it and, incidentally, it was never in New York! People sometimes think it was, because of the subtitle, "The Little Theater Off Times Square," but that, of course, was part of the illusion of radio, you know.

You played opposite Barbara Luddy.

Always.

Did you ever play opposite any of the other leading ladies?

I did, but not as the leading man. I played on the show with June Meredith and, I believe, Betty Lou Gerson, and I think they were the only two before Barbara came on. Barbara had the longest tenure, shall we say. She was on the show from about 1936 until it went off in the middle Fifties. By then it had moved to Hollywood for the second time.

For the second time?

It came out here in 1936 from Chicago when Don Ameche, who was the second leading man on the show, came out to go into pictures and, of course, almost immediately his agent, as I understand the story, asked for a lot more money, because at the time he was a very hot property. Campana had a budget beyond which they couldn't extend themselves, so they started looking around for a leading man. It's kind of a cute story. I became the leading man on *First Nighter* even though I was – now I must be specific about this – the leading man already for two years on *Grand Hotel*. When Don left the show, Campana started looking coast-to-coast for an actor to play the lead and they auditioned theatre people, radio people, oh, my golly, from coast-to-coast, movie stars, and they couldn't find anybody they wanted.

Well, I knew what they wanted because I had worked with Don on four different shows: *Betty and Bob, Grand Hotel* and *Jack Armstrong* and *First Nighter.* And it occurred to me that what they wanted was Don Ameche! It was very simple. Well, our voices weren't dissimilar and I knew his work so well. So, I went down to RCA and I talked to dear Betty Mitchell, who is now gone, a young lady who was the hungry actor's best friend. And I said, "Betty, I'd like to listen to some tapes of Don Ameche" or, rather, "discs." (We didn't have tape in those days!) And she said, "Okay, honey, what for? You've worked together so much, what do you want to hear him for?" And I told her and she said okay. She gave me a studio, sat me down with a bunch of 16-inch discs and let me listen to them.

Then, I immediately went up to the 19th floor of NBC and auditioned for Campana because I had gone to them and said, "Look, I'm the leading man on your other show; why don't you at least give me a chance to read for you?" And they said, "Well, we never thought of it." So I read for it and I played Don Ameche. Pure and simple. I even did his laugh, sort of a strange laugh he had, you know. And that's how I became the leading man. They said, "That's it!" And they didn't know what I was doing. It never occurred to them. And over a period of about four weeks after I started on the show, I weaned away from Don's delivery and became myself.

I would have thought that maybe they would have liked to have had different stars coming in, instead of a leading man and leading lady.

Well, that happened, as I understand it. I left Chicago in 1943. Well, when I left the show, Barbara and I had become so popular and so firmly ensconced on the show that they couldn't find somebody to replace me. See, history repeats itself!

So, they rotated four different leading men who were pretty well-known people around Chicago and finally they decided on Olan Soulé, who then became the leading man for eight or nine years, until the show went off the air.

You mentioned Jack Armstrong. *I've never heard of DON Ameche on* Jack Armstrong. *JIM Ameche was Jack Armstrong.*

And Don was on the show. He was hot around Chicago in those days, the early [and] middle Thirties. He played Captain Hughes. And when he played Captain Hughes opposite [his brother] Jim Ameche, who was playing Jack Armstrong, nobody knew who the heck was playing who! So, they had to replace him and that was the first replacement of Don that I was part of and I didn't realize that. And I was George Hartford, Bob Drake's bosom buddy on *Betty and Bob,* and when Don left that show, I became Bob and, then as I said, *Grand Hotel* and *First Nighter.*

First Nighter *was so popular that a couple of other programs did fairly good imitations.* Curtain Time *was one of them, and* Knickerbocker Playhouse.

And *Grand Central Station,* which was not a theatre format, but much the same type of thing, the structure of the show.

I never thought about Grand Central Station *in that same light.*

They had a framework as we did – theatre – they had *Grand Central Station,* and then their drama unfolded from that framework.

When did you first come into Chicago?

I started in radio on my birthday, April 16th, in 1931. I had been there for a number of years before that, playing vaudeville and carnivals and amusement parks and community theater, little theater, stock, tent shows, everything. I started in England, where I was born. I was born in London and my mother was an actress, God bless her. She was in motion pictures there and my brother and I worked with her when I was three-and-a-half years old. We came over here shortly after that and had our English accents beaten out of us by the kids on the West Side of Chicago, going to school, you know. So, I'd been in it a long time, a long, long time.

Where did you go to high school?

I never finished high school. I had to quit and go to work. We were pretty poor when we got to this country. Anyway, I went to Lakeview High.

Edgar Bergen's alma mater!

That's right. He preceded me by, I guess, by about eight or 10 years, so we didn't know each other in school. But I was an honor student and I won scholarships and I was never allowed to skip grades. That, I'm thankful for because I think you miss too much. But the scholarships I was not allowed to accept. My father was a tough man, God rest his soul, but he was a tough man and he didn't believe in the theatre and he didn't want my mother to be in it and he didn't want me to be in it. I won [the scholarship] for my singing abilities and that kind of put a crimp in me for a while. I never sang and I've been singing recently and I used to sing on *First Nighter* now and then. People are always amazed to find that I can sing.

I didn't know that you had sung on First Nighter. *Did they often do things with music?*

Not too often. One that I happen to have a recording of was [as] a young romantic Mexican millionaire's son and he also sang. He sang under Barbara Luddy's window with a guitar and that sort of thing!

What was your first radio job? Was it in Chicago?

Yes. The first show I ever did was on WCFL, the labor station there. It was called *The Night Court.* It was a show with two men and a woman [who] were the regulars. They had built this show. And in 1931, you know, just about anything went. One played the judge and one was the defense attorney and the other was the prosecuting attorney. And then people like myself came in and played – in those days we had no minority stereotypes – so you played the Italian, the Japanese, whatever, you know, with heavy dialects. And it was a copy show, sort of a traffic court sort of thing. And that was the first show I ever did. There were many other shows. Oh, gosh, they piled up so fast.

I was the original leading man on *Helen Trent,* Grant Douglas, before Gil Whitney came. I was on the audition. I helped sell the show in June or July of 1934. Anne Ashenhurst, later Anne Hummert, wife of Frank Hummert of Blackett, Sample and Hummert, which later became Dancer, Fitzgerald and Sample, an advertising agency, came out [to Chicago from New York] to cast the show and we made a live audition which, I guess, was piped back to New York or wherever for the sponsor. Virginia Clark was Helen Trent and, I'll never forget it, I'm this dashing leading man and I come down the hall in this, I don't know, apartment building, hotel, whatever, and I hear this lovely voice. (Virginia sang, too.) And she was singing and it arrested me, you know, and I came up to the door and I listened to hear her sing and then I sang back to her through the door. I was on the show for a year or so, but that's so long ago nobody remembers it.

You were on a few other soaps. I guess anybody who was on a soap opera was on a lot of soap operas.

Yes. People who were trying to get into the business and couldn't make it for one reason or another used to say it was a closed thing, a clique. Well, it wasn't that, but if you had the sometimes peculiar capabilities which made you a good radio actor, you were used a lot because it was a matter of time, more than anything else. And time is money. And if they knew that they could call you and you could do any number of voices, they would rather use you than take a chance on somebody new. It's still the same thing today, you know, and radio stands me in good stead today, because I do a great deal of voice work.

What have you done on television?

Well, I started on television in Chicago in 1939, on W9XYZ, the Zenith experimental station.

In 1939? You weren't playing a test pattern part at that time?

No! As a matter of fact, I was hosting and playing the leading man on a series of 45-minute dramatic shows and, if I may say so, this was pure hell. There was no air conditioning, it was a very small room, maybe twice the size of the room we're in, and it must have been 140 degrees. I was a thin young man and I lost eight pounds on the first show! I had to host the thing in tails and then, with no incidental music, no way to segue out of one scene into another, I hosted the thing and crawled out of one scene, undressing and getting into a business suit from tails, and came right into the next scene as the lead of the show. Well, 45 minutes of that, boy, I'm telling you, I was worn to a frazzle. And this went on for a few weeks and that was enough of that!

That must have been one of the very first dramatic things ever on television, period, let alone Chicago.

I suppose. I really don't know, but 1939 was pretty young for television.

You talk about First Nighter *and your identification with that program, but there's another program that you're rather well identified with:* The Thin Man. *You and Claudia Morgan.*

Claudia Morgan, a lovely girl, the daughter of Ralph Morgan, the famous theatre and motion picture actor and niece of Frank Morgan, even more famous. I did *The Thin Man* for about five years and I did *The Falcon* for, I don't know, three or four years, and just about every other show that was ever on the boards. I co-starred with various people on several *Lux Radio Theatres* and, incidentally, in those years, the middle and late Thirties, *The First Nighter* had a very small budget. And we had two hours of rehearsal on that show, including the music rehearsal, and it was a full network show. We played to, I don't know, 25 or 30 million people, which was a tremendous audience in those days.

We were neck-and-neck with *Lux Radio Theatre* for years. They would be top in the polls or we would be top. We alternated back and forth and they had a tremendous budget. They had to have, with all those movie stars, you know, who were guesting on their show. And we had ratings up in 27, 28, you know. And Barbara Luddy and I were voted as the top dramatic actor and actress in America. It was a beautiful time, beautiful.

Where did The First Nighter *scripts come from?*

From the free-lance market. And they had a special formula and they had a moral code, a very strict moral code. You didn't say "God" or "damn" or "darn" or "heck" or anything like that. The leading lady and leading man did not smoke or drink, no gambling. A very circumspect sort of formula, moral code.

The shows were submitted by [scriptwriters] to a sort of a jury of people consisting of a lady novelist, Florence Ward – God bless her, she was a lovely woman – and Bill Crowell, who at that time was the vice president and nephew of Emil Oswalt, the president and founder of Campana, which is now part of the Purex Corporation, and maybe one or two other people. Oh, Tom Wallace, God bless him, a wonderful man who was the head of Aubrey, Moore and Wallace advertising agency, who had the account.

They would set up a music stand in the studio and they would call Barbara and myself and whatever character people who worked on the show more or less regularly, and they'd call them in for one of these readings. And we would read six, eight, 10 or 12 scripts in the morning or an afternoon, all grouped around this one microphone with the one script [on the music stand] and it was a "cold reading." Nobody knew what he was doing until he did it! Actually, we had to give a performance as much as we could so that they could get a feel for the show. It was great training, tremendous training, even though we'd been in it a long time. It made you so facile as far as sight reading is concerned. Anyway, we would read the script. They would make notes in the control room. Then if they needed fixing, they'd send them back or possibly Florence Ward would do some fixing, because she was, I think, employed by Campana in this capacity.

As long as we're on *First Nighter*, I'd like to mention a couple of other things. Francis X. Bushman, the famous theatre and motion picture idol, was at one time Mr. First Nighter. The show originated and was created by a man named Charlie P. Hughes, who was the original Mr. First Nighter and used to be wheeled out. They wheeled out a beautiful gold and red plush theatre box onto the studio floor and then Charlie would come out in white tie and tails and top hat and his stick and would sit in the box with a microphone and introduce the show. And Charlie's ladyfriend was June Meredith and she was the original leading lady. The original leading man was a dear friend of mine, Jack Doty.

Two names come to mind, associated with the First Nighter *program. Rye Billsbury...*

He's Mike Rye now. He was Mr. First Nighter for a while in Chicago and he was also Jack Armstrong after Jim Ameche left it for a while.

...and Eric Sagerquist.

Oh, God bless him. He's long gone now, but he was the original conductor and arranger and the music meister of the *First Nighter* orchestra.

There was a very special sound to the theme of the First Nighter *program and I guess it was the use of violins more than anything.*

Yes, it was the instrumentation, actually, to make it sound as much like a pit orchestra as possible. You know, radio is a wonderful medium. It's a shame that radio drama, what I am speaking of, it's a shame that it's gone. It did something for actors, and I have said this many times, that has never been done before or since in all history for the journeyman actor, the lay actor. And that is, it made him an upstanding, home-owning, stay-in-one-place, family-raising, tax-paying, bill-paying, good-credit-risk individual. It did all these things for actors who were not big stars. And you had a steady salary and you became famous, and people loved you and you had people name their children after you. My gosh, I must have, I don't know, 50, 60, 70 kids named after me. Kids! Now they're 30 years old! And they become so familiar with your voice. It was a great I.D. point for me in the theatre in New York and also when I went into pictures in Hollywood, because people didn't know my face, particularly, but as soon as they heard the voice, they knew who it was, and it was a great tie-in for me. Even today, people over 35 remember me and are familiar with my voice. Telephone operators...

Just at random? You pick up the phone to make a call and they say, "I know the voice"?

Yes. "Are you – er, what was that show you were on?" A lot of older ladies, you know, middle-aged ladies, are telephone operators and they know voices. Traveling around the country, you sign your name on a credit card in a gas station or something and they remember you. And you have friends everywhere. It's beautiful, not only as an entrée to a lot of things, but just the fact that there is a warm feeling in the recollection of the things you did and they heard you do.

Those were good days and you contributed an awful lot to them.

Well, it did a lot for us, too. I mean, there was a great deal of reciprocity there, although we didn't think of it that way. We were having a ball. We were the busiest people in the world. For two solid years in Chicago, I did 45 shows a week, every week! And that's a lot of shows, believe me. Almost seven days a week.

That was including repeat broadcasts?

Yes, some of them.

Was First Nighter *ever on a repeat basis? Did you have to do that twice?*

I really can't remember, but I don't think *The First Nighter* was. We were on at 9:00 as a rule and that was a pretty good time, coast-to-coast. *Thin Man,* yes, *Inner Sanctum* most of the shows from the East had to have a repeat for the West Coast. And a lot of those, *Fu Manchu,* I believe, we used to do. That's very early. That was my first commercial, sponsored, show. And I had to ask my producer-director at WCFL – that was in 1931 – the difference between a sustaining and a commercial show. I didn't know.

You could tell by the size of the paycheck, couldn't you?

Well, it wasn't much different in those days. I did, as I said, my first spon-sored network show: *Fu Manchu* and that was a big deal! Oh, boy, that was the biggest show around! It had just gone on and I'll never forget. I played a young Jewish art shopkeeper who was poisoned by the golden needles and the golden pomegranates in this beautiful carved box, and I don't know whether I was trying to steal it or what, but I got my fingers caught in the pomegranates and it killed me and I screamed and – oh, it was a great death scene! But it was a big deal, coast-to-coast. Jack Daly was Fu Manchu, Bob White was Dr. Petrie and Charlie Warburton was Inspector Smith or something like that. Anyway, they were the three leads and a girl named Sunda Love was on it as a Chinese character, Fu Manchu's daughter or something like that!
You had to "dress" on that show. It was my first dress show. Up to that time I had not made any money in radio. I was in it for eight months before I made a cent and then I started making $2 a show or $1.50 a show or something like that. And I made $15 on Fu Manchu with a repeat! But this is a long time ago. I had to buy a tux, and a tux means shoes and socks, and a shirt and a bow tie, the whole works, cuff links, and I don't know how I did it. I was never a scrounger, I didn't know how to do those things. I wasn't a con man, but somehow I got this outfit for $15 so I didn't make anything on the show, you know, 'cause I was very poor in those days. I remember when 15 cents was a heck of a lot of money. I was studying sculpture and I needed some sculpting tools and I went to the art store and took one look at them in the window, and it said "15 cents" and I gave up. I made my own!

Well, I'm glad that you sculptured yourself a career in radio.

Thank you very much and God bless all those people who still listen to us.

Les Tremayne was born April 16, 1913 and was 60 at the time of our conversation.

Barbara
Luddy
and
Olan
Soulé

Barbara Luddy and Olan Soulé co-starred for 11 years on **The First Nighter Program.** *The three of us met on February 17, 1975 at Olan's home in Woodland Hills, California. I asked Barbara if she was with* **First Nighter** *when it went on the air in 1930.*

 BARBARA: No, June Meredith was. June Meredith and Jack Doty.

OLAN: Well, Jack Doty did it for a very short time and then Don Ameche.

BARBARA: And then Betty Lou Gerson replaced June Meredith. They came out here when Don got his Fox contract.

OLAN: And became Alexander Graham Bell!

BARBARA: *The First Nighter* auditioned every ingénue in town to do the six weeks they were going to be here. And I got it. Then Betty went back to Chicago for the summer hiatus. She got off the train and married Joe Ainley the very day that she got back there. So since she had just gotten married, when they went back on the air in September, she didn't want to come out here and leave him. So they got me. I did it with Don Ameche for nine months and then we went back to Chicago. Who turned out to be our director? Joe Ainley, the one she'd given up the show for! Then Les Tremayne and I did it for about six years. Then Olan and I did it for about eleven.

You started in 1936?

BARBARA: September of '36. I went to Chicago and I got there the first of June in '37 and was there until June of '46. I rounded my nine years off nicely, to the day.

Olan, when did you come into The First Nighter *scene?*

OLAN: In '43, really. It was just 10 years, I guess, because we came out here in '47 and it went off the air in '53.

BARBARA: That's right.

OLAN: That was the last 10 years it was on. I had the pleasure of being with Barbara longer than any of the other leading men.

BARBARA: My pleasure!

So you both spent a long time in Chicago with it.

OLAN: Yeah, Biddy was there from '36 on.

BARBARA: Thirty-seven.

OLAN: Thirty-seven?

BARBARA: Yes. I started out here in '36 with Don and went back there in '37.

OLAN: Oh, I see. And then Les went to New York in '42 or '43. Then I started with her. Then we came out here.

BARBARA: You had been on the show a lot, before you began to co-star in it.

The "little theater off Times Square" never came from Times Square, did it?

OLAN: Never came from New York! As a matter of fact, in our format, in the announcer's copy at the end of the show, there was always a note which said, "Announcer: do not ad-lib that this has been a Chicago origination."

BARBARA: And the same thing out here. They were not allowed to identify it as being a Hollywood origination.

OLAN: Because they wanted the illusion of the "little theater off Times Square" in New York, of course.

Mostly the show consisted of romantic comedies. But every once in a while you'd get into a kind of mystery-comedy or even something a little more serious than that.

OLAN: Yes.

BARBARA: It went from farce through comedy to fairly serious love stuff, and occasionally, a mystery. They tried to vary them each month.

Was it always sponsored by Campana products?

OLAN: Until the very end of the thing out here. Campana decided they no longer needed it on the air, and they sold it on a royalty basis – they still own it – to Miller High Life Beer... which was strange.

BARBARA: Which was really strange for *The First Nighter,* because there was never a mention of drinking. None of the ladies every smoked, and once we said "darn" in the script and we got so much mail you wouldn't believe from people saying, "When you say 'darn' you mean 'damn,' and that's just like swearing." Remember that?

OLAN: Yes, that's right.

BARBARA: So, when we were sponsored by a beer, that was really a step.

OLAN: Campana was a family affair. The Campana Company. It was close knit. They couldn't stand it when the show came out here with Don. They couldn't stand to leave it out here. They had to have it back there in Chicago. Remember our play readings, Biddy?

BARBARA: I'll never forget them.

OLAN: The way they selected [the scripts], when you had to stand in the hall in the middle?

BARBARA: I'm short, and our scripts were submitted by any and all writers.

OLAN: One copy. One copy [of each script].

BARBARA: And we had a reading each week to select which ones we would use. I'm not quite four-eleven, so I'd be right there in front by the one script.

OLAN: A copy on the music stand.

BARBARA: And everybody had to read over my shoulders. [These readings] were usually fairly early in the morning, around ten or so. I don't think they had things like Certs and so forth then! It used to get pretty heavy sometimes!

That's how they would audition scripts? Someone would listen to the actors reading it and say, "That sounds good." Right?

OLAN: Yes. We would read five or six shows at a time and the committee would be in the control room listening: Joe Ainley, our director, and the president of the company, Rich Kroll.

BARBARA: And Mrs....what was her name?

OLAN: I was going to ask you. A dear lady.

BARBARA: A very nice lady, who was a big wheel in the company. She would always be there, and so was dear Tom Wallace, who was our producer.

OLAN: Oh, yes. From the agency.

BARBARA: And they would select them.

They must have done a good job, because everyone really liked that show.

OLAN: Yes, they did.

That's what radio could do. The sound effects, the set-up of "the theater." Listeners could see the ticket taker and the usher. They could see the house lights dim and the curtain going up.

OLAN: It was a complete picture.

It was beautiful!

BARBARA: Most people who have ever mentioned it to me always thought I was a tall blonde instead of a short brunette.

OLAN: I didn't know that.

BARBARA: I had so many people meet me and start to shake hands up right here. "I thought you were a tall blonde."

OLAN: A lot of people I met had a different idea of the way I looked, too, because I used to play the handsome football heroes, you know. Here's a good example: When the show moved out here in 1947, we bought a home here in the Valley. Naturally had to move things out from Chicago, but we had to buy some extra things. We were buying some patio furniture at the time, which we hadn't had in Chicago. We picked out the furniture, bought it and I wrote a check for it. The man looked at the check and said, "Olan Soulé from *First Nighter?* I said, "Yes." I was beaming, of course. He said, "Well, my goodness, I've listened to you for all these years and now to finally meet you." He looked me over from head to toe and said, "I don't mind telling you, I'm sure disappointed."

The listener provided the pictures!

OLAN: The wardrobe and everything.

BARBARA: Someone has referred to it as the theatre of the mind. I believe that to be a very accurate statement.

The hero was always as handsome as you wanted him to be and the heroine as pretty. And the bad guys could be rotten. Olan, did you ever play a bad guy on the radio?

OLAN: No, I don't think so. I only played one on television. I did one heavy on television.

BARBARA: What was that? I didn't see it. You should have told me.

OLAN: It was a long time ago. I don't remember.

BARBARA: I don't remember you being mean!

You folks shared a lot of radio things in the Chicago area back in those good days. You were on The Chicago Theatre of the Air *together, weren't you?*

OLAN: Yes.

Colonel McCormick's special Saturday night pet there.

OLAN: Where he used to get to make his speeches. He'd speak about the Civil War.

BARBARA: And he always wore tails. Such a handsome man.

OLAN: Yes, he was, and a nice man. Incidentally, speaking of *Chicago Theatre of the Air,* I was doing a [voice-over] looping out here a while back on *Other Side of the Mountain,* I think it was. There was a young fellow there who was the director and he got to talking about the radio days. He was interested in the old radio days – *First Nighter* and various shows. I said, "I have a book about old time radio performers that I'll give you, if you'd like it." His name was Larry Peerce. I was going to autograph it to him, so I said, "How do you spell your name, P-I-E-R-C-E or P-E-E-R-C-E?" He said, "No, P-E-E-R-C-E." I said, "That's like Jan Peerce, the way he spelled his name." He said, "I know. That's my father. I know that you used to work *The Chicago Theatre of the Air* together many years ago when he was with the Metropolitan Opera."

BARBARA: Marion Claire [was on that show, too].

You were the voice of Marion Claire. She would do the singing and you would do the acting.

BARBARA: Not all the time, but I did it, I think, the majority of the time.

OLAN: A dramatic cast and a singing cast. We always dressed. It was white tie and tails.

BARBARA: You bet your boots! We always dressed for *The First Nighter,* too.

OLAN: In Chicago, yes.

BARBARA: You betcha.

OLAN: Always evening clothes.

That added to the illusion for the studio audience.

OLAN: Sure. It made the show seem more important. I don't know, I liked it better. We never did dress it out here. Things are more casual and informal.

BARBARA: Sometimes [here] I'd wear a cocktail dress, but short. There we wore long evening gowns and the gentlemen were in – the minimum was a tux.

OLAN: That's right.

BARBARA: On New Year's Eve, it was always tails.

This was before the advent of tape and recording.

OLAN: That's right.

BARBARA: We were all live. Our show was never recorded as such. But there was a man, [Urban] Johnson, at WBBM... whenever any one of us had a part we liked especially well, we would pay him to record it for ourselves.

OLAN: On acetate. A quickie.

BARBARA: They're beginning to deteriorate.

OLAN: I used to have Urb [record] shows every once in a while, as Biddy says.

One of them was *Bachelor's Children,* a show I did for a long time there, for 11years. We didn't have any tape then. It was all live. A live original show and a live repeat for the West Coast. Our first show was at 8:45, I believe, in the morning, to 9:00 in the Wrigley Building, WBBM, CBS. An agency hired me to do a 15-minute show, once a week at 9:00 on Monday morning at WGN, which was directly across the street. The studio was on the 11th floor.

BARBARA: Colonel McCormick's studio.

OLAN: McCormick's studio, yes. I was also doing a show there at the time called *Wayside Theatre,* which was on Sunday, sponsored by the Chicago Motor Club. Pat Dunlap did a lot of the leads in there with me. She played my wife in *Bachelor's Children.* So I had Urb record this *Wayside Theatre* Sunday show. I was anxious to hear it Monday morning. Now, mind you, I've got this show directly across the street to do at 9:00, immediately following *Bachelor's Children.* The way we worked it, on account of not being able to rehearse Monday morning, we rehearsed it on Friday. Then the agency man would walk through it, read for a last-minute rehearsal before it went on the air. I came across the street and did it cold Monday morning without a rehearsal. So, I had Urb record *Wayside Theatre* and I was very anxious to hear it. After *Bachelor's Children* went off the air at 9:00, I ran down in the basement to his place there and got the record and sat and listened to it. That afternoon, I came back for the repeat of *Bachelor's Children* and Bob Bailey was sitting there. Bob said, "You know, I heard a show this morning that you sure would have been good in." I said, "Oh, what was that?" He mentioned the show that supposedly I had done at 9:00 and I had forgotten to go do. That was one of those shattering experiences!

How about those repeat broadcasts?

OLAN: We didn't do repeats on *The First Nighter.*

BARBARA: One summer we did.

OLAN: Is that right?

BARBARA: Yes. The reason I remember it is because Tom Wallace and Joe and I would always go to a Chinese restaurant for dinner between the shows. One time they took me to the burlesque between shows!

Did you get in for half price? You're only four foot eleven!

BARBARA: I don't think so!

Olan, you should be familiar with Chinese restaurants. You played a Chinese cook on Little Orphan Annie, *didn't you?*

OLAN: My first network part.

BARBARA: What was his name?

OLAN: Aha. His name was Aha, the Chinese cook. It was very important, because it was a $15 job. I couldn't louse it up. I couldn't lose it. So what I used to do is go down and get a script. Actually, they didn't write any dialogue for him, so I'd write dialogue to fit the scene, and then take it to a Chinese restaurant up on the North Side, and get a waiter friend there to give me the Chinese phonetically. I would do half-baked Chinese to make it sound important.

If that was your first network show, what was your first experience with radio?

OLAN: My first show was *Uncle Quin's Scalawags.*

Quin Ryan?

OLAN: That's right. Mary Afflick, that's the name I've been trying to think of [from *The First Nighter* script audition booth].

BARBARA: Mary Afflick, that's right.

OLAN: She was married to Curley Bradley, who did *Tom Mix.* Mary was the writer and director on this show. That was my very first show there. In getting started, I'd been on the stage before. In 1933, at the time I started in radio there, the best offer that I could get was two-a-week stock in Zanesville, Ohio, for $25 a week.

BARBARA: Oh, my word. Two-a-week!

OLAN: Two-a-week and furnish your own wardrobe! So I said, "Well, we can be hungry here as well as in Ohio. This was during the NRA, National Recovery Administration, years. I got a job in the office of a steel company, the Edgar T. Ward Steel Company, on the South Side of Chicago, for $65 a month and worked there for six months while I started trying to get radio auditions. I'd tell all kinds of lies to get away. One time Mr. Bothwell, the manager, said, "Soulé, you've been gone more than you've been here. If you have to leave this time, don't come back." So that was my entry into radio. We got about 10 bucks a head at the time. Then I started getting other jobs with Blair Walliser.

I don't want to talk too much here, but a crazy little story about *Orphan Annie* and *Jack Armstrong*, in which I played Coach Hardy and these repeat shows. Jack Armstrong was on at 3:30 and 4:30 in the Wrigley Building on Michigan Avenue. Orphan Annie was on at 3:45 and 4:45, immediately following on the 19th floor of the Merchandise Mart. Norma, my wife, used to bring a car down to the back end of the Wrigley Building, the lower level there. I'd run down the steps, into the car, drive over to the Merchandise Mart and the [elevator] starter would shoot me up to the 19th floor. I'd run into *Orphan Annie* just as Pierre Andre would be droning out the last few words of his lead-in. I always made it, but that was a crazy thing. Sometimes, naturally, the parts would come in for a run at the same time.

You also were involved in Captain Midnight *and some other things too, weren't you? You did a lot of the kids' shows.*

OLAN: Right. I worked in *Captain Midnight* there with Johnny Coons, my old and dear friend there. Ed Prentiss was Captain Midnight there. He's now out here. Then I worked in *Captain Midnight* 20 years later out here, in film, incidentally, and played the same character.

BARBARA: I didn't know that.

On TV?

OLAN: Yeah, the same character.

That's right, but they changed to Jet Jackson, *didn't they?*

OLAN: Well, that was the rerun title. *Jet Jackson* was the rerun title.

BARBARA: I didn't know that. You never did let me know. I would have watched.

OLAN: Dick Webb was Captain Midnight and Sid Melton was Icky.

BARBARA: Did you know [Olan] was Batman?

Batman?

OLAN: I played Batman in *Super Friends*, an animated cartoon that's on Saturday mornings on ABC. I played Batman in a *Batman* series three or four years ago, a cartoon series. Just the voice.

You bridged the gap very easily from radio to television.

OLAN: I've really been blessed with that, going from one aspect of it to another. Stage and radio, then pictures and television, finally commercials – where the money's buried!

Hardly a week goes by when we don't see Olan Soulé on the screen someplace. How many Dragnet *TV shows did you appear in?*

BARBARA: You made dozens of those.

OLAN: An awful lot, yes. Do you know, that as long ago as the old *Dragnet* shows were, I still have more identification there than on anything else? I'm a "What's-His-Name" in pictures. People say, "Oh, there's What's-His-Name!" A lot of us had the same experience. The stars are known and the featured people in pictures and television, but a lot of us, in some cases the mainstays of things, are really not known by name.

BARBARA: We worked more often than the names did.

OLAN: We kept busy.

Barbara, you were in a lot of soap operas in Chicago, too, weren't you?

BARBARA: I was in [*Road of Life*] and *Woman in White*, an Irna Phillips series. I was Doctor Brent's wife and that wasn't a very good thing to be, because he was always having problems. They had to kill me in *Woman in White.* I was a bad girl.

OLAN: Why, Biddy!

BARBARA: I was. I had an illegitimate child, and they had to kill me! The audience absolutely insisted upon it.

OLAN: Oh, really? My goodness.

BARBARA: Yes. Irna Phillips tried to straighten the character around and, after I'd had the baby, make me a responsible type character, and clean me up, as it were. But the audience would have no part of it. They got so many letters saying, "You've got to get rid of her." So they killed me!

That was the end of it then! Today, on television, anything goes.

OLAN: Of course.

BARBARA: Oh, good gracious! The things I watch now shock me, in relation to the things we were not allowed to do.

OLAN: Oh, the taboos then, they would be nothing now.

BARBARA: We would be a real sissy-type show.

OLAN: Yes.

What was your first job in radio?

BARBARA: My first job in radio was when I came back from Australia. I'd been over there for a year in Australia and New Zealand with Leo Carrillo. I was in the theatre – theatre and pictures. I came back in 1930 and we opened in San Francisco in *The Badman*. The second week, instead of our salary, we got a notice of bankruptcy. That was when all the theaters all over the country were closing. So I came back here [to California]. This had been my home. Gale Gordon and I. He was beginning to be interested in radio. I'd been away for a year, and I didn't know anything about radio, actually, except before I'd left I'd heard a couple of crystal sets. As for dramatic radio, I knew nothing about it. One man, Gene Carmen, wrote a series that was based on a young couple at the breakfast table. We did that at 7:00 in the morning for six months on KNX for free, just to break into radio, which we did eventually.

We both started working with Kay Van Raproute. She was a magnificent writer. After I started working with Kay, the regular fee was $5. Kay would get $150. Barker Brothers was her sponsor, a big furniture company out here. They would only pay us $5, but Kay got $150 a week for writing, directing and starring in it. She paid us each another $5 out of her own pocket. So we got $10.

There was a recording company out here that is doing very little now, C. P. MacGregor. About the only thing they do now is *Heartbeat Theatre,* which is for the Salvation Army. They still pay scale. But at that time, they paid $3 a program. It was on wax. It was recorded.

OLAN: Regular pressing.

BARBARA: Oh, my word! If anybody made the slightest error, the whole blamed thing had to be done over. I remember one night we were doing a series for John Hancock Oil. Gale Gordon was the villain. True Boardman was the hero and I was the heroine. We recorded all night long. We'd start at 10:00 at night and do the five shows for the week. We had numerous little things go wrong. Then they'd have to shave the wax master and start all over again. We got, finally, to the very last. We had four of them in the can and we were up to the last line of the fifth one. Gale Gordon as the heavy was supposed to say, "I'll get you yet, Don Hancock." That was True's name [in the script]. He said, "Dan Hoecake." Nobody was angry. Everybody was just too tired to be mad. We just collapsed all over the place. But we were there until 8:00 from 10:00 the night before.

Why would they start at 10:00 at night?

OLAN: So she would be available, probably.

BARBARA: Yes, because other shows were beginning, and at that time, *Lux* was beginning. Then there was *Shell Chateau.* These were network things. *Lux,* for instance, took five days of rehearsal. They paid you $50, but you actually got $10 a day. On *Lux,* it was always motion picture stars. I was one of the few exceptions. Paul Muni wanted me to play Mrs. Pasteur in the Louis Pasteur *Lux* production. It was unheard of in those days to take a radio person. Francis Lederer – he has a big home and art gallery out in Canoga Park – also liked me as his leading lady whenever he did a radio program. Other than that, it was always just the picture stars.

How did they know to select you? Had they heard your work on other programs?

OLAN: They knew your work, probably.

BARBARA: Mr. Muni and Mrs. Muni had heard me on *English Coronets.* I was playing Lady Jane, one of Henry's wives. Francis Lederer, they auditioned and he chose me. From then on, every time he was on, for about three years after that, he'd always ask for me. One time, it was quite strange. Louella Parsons had *Hollywood Hotel* out here. Well, he asked me to be his leading lady and it was dandy. I was real pleased. They paid 25 bucks and it only took two days' rehearsal. *Lux* paid $50, but for five days.

Back to the reason why we recorded at night. We rehearsed the dress rehearsal before the show. I saw this very Fifth Avenue-ish looking advertising man sitting over in the corner, who had been watching me. There was no place else to sit down but a seat next to him, so I sat there. I said, "I understand they pay $25 for this show." He said, "Well, you're not getting paid." I said, "Why?" He said, "Because you're getting billing." They were saying, "Francis Lederer, starring in so-and-so, Barbara Luddy as his leading lady." I said, "Never mind the billing. I want the money."

OLAN: Now you've heard the money figures tossed around. Now you know why we started AFRA. This is the reason, because of the abuses.

When did AFRA come in?

OLAN: Nineteen thirty-seven.

Before that, whatever they could get you for...

OLAN: For $2, $5, you bet!

BARBARA: *First Nighter,* I must say, sadly, when I was out here with Don, men had to wear dinner jackets. Hans Conried was just a young boy. He was 19. Our show was the first one he was on. He had to go out and buy a dinner jacket for that part and he was paid $15 for a coast-to-coast program.

You were on Grand Hotel *in Chicago, weren't you? You did that together.*

OLAN: *Grand Hotel.* I used to call it the Saturday format, or the daytime format. It went on in the daytime, didn't it?

BARBARA: Yes. We did that occasionally, but you did it more often than I.

Tremayne did it more often than either of us. Anne Seymour and Tremayne, Betty Lou Gerson...

OLAN: But you and I did *Grand Hotel.*

BARBARA: We did it sometimes. I think it was when they were on vacation or something. The same as Betty Lou would come over to *First Nighter* when I wasn't there.

OLAN: Were *Grand Hotel* and *First Nighter* on at the same time?

BARBARA: Both running at the same time, yes. I was usually called in only when Betty Lou or Anne Seymour were on vacation.

It was a dramatic anthology series, set around a hotel.

OLAN: The same type of thing, exactly, just a little different format, that's all. I remember once I did a Mexican dialect in that. You know me. I've got a high voice and a low voice. That's it. We always had so many fine dialecticians; I never tried to do dialects. I had to do this Mexican. Joe carried me on his back.

BARBARA: Joe Ainley directed that, too.

OLAN: He taught me Spanish a word at a time.

Did either of you have to double much?

BARBARA: No, not on our own shows.

OLAN: Neither of us were ever very good at doubling.

BARBARA: The last time I had to double was about two years ago, when I did one of these *Heartbeat Theatres,* the Salvation Army thing.

OLAN: Heartbeat.

BARBARA: They pay $57 now.

OLAN: We love to do those, however, because you get a good radio cast together.

BARBARA: It's the only place we see our old friends. Everybody does it for scale.

Barbara, didn't I hear you on a Zero Hour *a couple of years ago?*

BARBARA: Yes.

OLAN: We both did some of those.

BARBARA: Yes, Elliott Lewis was doing them. They're off now, again. When Bob Hill was doing them, they went back to the old format that *Lux* used to have of having picture stars..

How about CBS Mystery Theatre? *They said that they were going to come out here to do a few shows.*

OLAN: They came out here and did a few but, of course, Hi Brown is in New York, headquartered in New York.

BARBARA: That's where he wants to be.

OLAN: When he was out here, I read in *Variety,* I guess, he was out here. Hi called one of the fellows at CBS, and I happened to be in his office at the time. I was trying to find out where to get him on the phone. So I talked to him. Hi said, "I know, I know. I couldn't get to everybody this time, only did a couple of shows." He used former New York people who had worked for him a lot. He said, "I'll get around to the rest of you the next time out." But he hasn't been back, as far as I know.

Would you like to get involved more with that kind of radio again today?

BARBARA: Oh, yes.

OLAN: Sure. It would be great.

BARBARA: Because, as we were saying earlier, you can be anything you can sound. People can build their own image.

OLAN: We could do the same characters that we did then, because our voices haven't changed that much. Physically, we've changed.

BARBARA: Physically, indeed.

OLAN: We couldn't do them in pictures, but we could still do them in radio.

BARBARA: I'm 67 years old now. I couldn't very well play an ingénue, if people could see me.

Well, you don't look like you're any age. You're still that four-foot-eleven gal...

OLAN: ...with the cute little voice!

BARBARA: Thank you!

You must have had some good times together.

OLAN: Yes, we did.

BARBARA: We did! Chicago, the nine years there, were among the happiest of my life.

Was it different when you came out here, from the radio point of view? There's always talk about "The Chicago School of Radio." I don't know what that really is.

BARBARA: I don't either, because I came from here.

OLAN: I think the reason for it being referred to that way is that for so many years, we originated more shows in Chicago than both coasts put together. Things started gradually falling apart. People wanted to go to New York, or people wanted to come to Hollywood. So it didn't originate as many shows. Of course, there aren't as many radio shows – period – as there were. But we did have a fine group of people there simply because there was a lot of work there. As Biddy says, she came from here, started out here. But Chicago was the center of radio.

BARBARA: You'd better explain that "Biddy," because it sounds peculiar. That's my nickname. B-I-D-D-Y.

OLAN: Yes, we've always called her and her daughter "Biddy" and "Little Biddy."

BARBARA: Little Biddy is three-and-a-half inches taller than I am!

Little Biddy is Big Biddy.

OLAN: Incidentally, since this is going to be on the air in Evanston, a lot of people back there will still remember this *Bachelor's Children* show that I mentioned that was on for 11 years, and will want to know where some of the people are. Hugh Studebaker, who played Dr. Bob, is out here, retired from the business. He didn't really get started in television. He didn't care much for television. He still likes radio. Marge Hannan, who played Ruth Ann, is no longer living. Pat Dunlap, who played Janet, my wife – I played Sam Ryder – Pat is now living up in Berkeley. Both Marie Nelson and Hellen Van Tuyl, who played Ellen, are no longer living. Of course, it's been a long time ago. The show was on the air from 1935 to 1946. Five a week, two shows a day. Bess Flynn – a lot of people will remember her – wrote the show. Bess is now living in Long Island. She is 90 years old, believe it or not.

BARBARA: Wow! I'm just a kid.

OLAN: That's right.

BARBARA: Wasn't her son Jack Armstrong?

OLAN: Charlie Flynn played Jack Armstrong part of the time, yes.

Olan, you were on Jack Armstrong. *You were Coach Hardy. And you were on* Chandu, the Magician.

OLAN: I did it in Chicago. But it was out here first before we did it there. It didn't have a very long run.

BARBARA: *Chandu* ran out here for five or six years.

OLAN: But I think that was before we did it in Chicago.

BARBARA: Yes, I'm sure it was. It started in about '32 or so.

OLAN: An entirely different cast.

You folks were both very well cast in the great days of radio.

OLAN: We loved it.

You're still doing some things today on radio, in television and in the movies. What's next for both of you?

BARBARA: I don't know.

OLAN: I don't know.

BARBARA: We never know from day to day.

The telephone rings, and then –

OLAN: That's right.

BARBARA: That's right. I've done quite a bit of work for Disney. I did Lady in *Lady and the Tramp*. Those things I love to do because, there again, it's the voice. I'm currently Kanga in *Winnie the Pooh*. All three of those. Roo is my baby. I played Merriwether, the little, fat blue fairy in *Sleeping Beauty* and Nanny Cook in *A Hundred and One Dalmatians*. I've worked quite a bit for Disney. About every seven years I get a new set of people who know me, because about every seven years they bring *Lady and the Tramp* out again. I started doing it in '53. It took us five years to do it before it was completed. But it's come around three or four times, and every time some little kid in the building who never heard of me will say, "Hey, I heard somebody who sounded like you."

OLAN: A new fan!

That's marvelous.

BARBARA: It really is. They sold *Winnie the Pooh* to television. That's nice, because residuals come from that. They can play it in the theater until hell freezes over and nothing.

You don't get anything from that?

BARBARA: No. It was made for that medium. It's when they make it for one medium and sell it to another, then they have to pay you. I made *Lost Light,* a very small part of a nun, with Lloyd Bridges and Anne Francis, in 1968. It was made as a pilot for a CBS series. But it was about that time that there was a great big to-do about violence in TV. It's much more violent now than it was then, but CBS didn't buy it for that reason. They sold it for theatrical release to motion pictures and I got a whopping, big check. It scared the daylights out of me, because they had made it for TV and then sold it elsewhere. They run it a couple of times a year now as a TV movie and I get residuals from that. Very handy indeed.

Well, it's nice when Mr. Postman drops off a little letter like that.

BARBARA: I did one *Dragnet* and I have had something like 15 residuals from it.

You've done so much to entertain so many people over the years in radio and television and the movies. We are glad to have this chance to chat with you in what might be the outer lobby of the little theater – way off Times Square.

OLAN: Yes, way off!

Barbara Luddy was born May 25, 1907 and was 67 at the time of our conversation. She died April 1, 1979 at the age of 71.

Olan Soulé was born December 28, 1909 and was 65 at the time of our conversation. He died February 1, 1994 at the age of 84.

Don Ameche

. Don Ameche had a long and successful career in radio before he went on to motion pictures and the stage. We met December 7, 1971 backstage at the Pheasant Run Playhouse in St. Charles, Illinois, where he was appearing in a production of Father of the Bride. *I asked him if he remembered appearing on a radio show called* The Empire Builder.

 Yes. Started September 1930. *Empire Builder* was the name of a crack train for the Great Northern Railroad and we did stories supposedly [true]. I don't know if they were true or not, but they all had locales somewhere along the Great Northern route.

That show was on, then, about the same time you were doing the First Nighter.

Yes. I started doing the *First Nighter* about March 1931. I didn't actually start the program. A man by the name of Jack Doty started it November 11, 1930 and I took it over, if I am not mistaken, in March of 1931.

Was this in Chicago? You did a lot of radio work in Chicago.

Yes. I stayed here until March 1st of 1936.

You really have the dates down pat, haven't you? Do you remember appearing in the cast of a program called Milligan and Mulligan?

Yes, that's right. That was on WGN. We did that for, I think, 26 weeks, if I am not mistaken. A man by the name of Bob White wrote it and produced it. We were on late at night, I think 10:30 to 10:45, five nights a week. A comedy-adventure type thing.

You were a detective?

Yes.

How about Betty and Bob?

I was on that also for, I would guess, at least two years. That was on NBC; a soap opera.

You were on Grand Hotel, *which also originated here.*

Yes, it did. That was sponsored by a product of Campana's and *First Nighter* was sponsored by [Campana's] Italian Balm, and I can't remember what that product was. It seems to me it was Drene, but no, I don't think that's right.

Drene brings to mind a thing that you did with Frances Langford and Frank Morgan.

Yes, that's right. Actually, Drene started out about the Bickersons. Danny Thomas was a part of the show and I was a part of the show and the original Bickersons was started by Phil Rapp, who wrote them all and produced them all. And Danny Thomas was the first of two segments. The Bickersons would be one half and I would work with Danny in the other half. But the next year we went with Old Gold and that's where Frank Morgan came in.

You were very much involved with the sketches on the Edgar Bergen and Charlie McCarthy show and you did a lot with W. C. Fields when he was a guest.

Yes, I did. Bill was only on 13 weeks. I guess most people forget that, but for the whole 13 weeks.

As a guest or as host of the show?

No, no no. I was the host, always the host, but Bill was just a guest with Bergen and McCarthy. The four of us worked, everyone – that was the first spot that he did. Later it became just Edgar Bergen and myself and Charlie. But he was part of the first. Bill was pretty broken down by that time. He was almost senile.

You remember a famous show that everyone refers back to all the time, with Bergen and McCarthy and Mae West?

I remember the Mae West episode? My goodness! I should say I do. I almost got thrown off the air for life because of that skit. The name of the sketch was... what was it? "Adam and Eve" I think was the name of it and Arch Oboler wrote it. Arch later became a very famous radio script writer. And it had been done before on the air and I was worried about many of the words that were in the script. So I called Danny Danker, who was then the head of J. Walter Thompson [the agency representing the sponsor of the show, Chase and Sanborn Coffee]. Danny came down maybe sometime around 11 or 11:30 at night and I told Danny that "all these lines have got to come out or I am not going to do the show tomorrow. I am frightened of it." So Danny said, "You stay here." I was downstairs and Danny went upstairs and spent the time with Mae and came back down and said, "Go home. Go to sleep. Everything is out." I said, "Fine, thank you, Danny" and went home.

The next day I came down and we did the show. And while I am introducing [Mae West] I could see her preening, you know, getting all set for this thing. And she didn't put any of the lines back in. She read them in the regular Mae West style, which was fine by me, and then did a skit with Charlie McCarthy. I remember distinctly, walking over to have something to eat with Edgar between rehearsal and show time, and I said, "Ed, I think you're crazy, saying all these things you are saying. [He said,] "So what am I going to do now?" I said, "I don't know, Ed. I am really frightened for you."

Well, the furor came not over any of the innuendos or anything like that; it was over, they claim, making fun of the Bible. And this was what it was all about. And this was what started it all and, oh my, it got to be a real ruckus. It went to the House of [Representatives in] Congress. It ruled her out! It threw her off [the air]. I don't think she was on for 20-25 years. It was a big episode on the air.

How did you make the transition from radio to motion pictures?

I had had a little bit of legitimate theatre background prior to going into radio, not a great deal, but a little bit. But that doesn't mean anything because the techniques are so entirely different: stage from motion pictures. I never felt that I was as good in pictures as I was in radio, so maybe I didn't make it as gracefully as I might have thought one time I did. I just didn't think I performed as well. I don't think I had as good a technique in pictures as I did in radio.

Did you prefer doing radio over motion pictures?

No, it wasn't that at all. It actually doesn't make any difference. It never did make any difference to me other than what I thought was good or had the chance of being good. No, I never had any preference, really.

Your first picture for 20th Century Fox, and I guess that was your first appearance of all, was Sins of Man *and released in 1936.*

Yes, it was. It started on March 1st of 1936. That's when I got there, March 1st.

How did you get the role? Who introduced you to motion pictures?

I came out and made a test for Metro, I believe, in August of 1935. And I was handled by a woman by the name of Dina Hushbugger. Dina was head of NBC Talent Bureau. Now, in those days, both Columbia and NBC had agencies where they hired you and you had to pay a commission to these agencies. And she arranged for this test at Metro and I made it and I saw it before I went back to Chicago and I didn't think it was any good at all. Some man on the West Coast by the name of Tom Oakey heard about the test – I don't believe he saw it – and he had a friend by the name of Scotty Dunlap, part of an agency called Dunlap and Frank. George Frank was the other partner. George went over to Metro one day and took a look at this test and he thought he saw something in it.

I told Tom Oakey to go ahead and contact George and see what he could do. So I got a call from George, who said that he had arranged for a test for me with 20th Century in New York, not on the West Coast, in December of 1935. So I flew to New York and made the test and flew back to Chicago. I believe it was probably in the middle of January they offered me a contract. It was for one picture and then five, one-year options after that. Forty weeks, they guaranteed you 40 weeks in those days out of 52, but it was a five-year contract, which was unusual in those days because they were all seven-year contracts.

But I had a radio show and it really didn't make a lot of difference to me whether I went or not. Although I really, deep inside of me, wanted to go in the worst possible way. And I also had a clause in the contract saying I could do two radio shows.

You stayed with 20th Century Fox for about eight years?

It was a little longer than that. It was about nine, I always think, but I am not sure.

What was your impression of Hollywood when you arrived on the scene?

Was I awe-struck? No. Did I enjoy being out there? Yes. Most of all, to come from a climate like [Chicago] in March, having gone through the winters that seemed to be much more severe in those days. I was never comfortable in cold weather. Never. Even though I was born in Kenosha, Wisconsin, I spent most of my younger life around here. I never really liked it. At the time, 1936, [Los Angeles] was such a clean city. I guess this was probably the first impression you got when you drove from the airport. I landed at Burbank Airport and drove right to 20th Century Fox and went right to work, as a matter of fact.

And the palm trees! The air was clean, the streets were clean, the houses were white or they were stucco and there was foliage galore and all this was quite impressive so far as I was concerned, anyway.

On the lot, 20th Century, all the time that I was there, was a very friendly place. They were very good to you. They would do almost anything for you to make you comfortable. If you wanted your dressing room done over, they would do that. I remember one time I was in New York doing a publicity thing on the

Kate Smith show for *Swanee River* and a forest fire came and it started down towards where I was living in the San Fernando Valley in Encino. Harry Brand, who was head of publicity, called me in New York and said, "Don't worry about the fire. We have two station wagons there 24 hours a day, so just put it out of your mind. Nothing will happen to your children or any of your possessions." And this is the kind of consideration.

They really took care of you!

Oh, they certainly did, and Zanuck was a most considerate man. I never once asked to see Darryl that he didn't see me. He was completely at ease with you and wanted to do everything in his power to make it easy for you.

I don't think we could talk about the career of Don Ameche without touching at least briefly on The Story of Alexander Graham Bell, *which you made with Loretta Young and Henry Fonda. I would guess that most people would identify you with that picture more than any other film. Is that a fact?*

I don't know whether *most* people... but a great number of people.

Would you tell us the reaction, initially, of the public to that film? I know it was a hit, but did you get letters as Bell?

I can't remember. First of all, none of us ever saw our fan mail.

Never did?

Oh, no, heavens alive. If you were getting probably 1,500 to 2,000 letters a week...

You mean the photograph that I sent for...

It was my signature, but –

– you didn't see it, really?

What are you going to do with a thousand letters a month?

Don Ameche was born May 31, 1908 and was 63 at the time of our conversation. He died December 6, 1993 at the age of 85.

Edgar Bergen

 Edgar Bergen took his ventriloquist act to radio in 1936 and entertained listeners for nearly 20 years. We met at his Sunset Boulevard office in Hollywood, California, on February 20, 1975. He told me that he went to school in Chicago.

I was born in the Chicago area. I went to Lane Technical High School for a couple of years and then I went to Lakeview High School to finish up. Then I went out on Chautauqua for the summer and then to Northwestern.

What was Chautauqua?

Chautauqua was a tent show sponsored by the businessmen of smaller towns. They would come in with a tent – they would put the tent up – college boys would run the tent and the show and they would have three-day, five-day and seven-day Chautauqua, and they would get all their entertainment in that one week. There'd be a matinee and a night show. The talent would change every day, so the people would give over their whole week to it. You'd see a different show in the afternoon than at night, so it just took every afternoon and night. Fine speakers, and inspirational. It was pretty well sponsored and endorsed by the people of the town.

Were you doing your act at that time?

Yes, I was doing Charlie ventriloquism and some magic and it was great training. It was good experience.

Charlie was born in your high school days?

Yes, my senior year in high school.

How did that come about?

Well, I had a papier-mâché dummy that had no personality. He didn't look like what [he] sounded like. I saw an Irish newsboy in front of the high school building, copied his picture in my history book – a sketch – and took it down to a wood carver, Theodore Mack, who made ventriloquist dummies part-time and [was a] part-time saloon keeper.

My history teacher was Miss Angel. She taught me medieval and modern history and she told me in January or February not to plan on graduating unless I improved a great deal, because I wasn't doing passing work. Well, I was booked for Chautauqua and I was more excited about that than I was about graduating.

In the last of March or April I got Charlie, and then I went on the students' program in the high school building, Lakeview High School. Our principal there was Mr. Brown, and we had a nickname for him, "Square Deal Brown," which he certainly didn't object to, and so I went on the student recital, figuring I would flunk out anyway.

Charlie [in the act] was a student, and he says, "School is rough, they really pour it on." I says, "What's giving you trouble?" He says, "Well, I got Miss Angel for medieval and modern history." I said, "That's a beautiful name, Angel." He says, "Don't let it fool you. She grows horns at examination time." And then I say, "Well then, I suppose you spend some time in Mr. Brown's office?" He says, "I'm in there so much with Square Deal, I have my own desk and sometimes we close the door and we just play checkers." I says, "Well you should be very flattered that Mr. Brown, Square Deal Brown, would play checkers with you." He says, "There's only one thing wrong; Square Deal cheats!"

Well, the next day I went to history and she says, "Remain after class." And then came the big surprise. She says, "I didn't know you had this talent. The world needs laughter more than it needs another history teacher. If you will try, I'll help you graduate." And that's how I got out of high school, graduated. So they say a man is known by the company he keeps? Well, my closest companion has been a dummy, and it's paid off!

That fall I wanted to get into Northwestern, and my chemistry was a little low, so I had to go back and face Square Deal Brown. And he says, "It's a shame to keep Charlie out of college because you're stupid." After two weeks of tutoring he raised my grade.

You went to Northwestern and while you were there, were you performing?

I would work Saturdays and Sundays in theaters around town and I played my first vaudeville theater; it was out on the West Side. I think it was called the New Marbro or something like that. They would have amateurs on Friday night, and then on Saturday and Sunday they'd bring in paid acts, professionals. And if the amateur was good – if any of the amateurs were good enough – they would be invited to stay over, and get $5 a day, and work with the pros. Well, I was billed as a magician and a ventriloquist. After the amateur show the manager came back and he says, "Bergen?" "Yes, sir?" He says, "If you cut out the magic you can stay." I said, "Oh, yes, sir." So, I guess I wasn't a great magician!

What kind of magic did you do, though?

Bad! Oh, I did the multiplying billiard balls, and the organ pipes and produce a fish bowl and drop the fish and break the bowl. I was appearing one place at some school on the West Side in Chicago and they'd built up a stage of planks on horses and I had a little magic stand loaded down with gimmicks and silks and coins and things and I stepped up on the stage and there was no bracing in between and the boards sprung, tipped over my magic stand and I said, "Well, that's the end of the magic." So I had to go on and had to do extra long with Charlie, or something.

What was the very first professional appearance of Edgar Bergen and Charlie McCarthy?

Well, that would have been at, I think, the New Marbro Theatre.

That was not an amateur program?

No. Then I played Saturdays and Sundays. In my early days I played a theater on North Clark Street. It wasn't high class then, but now it's been so long, maybe it's getting classy. The Near North Side, you know. And a little picture theater. And a little [man], Mr. Ginsburg, owned the theater and I got $6 a day for one day. So he paid me my $6 for the one day – I think it was Sunday – and he says, "You do a good act, Bergen. Here's 25 cents extra for your carfare." And I said, "Well, thank you." That took care of my carfare. You know, that was a wonderful thing. It was very generous, a very nice thing, to give me 25 cents just because it was a good act. This was a great, a nice, pat on the back.

You earned that quarter all your life, because it's been a "good act." After Northwestern, did you stay in the Chicago area?

Well, my mother and my brother lived on the North Side, up on Arthur Avenue I believe it was. And then I went into vaudeville and then I was all over the country. I went from Northwestern out on Chautauqua again the next time. Red Path Chautauqua. They had big offices downtown in Chicago. I belonged to the magic society there, so I would get some of the magic [tricks] there. Then I wrote my act.

I went in for an operation for appendicitis when I was a freshman at Northwestern, and while I was lying in the side room, getting ready to go in for surgery, you know, with all the fussing, and I says, "Gee, this would make a great idea for a ventriloquist act, operating on Charlie, you know. Strange time to be thinking of your act, but, and I ended up doing the "operation" and I played it for 10 years, all over America, Canada, Australia, England, Sweden. And I did a "tonsillectomy" on Charlie and I had a nurse and it played very well.

Did you ever play the Palace in New York?

Yes, and in Chicago, too. I played the Palace in Chicago, the old Palace, when it was two-a-day. Oh, and then, in the Thirties, vaudeville was dying out pretty badly then – there was very little of it around – and I was playing some nightclubs. I was the first talking act to do nightclubs and played the Chez Paree there. I enjoyed the real success right in my home town there, better than I ever enjoyed in vaudeville. I guess some of my comedy was a little fast, or a little subtle for them, and I was doing better there in clubs. I did so well that I headlined for the first time in my life at the Chicago Theatre. I'd always been the number two act, you know, feature, so I doubled. I played the Chez Paree late, then the Chicago Theatre.

At the same time?

Same time, yes. I did, I guess, two shows at the Chez Paree and three at the Chicago.

That must have been quite grueling for you.

I only had one day that was more active than that. That was in New York, and it was New Year's Eve. I was booked on Rudy Vallee's show in 1936, in December, and they said, "Come on for another week, would you?" I said, "Yes." And so that day, the 31st of December, I went out to Flatbush Studio, Warner Brothers Studio, and I made a Vitaphone short, a one-reel picture. Shot all day, came home and I was appearing at the Rainbow Room, in the nightclub, doing one show there at 10:00 at night and Rudy Vallee's second show. There was no time to get any food. I didn't drink in those days, but I bought some kind of a drink, like Angel's Kiss, with a little cream in it that made me drunk! I've gotten a little stronger since then; I have a little more durability. Anyway, I went up and did my second show on the *Rudy Vallee Show*, and then they asked me how would I like to round it out and make it 13 weeks. But then I went out and did a midnight show, a New Year's Eve show, at a private home on Fifth Avenue. And now, that's an awful big day!

Wow! Was that your very first entrance into radio then, with Rudy Vallee?

Well, it was the first time that they accepted me. I had been turned down by several people. I was turned down by NBC in Chicago. Clarence Menser – I'll give him credit for it! He was the manager of the studio there and I was playing the Chez Paree. I auditioned for him then and he says, "No, it won't go," he says. "They won't believe that you're doing the two voices and it would be confusing." I said, "Amos 'n' Andy are doing different voices and they accept it." And he says, "Well, that's different and your comedy isn't right." I say, "They're laughing at it at the Chez Paree." And he says, "Well, that's the Chez Paree." So a month or so later, I was on Rudy Vallee's show, and then [while] I was with him I was booked back in the Chez Paree in February. [Rudy] liked what I was doing so much that they piped me in from the Chicago NBC studio. And I went out of my way to go past his office and say, "Good evening, Mr. Menzer. I'm here." He became Vice President of NBC and he was only one of about three or four that turned me down. They wouldn't stick their neck out to put a ventriloquist on radio. You can't blame them too much.

What made you think that a ventriloquist act would work on radio?

Well, in the first place, it isn't ventriloquism on radio, really; it's the comedy, it's the material, and I thought I was awfully clever. I was sold on myself, you know! And they laughed at it and it was a good act – my gosh it was – it always went well. The big problem was when they said 13 weeks. I was to write a new act every week. I would work on an act for a month and play it out of town for a month before I'd bring it in vaudeville days into New York. Here you write a new act for 30, 40 million people around the country. It's something! There were no writers available in the beginning. No writer to write it with. All the early comedians were damn good writers like Benny, and Bob Hope and Fred Allen and Ed Wynn, and these people. They knew from vaudeville how to put things together.

It's the right kind of training ground.

Yes, it was excellent.

You were a fantastic writer, and a pretty good ad-libber, I think.

Yes. Well, with Don Ameche and with Bill Fields. They weren't afraid of it, [but] we used to live in fear that you might use some four-letter word and your career would be over because it was live radio. It was a long time before the agencies would accept an acetate, a recording, because they thought maybe it'd lost something in recording it. That has changed, of course, a great deal.

From The Rudy Vallee Show, *where did you go?*

Well, I was on his show four months, and then in May, Standard Brands, [who] owned the Vallee show, started my own show, our big show out here in California, and that was *The Chase and Sanborn Hour.* And it started with Dorothy Lamour, Nelson Eddy, Bill Fields, Don Ameche and myself. And that was it. That was a big, big show, and big budget. We had all the big names on, all except Greta Garbo and Norma Shearer. A few of those.

Was that an hour-long program in the beginning?

Yes, it was an hour.

When you first got started, did you always play in front of a studio audience?

Yes, we had, oh, 350 people there, something like that.

And there were you and Charlie and the whole cast. When did Mortimer come along?

Well, he was three or four years after Charlie. I was busy answering letters, "Is it true that Charlie's a dummy?" "Someone tried to tell me that you do the talking for both of them," and all that. So, I'd say, "Yes, it is." "Yes, it is." "Yes, it is." And then when I introduced Mortimer, it was the same thing, "We know you do the talking for Charlie, but I refuse to believe you do it for Mortimer, too." "Who plays the part of Snerd?" and all that. So, that was the thing all over again.

But you know, people say, "Isn't it amazing? A ventriloquist on radio! What a difficult thing." Well, it was so absurd, it was such a talking topic, that it was so ridiculous, it was a great plus! It was such a novelty! What kept the audience going, of course, was the *material* week after week. It doesn't make any difference whether I moved my lips or not for those 350 people, or what the dummy looked like, really.

Then I made pictures, made about 16 or 18 feature films, and 12 one-reelers, so then they got to know what Charlie and Mortimer looked like. When Mortimer came along I started with the voice, and it had to be a stupid face because the voice was stupid. But still, he had to be likable. I wouldn't want an ugly face on this character. Not too bright, but a nice boy, you know. So I studied phrenology and character analysis with the features of the face. Mortimer's a combination of weak features. He's scientifically stupid!

Did Charlie always look the way he looks today?

No. When I had him in vaudeville he was a newsboy. But then vaudeville was dying and in '32 or '33 I was booked to play a nightclub, The Helen Morgan Club in New York. I had gotten permission from *Esquire*, Esky, and I was going to have an Esky dummy made up. And I was writing some nightclub material and Esky and I, we would be doing the town and chasing the girls. Then I wrote [*Esquire*], could I get a copy, a plastic head or something of Esky. I'm awfully glad I did that, too. They said, "We've changed our mind, we want Esky to be known as a magazine and not as a ventriloquist's dummy." That was a stroke of good fate. I would have been paying royalty from now on for permission to use Esky. So there was nothing for me to do then but put a top hat and tails on Charlie and a monocle on him, which is ridiculous for a boy, but...! So then he became a girl chaser, you know, and so he had all these romances with Marilyn Monroe and Dorothy Lamour and all that.

All the glamour girls were on the show.

Yes.

Even Mae West was on the program.

Yes, yes. We'll never forget that one, yeah.

Tell us about it.

Well, we rehearsed our script and it sounded cute, you know, but Mae was holding back a little bit, not in anything she said but she says, "Why don't you come up and see me some time?" Well, when she says it, you know, you're right in the bedroom! And so, if she says "Hello," you know there's more to it than small talk! So we had some lines, such as, she says to Charlie, "Why don't you come up and see me some time?" and Charlie said, "What do?" and she said, "Oh, I'll let you play around in my wood pile." Well, that's kinda cute... till she said it! And then Charlie says "Well, I don't know whether I should or not. I'll have to think it over." Then she says, "Well, that's all right. I like a man that takes his time."

Well, now! There we got into all kinds of trouble. And the network apologized, Chase and Sanborn apologized, and I went and hid for a week. And the net result was our rating went up two points! So we weren't really too sorry.

Wasn't there a sketch on the show, an Adam and Eve sketch? Was Charlie involved in that?

No. Don Ameche was in it. I don't even remember what the sketch was, but I should.

What about the movies? You said you were in a lot of Vitaphone shorts, and some 16 feature films?

Yes, yeah. Well, I did two pictures at RKO with Fibber McGee and Molly: *Look Who's Laughing* and *Here We Go Again*. Then I did *I Remember Mama* with Irene Dunne. That was where I played a Norwegian undertaker. Charlie said he was such a dumb undertaker that they had to get a Swede to play the Norwegian undertaker! Then I did a couple out at Disney, and then we did, oh gosh, *Charlie McCarthy, Detective* and Sam Goldwyn, *Goldwyn Follies*. Oh, there were quite a few pictures.

While you were on the radio did you continue to do nightclub appearances?

No. I couldn't get out of town in those days, because I would do the show

Sunday night and take my bows, and then have a cup of coffee, relax and do a postmortem on the show with the writers and they'd say, "Well, we all meet tomorrow at 10:00 at the office." Then you start all over again and you write for the next week's show, for your guest, and you write in Ameche and you write in Ray Noble and all these people. It's a heavy schedule. So I was always on the writing team, overseeing that and then I developed writers as they came along.

Then working on a picture like with W.C. Fields, *You Can't Cheat an Honest Man*, the circus picture, we'd go out to the studio and we'd get our make-up on and we'd go out on the set. Fields would get out there and he'd have a writer and I'd have a writer and a script girl that would take down shorthand and then we'd say, "Well, where did we leave off yesterday?" We knew the outline of where we were going, and then we would develop the comedy sequences. Many days we wouldn't get a take until after lunch, but some days we'd get three or four takes from 11:30 to 12:15. Some days we'd get a few takes and that was no complaint. I'm not ashamed of that picture. It's played here in Los Angeles 35 times that I know of and I remember when it was the late, late movie and then it was the late movie, then it went into prime time.

The comedy between W. C. Fields and Charlie and Edgar has always been extremely rare. When did you first have such a confrontation between Charlie and Bill Fields?

Well, when I went on the Vallee show, Bill Fields sent me a wire. He was in the sanitarium at the time and he complimented me on my timing and on the comedy. And so, it was a natural to invite him. He was on the first show.

On the first Chase and Sanborn show?

Yes, and he got out of the sanitarium then and the first routine was *clang, clang, clang*. You know, the ambulance bell. "Agony Wagon" is coming, you know. I said, "You were quite sick weren't you?" and he says, "Oh yes, they took a lot of X-rays. Six reels of X-rays." I says, "Well, what did they find?" and he says, "They found I had a hollow leg." Just great material! And he could write. I had just great respect for him, because he could write comedy, he could play what you wrote for him, and he could do pantomime. He enjoyed sneaking toppers and kind of dirtying up the script, which we both enjoyed doing!

Did you often write just for him, or did you always write together when he was on with you?

Well, we would have a meeting and discuss what the situation would be. Charlie puts a skunk trap in his garden, as a practical joke, you know, and so he trips over it, and he not only sprained his ankle, but he fractured his flask! So then we would talk about that and then he would write some jokes and we would write jokes and talk. I would have the notes with the shorthand girl taking shorthand, and we would take those notes and then Bill would send his jokes in and we'd put it all together. Bill would forget which jokes he wrote and which he didn't write, so sometimes he'd say, "The first joke is not very good, so we'll get rid of that and just go to the others." Well, everything depended on the first jokes, you know. So any time we wanted to keep a joke in – his memory was bad, of course – all we had to do was say, "Oh, no, Bill, that's one of your own jokes." He says, "Oh, it is?" And I say, "Yes, and it sets off the other jokes." I wanted to keep it fair, I wanted to keep him happy and I didn't want him to play second fiddle to Charlie, 'cause that would be an insult. So we went on and off this way for four or five years. He'd come on and off, depending on his health, you know.

Did he ever –

– take a drink?

His health problems were legendary.

Yes. Well, he would bring a thermos bottle of martinis to the broadcast and sip through the broadcast. But never the slightest signs of drinking, no! He had no use for a guy who couldn't hold his liquor. There was an elegance about Bill. He had his cane, and his derby and his spats and he kinda felt it a little bit, too. He liked to play with words, big words. In the old circus picture the sheriff was coming, and he says, "Well, kids, if we get separated, we'll all meet at the Grampian Hills." I said, "Where did you dig up Grampian Hills?" I've never heard of it, have you? It was a funny word. And he said, "I was over in England and it's up near Scotland. They have Grampian Hills."

And then the "Upper and Lower Antilles." He'd always bring that in for some reason. He was such a success!

Was there ever much real ad-libbing between you and Charlie and Fields?

Yes. They would get a little nervous, but we would ad-lib and have fun. And they would always come in and raise two or three fingers, or one finger you know, one minute to go, get back to the script, wrap it up, you know. But he didn't always have to come up with great jokes. It was just the maneuvering and the inflection of playing around that it worked so well with Mortimer, Charlie and Bill and Ameche.

When did Effie Klinker come along?

She was the last one to come along and I guess that would have been about, 1947, '50, in through there.

Why Effie?

Why not? Well, she was really better in personal appearances, but we had fun with her. She was just a change. We never used her too much. Then I have another one that I never use on radio, and I only used her once on television, and I use her mostly in Las Vegas and in club events, because she's a life-size one that I dance with, you know. And she's very expensive. Nearly $4,000, you see. But she has to go to the beauty parlor to have her hair done, and her dress has to be pressed and – but she's beautiful, real dentures and lovely glass eyes. I dance with her. Oh, and she's so lifelike and so nice that they used to gamble whether it was a girl or whether it was a dummy.

What was the name of your dance partner?

Podine Puffington. I named her Podine after a newspaperwoman in New Orleans. When I went on a television show with her, she wrote me and she says, "My brother is a lawyer and I took this matter up with him about you calling that dummy Podine. And I said would you handle the case? And he said he refused to handle it, because he wouldn't know which one was the dummy."

What was the first thing that you did in television, aside from maybe being the guest on some of the variety shows?

Well, I guess the first thing would be *Do You Trust Your Wife?* I played that for two years and then we got in sponsor conflict. It was an expensive show, shot with nine cameras. One of the sponsors couldn't afford to go on with it and then the other one couldn't afford it, so unfortunately, it broke at the middle of the season and we were left out in the rain.

Is Charlie around? I'd like to ask him a couple of questions.

Yeah. (calls) Charlie!

CHARLIE: What do you want, Bergen?

EDGAR: Would you say hello here?

CHARLIE: Yeah.

EDGAR: It's to our friends up in Evanston, Illinois.

CHARLIE: Oh yeah, I remember Evanston, yeah.

Charlie, I wonder about the time you decided that Bergen wasn't a good boss, and you were looking for a job with Fred Allen.

CHARLIE: Oh yeah, yeah. I remember it. Fred would have been a better man, really. A better partner.

EDGAR: Yes, I remember that too. Remember, Charlie, how you ran an ad?

CHARLIE: Yeah. In *The Hobo News.*

EDGAR: Yeah.

CHARLIE: And Fred answered it.

EDGAR: Yeah. And then, Charlie says... what was it?

CHARLIE: Oh yes! You haven't been working very much lately, have you, Mr. Allen?

EDGAR: And [Fred] says, "No." He says he had several successful years on radio, and he saved his money so he has something to fall back on.

CHARLIE: Yeah, and now you've decided to get up off it!

EDGAR: And then Fred asked him, "If I work with you, would I get any jokes? Maybe just a little titter?" And Charlie says...

CHARLIE: Well, maybe a little snicker now and then, yeah.

EDGAR: That's right. Yeah. And then [Fred] says, "Oh, thank you, Charlie." He says, "Let me kiss the hem of your tuxedo."

CHARLIE: It's a tail coat, Mr. Allen.

EDGAR: "Oh," Fred says, "Well, I'll blow you a kiss." Then he says, "Charlie, if I put a rubber beret on your hat, I could use you for a plunger." He says, "I could put a ring in your nose and use you for a hitching post." And Charlie says ...

CHARLIE: "If I put a ring in your nose, you couldn't talk at all.

EDGAR: You know, he had a nasal quality. Oh, he was a great joy to work with.

Charlie, did you like working in the movies?

CHARLIE: Yeah, we had a lot of pretty girls.

EDGAR: Yes. In two or three of the RKO pictures, girl scouts.

CHARLIE: Yeah, they were good scouts too, Bergen. Good girls!

People who would go to the movies could see Charlie dance and run around a little bit. Was it Here We Go, Again?

EDGAR: Yes. *Here We Go, Again.*

CHARLIE: Yes, I have understudies play the smaller scenes, you know.

EDGAR: Well, as a matter of fact, we have a number two Charlie where in one picture he had to slide down a banister and there was some danger of him falling off, so we used a stand-in, a number two Charlie, for that. When I went to Viet Nam, we did 23 shows there. I had to go, but I took a number two Charlie!

Charlie, what about Edgar Bergen always playing the love interest in many of those movies? Edgar was the romantic lead, as a matter of fact.

CHARLIE: Well, thank goodness there hasn't been too much of that lately. He was never very good at it, actually. He did a lot of deep breathing.

EDGAR: Yes, well, I was the bashful lover most of the time.

One of the best things that you two did on the radio show was when you would tell Charlie a story. There were some pretty good stories.

EDGAR: Yes. What we did with [my daughter] Candy, when she was six years old [and] it was a Christmas show, they took alternate lines. It was the night before Christmas, and all through the house, and Charlie says...

CHARLIE: ...nothing was stirring, not even a louse.

EDGAR: A mouse.

CHARLIE: Mouse?

EDGAR: Yes. And the stockings were hung by the chimney with care. All right, Charlie.

CHARLIE: Oh, yes. And believe me, the room could stand some fresh air.

EDGAR: And then, on Donder, on Blitzen...

CHARLIE: And what do you know, Dick Nixon. Nixon came in and paid two-twenty to show.

I wonder, Charlie, do you think we can find Mortimer someplace here?

CHARLIE: You're just wastin' your time. If you want something stupid, he can deliver it. Oh, Mort!

MORTIMER: Yep, Charlie?

CHARLIE: Come in here. Make a fool of yourself. You specialize in it. Come up here and say hello.

MORTIMER: Hullo. That looks like a microphone. Yeah. I'm broadcastin', huh?

Yes! You're on radio again, Mortimer.

MORTIMER: Well, I'll be darned.

EDGAR: Yes. Well, aren't you going to say something?

MORTIMER: Well, I said hullo.

EDGAR: Well, aren't you going to say hello to me?

MORTIMER: Yeah. Hullo there, mister... mister...?

EDGAR: Well, you know who I am, surely.

MORTIMER: Oh, yeah. Hullo, Shirley.

EDGAR: No! Bergen.

MORTIMER: Oh yeah. Shirley Bergen.

EDGAR: No, no, no. Edgar Bergen.

MORTIMER: Well, make up your mind. Gee…

EDGAR: Well, you know, I don't have to tell you that Mortimer is pretty stupid.

MORTIMER: Yeah. But I've made a success of it.

EDGAR: Yes, he's done that, and he's helped me, too, as a matter of fact.

We're grateful for all of the time you spent entertaining us and so many millions of people all around the world.

It's been a very happy life. I tell you, if I had my life to live over again, I would like to do the same thing. Of course, I ask Charlie that and he says, "If I had my life to live over again, I'd like to make the same mistakes, only start sooner!"

You know, I had dreams of being a doctor when I started out in college, but I dreamed too much and studied too little, and so it's hard to say how many people are alive today because I'm not a doctor. But I've no regrets and that's nice to say.

Edgar Bergen was born February 16, 1903 and was 72 at the time of our conversation. He died September 30, 1978 at the age of 75.

Ken Carpenter

Ken Carpenter was one of radio's foremost announcers for nearly 40 years. We met in his Brentwood, California, home on February 19, 1975. I asked where his career began.

Well, I started here in Los Angeles on a local station, KFI. That was back in 1930. We came out here, my wife and little baby, in 1929 just looking for a job. I'd done some radio work back in my hometown of Peoria, Illinois, but I'd done some advertising work in department stores and things like that and I was looking for a job here in advertising. I ran into a man in an advertising agency whose lights were turned off – they couldn't pay their light bill. Just the beginning of the Depression in 1929, 1930 this was, and he said, "You've got a nice speaking voice." Luckily, being an advertising man, he could get me an audition. So I took an audition at one station, KHJ. They'd just hired a man away from KFI, so [the advertising man] took me over to KFI and I took an audition there. Fortunately I'd had some German in high school, and Spanish. Their audition, at that time, was largely musical and you can't fake German when you're doing German musical terms. So I just hung around there for about three weeks sitting out in the lobby until they finally put me on steadily.

That was my start, locally, at KFI in 1930, which was a very good place to work, because they had the NBC hookup here. At that time NBC had no studios here and any work that was done on the network for NBC, KFI did it, so I was able to get some start on the network at that time. Then I went to NBC as staff announcer here when they opened in Hollywood in 1936 and stayed there until 1942. Then I free-lanced from then on.

We've heard many stories about the NBC announcer's test. Did you have to go through all that?

Not when I got my job at NBC, no. They [had] just opened up down here, and by that time I had some reputation. I did Rose Bowl games on radio in 1934, '35, '36. These were leased over NBC, of course, so I had a certain amount of reputation. I started doing some network shows when they first started originating commercial shows from NBC out here. I went to some auditions, of course, but not as staff. I didn't have to, 'cause my name was fairly well known by that time.

You said you worked for NBC until about 1942. When did you join The Kraft Music Hall?

Well, that was in about 1935, when they moved it out here. It was Paul Whiteman in New York, and they came out here. Bing was doing some guest appearances on the show, [but] it wouldn't originate from out here. Then they decided to bring the whole show out here, with Crosby as the chief person and I won the audition for that. That was in 1935. Shortly after that I left KFI, because I was doing a lot of network work. But for the major shows, you auditioned, yes, of course. But later on, you'd get a reputation and you didn't have to. They want you.

You stayed with Bing Crosby almost through his entire radio career.

Yes, just about. I was with Bing even after he left NBC and Kraft. We went on for General Electric and Chesterfield and Philco, and then into daytime shows, so those spanned quite a long time, yes.

You moved with Bing to ABC when he decided to do tape.

Yes, that's right. I was free-lancing by that time and could move anyplace. The reason he left NBC was because they wouldn't let him do tapes, you see. He was really the one who broke that barrier, because his little firm hired Jack Mullin, the man who got the tape – liberated the tape, as they say – from Germany at the end of the war and brought the first tape machine over here [that] we used. And Bing, of course, properly so, being a singer, wanted to do at least his musical numbers so they would be perfect. He wouldn't have to worry about the talking part of the show. NBC would not allow him to do any tape or recordings of any kind and he said "Goodbye." That broke the barrier and then tape began coming in, because everybody demanded it then.

You say you actually used the machine they brought over?

Yes, you betcha. With German designations on it.

Whatever happened to that machine?

Well, that's probably in a museum someplace. An Ampex museum!

It really did revolutionize the business.

Oh, completely. The Armed Forces Radio Service – who I did a lot of work for during the war on *Command Performance* – perfected using the platters and making cuts in it. They had very skilled men who would, in fact, almost do what we do on tape nowadays, because they got very good at it. So it had really been perfected there, breaking things up so you wouldn't have to do the whole show live all the way through.

I always thought that the reason Bing Crosby wanted to use the tape was a convenience thing. Bing, being very casual, just wanted to –

He was very casual on the live show. We were very casual and convenient on that. No. He wanted the proper voice quality and didn't want to have to rely on it being right during that live time on the air. That was the main reason, a perfectly good reason, of course. All singers have used it since.

Was it really a spontaneous kind of program or was it totally planned?

It was written spontaneously, let me say it that way. The chief writer, Carroll Carroll, was able to write in the way Bing talked, naturally. He was really the first one to pick it up and caused the image. Bing had done a lot of motion pictures, but he had a very whimsical way of talking, a very interesting way of talking. This particular writer picked that up and put it on the radio show. Then motion picture writers adopted it after that. But it was written in that style [with] very little rehearsal, practically no rehearsal. Of course, ad-libs were thrown in, but it was pretty much according to script. But it was a script that was written to make it sound spontaneous.

You did much more than being an announcer on the show. You'd be a spokesman for the product, but there was always a certain amount of banter between you two.

That's very fortunate for me, very fortunate, because as an announcer, that's fine, but once you get to be, as Harry Von Zell and Don Wilson and a lot of other people were, part of the show, then it is a much more important thing, of course. And a lot of fun! We always had a station break routine. That's when we had to have station breaks with chimes in those days, and we had routines worked up around [them]. I was always a student, at "KMH Musical College" and we had special songs written for it. "Hail KMH" was our college song. John Scott Trotter wrote that. He was the orchestra leader and always was. One time I was called "Stacy Unbreak." That was one of many ways we got into the station break.

In the beginning The Kraft Music Hall *was an hour.*

Well, yes. All through the Kraft era, it was an hour. Then when we went to other sponsors on ABC, it became a half-hour show, yes.

Weren't there some Kraft 30-minute shows?

No, not with Crosby. There were some half-hour shows in the summertime, sometimes, things like that.*

One of the things that strikes me about the Kraft shows was that they were very, very heavy on patriotism during World War II.

Well, I think you find that most radio shows were pretty heavy on that during the war. There was an effort, a spontaneous effort, to bring that sort of message to the public, and I think radio did a tremendous job during the war selling war bonds and everything. Of course, the greatest job it did, in my estimation, why I was so happy to have been a part of it particularly during the Second World War, is that it pulled the country together, because every Tuesday night there was *Fibber McGee and Molly*, there was Bob Hope, all over the country. So it brought a closeness to people. They knew they were all listening. And they were, to the same thing at the same time. It was a very, very wonderful thing, I think, holding the country together.

That's an interesting point. Everybody listened to it at the same time, with the exceptions of the repeat for the West Coast.

At one time, when we were live, we'd do two shows. One for the East Coast about 5:00 in the afternoon and that'd be 8:00 release in New York. And then we'd do a show out here at 8:00 at night. Same show, done live again.

One of the great MGM stars, Frank Morgan, you remember him, great personality. He had a show with Meredith Willson's orchestra. "Meredith!" he'd call. Remember? After the show for the East, Frank would go across the street and enjoy himself for two or three hours. The [audience] on the West Coast at the 8:00 show heard some of the funniest shows ever. You couldn't understand a word he was saying! They were howlingly funny! That was a reason for the use of tape, so we didn't have to do that anymore.

Why was NBC so much against using recorded programs?

Well, it just was against their policy, that's all. You know, you build up a policy over a long period of time and take pride in everything live. But the bond just had to be broken, as many other things have been broken since then.

Were you working for Armed Forces Radio at that time?

---

* *The Kraft Music Hall* with Bing Crosby was a 30-minute program from 1942-46.

No. I was free-lancing at that time. You just went over there to Armed Forces Radio and did your job. No pay expected. They had a wonderful staff of people in the services. Very strange-looking soldiers, I'd say, because they were writers and directors, producers, everything, but they did a beautiful job of entertainment, and were very meticulous in their work. All the performers worked for nothing, but they had a big staff of people that were in the services doing the work.

They recorded all of those shows, but they were done before a live audience.

That's right, yes.

Who made up the audience?

They'd give out tickets at the USO and various places. Tickets were in great demand, because of all the big stars. I recall one show [with] Bing and Frank Sinatra and Bob Hope, all three of them. Shows like that, with all kinds of stars [who] were glad to do them, were great shows that were never heard in this country. Tremendous shows, just for overseas.

You were mostly the announcer on that series.

Yes, *Command Performance.* I worked in skits, too, quite a lot.

Is it true that Command Performance *and most of the Armed Forces shows came from the same studio where* The Lux Radio Theatre *was broadcast?*

For a time, yes. It was always at CBS on Sunset and Gower, where *Lux Radio Theatre* was done for a time. It was done originally in a theater on Vine Street.

How long were you associated with The Lux Radio Theatre?

I started in about 1943, I think, and I was with it until its demise when they went to *The Lux Video Theatre,* then moved over to the television end of it, and that was quite an experience. The early days of television were like the early days of radio to a certain extent. You tried things. Everybody was learning and the thing that I enjoyed – and it was tough – it was all live, completely live in those days. We had a kinescope for the repeat out here, but the show itself, the hour *Video Theatre,* was done completely live. A dramatic show, tough on the actors. I don't know how they did it, 'cause learning their moves, not only their lines and acting, but their moves, where they had to be and changing their clothes behind sets, dressers dressing them, was a very difficult thing to do. But once you did it, you had a great sense of accomplishment that you could do it.

They must have been out of breath running from one set to another.

They were at times, oh, yes, you betcha. It was quite a sight.

I grew up listening to The Lux Radio Theatre. *It was really a star-studded show.*

It was. You see, the agency, the J. Walter Thompson Company, that produced the show, had a good 'in' with the motion picture studios, particularly MGM. At that time the motion picture studios – Metro Goldwyn, 20th Century, and Universal, all of them – had contract players. They had stars, or young stars particularly, under contract and they would get them to come on the radio show, you see, for not a great deal of money. And it was really part of their contract to do that. The other big stars, they'd just pay them, but they got many of their players from the studios, because the studios said "Do it!" Then when the contract system ended that ended and there was just no more available talent.

Did the studios have an arrangement with J. Walter Thompson to provide them the story, probably for not a heck of a lot of money?

Well, they'd take an original screen story and we had a writer who would adapt it for radio. That was the only payment, as far as I know. I don't think they charged a great deal for the use of the property.

You worked for a long time with Edgar Bergen and Charlie McCarthy.

Oh yeah, yep.

I have never heard anyone speak so clearly and so quickly as you at the beginning of those Chase and Sanborn shows.

Well, that was your job, of course. I remember the introduction for Eddy Duchin, "the inimitable piano fingers of Eddy Duchin." Now, you wanted to say that one real fast, and as the announcer, I did it for some time. You would just stand there and blood would pour down your face. In an up-voice, too! That was a brute.

You really earned your money! You worked with Truth or Consequences *for a while. Did you have to warm up the audience?*

Oh, sure. We had a great audience warm-up. Of course, everybody participated. Ralph and everybody else. They had a lot of gags, lots of stunts, and one of the greatest warm-up stunts, I think, that's ever been used. We had a plant, a guy down in the front row, and Ralph, just before we went on the air, announced, "And now, ladies and gentlemen, we are about to start the performance. The doors will be closed to the studio so no one will be allowed to enter or leave while the performance is in progress." This plant, this stooge, gets up and says, "Oh, no, I'm getting out of here," and starts running down the aisle. The producer, Ed Bailey, has a .22 target pistol with blanks and *BLAM!* he shoots right back and the guy staggers on down and out! That will wake up an audience any day. That's the greatest waker-upper I ever saw! Wonderful warm-up.

When that show would come on the radio, the first thing you'd hear would be loud laughter.

Yes, because we always had some stunt going on, some guy trying to get into a corset or something. That was it!

The timing was such that the laughter would come in at just the right moment. You never got involved in any of the stunts, did you?

No, not in that sense, no.

Besides The Lux Video Theatre, *what were you involved with on television?*

Well, I did quite a few commercials, of course, and one year there was a Ford program, an hour program, a TV show, and I did the announcing and commercials for that. And there was one year for Kraft with Milton Berle, a half-hour show, and some commercials, but that was about the extent of it. Some openings and closings off camera, of course, but not too much as a personality on camera, no.

Did you ever do much work in films?

Yes, quite a bit, but always as myself, always as an announcer or something like that, not as a performer.

In the story, you were the announcer.

That's the way I was used, yes. And I did a lot of voice-over stuff, like *Speaking of Animals* and *Odd Occupations* and things like that. They used to have shorts that went on in theaters. They don't have them much anymore. Very interesting work.

What did you enjoy the most?

Oh, I don't know. I enjoyed the whole thing. Radio was a wonderful time to work in those days, a great time, 'cause that was it. People had that for entertainment and the great thing about radio, above television, was, it was consistent.

When a show went [on] and stayed in the same spot year after year after year, I think it sold merchandise regardless of ratings, just because it was there. I think it's unfortunate that they switch shows around so much. You get used to a TV show on a particular night. You look forward to it and all of a sudden it's on a different night. This didn't happen in radio. It stayed in the same place.

[I enjoyed] that sense of continuity and the very wonderful people I worked with, all the way through, from the network personnel to agency people to actors and everybody. We have a group out here of Pacific Pioneer Broadcasters and we have 800 members, people who have 20 years in radio or 15 years in television, in any capacity. That includes musicians, script girls, everybody who worked in the medium. And we have a big time. These people love to get together and see each other, you know. We're very close, 'cause you worked in studios that were close to each other. NBC and CBS were just down the street.

Did you ever work in Chicago?

No, I never did. I always worked out here. I stayed out here particularly because, in the mid-Thirties, some of the shows started coming out here. Jack Benny came out to do a motion picture, went back to New York, then finally came back here to stay, 'cause he liked it better out here. And all the people like that started having to come out to do a picture. Then they decided they wanted to stay out here. That's when the radio productions of the big shows, comedy shows particularly, started coming out here to the Coast. And I could see that coming. That's one reason I always stayed out here, 'cause I knew what was coming out here.

Did you enjoy working before studio audiences?

Yes. I don't mind working for an audience. I hated the warm-up part. To warm up an audience for Milton Berle, that was a miserable experience. Berle had nothing to do with that, but, you know, they were waiting for him! Who are you? But some guys like it and some guys do it. I never liked to do it. It was tough to do, but as far as the audience itself, working with it, well, that's great. You're working in front of an audience and getting laughs. That's the best! You never get over that. That's why actors and comedians never quit. They love it!

How long would a warm-up take?

Oh, about five minutes. I'd take less than that, 'cause I hate to stand up there to tell people to laugh when we hold up a sign. If I'd been in the audience, I'd refuse to [laugh], I know. That's my mentality. But you had to do it. As I say, some guys had a whole string of jokes, and they'd tell 'em, you know.

What have you been doing lately?

Well, I've been retired for quite some time now, but I keep active in AFTRA, the union of performers, and in the Pacific Pioneer Broadcasters. We have five luncheons a year. We're also collecting memorabilia, a beautiful collection of tapes, recordings, and everything. I'm vice president of that. So I keep my hand in the industry and a few little things like that, but most of the time I'm gardening, golfing, and thoroughly enjoying my senility!

Suppose someone said, "Ken Carpenter, we're going to try something new on radio today. We're going to have a live variety show with a popular singer and it's going to have some comedy spots and we'd like you to be the announcer." Would you do it?

Oh, sure! Oh yeah! Love it, of course, no question about that. You're always glad to get back in the business.

Ken Carpenter was born August 21, 1900 and was 74 at the time of our conversation. He died October 16, 1984 at the age of 84.

Norman Corwin

 Norman Corwin was one of the most prolific contributors to radio in its Golden Age and continues to add his talents to radio today. We met on August 6, 1976 in his Westwood, California, home, where I asked the writer-producer-director if he considered himself a 'triple threat' man.

Yes. It's a question of whom I'm threatening, but I have operated in all those three capacities, and did so practically from the beginning of my career.

What was the beginning of your career?

I went over to CBS from my job as a public relations man for 20th Century Fox. That's the fancy tip for it, that's the euphemism. The actual term is flack. I was a publicity flack for 20th Century Fox Pictures in New York City. And while there, I listened raptly to the product of a station known then as W2XR, later to be known as WQXR, which is now the *New York Times* station. And that was one of the first of the many stations that, I'm happy to say, have sprung up around the country in the years since, which was dedicated to classical music and to programs of a higher IQ. It seemed to me that they had a very well-balanced program, except that it lacked anything to do with the most ancient of the arts, and that was poetry. So, I wrote them a letter proposing that they do something about that. They said, "Would you like to come over and audition an idea for us?" So, one day at a lunch break from my work, I went over and did that, and that resulted in an offer to do a 15-minute weekly program on poetry. The pay was all of nothing a week. The price was right from the standpoint of the station and I was there with a program in New York City. And, through a series of serendipities, somebody at CBS heard me, and thought that I would be an interesting addition to their staff, and they engaged me as a director, not knowing that my chief interest was writing. And so, I parlayed those talents and became my own producer as well, and in very short time, I was able to latch onto some opportunities that found my programs getting attention in the national publications – *Time* and other magazines – and there I was, on my way.

You were reciting the poetry, yourself, on the air?

It was more interpreting rather than reciting.

You were doing that and they hired you to become a director. Now, is that typical logic?

Oh! A good question, a very sound question. There was an omission from what I told you I did on my poetry program [and that was to] dramatize certain poems. I engaged not even professional actors, but friends of mine to come up and take roles. And I, the term I used, which makes me blush now, was I augmented and orchestrated the poetry. In other words, in *The Death of the Hired Man,* let's say, of Robert Frost, which is a dialogue. I didn't violate the intentions of the poets, the originals. The program that was the catalyst was a 15-minute adaptation of *Spoon River Anthology,* and with a pretty good ear and eye, I cast five or six people and they were so effective, the program was so effective, that CBS said, "Let's talk to this guy." And of course I had directed as well as served as the program's Cicerone, so to speak.

You did something for CBS under the title Words Without Music. *That was right after you moved over there?*

That's right. That was similar to this. It was an outgrowth. When I went to CBS as a director, for the first few months I directed the work of other people. I did some adaptations, a very minor character, but I more or less learned the network console doing that. And after about three or four months I went to the top man in programming, and I said, "I have an idea for a poetry program, and will you give me a couple of hundred dollars?" which is all it took in those days to make you an audition record, the equivalent of today's pilot. He said, "Sure" and I did. I turned the record over to him. He listened to it, called me into the office and said, "Gee, I like this. How would you like to go on the air on the network after the Philharmonic concert every Sunday afternoon?" I said "Great." "What'll we call the program?" he asked. I said, "Well, I thought *Poetic License.*" He said, "No, the term 'poetry' will scare people away. What about *Words Without Music?*"

Well, I thought it was a banal title, but who are you to argue with a vice-president in charge of programming when he's just offered you a silver platter with a half-hour network time. I was a rookie! I was a kid, really. And then I said, "Oh, that sounds pretty good, but why without music?" He said, "Well, we don't have the budget for music." So he thought for a moment and said, "How about calling it *Norman Corwin's Words Without Music*"?

Well, here in one stroke he had accomplished for me what the highest-powered agent in the business could never have accomplished. Can you imagine walking into the office of a big network executive and saying, "Yes, I know this kid is still green and has hay sticking out of his ears, but what about giving him billing ahead of the program on a national network?" The man would have said, "That door leads to the corridor, which leads to the elevator. Good bye, Mr. Smith," instead of which he proposed it. His name was William Lewis, William B. Lewis. He's a sainted man in my life, because he gave me that great opportunity, that great push and the impetus of the name was, the name billing, was tremendous.

From there on it became the following series: *Twenty-Six by Corwin,* and there was *Columbia Presents Corwin,* and there were two of those, so when my books came out they were called *Thirteen by Corwin, More by Corwin,* and to this day, I have a column that runs in *Westways* magazine out here on the Coast, circulation half a million subscribers, and they call that column *Corwin on Media.* So the name, that whole thing, started with Bill Lewis in that office that day.

He must have had a tremendous amount of confidence in you, and you must have – actually it sounds rather simple as you describe it – but I'm certain that your reputation had been built pretty well by the time this happened.

Not by the time it happened, oddly enough, because the programs that were to get national attention were not yet written. They came out of *Words Without Music.* And it wasn't so much that he had confidence in me – I wasn't singled out at that time; it was that he believed in encouraging creative talent and that was one way of doing it. And he encouraged others who went various distances under that encouragement. I think I perhaps went pretty far within his lifetime. He died a couple of years ago. But I went pretty far, I like to think. I'm vain enough to think that I went pretty far in justifying that faith. I profited [and] was extremely lucky, extremely, because if I had come by two years earlier or two years later, I might have missed that opportunity. Things change. The tides of commercial broadcasting are so heavy and move so swiftly that all might have been washed up. Has been washed up. No young man can sit in an office now in broadcasting and get that kind of treatment. Not a rookie.

There isn't anyone today who would encourage talent that way, either.

In certain levels there are. I think maybe rock singers and performers of that kind. I mean, where did John Denver come from? Where did any of these kids come from? But that's quite another matter. That's a whole different species. But as far as dramatic writing and directing and producing are concerned, yes, I think you're right; the picture's changed.

What was the reaction of the people listening to Norman Corwin's Words Without

Music, *when it did go on the network? How did you meet that reaction?*

In the first place, listeners were agog. There had never been anything like it. It was a program for people who cared about language and ideas and drama. It was not the kind of program that would appeal to Bob Hope's audience. Indeed, my programs were run opposite Bob Hope for a long time. And Bob Hope was the number one rated program on the air, it was, for years. But CBS felt properly that our audiences were mutually exclusive, and they never even bothered to take a rating of my shows. Later on, some of the big so-called blockbuster shows where I was on all four networks at once, or when I had some big special commemorative program on CBS, they did take ratings. But it was never a question – and here again I was lucky in the timing – there was never a question of the viability of my program based on numbers. That's why I was able to endure. That's why, for the entire sweep of Radio's Golden Age, which was the shortest golden age in history, I was free of the harassment that so many writers and directors and producers and networks face today. They are tyrannized by the rating system; by numbers. It wasn't so then.

You worked primarily either for or through CBS during most of the Golden Age.

That is right. Yes. Right.

You mentioned a 'special' that you would do would be heard on other networks simultaneously with that of CBS. You were really one of the very few people in radio who developed specials.

They wanted something special, right. I don't know whether it began with a lust for prestige, [but] it began with a conscionable attitude toward broadcasting. They felt we ought to have a program on the day or night when the Germans surrender, when the Nazis surrender. That was V-E Day. So they asked me to suspend the series that I was then working on. It was the second edition of *Columbia Presents Corwin*, and I was at perhaps number 21 or 22 of the intended 26 [programs] and they said, "Norman, would you stop, knock off and immediately begin work on a program to be ready on the night of victory in Europe, because we have information from Washington, from the White House, that they expect this to be imminent. So I did. There was no time to be lost, and I prepared *On a Note of Triumph.*

And that was such an outstanding program. You had to repeat it within a week, didn't you?

That is right. Yes.

And of course, no recordings were involved or anything, so you just did the whole thing.

Well, the second one was recorded.

But the second one was not broadcast as a recording.

No. There was a network injunction against that. It was forbidden to use a recording, any kind of recording of the voice. You couldn't even use recorded music, so all my music had to be live and was original. My scores were written, composed, for my shows. None of this canned music stuff.

On a Note of Triumph was an hour-long program and it must have been sensational for radio at the time. What kind of response came out of that to prompt the network to repeat it, just five or six days later?

Well, it was the most phenomenal response, I dare say. It would be easy to say this if it were some other man's program, but I can tell you very candidly that the kind of impression it made both on the listening audience of the general public and within the radio industry was extraordinary in that the president of Mutual Broadcasting, a competing network, sent a telegram to [William] Paley saying, "When radio distinguishes itself in this fashion, it is good for the entire industry, and we want to congratulate you and thank you," and you know, that kind of thing.

The program originated here in California, but at New York, at 485 Madison Avenue, the headquarters of the network, a memorandum went around the following day saying, "For those of you who missed that broadcast last night, we are suspending work for an hour, between three and four this afternoon, and all of the audition rooms will be available to have that program piped into these rooms, so that those who missed it can hear it, and those who heard it can hear it again." It was given that kind of treatment. It is a little hard, in the light of the technological and productional advances that have been made since that time, 30 years ago, to estimate the degree of novelty and excitement that that generated. It was quite new and the devices which I used and the kind of rhapsodic sweep of the concept were entirely fresh. And emotionally, I think, you have to put yourself back in that day also. We were triumphant over one of the two enemies and yet the war was continuing and it was rather a peculiar form of celebration. I had to walk a tightrope between not being over-celebrational, because men were still dying and mothers and fathers and brothers and sisters had men who were still out there at the hazard of their lives, fighting for their countries. So it couldn't be a rip-roaring, confetti-strewn celebration, could it?

As I look back on the piece today and, more importantly, as others look back on it, it had a kind of unconsciously prophetic character. It said, in essence, what have we won and what's going to come of it and is this going to happen again? It examines some of the questions which today are still very much alive. So that last year, on the anniversary of V-E Day out here in California, the San Francisco city schools had the program piped in their classes twice that day and it was on the San Francisco municipal FM station twice that day. And that's 30 years later. I intended that program to serve the needs of one evening, of one hour, and that it is still alive 30 years later is very gratifying, of course. An LP, the first LP album of it, has since been issued, interestingly enough, of the second broadcast, the second of the two, which is the version that is available on the original 78 r.p.m. album that was issued by Columbia Records.

That was done a short period after the program, wasn't it, when the 78s came out. That's a collectors' item, by the way, to have that album with the 78s.

Yes it is, right. That was issued during a time of extreme shortage of materials of shellac, as they say on the radio, in the record industry. The original edition of 13,000 albums sold out and they did not reprint because of the shortage. Then, by the time the shellac shortage had ended, so had the war and so had the acute interest in the program. And so it lay dormant until this current season, when a recording company named Mark 56 Productions out here in California issued an LP that is now available for public sale.

However, it is not the same production. It is the first of the two. In between the first and the second there were variations. I made changes, not very extensive changes, but I did change certain readings, the emphasis. I wasn't particularly happy with the way that great actor Martin Gabel had concluded it. I felt he had become a little soft in the coda of the piece, which was a kind of apotheosis. The student of production would find interesting points of dissimilarity between the two.

It's really wonderful that something a man creates out of his imagination and his mind can last for 30, 40 years, or forever, because I think this really will last forever.

I think archivally it may last a good, long time, but of course in literature and in music and in painting we are accustomed to things that last much longer, I'm happy to say.

Did you write something similar to that for V-J Day at the end of the war?

No. They called me up and gave me about six hours' notice on V-J Day. *On a Note of Triumph* took weeks to do and hard going. It had to be researched, it had to be rewritten, it had to be cast, and the score and everything. They called me and said, "Would you go on the air with something on V-J?" I had 15 minutes' notice and I did a 15-minute thing. But in those days one was very rich in the talent resources, and I had no less than Orson Welles and Olivia DeHavilland do that for me. That was called *Fourteen August*, which is published. It appears in the last of the three collections called *Untitled and Other Dramas*. It's a slight piece but a thoughtful piece. No fireworks in it.

Did Twenty-Six by Corwin *follow immediately* Words Without Music *on CBS in chronological order?*

No, not quite. After *Words Without Music* I directed but did not write a series called *Pursuit of Happiness*, which was a variety show that again was in my old *Words Without Music* slot right after the symphony orchestra, Philharmonic, and that's where I first had contact with the reigning stars of the day, all the big Broadway and film names. This was written by a number of people who contributed and I was sort of script supervisor and director. In a sense, I produced it, although nominally it was produced by somebody else. And then came *Twenty-Six by Corwin*.

Now you had a completely free hand to do as you wanted in that series?

Absolutely.

And you did some fantastic things.

I like to think that most of them were good, ranging from good to fantastic, if I may borrow your term.

Which of the Twenty-Six *stand out as works of most popular acceptance?*

There would be *Untitled*, there would be *The Odyssey of Runyon Jones*, there would be *My Client Curley, The Long Name None Could Spell*, which in a sense was a precursor of *On a Note of Triumph*. *The Long Name None Could Spell* was about Czechoslovakia and, in its texture and its thrust and the tilt of its language and its ranging concepts and its mobility, it had some of the character, it was a warm-up for *On a Note of Triumph*. I wasn't conscious of that fact, but later, putting them together, you can see, if you stood them side by side, you'd say, "This is the overture to *On a Note of Triumph*." Another [was] called *There Will Be Time Later*, and there were some fantasies, some comedies.

One of them, *Daybreak*, had to do with the concept, which was then fresh, of an apparently stationary object which travels the same speed as the rotation of the earth and it was at a point over the earth which a satellite might have now. By staying in that point, you'd be in a zone of perpetual dawn or twilight or noon, whatever time you chose, and this was *Daybreak*, and it went around the globe as the earth turned and they would drop down to Earth for little vignettes how the day was received in these various places. Now, that was a program to be followed on your atlas, and had a good score, and it was a very happy combination of circumstances. That one of the *Twenty-Six*, [was] selected to use in a book called *The Three Readers*, an anthology compiled by Carl Van Doren, Clifton Fadiman and I believe, Van Wyck Brooks, each of whom selected his own favorites out of literature of all kinds, and I was very honored to find myself in there with Thomas Jefferson and a few others.

How marvelous.

Then there was a program called *Double Concerto* about two men who, if it were not for the other, each would have been the world's leading interpreter of Brahms, and they had a terrible rivalry. One was a Spaniard and the other was a Hungarian and it was a funny piece.

Was The Plot to Overthrow Christmas *one of the* Twenty-Six*?*

No. That was the first program I ever wrote. The very first original script that I wrote for CBS. That was on *Words Without Music*. Now, *Words Without Music* was principally adaptations of others' writing and I contributed only two or three original works to that. Mostly I adapted the ranking poets, alive and dead.

The Plot to Overthrow Christmas was an accident, really, because the program fell on Christmas Day and the man who was attached to me from the CBS publicity department said, "What are you going to do on Sunday? I see you have a program on Sunday. You going to do anything about Christmas?" The idea had never entered my head and I said, "Yes, it is Christmas, isn't it, on that day? Well, yeah, I guess maybe I will." And he said, "Well, I have to send out this release." (It was three or four weeks in advance.) "I have to give it some title. Want to name a title?" And off the top of my head I said, "Yeah, *The Plot to Overthrow Christmas*." He said, "You're kidding?" and I said, "No, no. Put that down and I'll meet it."

I went home. Then the time came and I sat down and I began it simply enough by saying, "Did you hear about the plot to overthrow Christmas?" That's the first line. "Well, gather ye now from Maine to the Isthmus of Panama." It went on from there.

Now, that was the first script I wrote, followed three weeks later, a month later, by *They Fly Through the Air With the Greatest of Ease*. And it was *They Fly* that first broke into the national press. *Time* magazine had a picture of me and a review of the piece and you know, that is kind of a mark of arrival, or was then, that you are noticed by a national magazine enough to have a column and a picture and all.

You did a series called So This is Radio*?*

That was an outgrowth of a program that I had written on the 25th anniversary of broadcasting in America called *Seems Radio is Here To Stay*. CBS asked its staff, in a general mimeographed memorandum, did anybody have an idea for a show on that day? And of course, most of them were busy with their programs and that memorandum went right into the waste basket.

When I was young and eager and a freshman, and I thought, "Gee, let's see what we can do with that," and I wrote a program called *Seems Radio is Here To Stay* and it had a lot of notice in the industry. CBS was so proud of it that they issued a private edition, a publication, very handsomely done – I will show it to you when we put the microphone down – and they sent it out to 2,000 public figures and broadcasting bigwigs as a kind of in-house thing. Now, because of the success of that, they felt emboldened to do a series called *So This is Radio*. I have blocked that from memory; I was not happy with that series. I think that it was too much of the same thing, and I won't burden you with the details of my disenchantment with it.

Just one question about it then: did you get direction from the network on that?

No, no. The network was heaven in those days. I was given absolute freedom. I was an entity and nobody bothered me. They were cordial and helpful and cooperative and supportive. One could not have asked for finer auspices under the Medicis. The Medicis.

It's marvelous to hear that. It's wonderful to hear that. I doubt that there's anyone in network broadcasting today who has that kind of freedom. People have the freedom to create whatever they want, but whether or not it gets on the air is another thing today.

Well, the whole picture has changed. The emphasis now is numbers, it's audience. Now and then they do fine, fine things on radio and television. Not radio so much. They really killed that dear, old girl.

Norman Corwin was born May 3, 1910 and was 66 at the time of our conversation.

Jack Benny

1989 RADIO HALL OF FAME *. Jack Benny was in the Chicago area for a series of concert appearances at the Mill Run Playhouse in suburban Niles, Illinois. We met on September 3, 1970, following his short rehearsal with the band and just a few hours before his opening night performance. I asked if he remembered his first words on radio, on the* **Ed Sullivan** *show.*

Was it Ed Sullivan or my own show where I said something like this: "This is Jack Benny, and there will be a slight pause while you say who... who cares..." or who knows ... or something? I don't know. It was something like that, yes.

You were on the Ed Sullivan *show in March 1932 and then later that year, in May...*

Right. In May I started my own program. I got it through the *Ed Sullivan* show. Canada Dry Ginger Ale. They heard me on the *Ed Sullivan* show, and as soon as that show was over, they called me and they made me an offer.

And you had a sponsor on radio and TV ever since?

Ever since.

What did you do on that Ed Sullivan *show?*

What happened was, I was in New York and Ed said, "Jack, why don't you come on my show? He did a sport show or something. I said, "What will we do?" He said, "Let's you and I sit down. We'll write something." So I forget what it was, a couple of questions. He was doing a sports thing. So we sat down and there wasn't much to the show except a little talk. But evidently the agency for Canada Dry Ginger Ale perhaps liked my speaking voice, 'cause that's all he could go by, and they made me the offer right away.

And that was for what length of time? Was it a 13-week series at that point?

That was 39 weeks, I think, with Canada Dry Ginger Ale. I think it was, or I don't know how many weeks it was.* But they really didn't want – see, I insisted on doing comedy commercials; otherwise I didn't want to do radio, television, nothing. They were afraid of the comedy commercial [and] we had some very funny ones. Even though they had a lot of marvelous letters telling them how good the commercials were, 'cause [the listeners] never heard commercials funny like that, [Canada Dry] still didn't like the idea. So they wanted me to do straight commercials and I said, " No, I don't want it." And they even wanted *me* to do [the straight commercials] you know. It was something like that, and so I could see we were going to have a little problem. I said to my manager, "Let's look for something else, because I don't think they're going to keep me if I stop with comic commercials."

You had insisted on the comedy commercial right from the beginning?

From the beginning! Right from the very first show.

When you had the Sportsmen on The Lucky Strike Program...

Well, that was Jell-O, Lucky Strike, everything, yeah.

...you wrote most of those, didn't you?

Yes, with my writers. Sure, I wrote every one of them. When we started for Jell-O, the Jell-O commercials saved Jell-O, because Jell-O was going out of business, almost, on account of Knox Gelatin was beating the hell out of them. So they wanted the comedy commercials, figuring that that could be the one thing that would save it. And by golly, it did. It did.

How long were you on for Jell-O?

For a long time [for] General Foods, Jell-O, and then when we had enough of that, we went on. We stayed with them for Grape-Nuts Flakes, and Grape-Nuts, and all this and that. Then I don't know what happened with that. We were on for years and years, and years, and then I went with Lucky Strike. I think Lucky

---

* Jack Benny's radio sponsors were Canada Dry (May 2, 1932–January 26, 1933); Chevrolet (March 3, 1933–April 1, 1934); General Tire (April 6–September 28, 1934); General Foods for Jell-O (October 14, 1934–May 31, 1942); General Foods for Grape-Nuts and Grape-Nuts Flakes (October 4, 1942–June 4, 1944) and Lucky Strike Cigarettes (October 1, 1944–May 22, 1955).

Strike made me a bigger, better deal, whatever it was, so I went with Lucky Strike.

What happened was, the last year that I was with General Foods, so I had a few shows that weren't as hot, but I still had a lot of great shows. So they practically said to me, "Watch it a little bit 'cause some of the shows..." As though every show had to be perfect, you know. See, I spoiled them. And then they went back to New York. Now, they didn't have an option. The thing was over, but they did want to give me a new contract. But the way they said to me, "Just watch it a little bit," I got mad.

So I said to my manager, I said, "Let's get another sponsor; I don't want to be with them" and we wired 'em *on the train,* as they were going back, that we will not be with them anymore. Because right away I had, like, four or five big offers from Lucky Strike, from everybody, and we grabbed Lucky Strike immediately. Then of course, Jell-O came back and said, "We didn't mean to hurt your feelings," and all this and that, but it was too late. So then I stayed with Lucky Strike for years. I went on television with Lucky Strike. Then we had a few different sponsors for television.

Weren't you on for an insurance group?

Yes, I was, for quite a while, for State Farm Insurance.

Is it true, Mr. Benny, that NBC once gave you an option on the 6:00 or the 7:00 time slot on Sunday nights?

Yes, they told me that as long as I would stay with them, I could have that time. Now, this was not in writing, but it was a definite agreement that I could have that time as long as I wanted to stay with them. But when I moved to CBS, CBS gave me exactly that same time.

I've always asked this question of old-time radio fans: What was on opposite Jack Benny? And nobody ever remembers.

No, because in those days nobody would go opposite [us]. They couldn't hit or match [us].

So, I moved and I didn't want to leave NBC. I loved NBC, but I had to make some kind of a deal where I could make some money. Because here I was, making a terrific salary, and it was all salary. I couldn't make a deal for a company. Well, I wouldn't care if I got a million dollars a week, that wouldn't do me any good, what good would that be?

It would be all tax, right?

Sure. So the ones that made me the deal, and came right through with it quick, was CBS. Then, of course, when NBC realized that I was going to go, then they were ready to make the deal, but I didn't want to play one against the other, so

I merely took CBS.*

Well, CBS had generally raided NBC at that time, didn't they, with these production company deals?

Yes, once I got on, but NBC was really the first network. Then, when I moved over, a lot of shows moved over and that made CBS the one on top. I made them *millions*, CBS, by that move, which I didn't know or didn't think, you know.

How did you get hooked up with Rochester?

We just auditioned a couple of black men, a couple of Negroes to play the part of a porter on our train. I liked Rochester the best, so I hired him. I hired him only for one show, and he was a big hit. Then I hired him for another show, later. Nobody even thought of taking him, because I hadn't signed him up yet. I thought I'd keep him steady.

He was certainly a big hit. He is occasionally on some of your TV programs.

He'll be on my next special. You'll see it November 16th, something like that.

Is it true that Mary Livingstone, your wife, really was a clerk in the May Company?

Yes, she sold hosiery in the May Company. But she's going to be on my next special and it's very tough to get her in a show. But, by gosh, she's going to be in it!

That's great! She stopped appearing with you even in the days of radio, didn't she?

No, no, she went even into television with me, live. Then she got very nervous and she didn't want to work anymore. She told me she didn't want to work. So I let her go.

I want to ask you a couple of questions about the Jack Benny legend. Do you remember when you fired the Sportsmen, and you hired Bing Crosby, Dick Haymes, and Andy Russell and Dennis to substitute?

As a gag, you mean?

Right, as a gag. There was a lot of reaction to that program. Wasn't it a rare occasion for Mr. Crosby to let loose with his off-stage comment on that show? Do you remember?

---

* Jack Benny moved to CBS on January 2, 1949 after broadcasting on NBC from 1933–1948.

Oh yeah, oh yeah! What the hell was that?

That was exactly that!

Was that it? Something that you couldn't say then. You could say it now, but you couldn't say it then! He said, "Who the hell picked this key, [Dennis Day]?"

Did you really live next door to Ronald Colman?

I lived a block away. We made it next door.

Were you good friends with him?

Yes, very.

Do you remember the time you lost Ronald Colman's Oscar? Do you remember that story?

Yes. I don't remember the routine now, but I remember the incident.

Was that tied in somewhat with the episode of when you were robbed? The great, famous Jack Benny episode where the fellow came up and said, "Your money or your life?" and there was that long pause and all that?

Well, no, that was a different show.

When was that, do you recall?

I don't remember any of the dates. I don't remember the years, dates. All I remember is the first time I started. And I remember my first television show, the date of that and that was all. I only remember the first dates.

When was that?

Well, it was in October or November of – I said I remember the exact date! October or November of 1950. That's why this is my 20th Anniversary [in television].

And this is also the 38th Anniversary of your first radio appearance, 1932; that was when you first started. At that time, back in 1932, you were on Broadway in Earl Carroll's Vanities.

Yes, but I was in the *Vanities* before I went into radio.

And you were on the vaudeville circuit even before that.

Yeah, yeah.

That's how you met Mary? You were in L.A.?

Yeah, playing at the Orpheum Theatre in Los Angeles. Mary was working across the street at the May Company.

When was your first film?

Nineteen twenty-nine. *The Hollywood Review of 1929.* We shot that in 1928. That's when they used all the stars of MGM.

What about the famous Benny-Allen feud? Was there really, in fact, a feud?

Well, only a friendly feud, of course. We didn't plan it, though. It came up by accident. Fred said something one night on his show, and I picked it up the next week. He picked it up, and then I picked it up. We were in the feud about eight months before we even did anything about it and the feud went on till he passed away. We would go on each other's shows. He was probably the best comedian, the best one, to ever have a feud with, because he was the funniest. He was a great writer, that's why, a great wit.

At the end of your program Don Wilson used to say, "Jack will be back in just a moment, but first – and then he would go into a commercial. Then, invariably, you would be out of time, and, after the commercial, he would return and say, "And now here's Jack" and you would end up with –

"We're a little late, folks."

We're grateful for this opportunity to speak with an idol of ours for many, many years. And you look really good for a fellow 39 years old.

I don't look 39, either way you want to go!

Jack Benny was born February 14, 1894 and was 76 at the time of our conversation. He died December 26, 1974 at the age of... 39.

Don Wilson

Don Wilson was voted the top radio and television announcer in the United States for some 15 consecutive years and was, for 35 years, the announcer on **The Jack Benny Program** *on radio and TV. We met on June 9, 1980 while he was in suburban Chicago with the revue* **Big Broadcast of 1944**. *I asked him when his career began.*

 I don't mind saying it, 1923. Crystal set days. You wouldn't know anything about that! But, I remember the first radio set that I ever made myself was made out of an oatmeal box with a coil of copper wire, a galena, a cat's whisker and an earphone, a set of earphones like we're wearing right now. If you were lucky, your signal was heard six blocks down the street! That's the way it all started, in that very embryonic, early fashion. It developed there to the battery-operated sets, and then, of course, to the Atwater-Kents and all the others that came on the market as the electrical sets.

It's a cliché now, but were you bitten by the radio bug as you listened on the earphones of the crystal set in those early days?

It was intriguing. I was terribly intrigued with it. I got into it – if I may be just a little personal right now – I was a serious student of serious music during my days in high school and college. My high school days and all the elementary educational days were spent in Denver. I went to the University of Colorado at Boulder, Colorado. But I used to try to sing a little bit. Well, they finally found me out after I got into this thing called radio, and I had to drop out on the singing, but they permitted me to "yak." So I've been talking ever since. Can't carry a tune in a basket!

You were part of a trio back in the Denver area?

Yes. If I might brag a little, it was a very successful operation that we had. We were all in business in Denver, and I'd been studying with a very well-known coach in Denver. I didn't know it at the time, but the other two boys in the trio were doing the same thing. It was the vocal coach in Denver who suggested, because they had lost their lead voice, that they might like to talk to me. She thought perhaps I was a likely prospect. So I joined them and we were busier than bird dogs. We made a lot more money in radio, even in those days, with the extracurricular things that we did, appearances of all kinds, including fill-ins at the Orpheum Theatre. Whenever an act couldn't appear, the trio would be engaged to play a week here and a week there.

Did you have a name?

Originally, it was the Columbian Trio. Then that was changed to the Civitan Trio when we all became members of the Civitan Club, a service club like Rotary and Kiwanis and the rest of them. Then one of the commercial accounts that we had about 1925 in Denver was for the Piggly Wiggly Stores, and we became the Piggly Wiggly Trio. Then the trio decided they would migrate to the "land of milk and honey," to California. So the vice-president and manager of the Piggly Wiggly Denver unit was the owner of the San Francisco unit. He put us under contract. We went into San Francisco, and the manager in the San Francisco unit sold us to Franchon and Marco, which was the leading presentation house on the Pacific Coast at that time. We'd open up, as we did, on Market Street at the big theater in San Francisco. Then we played the surrounding communities wherever Piggly Wiggly had an outlet.

Were you doing radio at the same time?

Yes. We were appearing on radio as the Piggly Wiggly Trio. It didn't cost the station – KFRC, the Don Lee outlet in San Francisco at that time – it didn't cost them anything for the talent because Piggly Wiggly was underwriting it. But Piggly Wiggly always got credit when we were on as a trio, a duo or a single. That was an exchange-of-services basis, you see.

What were the radio stations like in this, the first decade of radio broadcasting?

By the time I'm referring to now, during the Piggly Wiggly days, some of the transmitters had become quite sophisticated and were doing a great job. The big problem was programming. For instance, when General Electric came into Denver and built KOA, which became one of the really high-powered giants in the business, you could only use music that was in public domain. So "Jeannie with the Light Brown Hair" got quartered and sawed in a million different pieces all the time by anybody that went on KOA's air.

It was interesting. You opened up in the morning and swept out, and you appeared on the air. You wrote shows, you produced shows and appeared all during the day in whatever particular facet of the radio activity of that station was doing at that time. This was KHJ I'm referring to now, in Los Angeles. It was a lot of fun growing up, or trying to grow up, in the radio business. It's such a great industry to be associated with and to have the privilege of starting in, in the embryonic form, as radio was, relatively speaking, in those days, and trying to grow up with it. To make the transition from radio in about 1949 or '50 into television, and to try and grow up and become abreast of things in that monstrous medium today has been a liberal education. I so often feel that the longer I'm in it, the less I know about it.

What was your very first job in radio after the Trio ended? I know you were a sportscaster.

Yes, I wound up on the Rose Bowl for several years. I don't know whether you're familiar with that or not. When [Graham] McNamee no longer came out for the network, KFI, being the flagship station in Los Angeles, originated games on the Pacific Coast for the NBC West Coast division. I was involved in that, and that got me into the Rose Bowl. I did the Rose Bowl for about five years. McNamee no longer came out, and I inherited the play-by-play. I'd had a little experience in football in high school and college.

Was that the beginning of your radio work as an announcer or sportscaster?

Yes, virtually, it really was. I'd done a little bit prior to that, but not anything of any great importance at that time. But it was a lucky niche that I fell into. Then, as a result of the exposure on the Rose Bowl Game for several years, NBC, New York, hired me as a sports announcer in the New York division. I went east in 1933 to fulfill that commitment. Benny picked me up in the spring of '34.

Between 1929 and '33, you and Ted Husing were the two top sports announcers from coast to coast.

Ted Husing was the greatest sportscaster in the business, bar none. I knew Ted. I got to know him very, very well. He was invaluable help to me. I was told by the boys at NBC, "Look out for Husing. He's high and mighty and sits in a little, white castle all his own, won't talk to you." Ted and I met at Soldier Field in Chicago. I had been sent back from New York the second week I was on the staff at NBC to do a Northwestern-Stanford game.

I was standing back of a revetment in the stadium there at Soldier Field trying to stay out of that cold wind off of Lake Michigan. Here I am in a West Coast overcoat, which would be a lightweight topcoat back in this country when the wind from Lake Michigan hits you. A car came in, went around the track, and a head came out the right-hand front window and said, "Don't you want to come over and get out of the wind?" So I hightailed it over and sat in the back seat. I looked at the chap back of the wheel and I said, "Aren't you Ted Husing?" He said, "Yes, I am, and you're Don Wilson, aren't you?" We met at that particular time and under those circumstances.

Ted was instantly the exact antithesis of what he'd been described to me. He was the most generous man that you've ever known about in your life, and he was the most knowledgeable. He said, "If I can help you in any way, Don, don't hesitate to call me. If we're on the same game, I'll come to your room and I'll go over the scouting charts with you." That's exactly what Ted did. He was a great, great help. He was the greatest sportscaster in the business, in my book, in anybody's league.

When you were in New York doing sports, Jack Benny had been starting on radio. His first bit with radio was with Ed Sullivan, and a few months after that he got his own show.

He was on for Canada Dry beverages. That was his first year as *The Jack Benny Show.* Then the second year, he was signed by Chevrolet. The contract was terminated at the end of 26 weeks. Now, so the story goes, and I think it's an awfully good story, but I won't vouch for its veracity – that the advertising manager of the Chevrolet Division of General Motors concluded that their product was so high-classed, that they should be represented on the air by a symphony and not by a comedian. So Jack's contract was terminated at the end of 26 weeks. It was at that point, in the spring of 1934, that he held an audition for an announcer to carry on with him for the rest of that season of 13 weeks. I just got awfully lucky and got the job. I was thrown into a general audition with all the other stock boys and the free-lance men around town. The only answer I could give for how did it happen. Nothing really dramatic about it, nothing world-shattering took place, except I think perhaps I laughed in the right places when I read lines, and that got me the job.

When you had the opportunity to go in for this audition, did you think that this would be a positive thing for you, to become an announcer? Jack Benny was pretty big on radio at that time, but still...

I really didn't know enough about what I was trying to do or what was going on to be able to make any kind of a deduction. But it didn't take me long to realize that it was the happiest move that I would ever have the opportunity of taking advantage of, and I snapped at it.

Well, we're glad you did, too. You were preceded on the Benny show by three other announcers.

Maybe you remember who they were.

I did some digging to find out. George Hicks was Jack's first announcer.

George Hicks, a very good friend of mine.

And Paul Douglas, who became an actor.

Oh, yes, that's right. I'd forgotten Paul.

And a man with an exotic name by the name of Alois Havrilla.

Alois Havrilla was a Czech, one of the top people at NBC. He was on, but he couldn't make the transition when that 26-weeks changeover took place that I referred to, because Havrilla was doing the *Firestone Hour,* and General Tire bought Jack Benny for 13 weeks to fill out that '34 season. So that's the reason Jack was looking for another announcer.

So your first commercial for Jack Benny was for General Tire?

That's right. Bill O'Neill, the President of General Tire, was the man responsible for hiring Jack.

When you started to work for Jack, were you hired by the network or by the agency, or by Jack?

I was on staff at NBC, as everybody on the announcing staff had to be. I was under their management. But Jack was the man that did the hiring. He negotiated the whole deal.

Did he set your salary then, at that time?

Well, I guess you would say he did. Jack had such a reputation of being a skinflint. All I can say is, the Jack Benny that I knew had all the great attributes of a great human being such as generosity, tolerance, interest, and he was back of you 100 percent. As time went on, I wasn't the recipient of his penuriousness, which he was so reputed to be on the air.

Yet, over the course of time, on radio and even into television, there were so many stories around Don Wilson's salary, which was next to nothing. He'd lock you in a room until you would sign a new contract at the old salary. All of that sort of thing.

They were great, great days.

They were fantastic.

And the Big Broadcast of 1944, that we're doing here at the Mill Run Theatre, is reminiscent of that great era, the *Golden Era of Radio,* which I was fortunate enough to be a part of, and be a part of the Benny operation in the doing.

In The Big Broadcast, you come out at the top of the show to warm up the audience. You had the same role for the Benny show over the years.

That's right. Then, I sort of emcee the [Mill Run] show. I introduce all the acts as they come on, and so forth. Harry James, of course, is a top star. He does a certain amount of introducing at the end of the show. I might mention in passing, and I'm bouncing around sort of hither, thither and yon, Harry and I did the *Chesterfield* show together in 1942. I did *The Chesterfield* [*Supper Club*] with Glenn Miller. And when Miller went into the service, Harry took over and I continued on. So Harry and I worked for Chesterfield at that time, and we haven't worked together in all these many years since, until the institution of The Big Broadcast of 1944.

You worked for Chesterfield and then, while you were doing the Jell-O show for Jack, we forgot about Chesterfield and then you moved over to Lucky Strike.

Well, we were on for General Foods and Jell-O for 10 years. Lucky Strike came after them. Lucky Strike sponsored Jack and the Benny show for 15 years. They had the greatest longevity of any client on the show. General Foods being 10 years for Jell-O [and Grape-Nuts], and 15 years for Lucky Strike.

It's amazing. Jack Benny had Jell-O for 10 years and Lucky Strike for 15. Today, here in the 1980s, you're lucky if you get a sponsor to pick up a 30-second commercial during a television special.

That's right. My, how times have changed!

They really have. The sponsors took pride in the programming in those days. There was always the hue and cry – I'll editorialize for a second here – that once they got the network programming out of the hands of the sponsors, the audiences would have better programming. Eventually, through the Fifties and Sixties, the programming moved away from the sponsors who really produced the shows through their advertising agencies...

You got it.

...to the point where now the networks are producing the shows, or paying for the shows to be produced, and the sponsors don't really have any interest in it other than the sheer numbers they're getting out. Whereas in the old days when you were there with Jell-O and Lucky Strike, I believe, the audience, in their response to the sponsor, fortified the sponsor and kept his interest in presenting that program.

I think your analysis is very well taken. I don't think anyone can dispute it.

Did you have any experiences with an audience responding to a sponsor, either positively or negatively, about anything that was on the show?

We never had any difficulty in all the shows that I did, particularly with the Benny operation. There was never that conflict between the show and the client. The sponsor, I think, was very well aware of the fact of Benny's integrity and his great showmanship, and his devout attention that he gave to taste that he did on the show. That was one thing that got Jack a great children's audience. He never tolerated anything on the air that was the least bit off-color in those days. It was a show that the whole family could listen to with no compunction whatsoever.

We enjoyed Jack Benny because Jack Benny was so different. He was the star of the show, but he didn't have all that many gag lines.

No. Jack has often said, "I'm the biggest straight man in the business." Jack had a basic philosophy, if I may divert here for a moment, as I analyze it. It was obvious that this is his philosophy. The bigger he could make the supporting people who worked with him on the show, the bigger it made *The Jack Benny Show,* and the bigger it made Jack Benny. Now, this is a leaf that I don't think any other comedian ever took out of Jack's book. It was so sound and successful that I'm surprised somebody else didn't pick it up. But that was Jack. That was the generosity and the thoughtfulness and the great showmanship that was reflected in Jack's operation in all the years he was on the air.

When you read what someone has written about The Jack Benny Show *they always say he surrounded himself with all the stooges. He would say, "Mary and Dennis and Phil and Don and the others."*

Don't forget Rochester.

Rochester, of course! Yet, if you think about it, really, Jack was the stooge and all the others couldn't be stooges. A stooge, in my mind, is the guy who always gets the bad end of the joke, or the bad end of the story. And that was always Jack.

You brought up a reflection there that sparks a memory in my brain right now. There was one radio show many, many years ago that I can recall very vividly, that Jack did not speak one word on the show or on a microphone until the last five minutes of the show. This was the great generosity of this great man. [With] other comedians, if in rehearsal a supporting player got the laugh line, the star had that line on the air, not the supporting player. Jack was the reverse. All but five minutes, Jack was not on the air. We talked about him. We kidded him. He sat, with that kind of sheepish expression on his face, on a chair to one side. All the gags bounced off of him, but he never uttered one word, which is an amazing trait, really.

He had to have an awful lot of confidence in himself and his whole program.

Certainly he did.

He was a contributing writer, more or less, to the show.

Jack was a great editor. Jack was a creative mind. He created a lot of the basic ideas, just the thought, and turned it over to the writers for development. Of course, Jack always engaged the greatest writers in the business, in my opinion. The show just took off from that basic, rather simple, formula. Jack was a great blue pencil man. He could tell you from here to doomsday whether or not it was a gag that belonged on the show, that fit the characters it was given to or didn't fit the characters. He knew what it was all about.

Did you ever work with Eddie Cantor?

Yes, I did for six weeks at a time when Harry Von Zell – a very close friend of mine over the years; we're contemporaries – could not make an eastern trip with Cantor, so Eddie asked me if I'd fill in for those six weeks. Now, the Benny show had terminated for the season, and I was at liberty to do that. So I worked straight for Eddie for those six weeks.

You were working mostly for Jack Benny, but you were not exclusive to Jack.

That's right.

At any time?

Virtually so. I did not have a contract *per se* that tied me down exclusively, but in its application, it perhaps was an exclusive contract. That was due, in the later years, to the fact that Jack's recording sessions, or his on-camera TV appearances were not too predictable because he had other things going, particularly his concerts with his violin. So the schedules for the radio shows and the schedules for the TV shows had to be governed ultimately by his availability. So the rest of us made our time available to him. That excluded me particularly, as I recall, from doing a lot of other shows that were offered because I couldn't guarantee delivery of myself.

In the 1950s, Jack turned to tape for most of his shows, but prior to that, basically, those were all done live.

In the early days they were, and then finally for the repeat show, they went to the transcriptions. We used to do two shows a Sunday, one for the East Coast and one for the West, virtually. That was a bit much. Finally, when transcriptions came along, and we were able to do the show once a day, and the repeat show being played off those transcriptions, that was a great boon, really. Then, of course, tapes came along later.

When you did the shows twice, if Jack had the 7:00 time spot, you were probably doing it at 4:00. It was always on the West Coast, in Hollywood. You did it at four for the Midwest and the East and then again at seven for...

Seven was the New York time.

Was it heard at seven on the West Coast as well?

No, not as a general rule. The repeat show was.

When the West Coast heard The Jack Benny Show *they heard it at 7:00?*

Yes, Pacific Coast time.

Pacific Time, right. But what they were hearing, initially, was a repeat broadcast and later, a transcription.

Yes, you could say that.

When you had those two live shows, you obviously had time between the shows.

But it was well-consumed time, because there were rewrites that went on during that time. Things that Jack and the writers and producers thought might pay off, frequently did not pay off, so those are little changes that were made, so that when we did the repeat show it wasn't identical to the show we had done earlier.

So, maybe the West Coast, when they got the second shot at it, maybe they got a better show than we did here in Chicago.

Well, that's altogether possible, I think. I can't argue with that.

I don't think there ever was a bad Jack Benny show.

I think your point is well taken. Babe Ruth never hit a home run every time he got to bat either. I don't think anyone on radio ever hit a 100 percent, but Jack's batting average was extremely high. Believe me, it was high. I don't say that because I had the privilege of being associated with that great man. It was a fact, and well recognized and known in the industry.

You're a resident of Palm Springs. When did you take up residence there?

About 12, 13 years ago. We got out of the Los Angeles rat race, as we call it, and decided that we'd make our home in Palm Springs. So, that's what we've been doing.

Palm Springs was the real or fictional setting for a number of Jack Benny shows each year.

That's right. In the old radio days, we used to go down two or three times a year. We'd do a show from Palm Springs and related to Palm Springs, or the trip to Palm Springs. But it all had something to do with Palm Springs.

The most memorable one for Jack Benny radio fans is a show he would do the first or second week in December from Palm Springs, and it was the Christmas shopping show.

Oh, yes.

Jack would go in the department store and he'd be trying to buy gifts for all the members of the cast, but the whole thing revolved around a gift for Don Wilson.

Shoe laces! The generous man!

Or golf tees, or cuff links. Whatever it was, he would always go back and exchange, because he didn't know whether you'd like cuff links with "D" or "W" or "DW" or "Don." Is your middle name Harlow?

Yes.

Donald Harlow – "DHW."

We had a chap on the [TV] show, purportedly our son – Mrs. Wilson and I have no children – but they hired this chap out of the Pasadena Community Playhouse named Dale White and he played our son on the show as Mrs. Wilson played herself, my wife on the show, for 15 years.

She actually did play herself.

Yes, she did.

Lois?

Lois. That's right. She's the talent in our household, believe me. She's from the theatre, originally.

She did a lot of radio in the Forties, didn't she? Out on the West Coast?

Yes. She had been very successful in the theatre and looked upon this thing called radio rather down the nose, though, as theatre people are prone to do. She said it will never last. It's a single-barrel medium. The theatre, the live theatre, is the lasting medium. But when the theatre stock business kind of went downhill, and there wasn't that activity in stock around the country where she had done leads and character parts even as a young girl, she got involved through the persuasion of friends she'd been in the theatre with. She got involved in radio and whirled like a dervish ever since.

Do you recall some of the things that she did?

She was more or less a regular on *The Lux Radio Theatre,* which was the hallmark of great dramatic shows. She played the principal supporting part to the leads that came in from the picture industry for several years. She probably was on three weeks out of every four in a month. She was very popular there. She created the mother role for more kids that grew up in our industry: *Corliss Archer, A Date with Judy,* well, you name it. Lois had the voice quality that even as a younger woman permitted her to be able to do "mother" parts very, very effectively. She has a list of credits as long as your right arm.

The name she used on radio?

Lois Corbett. That's her maiden name.

How long have you been married?

We were married in 1950. How about that? How lucky can you get?

You're celebrating your 30th wedding anniversary.

We were married in June of 1950. Hey, wait a minute! There's an anniversary coming up and I'm not home! Maybe I'd better resign and go back home right now!

You ought to go to that Palm Springs department store and buy a gift for her! Over the years, as the announcer and the foil for Jack on his shows you, more or less, played probably the smartest member of the cast. Dennis was always a little...

He was a naïve kid.

Yes, and Phil was kind of brash, and after the gals and even tippled a little bit there.

That's funny! You're getting very polite there!

But you always had the brains. You were the one who had all the answers, and of course you...

When I blew, I blew it. I recall one incident where I was waxing very erudite on the air in introducing Jack. I'm talking about this particular situation, which I don't recall at the moment. When I got through, Jack said, "My goodness, Don, I didn't know you knew all that. Where did you learn it?" I said, "I read it in Dreer Poosen's column." Well, that created a whole new ball of wax. The crazy boo-boos that you make!*

That was not part of the script.

Oh, no, that just came out inadvertently.

It reminds me one time Fanny Brice had been off the air for two years. She and Frank Morgan were on together for Maxwell House. Now, Fanny is coming back with her own show, *The Baby Snooks Show.* I had a cold, declamatory, billboard opening in which I said, "The Baby Shooks Snow" and fell apart immediately! And the control room fell apart! We all fell apart and got a big laugh out of it, and started all over again.

I understand, that at one point, you said, when you were speaking for Lucky Strike Cigarettes, with their famous jingle back in the good old days...

Oh, here it comes. I knew you'd bring it up sooner or later!

*You said, "Be Lucky, go happy!"***

That's exactly what I said. That was at the close of a [television] show where we'd been doing a satire with Barbara Stanwyck and I was signing the show off from off stage, as a matter of fact. The closing scene, Jack went over and pulled the bell cord to summon the butler. Well, that caused a blackout. Jack did that pulling of the cord with so much alacrity, the whole ceiling fell down. So, that was the blackout of the curtain. The dust was blown all around and backstage – as you know, they're a little bit drafty anyway – a piece of plaster, or whatever it was, hit me in the eye under my glasses. I reached for it and made the boo-boo that you quoted. I was in the hospital for a week, and Lois got the job as the announcer on the show.

They made something out of that, too!

Every time somebody on the show would make a boo-boo, Jack was always quick to capitalize on it.

---

* The columnist's name was Drew Pearson.
** The line should have been, "Be happy, go Lucky."

I know Jack was an innovator in integrating the commercials into the comedy of the show.

Yes, Jack was the originator of that idea.

You were part of that with the Jell-O show.

Yes, for many years. I didn't do the so-called, "hard sell" announcing on the Benny show, although that was the job I was hired to do originally. But Jack started having the writers write me into the script. So, for a number of years, while I was always referred to as Jack Benny's announcer, even by Jack himself, the serious commercials at the opening and the close of the show were done by other people; I didn't have anything to do with them. Where I came in was the integrated commercials, or the comedy commercials, in the middle of the show, that we did with the Sportsmen Quartet for so many, many years so successfully. That was the part of the commercial that I really participated in, as well as other characters throughout the show.

Where did the Sportsmen come from? Were they a quartet before? Were they formed for this? Were they singing before?

They were a going quartet before Jack hired them, and very successfully, too. They made a great reputation for themselves, and it was all built out of a hum. Jack would ask them a question and in harmony they would hum. That was the thing that started their career on the Benny show.

And they'd start whatever song was popular and they'd do that normal lyric and then they'd come back with...

...a special lyric!

...for Lucky Strike Cigarettes. You toured with Jack during World War II.

I never went overseas with him.

No, but you stayed stateside and went to many of the military camps.

Yes, we were very busy doing that. We were thankful to be able to do it.

What kind of a reception did you get from the military personnel?

Just absolutely fantastic! They are the greatest audiences you ever want to play to. Great audiences, whether it was a military establishment of any kind, an army base, a navy base or a hospital or whatever it was. Those audiences, those kids, were great, great! Jack loved to do shows for the services.

You did a lot of work for the Armed Forces Radio Service with their Command Performance.

Yes, I started the *Command Performance* when that was instituted. Then when I went east, Ken Carpenter took over. When I returned, I started *Mail Call*. You're bringing back memories I thought I'd forgotten. Thank you.

You're entirely welcome. These programs were never heard stateside. They were produced for the large 16-inch transcription disks to be sent all over the world.

That's right, all over the world. They were great shows. Every top star in the business was on either *Mail Call* or *Command Performance* at one time or another or several times.

And they all worked for nothing, didn't they?

That's right.

How about the writers? Did the writers contribute some material, too?

Oh, tremendously. Jack wouldn't do a show without his writers helping him put it together. They did a lot of work.

They were marvelous. You weren't on just with Jack Benny on the Command Performance *and* Mail Call *shows. You were on as the emcee or the host or the announcer for a galaxy of stars. Did most of those programs come from that theater on Sunset and Vine where* The Lux Radio Theatre *was broadcast?*

We did several there [and] we did several of those shows from a number of different locations around Hollywood.

The Armed Forces Radio shows often had audiences. Were they mostly military audiences?

Yes, mostly. There were a certain number of civilians in the show, whether we were in one of the studios or whether we were on a military base of any kind. But, by far, the majority of the audience was military. The nice thing about it – Jack would come into an auditorium that we might be playing on a naval base or any military base, and if he found the brass down in front, he immediately arranged it, in his own polite way, where they got the brass out of those front rows and the GIs down, because that's where your audience was.

That tells us more about Jack Benny, doesn't it?

That's right.

I want to know a little bit more about you, too. Everyone associates you with The Jack Benny Show, *but you did so many other programs. You were involved, in the 1930s, with a program for Packard Automobiles, weren't you? Didn't you announce* The Packard Show?

I started that in Hollywood, and there again, Carpenter, whom I put in the radio business, succeeded me. He did more of the Packard shows than I did. I started them on the Coast and then went east and had to drop off of those and Carpenter picked [them] up at that time.

How did you start Ken Carpenter in the radio business?

Well, Carpenter had never seen the inside of a radio studio before. He was the son of a minister out of a town in Illinois that's very famous as a beer town.

Peoria.

Well, they brewed a lot of beer. Anyway, the head of a small agency in Los Angeles came to me one day and he said, "Don, we have a new minister at our church in Glendale. He has a son who wants to get in the radio business. Will you audition him? And I said – his name was Wilson too, incidentally; no relative – (first name Allen). And I said, "Well, Allen, I'll be glad to talk to the young man, but I have no place for anyone." So he sent Ken Carpenter in and I took a liking to him right from the very beginning. We had a long talk. I gave him an audition. He was a college man. He was a highly dependable individual. You could tell that from talking with him. I arranged it so I could hire him and put him on the relief shift at the noon hour and the dinner hour to pick up buttons because we were tied to the network at that time. That's how Ken started.

To "pick up buttons"? What does that mean?

"Picking up the buttons" means that when you've got a station break the announcers had to push their own buttons. You had a man in the studio control room, but you had to pick up your own button in order to activate your voice. You'd give your station call [letters] at that time, which was KFI in those days. That's about all you had to do.

In other words, when the network would take a break for station identification, or the music would be playing, you'd "pick up the button."

That's right, you've got it.

You'd turn on the switch and say the call letters of the local station and then they'd pick it up again.

That's right.

And for that, they paid you?

Well, that's what Ken Carpenter was hired for. If I may brag a little bit, I was Chief of Staff at that time. So, that's how it all happened.

You really have enjoyed your radio work, haven't you?

Very, very much.

Did you enjoy television as much as radio?

I think so. It's a different medium. It's an entirely different ballgame, and it's gotten so that a lot of the charm that we used to enjoy in the old, old days has been dissipated. It's a numbers racket these days. You used to go into a radio studio, or in the early days of television, and you knew everybody, but I mean everybody, and you knew them intimately. There was a great rapport. But that's gotten so it doesn't exist any longer. It's like a factory job these days. Maybe you see somebody. You've never seen them before or won't ever see them again. But there they are for that specific job.

Radio really was kind of a family association with the people behind the microphones as well as the people in front of the receivers.

Indeed it was. One of the great things about radio – and it will never be acquired by television because it's impossible – but in the radio days, through the listener's eye, his mind's eye, he lived the show with you. He re-created as the words came over the loudspeaker. He knew exactly what that individual looked like, although he'd never seen a picture of anybody. But, in his own mind's eye, he did. He knew what the situation was, what they were talking about. Again, the imagination played the part. That's one thing the young people, kids today, do not have that advantage that those of us that knew radio in the old days. Because their imagination is no longer stimulated as it was during the days of radio.

And those programs, created so many years ago, are just as funny as they ever were.

Just as good today as the day they were originally written! No question about it. That type of comedy, we no longer have. And bless the listeners' hearts for making it possible for us to succeed in it, because without the devotion of the radio listeners, and subsequently, the TV viewers, without that devotion that the public afforded us, we wouldn't be here today. We are indebted to the public for all the invaluable things that they did for us.

Well, the public is indebted to you and the radio people, too. One last thing. When we first met, I saw you lighting up a cigarette and I noticed it was not a Lucky Strike. Don Wilson lighting up a cigarette that's not a Lucky Strike?

When they quit sending them, I changed brands!

When the freebees ended!

Yes! It's been a joy talking with you. We've gone back over things that are very vague in my memory in some respects, but are pleasant to relate and chat with you about. Thank you for revitalizing my memory of many of those days.

Don Wilson was born September 1, 1900 and was 79 at the time of our conversation. He died April 25, 1982 at the age of 81.

Dennis Day

Dennis Day was associated with Jack Benny on radio and television for nearly 35 years, beginning in 1939. On August 11, 1976 my wife and I visited with the singer-comedian at his antique-filled Mandeville Canyon home in Brentwood, California. I asked what he had been doing before he started working with Jack Benny.

I graduated from Manhattan College and I had always loved singing. I was president of the Manhattan College Glee Club and I had done several appearances on a local radio show with Larry Clinton and his orchestra. I was one of those picked from about six or seven metropolitan colleges and universities to represent Manhattan College. I was on this program for about three times. After I graduated from college I intended to go into law school, because I thought I'd make law a vocation and singing an avocation. I never expected I'd be able to make a living at it.

But I was prevented from going to law school because I had an operation, and while I was recuperating, I started singing around local radio shows in New York City. Kenny Baker left *The Jack Benny Show* and someone suggested I send over an acetate of a couple of songs I had done on some of the local radio stations. So I did, and by good fortune, Mary Livingstone happened to hear the record and she liked the record. She saw my picture and all and brought it to Chicago to Jack. He came in and auditioned me and that was the start of the whole thing. They gave me a round-trip ticket to come out to California and audition out here, which I did.

And then, about two weeks before the program went back on the air after the summer hiatus, Jack signed me to a contract. It was a five-year contract with a two-week option: if I didn't make good in two weeks, he had the option to drop me. Then in the first year, it was for every 13 weeks. So they would pick me up after the first two weeks, for the next 11, then it was every 13 weeks. And I stayed with him for a full five years and then I went into the Navy in World War II. I spent two years in the Navy and then when I got out I went back with Jack. And I had my own radio show at the same time, for Colgate: *A Day in the Life of Dennis Day.* That went on for five years and then I crossed over into television and I had my own TV show for about three years.

Weren't you working with Cliff Arquette on that show?

Yes, Cliff Arquette, *Charlie Weaver:* "Yessss, that's my boy, Dennis . . . yeahhhhh!" We used to have a lot of fun and I'm sorry to see Cliff passed away. I guess it has to happen to all of us sooner or later. Jack Benny was a great loss when he passed away, because you never thought of him as an older man. He always looked so good, he thought so young. He was always full of ideas of what he was going to do, where he was going.

Six months before he passed away, my daughter Eileen was married and we sent him an invitation to the wedding. He wasn't able to make the wedding, the church wedding, but he did come out to the reception here at my home. He said, "I'll be there" and sure enough he was out here and spent about two hours visiting and then he had to go to another wedding reception.

He was leaving that night to go up to Portland to do a concert and then on to Seattle to do another concert and then over to Spokane. But this man was very thoughtful, very kind and very generous, contrary to the character that he was portrayed as. It was a great loss because nobody thought of him as getting ill. There was some talk of him not feeling well and everyone thought – well, because Jack always took excellent care of himself, he had a physical twice a year. And then he was doing a concert in Dallas and, just before going out on the stage, he got a seizure, cramps in the stomach, and his arm went dead. So they thought it might be a slight stroke. They examined him and there was no such thing. As a few months went on, they finally found out what it was and, of course, it was very insidious. He had cancer of the pancreas and, fortunately, he didn't suffer much. He went very fast, but I think the whole nation and the world was shocked when it happened, because nobody expected him, you know – [to die].

We think a man like that is immortal and can go on forever.

Yes. Well, he was a national institution. I never heard anyone have a bad word to say about Jack Benny. Everyone always loved him. He was a very kind and very gentle man. This is what's on his tomb: "Here lies a gentle man," which epitomizes, really, what Jack Benny was. A very kind and gentle man.

Did you find him that way on the first Jack Benny show that you did?

Oh, yes. Because, you know, I was scared stiff. After all, I had no great experience as far as singing is concerned with orchestras or appearing on [radio]. Here's the top radio show in the whole country and everyone was listening, so I was just very nervous and very scared. And I think that's why they brought in Verna Felton, who played the part of my mother. It was a buffer between myself and Jack until I got more confidence in myself on the show. So they used her in the first year, I would say, probably about 16 shows, and then finally I started to get a little more confidence in myself.

She was on quite a bit over the years in the role of your mother.

Yes. Well, they referred to her. Many times she wasn't even on the show, but Jack would refer to her. "Oh, your mother," you know, and I might say something about "She wants me to get a raise," or she was, always, you know, either a plumber's helper or a carpenter. She was a woman who could do anything and he would refer to her many times, or I would, and it felt like a living presence on the show.

Jack Benny was partial to tenors even before you came along.

Oh, yes, yes. Kenny Baker, and before that he had, well actually, between Kenny Baker and myself, he tried Michael Bartlett for a few shows.

Wasn't Frank Parker with him at one point?

For about five years when Jack first started in radio, back when Canada Dry Ginger Ale was his sponsor.

Why a tenor? Why not a baritone?

Well, I guess he liked tenors and it was good for him, I think, for the characters, too, that he created. See, Kenny Baker took over Mary Livingstone's character, that kind of silly, naïve type of thing, and then I had to perpetuate that same thing after Kenny Baker left the show. So I'd talk, "Yes, Mr. Benny." "Who, me?" "Oh, yes, please." You know, the silly, naïve kid.

It's like when I was in Chicago, I went swimming in Lake Michigan and when I came out, everybody on the beach was laughing. And he said, "Well, what were they laughing at? Your trunks?" And I'd say, "Ohhhh, trunks!" And we used to have these running things. You know, "Ohhhh....!" and whatever it would be, all through the years, and that was the fun part of it. Of course, it was the character that I played and, I guess I was [naïve]. Even though I was born and raised in New York City, I had never been west of the Hudson. I had been to Ireland with my aunt, who took me over when I got out of high school, but I had never been out west, so I was pretty green and wet behind the ears. I didn't know very much. I think I was, more or less, part of the character I portrayed on *The Jack Benny Show.*

Well, it was a great character.

After a while, when I got more confidence, I used to do dialects. During World War II, I used to do Rommel, popping out of a tank, and "ahhh...soo," you know, Japanese. We'd do all kinds of dialects and impressions. I did Parker Fennelly from the *Fred Allen Show:* "Howdy, Bub." All of these various characters.

You could be as silly as possible on the show and then, all of a sudden, Jack would say, "Sing, Dennis," and you'd sing "Granada."

And the public would accept it! Yeah, that was a phenomenon that is hard to explain. But they did separate the two: the fact that you couldn't have a good singing voice and then play a naïve, silly kid. [It was] kind of stupid in a sense, but the public always separated that fact. When he'd say, "Sing, kid," and then, after the song, [I would] go back into the same thing!

But actually all of us – Rochester, Phil Harris, Don Wilson – we only had about a page and a half of dialog on the show. But you better believe that it was the best dialog that possibly could be written, 'cause Jack knew it was good for himself and for all of the characters on the show. No matter how many laughs, he was very happy with all the laughs you might get. When the show was over, many people would say, "Hey, did you hear Dennis?" or "Did you hear Phil Harris on *The Jack Benny Show* last night?" It was still *The Jack Benny Show* because he was the catalyst who manipulated the whole thing. The jokes bounced off him; he was the butt of most of the jokes and we got the laughs. He was a genius in that sense.

In many cases, a show would be well under way before he would even make an appearance.

That's true, that's very true. And then he had a great facility of mentioning something. "I wonder where I put that book" or something like that, or "where Dennis would be" or whatever's going to happen. And, all of a sudden, when we're practically to the end of the show, that [line] would come in, in another roundabout way, that made an hilarious ending to the whole thing. He had that great facility.

In the early days when I was with Jack, he used to work with the writers on all the ideas and the dialog and everything else. And then, when we'd come in to read – usually on a Wednesday or Thursday we'd have our first reading – and after the reading was over we'd leave and go home. Then they would edit it and tighten it up and, my gosh, every time every script would be 200 per cent better once they worked it over.

Jack would work. "I don't like this, I don't like this. We've got to replace this or bring in new dialog. Let's keep this. This worked fine." He was a great editor of scripts. This is the great sense of comedy that the man had. Not only was he an editor, but what a timer, a master timer. He knew how long to milk a laugh and when to stop. This was a great thing about him.

It was an era, through the Thirties all the way up into the Fifties, when radio was in its heyday, 'cause everyone could imagine what a person looked like, what a situation looked like, in their own minds, by sound effects and by the person's voice.

People used to think I was a – oh, I get two different kinds of comments on what I look like [from] people who haven't seen me. One would say I was tall, six feet, with blond hair and a hayseed coming out of my ears. Or, the other would say, well, he's short and fat. These were the two opposites, but each person who listened to radio formed his own image of what he wanted you to look like, or what he thought you looked like.

That's because the listener participated. He had to supply the picture.

And the sound effects were all-important. I know Jack had a great sense of that. Many a time there was a slap in the face. I remember, once he was trying to get the sound effects man to make the proper sound. It just didn't come. And he kept, "No, no, that's not it." And, by George, when the sound effects man finally hit it, the right sound effect of the slap in the face, and Jack says, "That's it!" you knew instinctively yourself, in listening, that he was absolutely right.

He was very meticulous about his sound effects. Take the vault that he had. All those tremendous sound effects, with the chains and the alligators, created in your own mind what the vault in his cellar was. It was just amazing. I don't think you can really translate that [to television]. They tried. It came off very well, but I don't think it had the same impact as it did on radio.

Did you offer anything to the Benny radio show that wasn't in the script?

You mean to ad-lib? Well, sometime you might. But you better be sure that you knew what you were doing. Phil would ad-lib quite a bit. And Jack was a great audience. If something was really funny, he'd fall right down on the floor. He was just amazing.

You mean literally, he would fall on the floor?

Well, he'd just break up! I'm saying, you know, just break up and almost throw the script away and just put his head down and laugh, and just absolutely say, "Oh, that is funny! Oh, my gosh!" He was a great audience!

But we didn't do very much ad-libbing because you had a time structure in there. The show had to be off, and lots of times the audience may laugh a lot longer than we expected they would, and you had to get those commercials in – that was the important thing. Jack was the first one to do the integrated commercials way back in the Thirties, by "Jell-O again," and then we went from there to Grape-Nuts, and we went into L.S.M.F.T.; Lucky Strike Green Has Gone To War and all of that. He always integrated the commercials as part of the program.

It really was fun for the audience. We could listen and feel that everybody on your side of the microphone was having a good time with it, too.

Yeah, when you went there you enjoyed it. We didn't rehearse a great deal, because comedy loses its spontaneity if you do. Then it becomes too rote and planned, and Jack didn't want to do that. Never rehearsed a great deal. You may have one or two readings at most. I always got a great charge out of going to the Jack Benny rehearsals and the show itself, because you knew you were gonna have fun. And everybody did enjoy themselves. There was no animosity among any of us, you know. We weren't jealous of one another. We all got along just absolutely great. Everyone got his feature spot and, you know, the material was the greatest.

Did you have to rehearse on a Sunday? When did rehearsals start for you as an actor and singer on the show?

Well, I'd start at least on Wednesday. I'd have to get with the arranger, pick out the song, talk to Jack and Mary. I'd make my suggestions and then we'd have to get with the arranger as far as key and the routine, and then he'd have to make the arrangement.

Then, the next time I came in for rehearsal with the orchestra was on a Sunday morning. Usually around 10:00 I got there and the cast would probably arrive around 11:30 or 12. But, I would rehearse with the orchestra in my period of time. After I'd rehearse once or twice, that was all. He'd send the orchestra out. Jack would never let the orchestra sit there to hear the rehearsal of the comedy, because he wanted them to hear it for the first time, as well as the audience sitting in the studio and the people at home listening to the radio. That's why he loved Frank Remley. They always put a microphone under Frank Remley, because Frank was a great audience and he had an infectious laugh and he'd break up at anything that Jack or any of us would say. So you see, they kept the spontaneity there by dismissing the orchestra. They'd rehearse their cues for the bridges and things like that, but they didn't hear any of the comedy at all.

It seems to me that you could almost always hear Don Wilson's laugh on the air.

Yes, yes. He had a big, hearty laugh.

But he was part of the action in much of it and he must have been going through the rehearsal of it. Yet his laugh sounded like he had heard this for the first time.

That's right. As I said, we didn't rehearse that much, so it was almost like new to you. And I think all of us got involved in it and got carried away with it and enjoyed it.

Did you have to do a second show?

We did in the beginning. We did a second show until after the war. The first five years I was with him, we did one for the East Coast and then one for the West Coast. That was at 4:00 in the afternoon, which would be 6:00 in Chicago, and then 7:00 in New York. Then we'd come back and do one for the entire West Coast at 8:30 at night.

At 8:30?

Yes, 8:30 on Sunday night. And we'd do that show at that time. It wasn't until after the war that Bing Crosby, I think, was the first one who started with tape, and that's when we did. Well, it wasn't tape then, it was acetate.

But they started recording the show.

They permitted the recording of it and the replaying of it so we didn't have to do a live show twice.

When you were doing two live shows, did you lose the surprise element with the orchestra, then, on the second show?

Jack would change the script slightly. He would change some of the gags that didn't go or, if something needed punching up, they would change it. So it was slightly different.

So the West Coast might have heard a better show?

Yes. Also, Fred Allen would come on between the first and the second show, so Jack would have a comment about Allen, what he said, on the second show. So that made a little difference, too.

It was after the war and into the late Forties when you got your own show.

Yes. I started in 1946 and that went through the season of 1951. So I had five years. And then Jack continued in radio until [1955] and then they reran a lot of them. Then he went on to television, so I stayed with him until 1964 on TV when he had his regular show. After that, then he did specials.

While you were doing the Benny show, you did A Day in the Life of Dennis Day *and Phil Harris was doing the* Fitch Bandwagon *or his Rexall show. And Jack had no problems with that?*

No, no. It was understood at the time. That's one of the things about Jack. He would come on my show to help plug it, or anything like that. And he'd refer to it many times on *The Jack Benny Show*: "Oh, you got your own show?" and all of this sort of thing. Then when he moved from NBC to CBS, Phil didn't go with him and that's when Phil was terminated as far as the Jack Benny radio shows were concerned and they brought in Bob Crosby, and he stayed with it until the show was terminated in [1955.]

Once you got on television, in front of the cameras, did the people who thought that you were tall and lean, or short and fat... how did they react?

I never got any adverse reaction. They still accepted it, that I could be silly and everything else with Jack. It worked out fine.

You had your own television show, too.

My sponsor was RCA Victor. And I was live for the first year, year-and-a-half. And then the last year we were on film, but of course that was the kiss of death. They put me on opposite *I Love Lucy,* the number one show in the entire country, and I just couldn't get a rating at all and so that was the end of that.

During all this time, you occasionally popped up on the motion picture screen.

I did a couple of pictures at 20th Century Fox and RKO. The first picture I was in was *Buck Benny Rides Again.* So I've had a very varied and wonderful career.

Dennis Day was born May 21, 1917 and was 59 at the time of our conversation. He died June 22, 1988 at the age of 71.

Frank Nelson

Frank Nelson was perhaps the most famous "ye-e-esss" man on radio and television, appearing with Jack Benny for most of both of their careers. We met Februaty 18, 1975 in his very comfortable home with a fabulous view of Hollywood. I asked about the first time he worked with Jack Benny.

 The first broadcast I ever did with him was in June of 1934. At that time he was doing a five-minute insert for an eastern show. They had a little sketch where he was coming to California and he meets this fellow on the train, and Jack's telling him what a big shot he is and how he's going to California and he's really going to do great things out there. Jack says, "You know, you're a very personable young man. Possibly I can do something for you. My name's Jack Benny. What's yours?" And I said, "Clark Gable!" That was the opening sketch that we did.

And you were a regular with him all along?

Well, I started out, I guess, in the first year or two, just doing casual things with him here and there. And then, finally, it grew into a regular character. I was with him for many years under contract.

What was your first professional radio appearance?

The first thing that I did on radio was in 1926 in Denver, Colorado. There was a bank there that was going to do a 13-week series and so they held auditions at KOA. I was just a kid in high school at the time and I went out to KOA and this man looked at me and said, "Oh, you're much too young. This part is of a 30-year old man." I said, "Oh, well, they told me to come out." He said, "Well, have you ever read on a microphone?" I said, "No, I haven't. I've done theatre." He said,

"Well, as long as you made the long trip out here, maybe you'd at least like to read?" So, I had a deep voice then and so I read. There were 30 of us. When we got through, the next day they called back 12, and the following day they called back four, and the following day they called me and told me I had it. Now, I never understood the part, but I played it!

That was my beginning. Then I worked with KOA on various shows and then I announced for KFEL, which was a smaller station in Denver. Then I decided I was going to make my fortune and come out to Hollywood. I came out here the end of 1929 and started with Georgia Fifield – the "Georgia Fifield KNX Players." I had a letter of introduction to this lady and I went over to KNX.

And you've been here ever since?

That's right. The only thing I ever did in New York was *The Jack Benny Show.*

When he went to New York.

That's the only show that I ever failed to complete in my radio career. I've gone on in a stretcher, and I'm not kidding! I actually did that in Denver, in that early series. I got pneumonia and they took me out on a stretcher to play it one week. But the only show that I ever actually missed through illness or anything else, was the second broadcast of *The Jack Benny Show* in New York City. So, that's my Eastern career!

When you were first in Hollywood, after working with the KNX Players, where did you go from there?

We did so many things in those early days. We did a show called *Makers of History* down at KFI. It was written by Jerry Cady, who went on to write for 20th Century Fox. We did *Tapestries of Life,* which was about the statuary at Forest Lawn, and that's really the way I started back into free-lance radio.

I was doing announcing at KMTR and I got a call to go down and do a very highly dramatic thing called "Father Forgets," which is a father talking to his son, by his crib while he's asleep and apologizing for all the bad things he's done – as we all do to our children – how he yelled at him and so on. It was very dramatic, a tearjerker, and I did it in the middle of a comedy show and they got a tremendous response from it. At that time, the fellow who was doing *Tapestries of Life* was having a lot of trouble. He was getting his tongue wrapped around his teeth a lot and he was fluffing a lot, and so Jerry Cady called and said, "Look, would you be interested in doing the *Tapestries of Life?*" At that time they paid a lot of money for local radio. They paid $10 apiece, which was a big, big fee, because you were working for $2.50, $3, $5, which was fairly normal. A few at $7.50, but $10 was big money, so I said, "Gee, I'd love to." So, that started me back. And then he gave me *Makers of History* and so I was making $25 a week down at KFI, and I got out of the other job.

I did various things around town here. One that was very popular, a local show, was *The Witch's Tale*. Paula Winslowe, who was another gal from out here, and I did the leads in those for about two years. That was the most envied show in town at that time. Now, this was before there was any transcontinental shows out of here.

And then, finally, I had worked for John Swallow at KFAC-KFBD as an announcer. John became the first head of NBC out here. NBC, at that time, was just an office on the RKO lot, on the back lot, and we worked on sound stages initially. Then they built some sound stages strictly for radio right at the end of the RKO lot. But that was the beginning.

They had a show out here called *Hollywood on the Air*, which was an RKO show, the first unsponsored show out of Hollywood that was transcontinental. I was the announcer, I filled in as a bit actor, and then if somebody didn't show up, I played that part, too. I did that for about a year and a half, and then the first sponsored transcontinental show out of here was an original Marx Brothers show [*Flywheel, Shyster and Flywheel*] with Groucho and Chico – just the two of them – and I did that.

Georgia Fifield cast the show and she was their secretary and I was a regular on the show. As a matter of fact, I could have been in movies if I could have sung, because one day Groucho walked over and he said, "Look, Frank, can you sing?" And I laughed and said, "Sing? I can't even carry a tune." He said, "Oh, that's too bad." Because what they had in mind for me was – you remember the "Donkey Serenade"? You remember the gentleman who did it?

Sure. Allan Jones.

That's right. That's exactly what they had me in mind for in that picture and if I'd been able to sing, I'd at least had a crack at it, you know.

And you would have killed Allan Jones' career!

Well, I doubt that! He was much too fine a performer to have his career killed. But I was working with them at the time and they thought it would be a good idea to have me in the picture, I guess.

Those are the very early days and I used to have a running gag with John Swallow. I thought that eventually the big movie stars were going to bring radio out here. That is, transcontinental radio. And John never believed it, never believed it! I said, "You know, John, someday, really, we're going to have a lot of big-time radio out here." He said, "Not a chance in the world" and so, we had a running gag between us. When they finally had the studios at Sunset and Vine, the big NBC studios, and I'd walk down the hall and see John coming up the hall, I'd say, "John, ever think big-time radio will come to Hollywood?" "Nope, don't think so, Frank." We never changed it, never changed it in all the years we knew each other!

They were fun days, those early days. They were great days! I think radio offered so much more to an actor than television does, because you could do anything that your voice would allow you to do. You weren't trapped by what you looked like, how tall you were, how old you were or how fat you were, or anything else. You could just do anything that your voice would allow. And that let us play a great deal of varied type characters.

And you didn't need any time for make-up or costumes.

No! That was nice. And you read it, too. Although that wasn't as easy as we make it sound now. Lots of times we look back and we say, oh boy, what a soft touch that was, how easy it was. But it wasn't easy. It truly wasn't. You had to come into a studio and you had to create a character in a very brief period of time. And it had to be believable at least, and all those characters weren't the greatest in the world. But it kept you on your toes and it kept you working hard.

We did things, funny things. I remember I had a show at NBC, which was really one long block from CBS, and I had it at the last studio in the hall. That is, the closest studio to the CBS studio. I would conclude that show, sign that show off, and then run out the side door and have a page there who would have the door open. And I'd run out the side door, tear across the Palladium Ballroom lot, and slide through Studio A. They had big double doors there, and they'd have that open for me, and I'd slide through to the middle of the stage and take one deep breath and say, "Ladies and gentlemen, from Hollywood..." and open the next show. Boy, I'll tell you some days I thought I'd never get the words out. I wouldn't want to try it now! But I was a lot younger then!

Everybody really had to run around! You didn't have any long-range contracts. You did what you could.

That's right. Oh, yes, there were contracts, but not too many, you know. An awful lot of it was free-lance. And I did shows where I'd say, "Well, I can't make any of the rehearsals. What's the part?" They'd say, "Well, it's so and so..." I'd say, "Well, if you want to mark the script, I'll come in and do it." And then I'd actually go in and do it, on the air, for the first time. But it was a comedy show and, you know, the gags and things that you at least were easy with and familiar with. But, it wasn't quite as easy as sometimes we make it sound in retrospect.

We're so familiar with the character you played and, I'm sure, created on the Jack Benny series. Yet, he wasn't always the man behind the railroad counter or the floorwalker.

Jack always referred to him as his "nemesis." Well, the nemesis character – because I played a variety of things – were all the same fella. He never had a name, like Mr. Kitzel, but if Jack ever referred to him by name, he just called me my name, Mr. Nelson. I'd meet people on the street and they'd say, "Hey, you're that fellow on *The Jack Benny Show!*" I'd say, "Yeah." They'd say, "What's your name?" because they really didn't know.

You also worked on some of the biggest network comedy shows, doing other things, too.

Oh, sure, sure. I was in the *Blondie* show. I was the next door neighbor, Herb Woodley. I was a regular on that. And I worked with Eddie Cantor. I worked with just about anybody you want to name in the comedy field. I wasn't a regular on all those shows, but I worked them all.

Whenever they needed a good comedy foil!

Well, they used to have a standard thing. You'd go in and the writer would say, "Now, be as funny on this show as you are on *The Jack Benny Show*." And, I'd always say, "You write it as funny and I'll be as funny, 'cause I'm just as funny as the material. That's as funny as I am."

You were with Parkyakarkus, too, weren't you?

Yes, yes. I was a regular with Parky. I did a running character, I can't even remember the name of it now. It was not a long series, it didn't last long. And Parky, of course, unfortunately, had an operation that wasn't successful and he ended up in a wheelchair for the rest of his life. He had a back problem.

How did you land these shows? You get a job with Jack Benny, for example. Do they just come to you or did you have to go out and hunt for them?

In the later days, you just got the calls. Now, I'm not saying all actors did that, but I never went out after jobs. I didn't call directors just to say, "Why don't you use me on your show?" or anything like that. But in the very early days, back in those earlier days that I was talking about when I was doing the $5 shows and the $3 shows, and that type of show, then you kept a little book, boy, and you knew exactly when that director cast and you'd call him up. You knew whether to tell him a joke and hang up or whether to ask him for a job or what to do. And, oh, I was famous for my little black book at that time, because I knew them all and I knew how to approach them. And you had to do that then, because you were fighting for very little money. And if you didn't go around and see them and remind them that you were alive, you just didn't get the calls. But as the business got bigger, and there were more people listening to the shows, more people would catch that show and say, "Hey, why don't we use him next week?" and so on. So, I think that's the way our calls came, mainly, in the later days.

I'd like to find out what it took to put on a Jack Benny show.

The Jack Benny Show was really quite easy to do. I'm talking now from the actors' standpoint. Obviously, the writing was meticulous. Jack had honed a lot of that writing. He sat with the writers a great deal. If it came down to a rock bottom decision as to a joke in or out, it would be very often Jack's decision that made that happen. But for an actor, it was a very simple show to do. You'd go in, say on Saturday. You'd read through once. Just sit down, read the script straight through, get up and leave. And you'd come back in on Sunday. You'd read once, around the table, go and read it once on the "mike," and that's all until show time. It was just that easy to do.

Jack knew his people, and they wrote for those people. And Jack had a great, great thing that I don't think any other comic in the business had. If you were to pick up a Jack Benny script and read it, you'd say, "Well, wait a minute. Where are Mr. Benny's jokes?" because Jack didn't do jokes. He did looks, he did takes, he fed, really, the actors around him. That's the way he conducted his show. The big jokes were in the hands of the people who surrounded him, which was most unusual. It shows that he had tremendous confidence in himself.

There was one man – I could name him and I won't – who was very famous as a comedian and when you would do the dress rehearsal, if you had a big joke that got a big laugh, when you came back to do the show, you didn't have that joke. *He* had the joke. And very often he couldn't understand why the joke didn't play on the show like it had in the rehearsal. And the reason was, it was built for you and it wasn't built for him. But he never learned that lesson. But Jack, on the other hand, had no such insecurity, and so he gave those jokes to his people. He surrounded himself with characters that people expected to hear. As soon as he said, "Oh, Mister – " people said, "Oh, boy, here it comes. He's gonna get it!" And if he said, "Excuse me – " and the fellow said, "Sí," you'd say, "Oh, boy, here it comes. Now they're gonna do that routine!" The people were in on it and I think they enjoyed being in on it. I guess the fact that the show stayed on top all the years that it did proved that.

How long were you with Jack on radio?

From the time he started his own show out here, I worked with him. I did not work regularly right at the beginning; I worked just spasmodically. But after about two years, I guess, I was pretty steady. We'd do 39 shows in the season and I'd do, oh, anywhere between 25 and 30 of those shows.

That's pretty regular! You made a nice, easy move into television with him, too.

Yes. Well, television came along, you know, and you had to go with it. I kind of wish this [radio] business were still here, and I kind of think it would have been if we hadn't the same people in charge who were going to be in charge of television. I'm talking about the networks. I'm talking about the ad agencies because I think then you'd have seen a big fight between the two. I think they would have each fought for their share of the audience. And I believe, today, there is a very definite place in this country for good radio. But I guess the networks aren't much concerned about that, 'cause they're making more money this way.

Radio in itself is an art form and should be able to provide the public with comedy and mystery and drama.

That's right. There should be a great deal more variety than there is today. Today we have talk shows, we have news, but where are the kinds of things that we did in radio before? They're gone.

You've been part of so much of the great radio days and there's a lot of people out there who want me to say thank you for all the fine performances you've turned in over the years.

Well, that's very kind of you, Chuck. It's been a gratifying business to be in, and it's given me a lot of pleasure and I'm glad it's given other people pleasure, too.

If you were to be offered a job on another kind of Jack Benny radio program, and you were asked if you could spare some time to work in it, what would you say?

Oooohhhhhh, can I!!

Frank Nelson was born May 6, 1911 and was 63 at the time of our conversation. He died September 12, 1986 at the age of 75.

Phil Harris

Phil Harris was a star of the bandstand before he became an important part of **The Jack Benny Show** *and star of* The Phil Harris-Alice Faye Show *on radio. We met on June 15, 1988 in his home at the Ironwood Country Club in Palm Desert, California. I began by mentioning that he had spent some time in Chicago over the years.*

 Oh, yeah! My first trip to Chicago I never will forget. I'm in New York and they're bookin' me – the Music Corporation – and they're bookin' me into Chicago at the College Inn. I'm supposed to follow Ben Bernie, who is a tremendous success, and he was going over to Pabst's Casino during the World's Fair...

The Century of Progress.

...and I don't know how big this guy is because they brought him out to California, I think, when I was at the [Coconut] Grove or someplace, and they put him in the Roosevelt Hotel and he laid a soufflé. And then they put him in another place out there and he laid another bomb and he went back with "Yowsa, Yowsa" and he busted everybody in the College Inn! So they put me in to follow him and it was like standing in front of The [Super] Chief at that time! So anyway, I went in and all the guys were around in those days – big opening, you know, you had all the bands in Chicago – and I think the only thing that saved me was the World's Fair. So I had a very pleasant engagement and, like I say, it was a tough job to follow Ben Bernie, because he was the toast of the town.

Since then, other people have had a tough job following you.

Well, no, no. I mean, I don't think anybody's invincible. I'm just saying, how can a guy lay an egg two places in one town and then go to the other town and be the toast? It shows it could only happen in America, Chuck.

Phil, you're a Midwesterner, right? You were born in Linton, Indiana.

I just got back. This was our 10th anniversary at Linton. We put seven more children through college. We average seven a year and the town's only 5,000 people. We are the third largest PGA tournament, guest tournament, in the United States. We played over 500 players and I'm very proud of the guys [who] plan the thing every year and it just becomes bigger and bigger and all I have to do is just walk in; everything is all set up. It's put together by the friends who conceived it and it's turned out very successful.

How long did you stay in Linton as a child?

Up till I was out of grammar school, either 11 or 12, because I started high school in Nashville and I never finished. I was there about 20 minutes. That was long enough.

You were a musician. You played the drums, didn't you?

Well, I did until I heard Buddy Rich, Chuck, and that made me throw 'em away.

Your father was a musician.

My father was a good clarinet player, a legitimate clarinet player, right.

And you worked with him in the vaudeville days.

Well, my father was with circuses. He was with Hagenbeck and Wallace, and he was with Ringling Brothers. He loved it under the canvas. Up until the time he died he was my band manager, all the years that I was with Benny, and he still said that if it wasn't under canvas, it couldn't be any good. He went back to the carnival days and, like I say, the circus days. But my father just picked up the clarinet and started playing it. It was one of those things. It's a very intricate instrument and if you think everybody can play it, listen to Pete Fountain.

When did you start your musical career?

When, I guess, I was about five or six years old. For some reason or other I wanted to be a drummer, because all you had to do in a small town that I was in is go out and play under the street lamp and collect lightning bugs and put 'em in a fruit jar. What are you goin' to do? You know what I mean? And I'd already turned over a privy and, you know, played "long-tail fox," "spin the plate" and "who's got the bottle" and all that stuff. You know what I mean? So I just whittled out a pair of sticks and on the hard tables and with the rungs in the chairs, I had a ball. I liked it.

When I was a kid, my mother put me in an amateur show, like they do kids today, and I guess I just showed a flair for it, like my father, who was a coal miner. Came from a little town in Kentucky, Beaver Dam, and worked in the mine every morning, every morning at 5:00, down in the mine. And all of a sudden he saw a clarinet. That's like picking up a rattlesnake, you know. You don't fool with a clarinet. You make a note on it, if your nails are not clippped, you're going to squeak, you got a clinker on your hands, you know. So the same thing with me. For some reason or other I wanted to play drums.

You started professionally as a drummer.

I got $5 a week, yeah, in a local theater. I saw silent pictures, so I got a kick out of playing. I had a woman piano player and a woman playing a fiddle with a horn on it. You know, [it would] drive you out of the room. But you had to stay there anyway, you know. They did a whole show in the afternoon, then you'd do one of the supper shows, the one that is a brain-knocker. I got so that I'd see a guy [on the screen] and he's running around the corner and the car wouldn't start so I'd send [away] and get a ratchet. I'd take my $5 and I sent for drums. And then I saw the guy directing traffic. He blew a whistle. Boom! So I'd blow the whistle when he did. Then I got a wind machine. The first thing you know, for my own kicks, I'm cuing the pictures. Later on there is a guy in San Francisco who, years ago, went to Paramount and made a fortune doing the same thing that I was doing because I was getting a kick out of it! Because when the wind blew we had a wind machine and, before they had talkies, this guy made a fortune by cuing pictures, the drummer with every kind of sound – chimes, bells.

The Dixie Syncopaters. Was that an early group of yours?

That was after I got to Nashville, yeah, that was five guys. That's like a regular five-piece Dixieland band in those days. That's a lost art. There's no more bass drum. These people put pads and they put pasteboard. In my days the bass drum was an instrument. It's even in the symphony, you know what I mean. In my day you had to play a bass drum. You got piano, you got saxophone or clarinet, you got banjo, you got drums and if you're lucky you get a trumpet, and trombone – seven pieces – that's Dixieland. That's the original setup, but then you had to play bass drum because bass drum has a tone. It's got a sound. You put your foot on there and take it off and it's an instrument, but these people now, it might as well be like a cardboard box. It has no tone to it. All my life I wanted to have a bass drum made at the same size as a tympani so I could have things on it to tune it like you do a tympani, but I never got to it, or I don't think they've ever gotten to it, because now you have good bass players which, in my days, the bass drum had to have a tone, otherwise you're out of gas.

Where did the Dixie Syncopaters perform?

Around town at the country clubs, and everything, and we were right before Francis Craig, who had one big record, after we left. He was from Vanderbilt. We left town and went to Honolulu. They had sent for us in Honolulu. It's a long story 'cause, during vacation, a lady came through, Ruth Stonehouse, she's a big star, playing theaters. So we went with her on one-nighters. When she got to Denver, we met a guy, an organist, who was going over to open the Princess Theatre in Honolulu. He said, "I'll send for you" and we said, "Yeah." So he really did. Then we went to Hawaii and we opened the Princess Theatre and at that time they were hanging somebody on the screen and we're playing "St. Louis Blues" and the Hawaiians are going crazy, 'cause they never heard music like that. So that's what actually happened.

Who was Carol Lofner?

Carol Lofner. That's later; that's in 1928. So we went to Australia. J. C. Williamson could book you around the world, one of the big booking people. We had Remley, we had Chuck Moll, good alto player, came from Moscow, Idaho, graduated as an engineer. They're all gone.

Remley was in your band way back then?

Yeah. First met Remley on the boat. Remley was a left-handed ukulele player. Drive you out of the room! Can you beat it? Hell of a guy. We went to Australia together. It was very strange. They sent a guy over by the name of Phillips. There were four brothers that owned Luna Park in Melbourne. He came over to pick four guys to augment the Australians, because they were tremendous musicians but didn't know a thing about jazz. Now I'm working one place, Lofner working another place, Chuck Moll working another place, and Remley working another place, and this guy picks the four of us. We don't know anything about it. He went to this booker and that's the way we happened. So we all go to Australia and we spend a year in Australia and then the guys went back and I went with the band to Detroit to open the Addison Hotel. I went home to Nashville and I got a call, saying that Lofner and Remley and Chuck Moll were starting at Balboa and wanted me to come out and join 'em. So Pop Tooter said, "Will you stand in front of the band?" So that's how I started, singin' a couple of songs. He was responsible for what little success I attained as a band leader.

Had you done any singing before that?

Oh, yeah. Going to Australia, you got to sing. You were 21 days going second class on a bad ship.

When you came back –

I was a sideman again when I came back, and I went to Detroit.

When was the Phil Harris Orchestra developed?

The Phil Harris Orchestra was started in 1928, 1929 and then I went with Lofner. That's when I stood in front of the band instead of taking the guy's place. And then we went to the St. Francis Hotel in San Francisco in 1929 during the Crash and we spent '29, '30 and '31. When the Crash came, you had to duck when you walked out the door, because somebody was jumping out the window. That's when it really hurt. The only thing that saved us was Stanford, because all the students were going over to hear Anson Weeks at the Mark Hopkins. But then, after I stayed there three years, a man by the name of Frank, who owned the Ambassador Hotel, came to the manager of the St. Francis, who was a good friend of mine, Jimmy McCabe, and he said, "You should take this guy to follow Gus Arnheim." They're big! Talk about following somebody! So anyway, I left Lofner there and I went to the Coconut Grove and Mr. Abe Frank and I put another band together. The only ones I kept were Remley and some other guys and we went in to follow Gus and the Rhythm Boys and, thank God, we made it. I mean, it turned out all right, because a friend of mine, Artie Mellenger, who was in the publishing business, hustlin' tunes, said, "I have a niece that comes from Norfolk, Virginia. She's quite a singer and she's absolutely beautiful." I said bring her out. She was 16. Her name was Leah Ray. She's now married to Sonny Werblin, been married for years, and they have beautiful children. I would say she was a good 60 or 65 per cent of what little success I attained as a band leader.

While you were at the Coconut Grove you started getting into radio, didn't you? Some broadcasting?

Oh, we did radio! I did radio back in the cat whisker thing, way back, as a sideman in Los Angeles. I forget who it was, it's been so many years ago, but we did a broadcast when they used to put that thing, the wire, on the crystal set. And when I was broadcasting from the St. Francis we had the second most powerful station in the United States. There was only one more powerful, from Texas. They had Dr. Brinkley. But other than that, KGO from San Francisco. We got letters from Alaska, from all over the United States. There were so few stations, you know what I mean, and a tremendous amount of wattage. I don't remember. We'd go on at night, and the next day I'd get baskets of mail, baskets. Of course I'm talking about 1929 now, remember.

People were hungry for the new thing, radio.

And during intermission, I introduced [the music of] Bert Williams to [the listening audience]. We'd play a set and then I'd get the guitar. I'd get Remley and I'd sit down and I'd do Bert Williams tunes during the intermission and they happened to catch on.

You were at the St. Francis, and then the Ambassador, and you also did some work at the Wilshire Bowl.

Well, I had a piece of that. That was way later, after I was with Jack Benny. What happened was, after I got through at the College Inn, the Music Corporation started bookin' me around. You know, it's an octopus, and they control you, so I left them.* I didn't like the way they were operating for me. I'm not saying anything against them, but then I went with Ralph Phipps, who had his own little routine. There were two or three bands and we played the New Yorker, we went to Cincinnati, to Dallas and to the Roosevelt. Then we went to Galveston. [He] kept me in business until I later went back with Music Corporation.

Did you travel from coast-to-coast at all with the band, doing one-nighters?

I played a few one-nighters, but not coast-to-coast. I didn't fool around the East much. Well, I played the Waldorf, the Palais Royal, the Pennsylvania Roof, the Hollywood. I took Vallee's place for a while, and I also played at the New Yorker, but other than that I didn't do any one-nighters around the East, no. Then I went to Chicago, but every year I used to make all the theaters like Boston and Cincinnati and all those when I was on the three months off from the Benny show.

How did you hook up with Jack Benny?

Well, I met him at the Essex House years ago, and I had my own program. I was on for J. Walter Thompson with Cutex nail polish. I was staying at the Essex House and he and Mary were staying there too and we became friends. I think at that time he was with Chevrolet or somebody. A couple or three years passed and I'm on this thing I told you, at the New Yorker and then to New Orleans. I get a call in New Orleans that George Burns wants [me] as a band leader. So I go to Seymour [Weiss, manager of the Roosevelt Hotel in New Orleans] and I had a contract and I said, "Gee whiz, I got a chance to get back on the air with my own program" and he let me off. Two days before I'm supposed to leave New Orleans I get a wire back from Music Corporation that said don't bother, Wayne King is going to go with Burns, so I came back to California. I'd been here a couple of days and Jack Benny had heard about it and he invited me out to the Trocadero for dinner. So I go out there and he said, "What program are you on this year?" and I said, "Well, I haven't got one," and he said, "You're with me." That's the way it happened.

Just like that!

I just happened to be sitting in the right spot at the right time.

---

* Many musicians referred to the Music Corporation of America as "the star-spangled octopus" because of its size and control of the music business. The company later became MCA/Universal.

I want to talk about the Jack Benny radio and television shows.

You're getting a book right now, you know?

The price is right!

That's right. Don't know about the price. I hope I get one of these [tapes]. You know, I'm kinda having fun doing this, Chuck, because I would like to have it to send to my little library that Alice and I have in Linton, [Indiana] and let 'em put it away. Like I say, it's darn near a book!

Well, let's turn the chapter and continue. You told us how Jack Benny said, "You're my bandleader."

We were invited to dinner and we were sitting there and he wasn't even aware that I didn't have the program that I had when we were staying [at the Essex House]. Like I say, I was terribly disappointed, because I brought the band all the way from New Orleans and found out that they're using Wayne King, instead of me, on the Burns show. I don't even think that Jack was aware of that and if he was, I never found out about it, and I spent 16 or 17 of the most beautiful years of my life with him. A man who was one of a kind.

I think everyone would agree with you.

Well, what the hell – he proved that.

When he found out you were free and he wanted you for his show, how did your association with him begin, formally?

He had a manager, I don't know. Mendel Wallis was my manager for years. That's Hal Wallis' sister, who only handled three people that I know of. Gable was one and George Brent was the other one. I was pretty well-established too, so I don't think we had any problem.

Jack was exactly opposite of what he portrayed. In other words, he was very, very generous and his biggest asset on the air was being tight. But he was exactly opposite. One time he came to me and said, "Phil, you keep drinking like that and it won't be funny anymore." Understand what I mean? And he used to come to me maybe every four or five months and say go to so-and-so and get yourself some more money. I said, look, I'm getting plenty. All I'm saying is "Hello, Mary. Here comes Rochester." You know? I could phone it in, you know what I mean? He said, "Go tell 'em to give you some more money." Beautiful man. Beautiful man.

He knew the value of what you did.

He was a beautiful man. What the hell, anybody wanted to go to work with Benny.

You were actually conducting the band on his show for all the years you were with him?

That's right.

So you had more to do than just reading a line.

It wasn't hard, because after J-E-L-L-O, it was the same thing every week. The only thing I had was a special arrangement for Dennis Day to do the ballad, and then the only other things were little eight-bar phrases to break up the sequences.

There was a time when you and the band would perform a number within the show.

Very few, very seldom. No, no.

"Play, Phil."

"Play, Phil" was for Dennis, but no, very seldom. I had one that they talked about a lot was when they analyzed "That's What I Like About the South." But I think that was on television. See, I only worked with him, I think, once or twice when he went into television. I didn't go.

Was there any reason for that?

No reason, no. I was doing all right myself. I had my own show. To show you what kind of man Jack Benny was, Jack Benny let me do comedy exactly following him, so you can imagine what I had goin' – what kind of account I had goin' in. I had the highest rating in the world going in, the best rating. And I'm doin' comedy. That's how beautiful. You know I had two daughters. I mean, I'm doing a different type of comedy, Alice and myself. And then I'm running through the alley after they go to CBS. I'm running through the alley to warm my audience up and he puts me on the first 15 minutes so I can get out of there and go and start my own show. That's a pretty nice guy, isn't it?

I would say. You were both at NBC initially.

Then he went to CBS, and it's a block away, a block and a half away. I used to run through the alley!

And he'd let you get away.

First 15 minutes he'd put me on and then let me fly in there so I could warm up my audience at NBC. Never been done before. Never again. He was a beautiful man. I was seven years on my own program with Alice and for four or five of those, I was on Jack's too. Same time. Never be done again. The same thing, if you stop to look at it, you wouldn't go to a theater on Sunday unless the manager promised to stop the picture and let you hear *The Jack Benny Program.* They wouldn't go to the theater on Sunday.

You started your own show on The Fitch Bandwagon.

I played *The Fitch Bandwagon* and then from there that's when I went, I took Cass Daley's place. They were putting on all kinds of bands. So, what the hell, they ran out of people, so they called on me, you know. They used a band every week.

How did it change to comedy? To Phil Harris and Alice Faye?

Well, I'm on with Benny. I'm saying pretty funny things then, I think. And Alice Faye had been around a little bit, you know, she'd been a star for a hundred years, for 20th Century.

Who came up with the idea for a situation comedy?

Fitch. They wanted to try that 'cause they tried all the bandleaders and then they had, like, Cass Daley doing comedy, slapstick comedy, so then they wanted to go back to a family show, I guess. That's where we came in [with] Julius Abbruzio and Frankie Remley, who somebody else was playing. Elliott Lewis was Remley.

I had a chance to talk to Elliott Lewis and I mentioned this to him and I would like to tell you, too, that I think that you and Elliott, as Phil and Remley, were to radio what Laurel and Hardy were to the movies, and maybe what Gleason and Carney were to television, because you two worked so well together. You were just an absolutely perfect team.

I appreciate it, because, you know, I've always felt the same way. And I'll tell you something else about Elliott Lewis. He was a very astute guy and he said at the time, and he lived it out, that he would never work with anybody after me. And he never did. Yeah, we were like clockwork. See, he did two or three things on the Benny show when I was on that show and then when we came in, we fit together like a glove. Like he said, he had several occasions to work with other people and he said, "No, not after Phil. That's it." And then he went into producing, as you know.

Well, I don't think he could top that.

It was easy. It just used to flow, you know what I mean? Don't forget, he was a very important actor before he went with me. Like [Sheldon] Leonard, the Tout. These guys worked every week and so did Elliott. They did two or three characters, you know, they were working on all these shows. And Elliott's a good writer. He's a good producer. And Leonard did all right. Those guys all came up through the ranks. They knew what they were doin' because when you're around Benny, you're around a guy that – Benny used to have office hours in Beverly Hills and the writers had to be there at certain times and Benny sat at the table. Nobody took bits home like they do now. You do this and you two writers do this. No way. You sat right at the table and started this thing. Jack and I, we really got along. I've been in there sometimes when they had a line for me that would break the building down, and Benny would say, "No, that does not fit his character. I've been too long building it up." In other words, he protected, protected you.

You hear a lot about the shows. They had a guy on the air one time, they had him doing this, doing that, first thing you know, they burned him out. Benny said to me one time, "There's no way to kill you. I found you four stories down in the basement, I brought you out, I had you married, I had you drinking. I had you back on the booze again," he said. "There's no way to kill you!" Because people knew it wasn't true. See, that was Benny's whole stock in trade. You had to have something that he could magnify. In other words, after Kenny Baker left, we couldn't find a singer. Benny always wanted a tenor and we finally saw this picture and we went into the Bronx. McNulty is his real name and I went over, I had dinner over at his house. At the first rehearsal, Jack said, "Dennis" and Dennis said, "Yes, please." Well, that was it! See, he had to find something he could magnify and he magnified mine by being a ladies' man or a drinker. You know what I mean?

On the show, you were a very vain person: "Hello, folks, if you were down in the dumps you can smile because Harris is here."

That actually was it, because I was a very happy guy. Still am.

I can see that. Everybody would get lines to put Jack down on the show and Jack loved that. That's what he was looking for.

Oh sure. I never will forget, he came to me one time, I couldn't tell you what the line was, but after it was over, he said, "Phil, do you like this job?" And I said, "I certainly do. It's the first time I've ever had a home and the first time I don't have to go on the road." And he said, "Would you like to keep it?" and I said, "I certainly would." He said, "Well, don't ever say anything sweet to me again." That was his line!

How much rehearsal did you have to do for the Benny show?

Well, we finally got it down to where it was so oiled and so beautiful and so well-written, before we went into rehearsal we used to have a reading on Saturday afternoon. Then they'd make the cuts and we'd start on Sunday morning; at 9:00 we'd go through a rehearsal. We go back in the room, they'd cut it and fool with it, fool with it, and we'd go through it again and then we'd go to lunch. We'd come back and the first program would go on at 4:00 and the second one at 8:30. That's before tape, when we'd do it for New York and then we did it for the Coast.

It was a relatively easy stint, then.

The musicians were making about three times as much as they're making now, because now everything is put on the tape and once they got it, they got it. But these musicians, in those days, for one day alone, back there, a sideman, just a sideman, was making $90 or $100 for Sunday alone, 'cause we did a broadcast and a re-broadcast for the East and one for the Coast.

If you had a particularly good gag or a flub maybe, in the first show –

There's no way you can fix a flub. No way! They have tried every way in the world. You can't set one up.

In other words, if you screwed up on the first show you just –

It won't play, it won't play!

It comes off fake then.

That's right. I mean, that's my experience. 'Course, we never tried to set up one. Mary used to make one infrequently and it used to play or we all did, you know? As far as settin' a trap, it won't work.

Sometimes the writers would pick up on something –

Well, Benny had this gag – it was the most beautiful thing in the world – that he got hung on years ago. I never will forget it. It's "like a moose needs a hat rack." Now, he used that for years and he could never get a laugh with it, but it is very funny if you stop to figure it out. And then the other one is *The Horn Blows at Midnight.* You know, he liked to never live that picture down. But he wouldn't let people forget about it. His whole thing was he'd set up a line and then he'd go maybe five or six minutes and then he'd trip it. And then he'd go another five or six minutes and then he'd bang you with it again!

The running gag. He was a master of it. I want to ask you about Frankie Remley. You say he was with you from way back.

Well, he started when I first went to Honolulu, with the band I told you about.

He was in the band playing ukulele, left-handed. He was a nice guy, a beautiful guy, and a beautiful personality. Good looking guy, came from Fargo, North Dakota, and I just took a liking to him. So then I go over to Honolulu and I spent a year and when the [boys] all went back to school in Nashville, I didn't want to go, so I took the first boat back to the United States after the earthquake in Japan, about 1924. I didn't want to go home, so I took the President Pierce from Honolulu to San Francisco. I'd never been there before but I wanted to do something and, like I say, I was a pretty good drummer at the time. I mean, I could keep good time.

You knew Remley then?

No, no, no. I didn't even know who he is. He got off the boat. I don't know what the hell he's doin' so when I come to San Francisco I go to work with two or three bands and then I went to L. A, and now when I go to L.A. I meet him. He's thrown the uke away and gotten a banjo, which is worse, you know. Anytime you're playing banjo, you're the leader, 'cause when they turn that on you might as well leave town 'cause they got it made, you know.

Well, he took a lot of ribbing as a member of your band on the Benny show.

Oh, Benny loved him and they used to go on vacations during the summer. Benny loved to drive 'em places. He and the real Remley were very close friends. He liked Remley. He let me use his name on my program. Benny. I'll tell you something, God love him, he was one of a kind.

I want to thank you on behalf of all of your fans out there for all the great things you've done over the years. The work you did enriched our lives.

Well, that's very nice, Chuck, and it's a pleasure to meet you and to meet Ellen, your wife, and I just wish that when you play this thing you will say hello to all the fans in Chicago.

We certainly will.

Man, you got a book there, I tell you!

Phil Harris was born June 24, 1904 and was 83 at the time of our conversation. He died August 11, 1995 at the age of 91.

Alice Faye

Alice Faye was the co-star of **The Phil Harris-Alice Faye Show** *and had an earlier career as a glamorous screen star at 20th Century Fox. We met on October 28, 1987 while she was in Chicago as the "ambassador of good health" for Pfizer Pharmaceuticals. I asked about her latest role.*

Well, I'm in my fourth year and I travel all over the country visiting young elders – I don't call them senior citizens. And I talk about a better way of life as we age. I tell 'em about the Pfizer Five: Stay active and involved. Eat a sensible diet. No smoking. Exercising, at least two or three times a week – walking, stretching, swimming, for example. And seeing your doctor whenever necessary. And I've added a sixth: For God's sake, have a sense of humor! It works for me.

I can see it all works for you! I'd like to talk to you about your career. Before you got into show business, you were the daughter of a policeman, right?

That's right. I lived in New York City, on the West Side in what they called Hell's Kitchen. There wasn't anything hellish about it. It was a pretty nice place. I had a wonderful life. I had my very own fire escape that I could sit on out there and dream. I wanted to be a movie star. I hoped I would be. I graduated grammar school and got a job with Chester Hale at the Capitol Theatre. And that's where I really started, in the chorus as a hoofer! And I worked for NTG [producer-radio pioneer Nils T. Granlund], who had a place called the Hollywood Restaurant, and then I went into *George White's Scandals* and chorus. Ethel Merman was the star. Rudy Vallee was in it, and Ray Bolger.

You were singing?

No, just dancing in the chorus. Rudy decided he wanted a girl singer in his band, almost unheard of at the time, outside of Mildred Bailey. She sang with Whiteman, Paul Whiteman. Rudy decided he would have a girl singer, so he decided to have a little contest. A number of the girls were interested, so he made a record of our voices. I sang "Mimi" and, fortunately, he chose me.

Had you done any singing before this?

Oh, no, no, no, no, no. Nothing! He liked the quality of my voice and he took me with his band and then when the show closed – he was also doing the *Fleischmann Hour* – and then he went to California to do a film of *George White's Scandals* and I went along with the band. When we got to California there was some mix-up about the leading lady, an actress from Germany, that didn't work out. Someone from the studio had seen me on the *Fleischmann Hour* so they decided to test me, and they did, and I got the part and that was the beginning of my picture career.

Which was a very long and very wonderful career.

It was wonderful.

Once you started with the movies, then you left the band?

Oh, yes.

You had done quite a few of those Fleischmann Hour *programs.*

Yes, I did.

It was a major radio show. Rudy was known at the time for introducing new talent to the public.

Yes, he was wonderful. I liked Rudy so much. He was a good boss and taught you a lot of good things, like being on time. If you weren't on time, he docked you, and if you forgot lyrics, he docked you. He kept you pretty much on your toes.

He went on with his career and you were signed by Fox after the Scandals. *How did they sign you up?*

They started you at $750 a week, then worked you up to $1,250, then $1,750, then $2,000. That's the way they paid you then.

Fox really owned you, as far as your career was concerned. The legendary studio system. You'd have classes and all that.

No, I didn't do that. As a matter of fact, that's when I lied about my age. My mother said, "Someday you're going to be sorry" and I said, "Mom, when I'm 60, who's going to care?" But now I pick up the paper and they've got me three years older than I am. So now, I say, "Okay, Mom, you were right." But Ann Miller did it, everybody did it. We all lied about our ages and we didn't want to go to school on the lot.

Then you had a succession of films in which you starred.

I did a lot of B pictures with Lew Ayres. When I went to the big studio I worked with John Payne, Don Ameche and Jack Haley. Tyrone Power.

Tyrone Power and Don Ameche were your co-stars in a movie about Chicago, In Old Chicago.

Oh, I loved it! One of my favorites.

And then you brought new life into the music of Irving Berlin in Alexander's Ragtime Band *with co-stars Tyrone Power and Don Ameche.*

Loved that!

Typically, how long did it take to make one of these movies? Those were pretty big-budget films.

I think three months, three-and-a-half months, something like that.

It was always on the lot, never on location?

No, we never went off the lot, because we had our own back lot that was terrific –

Where Century City is now?

– that's where they had the Chicago Fire.

Was it hard to make those films?

Oh, no. I didn't think so. I loved it.

Had to get up pretty early for make-up?

That's your job. That was a wonderful job. Oh, I loved it. It was what I wanted and I was doing what I loved. And then, of course, you live with those people. I used to kid around and call Fox "Penitentiary Fox"! You live there. You get up at 5:30 or 6:00 in the morning and go right to the studio. Then you're made up and have breakfast on the set and shoot at 8:30. You're there day in and day out. The same wardrobe woman, the same make-up man and cameraman, the lights. You knew everybody. It was a family. It was, then, it was home and if you were to take me out of there I was lost. Until I walked out, walked out on my own. And that was something else.

A few years later.

But it was my home and those people were my family.

I read that Darryl Zanuck was not in favor of your working on the radio while you were under contract to Fox.

No, he didn't care much about radio. He wouldn't let us record – make records.

He really ran the studio with an iron first. Was he as tough to the moviemakers as Rudy Vallee was to the people in his band?

Well, I think you learned something from Rudy. You didn't learn much from Zanuck. He was bossy and he was a smart man, but we never agreed. I didn't get along with him that much.

Were you a rascal on the lot?

Oh, no. I did what I was told. When I got married, I thought after doing *Chicago* and *Alexander's Ragtime Band* I would do something more mature. He wanted me to do *Dolly Sisters* and I said, "No, I don't want to do that. I want to do something like *Laura*. I want to do something great." And he just didn't hold still for it. He did give me a wonderful script, *Fallen Angel,* probably one of the best things I ever did in my life, but when I saw it I couldn't find myself. I was on the cutting room floor. They were building up Linda Darnell, a beautiful lady and very fine actress, but I didn't see anything happening for me. I was kaput. They would just keep doing tired musicals, because the more musicals, the more money for the studios and they could lose money on all those dramas. So I just decided to get out. I couldn't get along with him. I walked out. It was my life. I decided to go home and raise my family and learn how to market and learn how to drive a car and learn how to have a dinner party, do the things I hadn't done. I was knocking my brains out doing high kicks with Betty Grable and where was I going? I just didn't want it.

You married Phil in 1941.

We're married 45 years now.

How did you meet?

We met through Jack Oakie.

Your co-star in The Great American Broadcast.

Oh, you'd like Phil a lot. We had had our differences before [we married]. I had a dog. We each had a Doberman pinscher. When I'd go to work, my dog would go down to a market in Encino. [The dogs] met and had a big fight, and so Phil called me and told me to keep my dog at home. I told him a few things and we didn't get along for a long time. And then we finally started dating and that was it.

About the time you left Fox and decided to become more domestic, up pops The Fitch Bandwagon *on radio. How did that come about? How did you and Phil get the job? He'd been with Jack Benny.*

He was still with Jack Benny when we were doing our show. It was offered to him. He asked me if I'd like to do it. I didn't particularly like to work with my husband. I don't believe in wives and husbands working together, but that's just my opinion. I worked with him, but we didn't hit it off too well while we were working together. He's a little rough.

During the whole radio period, from 1946 to 1954?

I made it. I wasn't too happy, but I enjoyed it.

You were excellent on that program and brought a lot of spark and life to the show.

It's like anything you do. You get better and better. A husband tends to pick on you where somebody else won't pick on you. Actually, that part I didn't care for.

In the beginning, when that show first came on, it was live and I suspect you had to do one or two broadcasts every week, a second show for the rest of the country.

Yeah, that's right, we did. I'd forgotten. We had it going then. When Rexall came in, we were really rolling then. We had tremendous writers, too.

Ray Singer and Dick Chevillat. You came in a perfect time for radio and by the time you left, so much TV had come in.

Phil wouldn't do it. I'm sorry, I think that's one thing I really am sorry for, that we didn't go into television. He didn't want to do it. He couldn't see another family show on TV.

It's too bad, because The Phil Harris-Alice Faye Show *was not another family show. It was a very special show.*

It was really funny!

Your personalities could have easily translated to television.

He couldn't see it and you couldn't tell him anything.

Television is *hard work. He did have a hard time, didn't he, for a while, doing the Benny show and your show?*

But Benny was great to him. He helped him getting through rehearsals and all that.

How much time did you have to devote to your radio show, generally speaking?

We had a rehearsal on Friday, and then we rehearsed Sunday morning, and then we did the show Sunday afternoon.

Two days.

Yes.

You never saw the script before Friday?

Never.

The characters were so well-defined. One of the highlights was your song, and Phil's too.

We had Walter Scharf. Wonderful, wonderful arranger, Walter.

You had Walter Tetley as the grocery boy.

A wise-cracking kid, Julius Abbruzio. He had a great delivery.

He was a master of timing. He didn't lose an inch with Phil or Frankie, Elliott Lewis. He was a small person, wasn't he?

He always reminded me of Johnny, who did the call for Philip Morris. Phil tried to go first class and tried to get the best you could get.

After the radio show went off the air you made another movie, back at Fox, a few years later; State Fair, *a remake.*

Yes. It was awful. I say the only good thing that came out of it was Ann-Margret. It just wasn't good.

In the early Seventies you teamed up with one of your Fox co-stars, John Payne.

Good News. Oh, I loved that.

I think you played Chicago.

We had a long run here. I loved it! It was so wonderful to be here.

How many times over the years have you played in Chicago?

Oh, with Rudy, *Scandals*, *Good News*, and Chicago Theatre personal appearances, many, many, many times.

Going back to 1937 for a minute, you sang with Hal Kemp and the orchestra, broadcasts from Hollywood. Did you sing with any other bands?

Just Rudy and Kemp.

You've had a fantastic career. I think you've enjoyed it.

I have. I love going from one thing to another and then this [Pfizer] door opened up. It was something else. I couldn't believe it. I was ready, because I have been taking care of myself, exercising and swimming. I went to a spa when I was 40, at Elizabeth Arden. I had a week there and I thought, where have I been, what have I been missing and I got into this exercising and I never left. This is for me. Wake up and exercise!

On behalf of all your fans I thank you for doing all the things you did to entertain us over the years.

I'm so happy everyone remembers. Thank you for remembering. I can't believe it sometimes. It gives me a big kick.

Alice Faye was born May 5, 1915 and was 72 at the time of our conversation. She died May 9, 1998 at the age of 83.

Elliott Lewis

Elliott Lewis co-starred on **The Phil Harris-Alice Faye Show** *as Frankie Remley and did a great amount of radio work before the microphone and behind the scenes. He was working on some special writing projects when we met at his office on the Paramount Pictures lot in Hollywood, California, on August 27, 1975. I told him that I felt that Remley and Harris were to radio what Laurel and Hardy were to movies and Kramden and Norton were to television.*

 Well, thank you. I remember those days with the utmost fondness. I don't know when in my life I have so enjoyed a job. It was just an absolutely marvelous job. When I realize that we did that for nine years, Phil and Alice and I, and Walter Tetley. It was just fun, wonderfully refreshing, the two characters and the way it played and the relationships.

The rapport that you guys had was marvelous.

Well, you know, Jack Benny was my teacher, really. I was here in Los Angeles when I was still going to school. I was going to junior college, and right across the street is the KHJ building. When I was 18 I worked over in that building, which was then NBC. It had just been built and I worked in that building for Jack Benny, and then on and off for him for all those years.

You mean on the air?

On the air, as an actor, never playing Remley, always another character, because Remley never appeared until he appeared on the Harris show. But Jack was always fond of Phil and me and of what we were doing and was most helpful and kind of guided us and gave us suggestions. I remember sitting down with him one day and I said, "Please explain something to me. I know that when Phil and I work that it's funny and the jokes are funny, but I don't understand why the laughs are so big. What are we doing?" He said, "You've found a wonderful thing in the relationship that you two have. The two of you say and do what everybody in the audience would like to say and do in a similar situation if they had the nerve. But nobody has the kind of nerve you two guys have, and that's what people are laughing at. They're just delighted." It always surprised me, you know. We'd say something like, "You stick Tetley [Julius] in the oven" and he says, "Let me out! Let me out!" and you just wait and say, "What do you think?" And the whole audience is screaming! It is, if you think about it, ridiculous. You don't leave somebody in an oven, but that we would even consider it and think about it and stand there and say, "Well, I don't know" and to talk about it, and this poor soul is in the oven, screaming and yelling and banging on the oven door!

There was one show where Phil and Remley were marching down the street behind an elephant, on Hollywood Boulevard. They wouldn't think about doing that on television.

No! We did one, I remember, that Dick Chevillat and Ray Singer wrote, where they buy a racehorse and the description of the racehorse was so hilarious. Of course, you couldn't do it on television. You can't get a horse as running slowly or more quickly because his stomach is dragging on the ground! But, you know, these men would buy this and then consider it. They're talking about it, saying, "Does it look right to you?" No! He thinks there's something wrong – a horse shouldn't look like that. A marvelous, marvelous relationship, very well written by Ray Singer and Dick Chevillat.

They wrote the whole series?

They didn't write the first 26 weeks or so.

It started on The Fitch Bandwagon, *didn't it?*

Right. And I wasn't on it at first; I was doing something else. And Remley, the real Frank Remley, was a left-handed guitar player who worked with Phil's band and on the Benny show. He was a dear, dear, marvelous man. Well, they decided when Phil and Alice had their own show to use Phil's best friend, Frankie. So they wrote it in and they said to Remley, "Here you go." And he got up and he couldn't read it. He was a guitar player, not an actor. So, I had worked with all of them for a long time on the Benny show and we all knew each other and were close friends. I was doing a show down the hall and Phil came in – they did the first show without me, they cut the Remley thing – and he said, "We're going to write Remley in on the second show. The script is ready and we have to establish the relationship. Could you come in and do it? It'll take you a couple of hours and that will be the end of it." And I came in and did it and we got the kind of laughs that I've been describing to you – which neither of us understood – and we did it every week for nine years.

That's how it happened. I think Bill Moser and Bob Connolly wrote the first 26 shows. Then Ray and Dick wrote it until, possibly, the last year, when they were off on something else. I have a memory of Marvin Fisher and Jack Douglas working on the show, 'cause I remember Jack wrote some wild, wild material. But Singer and Chevillat were responsible for the show.

The show started under the sponsorship of Fitch Shampoo and then Rexall came in.

Right, and then RCA had it in the last couple of years. We were working for the dog, His Master's Voice!

On the Benny show, whenever they referred to Frankie Remley, he was, of course, a lush, a drunkard. Now, was he really –

– Oh, no! No. He was a very sweet, nice, quiet man, a really dear man. He passed away some time ago – 15 years or more – but he was a dear man, a very nice man.

It's interesting how they made a fictional character out of a real person.

Yes, well, that's the secret of Jack Benny, who was the comedy genius of all time and who taught us all. That was his theory, that you made jokes out of nothing. They would make a joke out of something that started at the beginning of the half-hour show and by the end of the show you're laughing hysterically! Nothing funny, really. There wasn't a joke, just the gas man, and the car, and all of the things, the train to Cucamonga.

I remember a routine we did on the Benny show where every year Jack and the group go to New York and therefore is the scene in the railway station. And Frank Nelson is saying, "Yeeeess." He's selling tickets and Jack's in line and Mel Blanc is on the speaker going "...and Cu-camonga" and, you know, every year we did this. And I was always the man in line in front of Jack. And Jack is trying to get a ticket to New York. The first routine that we did, the reason that we then continued it, was that we took the lyric of "Glocca Morra" and all I did was read the lyric. Jack was very nervous about it and he said, "I don't know. You got to be crazy! Is that going to be funny?" and I said, "I don't know. It just seems to me that it's funny if I just ask Frank Nelson these questions: "How are things in Glocca Morra?" And he said, "Fine." And I say, "Is that little brook still rippling there?" And he said, "Oh, yes." Well, you could imagine! We're doing this, Frank and I talking, and Jack Benny is standing behind me, just staring at the audience with that look, you know, he did with the elbow! Well, what *is* funny about it? I don't know, but it just was funny. It was funny stuff.

Indeed!

Jack would create these characters and he would create them in the image of Phil and, therefore, in the image of Remley. He created Phil and Remley images and characters for them so strong that Phil and I and Alice and their real little girls were in a Santa Claus Lane Parade on Thanksgiving down Hollywood Boulevard one year. It was freezing cold and, without thinking, we each took a mug of coffee, hot coffee. The girls were all bundled up warm, and one of the kids sat on my lap and the other kid was on Phil's lap. And we stopped at one place and I reached to get the coffee. I was really shivering, I was so cold, and I picked it up and Phil, without seeing what I was doing, did the same thing. We had stopped and there were crowds on either side on the street and they started to laugh. They thought we were drinking booze! They thought we were stoned! And you don't know what to do 'cause you've got a little kid on your lap and the audience is laughing 'cause they think you're drinking whiskey, which we weren't. Hot coffee! But that's how firmly the Benny show created those characters, established those characters.

I remember doing one show Jack created for those characters. They were musicians who hadn't the faintest idea what they were doing. They knew no more about the music business – had no right to be musicians. This was so firmly established that on Phil's show, years later, we did a scene, that I still recall, of a music rehearsal that Phil is conducting. Remley is playing guitar and Phil stops and says to Remley, "Wait a minute. Wait a minute. That doesn't sound right. What have you got there?" And Remley says, "I've got a black dot and then another black dot" and the audience started to laugh. You'd figure they'd have to be musicians to know. They didn't, but they just knew that *we* hadn't had the vaguest idea what we were talking about. Phil says, "I think there's supposed to be three black dots." I said, "No, there's one here that's a white dot." And he said, "Where is it?" And I said, "No, that's a fly." All those music jokes! But people were laughing because the characters had been established by Jack.

I remember the biggest laugh we ever got. To show how little I know about what I'm doing, I had no idea we'd get this kind of laugh and it made me kind of nervous. The story, very simply, was that Alice says to Phil, "Remley is not your friend. He doesn't really care about you. He's a terrible, vile person who is looking to take advantage of you and you've got to be very careful." And Phil keeps saying, "No, no, no. That's not true." They keep arguing until finally Phil says, "All right, I'll tell you what. When Remley comes to the door this morning, you tell him I just died of a heart attack. And then you'll see what a friend I've got." Well, I thought, "My goodness, are we really going to do that? But, we play the scene in front of the audience. Doorbell. Alice goes to the door. She's crying and Remley says, "What's the matter? What is it, Alice?" And she says, "Phil just died of a heart attack." There was a long pause and then I said, "Alice, will you marry me?" Well, I tell you we could not stop the people from laughing! The studio was shaking! This explosion of laughter! That he had the gall... didn't even wait... didn't say, "Gee, I'm sorry." Nothing! Couldn't wait to get his hands on that money! And I thought, "No, we really can't do that." Ray and Dick said, "It's funny, do it. Just do it." Phil said, "Don't worry about it." Well, they were right.

Did you have to do a lot of rehearsing for the Harris show?

No. As a matter of fact, by the time we were in our seventh, eighth and ninth year, we were on tape; the show was no longer live. And we would tape the show on Friday for Sunday broadcast. We would meet at around noon or 11:00 in the morning on Friday and read the script around the table and make some cuts and changes, go get our lunch and come back and read it again on mike to balance it, make additional cuts and changes. I was producing and directing over at CBS, so Phil would go and do his business and Alice would do whatever she had to do. I'd go over and work on scripts for *Suspense* or *On Stage* or *Broadway's My Beat* or one of the shows I was doing at CBS, and then come back, dressed to do a show in front of an audience, at 5:30. The audience would come in at 5:30 or 6 and we'd do a little warm-up and do the show from 6:30 to 7. And Phil and Alice got on the train and went back to Palm Springs and I went home and that was it. So we would devote most of a Friday to it. But that was about all.

Of course, by that time the characters had been so finely refined and keenly developed.

That's right. And you're able to do in radio, especially in radio, comedy in radio, the kind of humor that you cannot do anywhere else. And once it is set up, the characters are set up and a situation is set up, and you have the kind of writing that we were getting from Ray Singer and Dick Chevillat, there are no problems. Everybody knows what they are doing or they wouldn't be there. And if it wasn't a good show and the audience didn't like it, it wouldn't be on the air. You know, you find out very quickly whether it's working or not. And as always in almost anything, but especially in show business, if it's going easily it's usually on the right track. It's not hard to have a hit; it's hard to have a failure, because it's rough. You know, you keep trying to fix something that you should just throw away. When it's going well, when all of the elements are together, wow! It's no problem, it just runs.

You mentioned producing and directing Suspense*. Did you do some of the writing, too?*

Yes. I did writing and editing and produced and directed the radio *Suspense* for about five years, I guess. And then, while I was married to Cathy Lewis, we did *On Stage* for a couple of years, and I wrote the openings and the closings and did the editing on it. And E. Jack Neuman, with whom I'm working here at Paramount, contributed I would guess half of the scripts during the two years we worked on that show. Also wrote goodness knows how many of the *Suspense* shows.

As a matter of fact, there was a thing we would do together that was kind of fun, because it was kind of a challenge in the mystery sense. I recall, driving to work one day, I had seen a scene in my mind which was a marvelous first-act curtain. So I said to Jack, "Somebody's chasing a man and he's in a fun house at an amusement park and he knows he can't get out the front door so he tries to get out, to find another exit. And at the back of this building there's an enormous animated figure, a great big, jolly kind of animated stuffed thing, and its arms are at its side and it goes 'Ho-Ho-Ho-Ho' and as it's doing 'Ho-Ho-Ho-Ho' the arms raise over its head and then the arms go down and the man describes this in the narrative." And I said because what he does is, he times it and the guys are chasing him and so he waits and the figure goes, "Ho-Ho-Ho-Ho" and the arms are up and he's going to make a dash. And so he waits and he times it and it goes "Ho-Ho-Ho-Ho" and he starts to dash and as he starts, the arms go BANG and cut him off. There's a door behind him when the arms raise and as he heads for the door and the arms come down and from inside the figure a voice says, "You didn't really think I was gonna let you get out, did you?" So I said to Jack, "I don't know who he is or how he got there or how it ends." Jack says, "Great idea, you really scared me." It was called "Giant of Thermopylae." It was marvelous suspense.

And it was on Suspense.

Yes. That was what we did on *Suspense*. We did a lot of them that way.

This was in the late Forties and early Fifties.

Yes. Before World War II I had been on *Suspense*, working with Bill Spier as an actor and a rewrite man and also writing originals. Then I was in the service, working for Army radio, Armed Forces Radio. I was in charge of what they called "Commercial Denaturing," which was a division with Howie Duff. We supplied 476 radio stations, Howie and I and three other guys, with 120 programs a week, which we took off the air, edited, took the commercials out, took out anything that dated the show. By editing, I mean anything that would be considered information that you didn't want broadcast worldwide. These were then placed on acetate discs and sent to the short wave stations. Then masters were made, printed and shipped all over the world, to these 476 stations. So I was busy doing that.

Then, when the war was over, I went back to *Suspense*. Bill Spier, who was doing *Sam Spade* and *Suspense,* wanted to do a picture in Europe with his wife, at that time June Havoc, and with James and Pamela Mason. Bill would produce and direct the film, so he wanted to get out of his deal and he suggested to CBS that I had done so much work on it, and since I was producing and directing another radio show for them at the time, called *Broadway's My Beat*, that I should produce and direct *Suspense*. They were agreeable and so that's when I picked up on *Suspense*. I think I did some of the *Sam Spades* for him, too.

On the show The Casebook of Gregory Hood, *you were Gregory Hood.*

Yes, Anthony Boucher's character.

Before you took over the role of Gregory Hood, it was played by Gale Gordon.

Gale and I had known each other for years and, in the true manner of show business, I was called one day to the Young and Rubicam Advertising Agency and they said, "We have a property called *Gregory Hood*. Have you ever heard it?" And I said, "Well, it's on the air, isn't it?" And they said, "Yes, but it's not working out the way we want and we would like you to be the star." And I said, "What happened to Gale?" And they said, "Well, we've told him and he agrees and you know, no hard feelings or anything. We're trying it, so come to rehearsal Monday and you're Gregory Hood." I said, "Fine." I walked into the studio and there sat Gale. Nobody had said a word to him. So I said, "Gale, why don't we go outside and have a cup of coffee and have a little talk," 'cause we were old friends. It was supposed to have been arranged, but I was the one who said to Gale, "I'm doing Gregory Hood now. I guess you're not." It didn't matter, of course.

Well, he had to scratch for work through the rest of his career, didn't he!

Yes! Well, he really was desperately looking here and there trying to find something to do. And then, when I was producing *The Lucy Show* on television, there we were, working together again. When we started the television series, *The Lucy Show*, that I produced, Lucy came back from New York and she and Desi had been divorced. We were sitting around with the writers and we said, "Gee, we need somebody for the Mr. Mooney character. Let's get Gale."

You followed him again on another series, Junior Miss. *You played Judy Graves' father.*

I think he may have followed me, because I remember doing that one with Shirley Temple. I played her father. And I played her father the week I was drafted! I was, like, 22! I was playing Shirley Temple's father and I did the *Junior Miss* show on a Thursday or something, waved bye-bye and Friday went into the Army. I think Gale followed me on that show, and then I think Shirley dropped out and they did another version of it later on.

How busy were you at your busiest?

I think I counted in one week I did 20 shows, in one capacity or another. Finally, in the late or middle Fifties, I guess, I was involved in the production, directing, acting, whatever on five weekly series. My desk at CBS looked like a joke! I was doing the *Harris* show as an actor, I was producing and directing *Suspense,* I was producing, directing, editing, writing openings and closings, and co-starring in *On Stage.* I was producing and directing *Broadway's My Beat* and I was producing, directing and writing the openings and closings and editing

Crime Classics. At one point CBS had three of those shows on back-to-back on Wednesday night. And, by taping parts of this one and sections of that one, because you couldn't record the music – music had to be live and put in when you went on the air – and having adjoining studios – Studios 1 and 2 at the old CBS – I was able to do it. I had a show on the air from 5:30 to 6, and a show on the air from 6 to 6:30, and a show on the air from 6:30 to 7.

It was Elliott Lewis night on CBS!

Yeah, it was ridiculous! There was no reason for that, it was just silly. But that's the way scheduling happened.

I'd like to back up to your Army career for a moment or so. You were working on editing and dubbing all those radio shows. Did you start that? Were you the first one to get involved with that?

I think Howie and I were, yes. Duff, when I say Howie. We were both in the service at different places and were called here by Col. Tom Lewis, who we had known when Tom was head of Young and Rubicam. And he needed people who knew radio and he had this thing starting and he needed people to take over the job that had been handled by Don Sharp, who had been an agent and a producer. At that point I believe Don was working for the Office of War Information and they were trying this but nobody had done anything with it yet. So, Duff and I were there and were called in and they said, "Now, here's what we want to do..."

As a matter of fact, some of the things we developed... well, I won't be bashful, some of the things we developed worked so well that I was given the Legion of Merit for developing new techniques in recording and broadcasting, only because there was no other way to do it. We had three civilian crews working seven days a week, 24 hours a day to reassemble these shows by the techniques that we developed: cut this, pick up here, and so forth. And this is before they had tape. We were doing this editing off of acetate. We got so that we could look at the turntable playing at 33 1/3 speed and drop the head on a word or on a spot. You look at the grooves and the right line and you'd know exactly where you are and what you're doing!

You picked up the shows as they were being broadcast?

Off the line at Radio Recorders. They were taken off the broadcast line. Howard and I would pick them up in an Army vehicle which was given to us occasionally. The rest of the time we were to use our own car and our own gasoline and were never reimbursed for it. And we had to be very careful, because we had a stack. These were not aluminum-based acetates, they were glass-based. And we had one guy cut in front of us on the way to the studio one night and we lost two hours of programming, because the records just slid and that was it! Nothing you could do about it, they were gone. They were glass-based acetates that we took off the air. We picked them up and what we tried to do with the immediate show is that we would make worksheets on a typewriter as the show was on the air, so when we picked it up and delivered that acetate to [C. P.] MacGregor's [studios] or to Universal or to the other part of the division of Radio Recorders, they had the worksheet and the crew knew exactly what they were going to do with it. And by the following morning that show would be ready to be broadcast short wave. We were watching a clock, timing, so that when a commercial began, this would be taken out, or a new opening would be put in, what fill material was to make up for what we deleted.

You always had to pad it back to 30 minutes again, right?

Right. Twenty-nine thirty. And it got to be quite a thing. As I think about it now, I don't know how in heaven's name we did it. Because as we were typing, we were listening to a show and watching a clock!

What you fellas did there, and you really didn't realize you were doing it, but you were really preserving the sounds of radio from the 1940s, because the networks never wanted to keep it. They just did it live and they didn't copy it.

Right. What we did, if we didn't have enough material coming off the line to make 52 weeks of something, we invented. So, we invented the *Mystery Theatre*. Now, the *Mystery Theatre* had to have a host, because sometimes it would be *Mr. and Mrs. North* or sometimes it would be *Inner Sanctum* or whatever was on the air that was a mystery show that we could use. So we had our own opening and our own closing. Now, whichever of us went down with the record, with the transcription, to make the show, also recorded an opening and a closing for that show. So we had to invent characters, because it was not the same person. There was Corporal X and there was Sergeant Y, and we did all these things. Whoever went down. It was Howard, or Jerry Hausner or it was me or it was Jimmy Lyons, who was part of our group and now runs the Monterey Jazz Festival.

But we all fell into patterns. Alan Hewitt loved opera and symphony, so he would edit opera and symphony. Jimmy Lyons loved jazz and knew all those people, so he did that kind of music. Howie and I did the dramatic things and the comedy things. Hausner did all of those and also 15- and 30-minute original shows for everybody. But we were kind of a lost group. We were in a side corner, because the big shows the Armed Forces Radio Service was doing were *Command Performance* and things like that. They did one *Command Performance* show a week while we were doing 120 shows and nobody even knew we were there. We were just off in the back somewhere.

Did you ever meet G.I. Jill, who did a little 15-minute show?

Oh, sure, Marty Wilkerson, Mort Warner's wife. Mort Warner is, was, the head man at NBC television for I don't know how long. And G.I. Jill was Marty, his wife. And Mort, who at that time was a G.I. with the rest of us, Corporal Warner, was kind of producing and directing his wife's little show.

I've heard lots of those G.I. Jive shows with G.I. Jill. What did she look like?

Marty was a very lovely looking young woman. She's a very attractive older woman now. They have grown children. Just a marvelous looking woman, warm, very attractive. To me, she always looked like what she sounded like.

She had to be every girl next door for every G.I. around the world.

But Marty primarily was a writer when she wasn't doing that. She wrote, has written many, many television things. She wrote *Robert Montgomery [Presents]*, wrote original material for it.

Let's return to civilian life. You were the lead in another version of The First Nighter Program, *called* Knickerbocker Playhouse.

Yes. They called me to go to Chicago in '39. I knew nothing about this program. I was working as an actor on a lot of shows here and one of the shows I was working on was called *Silver Theatre*, which was a Sunday afternoon drama. I was under contract to them. The AFRA contract stated that you could pay people, if you signed them to a 13-week deal, scale less 10 per cent. So I was under contract to *Silver Theatre* and *Big Town*. Now, on *Silver Theatre*, some weeks I had four lines and some weeks I was the leading man opposite whoever the leading woman was. One time, they had heard me as a leading man opposite Ginger Rogers or somebody, and they were out here. I knew nothing about this and my agent called me and said, "There are some people here from Chicago and they would like you to audition for them. There's some kind of radio show that they're going to be doing from Chicago and they're over across the hall and would you go over and read something for them?"

Now, I'm in the middle of a *Silver Theatre* rehearsal playing the lead opposite Rosalind Russell, a darling, lovely, gifted, talented lady. So I came in and must have looked puzzled and she said, "What's the matter?" And I told her and she said, "Well, we'll stop rehearsing for a little bit and go over and do it. It could be a big job for you." I said, "I don't know what to read." She said, "Let's read what we're doing." I said, "We?" She said, "Sure, don't tell them who I am. We'll go over there and read. I'll read with you."

We went across the street to this other studio and went in and I still don't think they knew who she was. She said, "Tell then I'm Miss Brown." So I said, "This is Miss Brown, she's going to read with me." And they said, "Fine, how are ya?" And we read the scene which we had been rehearsing for two days. They said, "Thank you very much" and I said "Thank you" and Roz and I went back and did our work. The following day I got a call from my agent and he said, "They want you. The show is called *Knickerbocker Playhouse* and it's going to come from Chicago and they want you to be the star. Do you want to go to Chicago this summer? It's a firm 13 [weeks]." I said, "Well, I've never been to Chicago. That sounds like it'd be a lot of fun. I'll drive to Chicago."

And I did. They said to bring a tuxedo, 'cause they get all dressed up. I checked into the Medinah Club, which was across the street from the Wrigley Building where they do the show. Then I got an apartment on Wabash. And the woman to whom I have been married for 17 years, Mary Jane Croft, was coming through town on her way to New York. She had been working in Cincinnati and that's when we met one another. Then she married somebody else and I married somebody else and she divorced and I was divorced and we've been married for 17 years. We met in Chicago in 1939 at 720 N. Wabash.

You've had an interesting career.

When you talked about Phil Harris – I saw Phil maybe a couple of years ago. He called, he was coming to town and wanted to know if I wanted to have breakfast with him, 'cause he's an early riser. He was in the band business so long, the two things he hates are staying up late and wearing a tuxedo. And his idea of heaven is if you go to bed early and you get up at 5:30 and you wander around and see a sunrise fresh, not just as you're ready to go to sleep. So we met and had breakfast and chatted and it's like we hadn't seen each other in five or six years just picking up where we left off.

I wish you guys could pick up where you left off. It would be great to hear Frankie and Phil again. They were great shows.

Yes, and a great time!

Elliott Lewis was born November 28, 1917 and was 57 at the time of our conversation. He died May 20, 1990 at the age of 72.

Howard Duff

Howard Duff starred on radio in **The Adventures of Sam Spade** *from 1946 to 1949. We met on August 25, 1975 at his beach house on Sea Level Drive, just north of the Malibu Colony, along the Pacific Ocean in Southern California. I asked him where his career as an actor began.*

Well, I started in drama school. We had a very fine playhouse in Seattle called the Seattle Repertory Playhouse. I worked in the daytime on a rather menial job at a department store and at night I was either rehearsing or playing a show. We did all kinds of things: Ibsen, Chekhov, Shakespeare, Noel Coward, Odets. We wanted to do good things. I don't say we always did them. Anyway, that's where I started.

Then I finally got into radio as a radio announcer in Seattle. I did news, I did everything. I finally gravitated down to San Francisco, where I picked up a couple of jobs down there as a newscaster and kind of an extra announcer at one of the stations. Then I latched on to a kids' serial called *The Phantom Pilot*, of all things – and this before World War II!

I did this kids' show for about two years and then I did free-lance work until World War II came along. Then I went into the Army for about five years. I started out in the Infantry, but eventually I got into the Armed Forces Radio Service.

Your voice crops up on literally hundreds of Armed Forces Radio rebroadcasts.

I did a lot of the announcing on some of them. Actually, Elliott Lewis and I started this department. We took all the best commercial shows off the air and then we had to take all the commercials out and certain editing references and then reassemble them.

You started this operation?

Elliott and I did. He was head of the department, actually.

How did that come about? Whose idea was it to rebroadcast?

A civilian was doing it before. A fellow named Don Sharp started it and then we took it over – Elliott and I – and then the department became enlarged. Then I went over to Saipan as a correspondent for Armed Forces Radio. I was there when the war ended and eventually got out of the service and into *Sam Spade.*

Just that easy?

It wasn't *that* easy, no!

How did you get into Sam Spade?

I was a free-lance actor and I'd worked with Bill Spier, who has done *Suspense,* as you probably remember, and they were auditioning for this new show. They wanted, they thought, kind of a Bogart type and I guess I was the one that they thought sounded more like they wanted.

Did you feel that you were a Bogart type?

No, I didn't. Eventually, I did, but I wanted to do my own set and I got into it. It was a very pleasant four or five years.

Did you get all the Wildroot Cream Oil you could –

– yeah, all that I could put on my head!

It seems as though there was a heck of a lot of ad-libbing.

Yes, yeah! I did a little. We had a group of people that worked together often and we got kind of a stock company. Lurene Tuttle, who played Effie, of course, and she doubled as the old landlady and a lot of other characters. She's marvelous! And we had all the top people in the business: Johnny McIntire, Jeanette Nolan, Ted Reid, to name a few.

Did this come out of Hollywood?

Yes. *Spade* was set in San Francisco. Everybody used to think we were in San Francisco, but actually it was here.

You were introduced on the screen in the film Brute Force *as "radio's Sam Spade." It said it right up on the credits.*

That sort of annoyed me at the time, because I just didn't feel that should be. I thought they should just let me come on as Howard Duff and let it go at that. But, as I look back on it, why knock it? What the heck. If it could bring a few more people into the box office, great!

That was a good motion picture debut. Was that the first time you appeared on the screen?

Well, I did a training film for the Army but you can't count that. I played a soldier for Frank Capra's unit, which was right next to us in the Armed Forces Radio Service on the old Fox lot.

When you were with Armed Forces Radio, did you have anything to do with the big variety shows that were produced primarily for military audiences?

No, that was another department. Most of those were done by fellows who had been producing the big variety shows at the time and high-priced writers: Jack Benny's writers, Bill Morrow and, oh, we had all the greatest talent to draw from in the whole world!

You know, by doing what you were doing, editing those shows and putting them on disc for play around the world, you actually contributed to saving thousands and thousands of radio shows.

I did?

Absolutely, because, you see, the networks never preserved the radio shows. They were all done live. Nobody bothered to record them.

All that acetate was destroyed.

Right. They went out on the air and you copied them, edited out the commercials and put them on discs and then the discs were shipped all over the world. Long after the war, long after radio had really kind of moved out of the picture, as it was, as we knew it in the Thirties and Forties, some of those discs were found by GIs who grew up listening to those shows. They made tapes of them and sent them back home. And if it hadn't been for you – well, that's probably the best thing that ever came out of World War II, the fact that those old radio shows were saved.

I wasn't really aware of that. I was wondering where [they came from]. You know, somebody said, "Gee, I heard one of your old shows on the air!" And I said, "Well, I don't know where anybody would get hold of a recording," because I asked CBS at one time if they had any, but no, they destroyed them all. I don't even have one lousy acetate [disc] from all those five years. Isn't it strange that after all those shows I made, I haven't one acetate to show for it.

I'll send you a tape if you like.

Thank you. I'd appreciate it.

You eventually wrapped up Sam Spade *near the end of the radio days.*

Yes. Well, that kind of went off, but it could have gone on and probably become a television show. But unfortunately, Dashiell Hammett went to jail for contempt of Congress during that time. That was the big "Red" routine going on and actually he had nothing to do with our show, but he created the character of Sam Spade. And I made *Red Channels** because I was a little too liberal for those times, apparently, and then the combination killed the show. You know, that was a time of great insecurity in the networks and the sponsors. Anybody who had kind of a vaguely liberal tinge was *verboten.*

Did being in Red Channels *hurt you a lot?*

Yeah, I'm sure. Oh, yeah. We couldn't get on the air for about two years. And the only way that I got back on was I just did any show that they threw at me. My agent said that the only way I would get back on was getting a sponsored show and eventually, of course, since I was really not guilty of anything, why –

– They finally had to go back to the talent!

I wasn't even *a good* liberal. I was just kind of a half liberal!

When did you first get involved with television?

Well, by the time we got around to '57 or so things had cooled down, so I could work. But it was still nip and tuck that I was gonna get on the air for *Mr. Adams and Eve,* which we did for two years [on television].

That was a fine show.

I thought it was kind of a bright show and not too sophisticated. We only made about 62 shows or something like that. In those days we made about 36 a year. Today they're making about 13 if they can get through that before being cancelled.

That's one of the big differences between radio and television. I know the

---

* *Red Channels* was a McCarthy-era publication listing names of writers, directors and performers suspected of being members of subversive organizations before World War II.

economics were different, but in the radio days they would give you a chance to do it. On television, if you're not number three or four in the ratings by the fourth program, that's it!

That's it! Forget it! You know, I think our first years in *Sam Spade* weren't any big smash or anything, but they gave it a chance to develop, until we finally developed an audience and as far as I know, we were always doing well after that.

It was a good show. It was well-written. Who wrote it?

All kinds of people. You know who E. Jack Neuman is? He's a producer now, but he was one of the early writers. A guy named Gil Doud and Johnny Michael Hayes, a well-known writer – we had the best. They were unknown at that time, but they have certainly done well since. I thought the writing on it was superior, most of the time.

You probably didn't spend three or four days rehearsing one of those scripts?

No, no. Far from it. We'd go down there, as I remember, about 11:30 on a Sunday morning and read it around the table and then we'd spend about a half hour – Bill and I – rewriting, cutting, and then we'd put it on the mike and go to lunch, come back, dress it, and put it on the air. Then, at one time we had to do two shows, one for the East and one for the West Coast and then, of course, when they found out that recording wasn't a dirty name – Bing Crosby was responsible for that – we'd do just one show and they'd just do the recording for the West Coast. Poor West Coast, they always got the second best!

Was Mr. Adams and Eve *the first thing that you did on television?*

Well, not the first thing, but my first series, yes.

You moved easily from one series to the next.

I did a show called *Dante* that lasted a hot 26 weeks! We had the misfortune of being opposite *Andy Griffith*, the smash of the season!

Was Dante *the show that was based on a couple of Dick Powell things?*

Yes, Dick Powell did it on *Four Star Playhouse*. Dante was kind of a gambler, an ex-gambler who ran a nightclub called Dante's. I thought it was a pretty good show, but I guess we weren't getting the numbers, so that was it. So the next show I did was *Felony Squad* – we got three years out of that one. I thought it should have gone a little further, but I guess people lost interest in it.

You bounced back to the radio scene for a brief while in the early Seventies with the Hollywood Radio Theatre/The Zero Hour.

Yeah, that was my old friend Elliott Lewis who directed and produced it and a lot of my old friends were on it: Lurene Tuttle and a lot of people, people I hadn't seen in years. I did two shows there and every show was old home week, and the stories would go back and forth.

From an actor's standpoint, of course, radio was beautiful, because you didn't have to worry about lighting and make-up and costuming or anything like that. You just got up there and you created your own costumes and your own imagery and drew on the written word as much as you could, and that was the art of it. And we just didn't know how great we had it then, until all of a sudden, it left.

It was great while it lasted. One last thing. From Sam Spade*, what was your license number?*

137596. You know, every once in a while somebody comes up to me and says, "What's your license number?" *137596!* I said that so many times that it's indelibly imprinted someplace.

Howard Duff was born August 24, 1913 and was 62 at the time of our conversation. He died July 8, 1990 at the age of 76.

Lurene Tuttle

Lurene Tuttle was one of radio's busiest and most versatile actresses. We met at her home in West Hollywood, California, on August 26, 1975. She told me that her career actually began in the theatre.

I started in the theatre in 1926. I was a full-fledged leading lady in 1928. Quite young to be a leading lady, you know, because I went to San Antonio, Texas, when I was 20 or 21, and became a leading lady in very heavy drama and heavy acting. From then on, I went to several places in the theatre. I went to Portland, Oregon. I went to Salt Lake City and became a famous leading lady in that town. There were fine stock companies in those days. I wish we had them now for young people to grow in. You don't have that kind of thing anymore, where you get money for learning. These days you have to pay money to learn, but in those days, you got good money. I was very proud of my position in the theatre.

Did you get to Broadway?

No, I never did. I was asked several times, but then I always had something here. I seemed to always have a contract. They wouldn't let me out of it or something. When I started in radio, then I really got involved. I would, so many times, be under contract to three or four companies at the same time. *Sam Spade*, after a while, I think about the second year, I got involved with *The Red Skelton Show*. So, I couldn't stay there to do the *Sam Spade* show. I would have to put my work, our dear little opening scene and closing scene, on record. It wasn't tape, it was record. We would put that on during rehearsal, and then I'd go and do *The Red Skelton Show*. So, I really wasn't there for the actual [broadcast]. They would just put my part on.

Well, they weren't in conflict with one another, were they? They weren't on opposite each other?

No, but my rehearsals were. You see, we would start to rehearse the *Spade* show at 10 in the morning. Then, I think, we went on at 5:00 to 5:30 here, and then they played a repeat, a transcription record repeat. So, at about 2:00 I had to go over to the Skelton show. Between 1:00 and 2:00, the others were sent out to lunch. Howard [Duff] would stay with me and we would record my opening and closing stuff. I have those. I bought those little records. I love to hear Effie and Sam. Oh, they're the most adorable love scenes ever written in the history of show business, I think.

Sam Spade, Howard Duff, remembers his license number.

137596.

Ah, you can't forget it either!

No, sir.

Those were the days, weren't they?

Yes, they were.

Let's back up a little, before Sam Spade. *What was your very first radio role?*

Well, a big radio role was the part of Ginny on the *Hollywood Hotel* show. I was chosen because I looked and sounded as if I could be the speaking voice of a coloratura soprano. Anne Jamison was chosen to play the singing role of Ginny opposite Dick Powell. She wasn't an actress, so I was chosen to be her speaking voice. All of the lovely operettas that we did, I was the leading lady opposite Dick Powell. That was a marvelous way to start radio, because it was leads. I had come right from stock company in the East, from theatre leads, so I wasn't ill at ease in these things. It was just easy for me, and we had an audience out there. It was like working, except that you had a script in your hand. You didn't have to learn it. But it was the same kind of show business to me.

Louella Parsons was involved in that program, wasn't she?

You bet she was. I just found an album the other day. I haven't heard it yet. They had some excerpts from the show which I'd never heard in all these years. I didn't know that anybody ever took any. At least, I didn't have any.

Most of the time, the shows that were broadcast in the Thirties and Forties were not recorded for preservation purposes.

No, not at all. They were live, absolutely live. If you made a mistake it was just too bad.

Some of those conversations on the air between you and Sam were great.

Oh, it was so funny! I listen to them now, and I know half of it was ad-lib. We were allowed to! Many musicians used to come down and sit in the booth. I saw Sammy Davis recently, and he said, "Oh, I'll never forget when I was allowed to come there and sit in the booth and watch you and Howard do *Sam Spade*." He said, "I wasn't anybody then, and I wouldn't have been allowed in there if somebody hadn't taken me. But, somebody took me by the hand and asked Bill Spier if I could come in and visit. I loved coming there." Louis Armstrong used to come and sit in the booth. And [other] famous people. It was a great privilege to be allowed, because it wasn't a very big booth; they didn't have very many seats.

And there was no audience, no studio audience.

No, not on that show. So the people who sat in the booth, many times Howard and I would mention them. He would say, "Did you see Dizzy Gillespie the other day?" I would say, "What was he doing over there? I didn't see him. Ah, I'm so glad you mentioned him, because..." and then we would go on. It was so cute. A lot of it was ad-lib. I realize now when I hear some of them. Of course, it was only, I think, about 13 weeks that I had to do that [recorded] doubling.

What about The Red Skelton Show? *When Red was Junior, you played Junior's mother.*

Mummy.

Mummy, right. Not Nammaw. Nammaw was Verna Felton.

Yes, right. And I played Daisy June, his girlfriend, Clem Kadiddlehopper's girlfriend. And I played Mrs. Willie Lump-Lump – he was the drunk. I played a lot of other parts on the show. I have some of those tapes, and they're fun to listen to. I really think his show was always better on radio than it ever was on TV. At least to me it was funnier.

Well, that's the old story of the imagination again. How long were you with Red?

Seven years.

Did you take over the characterizations on that show after Harriet Hilliard was on the show with Red?

Yes, she was on, and then GeeGee Pearson was on, and I was about the third one. I loved working on that show. Oh, it was fun. Red ad-libbed a lot, too. But he always came back to the cue. He would wander far away from the script, and then he'd always come back so you would know when you were suppposed to talk.

I understand he put on an after-show for the studio audience when the regular radio broadcast was over.

Yes, he did. At least an hour, sometimes and hour and a half. He got steamed up, you know, and the half-hour show didn't really satisfy him. So he kept the audience there afterward. See, we used to have a preview night. When we were on Fridays, we would have a preview on Thursday and he would go on and on and on. We'd have to stay there, because we had to wait till his after-show was over before we could listen to the record to see how things went. Then we came back the next day and did the live show. Always live. I don't think I ever went on that we weren't live.

You had to do two shows then, didn't you? For the West Coast and the East Coast?

No, in that case, no, because it was taken off on transcription and replayed. Many times we would do a 5:00 show, and that would be taken off on transcription and played later. In the old days, we did do two shows. We would have an afternoon show, a 5:00 show or a 5:30 show, and then come back and do it again at 8:30. Those were audience shows, too. We would wear street clothes in the afternoon and come back and wear evening clothes. It was a very glamorous business. Over at the Huntington Hartford, when I go backstage, I think of the many radio shows we used to do there. The *Lux* radio show went on there, and lots of radio shows went on there, because they were audience shows. That's why I felt that radio was not just a microphone-working kind of show. It was audience participation.

Weren't you on The Great Gildersleeve *at one time?*

Yes. I was the original [Marjorie]. I was on the opening show, and I worked on it for about two and a half years. Then they kept writing [Marjorie] younger all the time. She got to be about 16, and I felt that that was too difficult for me to go out in front of an audience and try to look 16. So, I think I gave my notice on the show.

Were you on the pilot show for Johnson's Wax?

I expect so.

It was supposed to be a summer replacement for Johnson's Wax, and then Johnson's decided against Gildersleeve. *Then Kraft Foods picked it up.*

I see. You know more about it than I do! I have lots and lots of tapes and things. I buy the albums and I buy the tapes, so it's fun to listen. Sometimes I hear things and don't remember doing it. I have a marvelous little mystery thing about a doll. I guess it was a voodoo doll. It was beautifully done and I can't even place the man's voice who did it with me. But it was a very exciting thing and I've listened to it several times. I like it very much, but I don't know when I did it, and I don't remember who did it with me. I have one with Gary Cooper. I have one with Cary Grant; "The Black Curtain" is the one I did with him. And I have one with Humphrey Bogart where he says to me, "I want to see more of you, Baby." My friends laugh! We love to listen to those things.

You were really all over radio, weren't you?

Oh, I should say I was! I used to do all kinds of voices, too. I still can. On a show over at CBS, Television City, I had to play a doll not too long ago. Somebody pushed the little string on the doll and I had to run upstairs and put my face into the microphone and be the doll while they were working the doll downstairs. Nobody knew the difference. Nobody knew I was doing it.

Howard Duff was right! He said, "You have to talk to Lurene Tuttle, because she's a doll!"

You know, he used to say such a cute thing. I used to ask questions on the show. I mean on the rehearsal, for real. Because I'm always saying, "I don't understand this plot." I would always say to somebody, Howard or Bill Spier or somebody, "I don't understand this plot." So they got to saying, "Down, Effie. Down, Effie." And that's how that phrase got started. It was really, "Shut up, Effie."

You played the nurse on Doctor Christian *for a while.*

Yes. Judy Price.

Was that before or after Rosemary DeCamp?

It was after. She got very busy in the picture business. So she sort of resigned for a while. I just took over while she was busy and then she came back, but that was a lovely thing to do. Jean Hersholt was a fabulous man, lovely to work with.

They asked the audience to send in a script. It was billed as the only show on radio where the audience wrote the script.

Yes. They were lousy, too!

How much tampering did the real writers on the show do with the audience scripts?

Quite a bit. They had to fix them quite often. A lot. They were really quite amateurish, but they had nice thoughts, they had nice plots. They just needed fixing. The dialogue didn't work too well.

The essential ingredient a writer has to look for is a good story line, something to work with, and then they can pull it together. So then the audience did participate; they wrote the story.

Yes. I would love to do radio again, but I would not want to do radio with some of the non-knowledgeable people running it. For instance, we'll take the show called the Frigidaire show [*Hollywood Startime*], which was directed by one of the best directors in the business, Bob Redd. We had the most beautiful orchestra in the world with all the finest musicians, and a fine conductor. We had the best sound men. We had the best mixer. We had the best engineer. We had the best everything and [it was] very carefully put together. Now, I'm afraid they'd be careless these days. I'm afraid they wouldn't realize the essence of perfection that you have to put in on one of those things. I would not like to see them do it unless they could go back to the old days of doing them properly.

You have at least 25, even 35 years between today and the day when the people who were doing it were day-to-day craftsmen at it. They knew what they were doing. You talk about putting it all together. The sound effects in those days, for example, were made on the spot. They never used tape.

No, no.

Occasionally they used a record with something, but almost always, they created the sound on the spot. Today, everything is on a little tape cartridge and they have to press buttons. It doesn't work.

It hasn't essence. We used to do dogs, you know. I've got to tell you a funny story. On *Hollywood Hotel* the sound man was supposed to do a little yipping, yappy dog, a little tiny dog, like a terrier. He sounded like a big dog. He sounded like a Newfoundland dog or something. The director kept saying, "It won't do. I can't have it." Olivia DeHavilland was sitting next to me, and she said, "I can do a very good dog." And I said, "I don't think they'll let you do a dog. This is an audience show. They won't let you. You're a star. You can't do a dog." She said, "I'm going to do it." She went over to the director in the booth and said, "I'd like to try doing this dog for you." So they put her behind a screen and she went on the show, and did the yipping dog. Isn't that the cutest thing? I'll always remember that.

Did you ever do animals?

Not very often. I once did, for Lawrence and Lee, on a show, "Alice in Wonderland," I did the dormouse, the little dormouse in the sugar bowl. I gave a fabulous interpretation of that. I can't re-create it because I have to have the words to go with it. They wrote such a cute little sequence there, so I'd have to have the dialogue. I've done animals, yes. One of the most interesting things I did one time on a show was Barnum and Bailey's first freak. It was an old lady, 120 years old or something like that, at least over 100. She drank heavily, so she was full of gin. Let me see, what other things I had to interpret. It seems to me I had three or four things that I had to do. She was black, so I had to conjure up all those things to do at the microphone. The people in the studio were just bursting. They wanted to laugh on the air, but they didn't dare.

I always felt that we had to work with an all-physical person. There are very clever people in the business now who are just voice characters. I would say, "Turn on voice 36 or voice nine, or voice 12 or something." But we always worked from the full person, at least I did, and I know that all of us tried to work that way, because that's the only honest way to do it. You have to have a person who lives and breathes and walks and is alive rather than just turning on a voice. You could conjure up, if you really had true imagination, anything that you wanted to be. That's why I loved it, too, because I could play opposite Jimmy Stewart or Fredric March or Cary Grant or Gary Cooper or Leslie Howard. On the air I could be the most glamourous, gorgeous, tall, black-haired female you've ever seen in your life. Whatever I wished to be, I could be with my voice. That was the thrilling part to me. I did several shows with Leslie Howard, who was a marvelous actor and a fine radio actor, too. I think I did "Intermezzo" with him one time, playing the Ingrid Bergman part. I wish I had a tape of that. I think it was on *Academy Award* or *Frigidaire,* one of those two.

On *The Lux Radio Theatre* they always had the male and female star, but on the *Frigidaire* show, or *Academy Award*, I would play opposite the big star. I would be going on for somebody else like Ingrid Bergman or Irene Dunne or any female star. I did a lot of things with female stars and also male stars on *Suspense.* I worked one with Rosalind Russell, and a marvelous one that I had with Joan Crawford, which was so good. Oh, she was so good. She was a good radio actor.

You were, too.

I loved it! I was with, by the way, Errol Flynn. You know that *Casanova* thing that he did. He was called Casanova, Casanova somebody.* I did foreign women with him. I'd come in and do some marvelous Hungarian wench. I remember Errol only as a very quiet, gentle, good actor who was very serious. When I read these things about what a wild man he was, I never saw him that way. I only see Errol as a symbol of excellence in every way. How in the world he ever

---

* Errol Flynn starred as Christopher Casanova in *The Modern Adventures of Casanova* on the Mutual Broadcasting System in 1952.

got a reputation as such a bounder or a libertine, I don't know, because I never saw him that way. I used to love to work opposite Ronald Colman, too. I have a picture and I should show it to you. It says, "Dear Lurene, Thank you for pulling me through so many broadcasts. Fondly, Ronnie." Not "Ronald Colman," but "Ronnie." Oh, it touches my heart.

I notice a lot of photos on the wall in your apartment.

Oh, yes. I have a pile over there, just filled with stars' pictures.

And all autographed, I'm sure, to you.

Oh, yes. I have one of Gregory Peck over there. I did a marvelous radio show with him.

I see a photo on your wall of the family that lived with Father. You were the mother in Life with Father *on television.*

Yes, I was. Dear Vinnie. Oh, I've had such lovely things to play. She was just perfection, she was the dearest, but also mischievous, lady. She had a lot of little plans and schemes and things which were cute. She was a very interesting person to play. I love to talk about having gone from *Life with Father,* after it was off the air, to Ma Barker. I did a movie called *Ma Barker and Her Killer Brood.* I had those terrible gangster sons. Ma Barker taught – she called him Johnny – Dillinger how to shoot. Oh, what a character she was! I loved playing her. I didn't have any problem shooting my machine gun. Hedda Hopper told me one time that the reason I loved shooting that gun was because I was after a lot of people that maybe made me mad at times, but I don't know. I don't remember being very mad at anybody!

You've enjoyed your show business career, haven't you?

Oh, I should say I have. One of the reasons, too, that I loved radio so much was because I always played opposite a very big star. That doesn't always happen now in TV. I just thoroughly enjoyed working with Chad Everett, for goodness' sake, in *Medical Center.* But I don't play opposite them the way I used to. You see, it was quite a thrill to play opposite Paul Muni on a show and have a role that was commensurate with his. To realize that you were co-starring with somebody who was supposedly a really big star. They were just wonderful. For instance, I did "A Star Is Born," with Fredric March; I did the Judy Garland part. I did "One Sunday Afternoon," with James Stewart. So I have all beautiful moments to remember, and I have many of them on tape so that I can re-create them in my mind.

They don't write really meaningful women's parts anymore. Not at all. Women are kind of discarded. We're just kind of pushed in the background a lot. They don't have the warm grandmas and aunts and people that they used to have, always, in a script. There was almost always a grandpa or an aunt or an uncle, or somebody of an older generation. But nowadays, they don't bring it in. I think younger people these days are really a little bored with older people. I think they're only happy with their peers.

Women were responsible, in many cases on radio, for some of the most dynamic shows on the air. Look at Agnes Moorehead in "Sorry, Wrong Number" from Suspense *and others like that. Did you ever do any one-woman roles on radio?*

Not all by myself. I did – just noticing the other night in my scrapbook – I did twins on *The Whistler;* I did a good girl and a bad girl. It was interesting because I had different microphones, one for the good girl and another microphone for the bad girl, so that I had really a different sound of two people. That was almost a *tour de force.* It was almost all by myself. There weren't very many more people in the cast.

Was that an aid to you, to have the two mikes there to keep your roles separate?

Oh, yes, because it was like night and day. These two persons were different, entirely different, even though they were twins. One was evil. I felt I had the time to physically become the other person as I moved from microphone to microphone. I had to. My imagination has always been very strong from the time I was able to talk. I had a stage father. Most people have stage mothers; I had a stage father! He put me on performing when I was just able to talk. So I performed and I have been acting since I was a year old. It's never been anything but just joy and part of life to be acting. I wouldn't think that I could do anything else. Although, when I got out of high school, I decided to work in a store. I was only 17. I sold so much and had so many friends coming in buying stuff in this store, and I brought in so much trade that he decided that I could be the buyer of the whole department. Well, that was too much for me. I said, "Oh no, I'm going off to college now. Sorry, can't do that." But it was lovely. An actress should be a perfectionist. An actress should have the epitome of belief in themselves. They should always do things well.

I have heard that you are a pretty good historian and documentarian.

I have everything written down. From 1937, I have every show I ever did, and the amount of money I got for it, so I could count up someday how much money I made in the radio business! Scary, isn't it? I have it all written down, all tabulated. If anybody says, "What show did you do on August 12, 1942?" I have it and they can't fool me on it. If anybody wants to fight with me on it, I could take it right to the government!

I don't want to add up all the money you earned in your radio career –

Let's don't. I'd faint!

I would faint, too! But how much did you earn for a Suspense *program, for example?*

Not very much. You see, the stars came in, backed up by a studio. For instance, we'll take James Stewart. He would come in and get at least $3,000, maybe $5,000, and my price would be $55. That was almost always the way. Radio persons hardly ever got very much over scale, $55. I didn't fight for it because I liked the volume; I liked being in a lot of shows. I didn't hold out for a lot of over-scale money, but I worked a lot and you add up about 10, $55 shows and you're not making bad money. So I worked it that way, just by volume.

Were you working for over-scale with Red Skelton?

Not much. I don't think much more than about $25 over scale. I probably got $125 for that show, even if I was there for two days. Maybe I was there Thursday and Friday and Sunday. I could have been there all day Saturday and all day Sunday. I probably just got about $150, maybe.

And while you were ad-libbing with Howard Duff, about the same I suppose.

Yes. I think it finally got up to $90, maybe $125, but not ever over that. Howard got a lot more than I did. You see, I still say it's a man's world. A man can get more money than a woman. I'm not a woman's libber, because I don't like that type of person. I think that we shouldn't shout and get very ugly about asking for favors. But I do think it's rather strange that a man getting a job will get more money than a woman, always.

Was this still the case when AFRA came in and equalized salaries? A man, you say, a star would demand more?

Yes. Always. In the case of Howard Duff, naturally, because he was the star of the show.

He had to be there live every week. You just recorded your stuff and cut out!

Well, only 13 weeks though. Three years of it, I was on there live with him. It was just those 13 weeks that I had to go over and do the Skelton show.

It was good that they would permit that.

I know. Well, Bill Spier was just dear about it. Effie, I think, was one of the dearest people I've ever played in my life, because she was patient. She always waited for him to come back. I think people were very aware of the fact that he chased around quite a bit, but he always came back to Effie. I wanted it to be kind of a symbol to girls who had itchy-feet husbands that if they'll just be patient they'll always come back. Don't be too demanding. Effie was just glad to see him. She loved him. It was very, very nice.

Lurene Tuttle was born August 29, 1907 and was 67 at the time of our conversation. She died May 28, 1986 at the age of 78.

Jay Jostyn

Jay Jostyn is best remembered as the star of **Mr. District Attorney.** *We met at the Masquer's Club in Hollywood, California, on August 25, 1975, many years after the long-running program left the air. I asked him if he could remember the show's famous opening lines.*

 "...and it shall be my duty as district attorney not only to prosecute to the limit of the law all persons accused of crimes perpetrated within this county, but to defend with equal vigor the rights and privileges of all its citizens."

And that was the voice of Mr. District Attorney!

"Mr. District Attorney..."

"...champion of the people"

"...defender of truth"

"...and guardian of..."

"...guardian of all fundamental rights to life, liberty and the pursuit of happiness."

You even remember the announcer's lines, don't you?

Yes! I received a letter from a school teacher in Aurora, Illinois, which I always cherished. She said that she was having an oral examination with her junior high school class, and one of the questions she asked – she had several of the parents in, because it was sort of an occasion – one of the questions she asked was where does the [phrase] "all men are entitled to life, liberty and the pursuit of happiness" come from? And she told me that without an instant's hesitation, the entire department roared, *Mr. District Attorney!*

Of course, they knew differently, and of course they knew that these were the words that came from our founding fathers some 200 years ago, when they were framing the Constitution.* We were on the air for about 15 years, and week after week, they had heard this. We were a top show for over 10 years, the top show on the air. We were never out of the first 10 in the 15 years that we were on the air.

That's amazing for a weekly, dramatic adventure show.

It's quite a record. We were very proud of it.

Did you say those familiar lines every week?

Every week, every week. Well, let's see, we did the show in New York, so of course we had to do a repeat performance. We did one at 9:30 on Wednesday night and then we'd do a repeat for the West Coast at 12:30.

Were you the one and only actor to be Mr. District Attorney?

No, no I wasn't. As a matter of fact, it started with Dwight Weist, I think. He was on as a summer replacement originally and then it started in the fall as a regular thing, and [Raymond Edward] Johnson played it. Dwight played it when it wasn't a commercial show, when it wasn't sponsored, and then Ray Johnson played it for 13 weeks, and they decided to make a change and I remember it was, I think the first of October that I went into the show.

What year was this?

Well, it was 1939. Yes. Somewhere around there, '39 or '40. They had auditions for it and I was fortunate enough to get the role of Mr. District Attorney and I enjoyed it for that many years.

I assume this was absolutely the very first thing you ever did on radio, right?

No, I can't say that, because I actually started in radio out here, out here in California. I did some recording and was familiar with it and then of course I was down at WLW in Cincinnati. I was there for a couple of years.

You were involved there on a series of programs called Moon River.

Moon River, yes. Worked on that. Of course, my wife and I went down there

---

* The phrase "Life, Liberty, and the pursuit of Happiness" appears in the second paragraph of the Declaration of Independence.

and we were both employed at WLW. She's an actress, or was at that time, in the profession. We were there for two years, and then I decided to go to New York. So that was it. And I remember very distinctly when I left WLW, I was doing the leads in about three or four different things. In *The Life of Mary Sothern,* I played Max Tilley, the lead in that, the lead opposite Mary. Of course I couldn't do the female lead!

And then we had another show called *Salute to the Cities,* and I was the sort of major domo of that. We had an orchestra, actually a band, and going through various cities in the United States and pointing out the places of interest in them. Then I did *Smoke Dreams,* which was another show, which was recalling [theatrical] shows that I had been to in New York, talking to my dog, Rig, and just remembering various things. The orchestra would go into familiar numbers taken from these musical shows that I had seen in New York. And then I did the type of thing in *Mr. District Attorney...* let's see, what was his name? He was an investigator of some kind.

Was that Foreign Assignment *with Vicki Vola?*

Yes, I did *Foreign Assignment,* but Vicki was the secretary on *Mr. District Attorney.* She was Miss Miller for many years. Before she got the part of the secretary, why, Arlene Francis was doing it. She was my secretary.

Did she play the role of Miss Miller?

No, a different name. It wasn't Miss Miller. They had changed the name.

Len Doyle was Harrington.

That's right. He played Harrington for many years.

Are those folks still active?

Vicki is. She's in New York. I heard from her just recently. But, Lenny has passed on. He was in, as I understand, some kind of an auto accident from which he seemingly didn't recover entirely. It just, you know, unnerved him or something.

You folks were regular visitors in millions of households week in and week out.

Yes, we were. We appreciate it.

Before your radio days, did you work in any other area of show business?

Oh yes. I started in so-called stock companies for about six years. I think anybody who is going to do any dramatic radio should have some actual experience on the stage, because I think it's very, very important as far as the interpretation of a part, a dramatic part, is concerned. I don't think you can do it just by getting up. You have your lines, of course, with you in radio, but it takes more than just the words; it takes an interpretation of the part, which you learn from stock companies and doing parts on stage. And I think it's very important for anyone deciding to do dramatic radio to have a background on the stage.

During your Mr. District Attorney *years, you were so very much identified with that role. Were you able to do anything else on radio at that same time?*

Yes, yes. I used to do a lot of shows. At one time, I know I did so many shows that particular week because, as I said, we had to do the repeats on the show and repeat them live. They didn't tape them. (They had no tape at that time.) And, I did, oh, 30-some shows in the week. They were mostly about seven, half-hour shows and the other quarter-hour shows.

You were on soap operas. Were you on the major evening shows, too, in other roles?

Yes, soap operas. Well, let's see. I was on *Second Husband* with Helen Menken. I played that for eight years, [as] Ben Porter. Let's see, I forget what the others were, but I was the father in *The Parker Family* for about five years, and that was with Leon Janney. That was on on Sunday nights.

Now, Mr. District Attorney *lasted almost to the end of radio, which showed, of course, its great durability.*

Yes. That's right, it did.

And it was transferred to television. Did you play in the television version?

Yes. The first year that it was on the air. At that time they had what they called the kinescopes, and they weren't very satisfactory. And then the title was purchased by the Ziv company. They just bought the title and ignored the cast that we had, I mean as far as anybody in radio is concerned, but they took it and made it into an entirely different show. In fact, it was practically a whodunit. They eliminated Harrington and Miss Miller. It wasn't the same show.

I think they had David Brian in that role...

Yes, that's right.

...and he had something that the original Mr. District Attorney *never had. I think he had a name. When you were Mr. District Attorney you were always "Chief," or "Mr. D. A." or "the D. A."*

Yes. I never had a name.

You were quite a crusading district attorney. You really were an investigator.

Well, it was more or less patterned after Tom Dewey, you know, at the time he was District Attorney of New York. I remember, on the 10th anniversary, Dewey was invited to a little party that we had at The Stork Club. I went over to the hotel to invite him and he said at that time – this was shortly after he had been defeated by Mr. Truman – he said, "Jay, you've been successful. Let me give you a little advice. You've been successful as a district attorney. My advice to you is not to try to advance politically!"

He had a little experience in that area!

Yes.

He never actually appeared on the program though, did he?

No.

Did Mr. District Attorney *always come from New York or did it move out here?*

No. It was always from New York.

You did get involved in television, although not as a district attorney. You changed the roles in the courtroom.

That's right. I became a judge [on] *Night Court.* I did that for about six years. That was a scripted show. It was taken from actual cases, as I understand, and I solved a good many of the cases.

You have been very much involved in a very important phase of show business. Your voice and your talent added to the imagination of millions of people to make some fabulously entertaining years. Thanks for everything you've done for the good old days of radio.

Not at all. Thank you, Chuck.

Jay Jostyn was born December 13, 1905 and was 69 at the time of our conversation. He died July 24, 1977 at the age of 71.

Virginia Gregg

Virginia Gregg was one of the busiest actresses on the air during the radio days. We met at a Pacific Pioneer Broadcasters meeting and arranged to talk about her career at the Beverly Hills Hotel on March 18, 1984. I asked if she got her start in radio in California.

It *was* out here, and it was peculiar. I'd always been going to be an actress. I grew up in Pasadena, so I worked at the Pasadena Playhouse while I was going to school, and did a little theatre work and so forth. But I also was a musician. I played double bass viol and I played four years with the Pasadena Symphony and then I got into a group called "The Singing Strings." It was three violins, cello, bass and piano. Girls, all girls. We went on staff at CBS for a year. We went on staff at the Mutual network for a year and a half. But I still had that little bit of a discontent. I didn't want *really* to make music my life; I wanted to be an actress. So they started having me do things with the group, like *Diary of a Young Woman,* and if they needed somebody around the studio. I did the *Rise and Shine Show* and just started with Morey Amsterdam and Mabel Todd. And suddenly I said, "I don't want to be a musician anymore," and I sold my bass that day.

Oh, so that was definite then?

So I would never go back to it. Yes. And then, it was quite difficult to make the break because people knew me as a musician, and everybody knows you can't do two things! But, I did have enough friends that I started on *Calling All Cars*, and some of the really good shows [like] *Lux Radio Theatre.*

You worked many, many times on The Lux Radio Theatre, *mostly in supporting roles. Did any of the stars ever fail to show up and Virginia Gregg got a big –*

No! Not on *Lux*. Well... once a star didn't show up for the second show. It was a live repeat. Our first one [was] to the East, second one to the West Coast, and somebody had to rush in and do him, but it's the only time I ever remember.

Gee, what happened to him?

He forgot the second show; he just forgot. In New York, they always have the two. They go New York, and one for this coast.

You did a lot of that, didn't you, two shows?

Yes.

One of the things that you did best on radio, I think, was being the girlfriend of the private eye, or the secretary.

Oh, I did a lot of those.

You were Nikki, Ellery Queen's assistant.

Yes, with Larry Dobkin [as Ellery]. When he first came out here. Larry is now a writer, director. I've done a lot of pictures with Larry.

And you worked with Dick Powell on Richard Diamond. *He would always come back to your place and then he'd sing a little song and there would be a cute little repartee between the two of you.*

Yes. [I was] Helen Asher. I doubled other parts, too, on most of those shows. Maybe if an old charwoman came in or something, I'd do those.

Did you free-lance most of the time through this period?

Well, in radio days, yeah, that's what you did. I was doing as high as five shows a day. But I did Brooksie with Bob Bailey.

On Let George Do It. *You also worked with him on* Johnny Dollar, *didn't you?*

Yes, I did. I [also] did *One Man's Family* for nine years. I did Betty on that.

Jack's wife. So, you really had a varied career.

But then, you weren't strictly under contract to those shows. You had to be available for when they were there.

You were lucky you stayed with it, then.

I worked at *Villa Vallee* [with Rudy Vallee]. I don't know how long that lasted. I guess it wasn't terribly long, but I did a running part on that.

Did you work with Jack Webb?

Jack Webb. I was in the [*Dragnet*] stock company [and] I did Nurse Parker –

– with Lionel Barrymore and Lew Ayres on The Story of Dr. Kildare. *That ran for quite a while, didn't it?*

Long time, yes.

You say you were doing five shows a day sometimes. What kind of a day did you have?

Busy. Very busy. Well, I didn't always do five shows a day, but you see, the studios were all very close. CBS and NBC and Mutual were all within walking distance, practically. So, if I was working with any CBS show, I would have somebody rehearsing for me at NBC.

Someone would rehearse for you?

Yes. Well, maybe you'd get a run-through or something.

How soon in advance would you get a script?

You never got a script in advance. In the early days, you went in and had a story conference, and a read-through, and you'd say, "Well, I don't think she would say this, or wouldn't it be better *if*..." And you could talk a show over and have a first read-through. When radio kind of faded out toward the end there, particularly with Jack, now Jack Webb really did have a stock company. He used the same people, and so did Jack Johnstone [on *Johnny Dollar*] pretty much. They would say such things as, "Now, next week you're doing an Irish." And I'd say, "I don't do Irish." And they'd say, "Sure you do." And I would get it and you "do Irish" or Chinese or whatever they'd tell you to do. We would go in, they'd hand us the script. Jack would be there. We'd start to mark the script. Maybe you wouldn't even get it all the way marked, and he'd say, "Okay, let's cut. Let's tape it." You'd hear yourself say the first few sentences, and you'd think, "Oh, that's my character." and if he didn't like it, of course, he could always cut it, and say, "No, you're off there. I want her more this or that, or try Brooklyn" or something else, and then you'd start again. But you didn't get a rehearsal. Not even a read-through at the end.

An actress, then, such as yourself, had to be very, very versatile to pick up on all that sort of thing.

Yes, radio people did.

Now, when you talk about taping the Dragnet *shows, you were fortunate to be involved in that good chunk of radio as it was so-called, "by transcription." You did have the opportunity to package it at a realistic hour, if nothing else.*

Well, that's true. *One Man's Family,* we would do shows for the week in one day. They were 15-minute shows.

You were on an awful lot of CBS shows during, perhaps, the last decade of radio as it really was radio. During most of the Fifties, you were on Escape *and* Frontier Gentleman *and* Have Gun Will Travel, *and I know you did so many shows. Before you played the girlfriend or the secretary to all these private eyes, on* Have Gun, Will Travel, *you were the girlfriend of Hey Boy.*

Oh, yeah! That was Ben Wright. He's marvelous. He's so bright and so talented, and I'm sure remembers a lot more than I do.

What was the best of the radio days for you?

I enjoyed the whole thing. I enjoyed the people in it, too. There was a lot of loyalty, camaraderie, we were together so much. In the beginning, I think there were 1,500 members of AFTRA, then AFRA. They figured about 400, 450 did practically all of the work. Of course, that wasn't very many, and we spent a great deal of time together, and that was before the days of tape, or even on tape lots of times you spent many hours together. But, we would have a break. You didn't have long enough to go anywhere, and we got to know each other very, very well, and our problems. They were like family. We'd hear about somebody who was having kind of a rough time, we'd go to one of the other producers and say, "Gee, Dick's having a hard time paying his rent. Do you think there's anything for him next week?" They'd get behind him, and he'd be working.

So, you'd all act as perhaps an agent for someone else.

Yes, for everybody else. We were very close and very loving. Very caring.

Did you have any disasters? Did you ever blow a show or something like that?

Oh, good heavens! I never blew a show, but I've sure blown enough lines. Oh, yes, like, "Doctor, here is your hypodeemic nerdle" and such. I did that one. In [a] book it says Cathy Lewis did it, but she didn't. I'd be glad to give it to her.

Did you start doing a little work in television after the radio scene –

Oh, yeah. I've done a lot of work in television.

What have you done?

Oh, here we go! I did about, I would say, 65 percent of the *Dragnets* on television, *Gunsmoke*, all the Westerns, *Bonanza. Jack Benny.* I don't know, almost everything.

You were just as busy in television as you were in radio. Let's talk a little bit about Dragnet *again, working with Jack Webb. You were part of his company, so to speak. It was an informal company, wasn't it?*

Oh, yes. It's just that he relied on these people. I'm sure he didn't set out to form a group, but it was very hard to break into that little company of his.

He looked, I think, for a naturalness on the part of his actors, and he wanted the audience, whether on radio or television, to identify with these people, or at least to listen to them and say, "That is really how this person would sound on that."

That's right. Yes, but that being so, strangely, I have done some of the broadest characters I've ever done for Jack. I mean, really broad, far out characters. Except, he felt that they were real. What he didn't want you to do was *act.* As long as you could be real in whatever you were doing, that was fine.

What kind of direction did he give you then, with that end in mind?

Not any more than he had to. Not character direction. He'd hand you the part and say, "She's a..." Or it was written out that way. If you got too far off, he'd bring you back.

And you knew what was expected of you, and he knew that you could do what he was looking for. How long did it take to a Dragnet *radio show, for example? Would it be a one-day thing?*

No, not a whole day.

Not even a whole day? Dragnet *came on in the late Forties, I think, when it started.*

Probably, Jack came down from San Francisco. I worked with Jack as an actor when he first came down. Before he had his own show in radio. When he was an actor here, in town.

Now, when Dragnet *moved to TV, you moved along with him.*

And also into features with him, too.

Were you in the Dragnet *feature film?*

Yes. I played the one-legged drunk. Did you ever see it?

I'm sure I did, but I must say, I can't remember the one-legged drunk.

If you saw the feature, the *Dragnet* feature, you know the opening where he's mowed down, walking down a hill? I was his wife. When they go to investigate, here she is out on the davenport with a drink, boiled to the eyeballs. And then when she gets up they find she only has one leg.

And you were out of it almost before the opening credits?

Yes. It was a marvelous part.

It tells us something about the loyalty that Jack Webb had for the people that he worked with.

Yes, he certainly did, and he was wonderful to work for.

You were on the Jack Benny *TV show. What kind of things did you do for Jack? There's all kinds of characters.*

Oh, I only did one of those. I didn't like to do live television. I loved Jack. He's sweet to work with and the company was marvelous, but I'm just not cut out to do live television.

Other features that you might have been in?

Well, my very first feature was *Body and Soul* with John Garfield. *Love Is a Many-Splendored Thing, I'll Cry Tomorrow.* My last one was *S.O.B., Operation Petticoat.* Oh, I've done a lot of them.

So, you're still very, very active in the business today?

I'm not as active as I once was.

Are you as active as you want to be?

Yes.

That's all that counts. What was, would you say, the best role you ever had, whether it be in movies, or radio, or television? The one that was perhaps the most challenge to you?

Oh, you know I don't really think there was one. I did a bag lady on *Lou Grant* that I liked an awful lot. That was just a couple of years ago. On skid row. I enjoyed her. She was just a little batty, but that was a good, well written [role]. Anything that's well written is fun to do, no matter what it is.

Day in and day out, you really are the backbone of the entertainment industry, a person like yourself who has the tremendous ability and can adapt well to any situation, whether it be radio or television or the movies, and you're always there and always adding the extra dimension of substance.

Oh, yes. I think that the character people, the supporting people, are most important.

And I don't suppose you have the pressures that the top, leading people have. Everything has to be perfect for them and all of that business.

Well, further than that, I never wanted to be a star. I'm not geared for that. I don't want to go into a restaurant and be surrounded. I have just enough of that that really makes me feel very good. People recognize me and are flattering, often. But I would hate that fishbowl existence. I'm not for that. I don't think any of them really enjoy it forever.

So, what's on the agenda now for you?

Nothing that's coming up now. I do the one remaining radio show quite often. And that's that Salvation Army show, *Heartbeat Theatre.* I love doing that. I like doing any voice work.

Well, you have a very fine voice, and I know you are so versatile with it, and we have heard so many examples of your work listening to many of the radio shows from those good days. Those were busy days.

Oh, they were busy but they were wonderful. I knew it at the time, too. I knew how wonderful they were. I was very happy in radio.

I want to thank you for all the things that you've done in the past. You've entertained a lot of people with your talents.

It's been my great pleasure. I have enjoyed it thoroughly.

Virginia Gregg was born March 6, 1916 and was 68 at the time of our conversation. She died September 15, 1986 at the age of 70.

Art Linkletter

Art Linkletter starred on and developed the popular audience participation program **People Are Funny.** *We met at his office in Beverly Hills, California, on August 12, 1976, where I asked how he was able to translate the highly visual aspects of the show to radio.*

We just described everything that went on and prayed for the day when television would arrive. And, of course, when television did arrive, we found out that it had many, many limitations and that a lot of the fun of *People Are Funny* was gone, because anticipation is greater than realization. Things that you could describe as being funny often weren't really that funny. So it was a very interesting experience to have spent 10 years in radio, waiting for television, and then to find out that it had many, many limitations on it.

Radio's a participatory experience and television is a passive, spectator sport where everything is laid out for you and you have no room for imagination, no room for heightened enjoyment of things, depending on your own cultural and educational background. It's all laid out flat. Whereas in the old days on *People Are Funny,* to use an extreme example, we would hit somebody in the face with a chocolate meringue pie. If you were listening to it, you could visualize that as aesthetically as you wished it to be or as crudely and burlesque as you wished it to be. When it was on television, there was no possible point of interpretation. There it was and it made some people angry and it made some people happy.

Where did People Are Funny *come from in the first place? How did it all begin?*

I was doing a number of radio shows in San Francisco. I was the Mr. Radio of San Francisco, doing 21 shows a week on seven stations: *Man in the Street, Who's Dancing Tonight* from the ballroom, and *Are You a Genius?* from Oakland, and many other programs. It occurred to me that a program built on psychology would be most interesting, since I was a psychology minor in college (an English major), so I devised a program idea called *Meet Yourself,* in which I would get people up to the microphone, have them answer questions or participate in a stunt and then have a famous psychologist from Stanford University come into the picture and interpret that person's personality. Is he an ambivert or an introvert or an extrovert or whatever he was, depending upon what the stunt was. And then we would go on to the next stunt.

I came to Hollywood one time on a chore that was not related to this and I ran into a man named John Guedel. He had exactly the same idea, only he had a psychologist from USC and he called it *People Are Funny* while mine was *Meet Yourself* – "Look into the mirror of your own self and find out really who you are." So John and I found that we were compatible. We were both writers, we were both idea men. He was a producer and I was a performer. So we pooled our talents, took his title, which was the better, more saleable title. We spent $15 each, which was a total of $30, borrowed a studio at NBC, assembled a cast of characters and made a pilot.

Well, the psychologist didn't work out, because we wanted him to be strong and definitive. We wanted to do a stunt and then he would give a complete analysis of that person. Naturally, a professional psychologist from a big university would only say, "There's an indication that possibly, under certain circumstances, this man might conceivably be this way." We wanted him to say, "He is thus and so." So we threw him out and left the stunts in!

We sent the record to a Chicago agent named Russell Seeds, who was having problems with the United States government over a program called *Sergeant Quirk and Captain Flagg,* because World War II was beginning and the show that he had on NBC for a tobacco company was a very tough show between a non-com and a captain, that is, a commissioned officer. So they were cancelling that show and just at that moment they needed something else and they picked up *People Are Funny* and we were off and running. So here was the birth of a show which ran for 19 years.

It ran on radio until from about '42 –

– Until about '53 and then went into television until about '61 or '62.

Was it on television at the same time it was on radio at any point?

Yes, at one time, just as *House Party,* which I did on CBS. I was on both networks.

That's a little unusual, isn't it, for those days?

Very. Especially during those years when there was so much competition between the two [networks]. But I was on five days a week on CBS, on radio, and then finally TV. And both shows were suited for radio or TV. And they, at one time, were on all four networks – the radio and the television on each two networks. So it was quite an adventure.

Was there any problem with doing that?

No. I just had to be sure that I was loyal and capable and did a good show of each. In fact, it was better for me, because each network was trying to make its show more important to me and to the viewer than the other network show. So I got reams of publicity and attention and all the things that make young, rising emcees happy.

You said before it was actually easier to do People Are Funny *on radio than on television. How did you find that transitional period?*

Well, as a matter of fact, what I did, to tell you the secret, inside truth, was, that I was so concerned about the worries of television and the transition that I went over to ABC and sold the Jolly Green Giant a show called *Life With Linkletter,* which was really a hidden version of *People Are Funny* under a different title. And so there I was, on all three networks: the real *People are Funny* on NBC radio, the substitute *People Are Funny* under a different title on television on ABC, and the *House Party* on radio.

Life With Linkletter ran for a year and a half before NBC decided that *People Are Funny* had the priority and wanted it on the air on television. We found, on *Life With Linkletter,* for instance, that if we gave a lady a skunk and sent her up Hollywood Boulevard on a mission, that the description of the expressions on the faces of the passers-by evoked a much better image in the listener's eye than the occasional blasé and even indifference with which you would greet a lady with a skunk on a leash on Hollywood Boulevard!

Was People Are Funny *live on television or was it on film?*

It was live at first and then it was filmed. It was better on film, because we could edit. And some great, great stunts didn't pay off the way they should have, because people didn't react the way they should have.

I'm amused at today's game shows which I see on TV. When a person wins money, he jumps up and down and squeals and yells and kisses the emcee and falls down and does all that stuff. That's not natural. That's not the way people react. That's all coached. That's not only coached but it's threatened. If they don't react that way, they're never seen. We never told people how to react.

Did you ever have any problems with people's reactions?

Our only problem was, they didn't react strongly enough. We'd give somebody a house or a car and they'd say "Thanks." We would put together two brothers who hadn't seen each other for 35 years, separated by family problems. We brought them together and they'd say "Hi, Joe" instead of crying. On the other hand, there were times we got gigantic response out of very little things. You just don't know. People are funny! They're unpredictable. And if you look at the shows across the board today in the daytime, you'll see that they are predictable and they are the same and they are reacting exactly like two peas in a pod, whatever show you see.

You were doing an audience participation show probably before anyone else was doing it.

Ralph Edwards and myself and John Guedel. We three: my partner John and myself and Ralph. He had *Truth or Consequences* and the two shows started at approximately the same time. We were fighting all the time about who got the ideas and who didn't and now, of course, we're good friends. But there was a lot of tension in the early days when we were both trying to make it. But we originated, between the three of us, about a third of all the shows you see today, like *To Tell The Truth, The Price Is Right,* and *Let's Make A Deal.* We were hiding prizes in boxes and behind screens.

I never did care for quiz shows. Never wanted to do a quiz show, although I've done some. But I always wanted to have audience reactions to people undergoing real life hazards and problems. We've done everything.

Were there any stunts that really backfired?

Oh, yes. We had people, for instance, who got mad on stage. We got two neighbors together one time and neither one of them knew they were going to be on the program and we had researched and discovered that they had a problem in the neighborhood and they feuded. And we thought if we got them on the air in front of a live coast-to-coast audience and confronted them with the childishness of a simple argument over a dog, they would get back together again. And we'd give them a wonderful prize of a trip to Europe together. Well, they would have nothing of this. When they found that the other one was on the stage, fireworks ensued and they wouldn't talk to each other and they wouldn't accept a prize and they made it even worse than it was before, because now it was out in the open nationally. That was a surprise, because they were both nice ladies and both reasonable separately. But it demonstrated to me very forcibly how Hatfield and McCoy feuds began almost from something they couldn't remember but at the end were killing each other over the growth of an animosity.

On the other hand, was there a stunt or an event on the program that turned out so much better than you had expected?

Oh, yes. That often happened. Everything happened on the show. In 19 years there's nothing you could mention that didn't happen, because we had people who, as a result of some stunt, changed their whole lives.

We did a thing where we took a sealed, plastic case with a telephone number and an address inside of it, and we dropped 12 of these into the Pacific Ocean. And they said the first person who breaks this open and phones us will get a $10,000 reward. Months went by and then one day we got a short-wave message from an atoll in the South Pacific. A native boy had found this on a beach in an incommunicable-type atoll and they waited for a month to get favoring winds so they could bring it to the naval base in a twin-hulled canoe. And the guy broke it open – they were afraid it might be a Japanese bomb! We flew this young man all the way from this atoll in the South Pacific to Hollywood, did a stunt with him, showed him things to do, gave him money to go out and buy whatever a guy would buy with $50 in an hour in stores he never even dreamed existed and come back and report. But anyhow, we gave him the $10,000 as a final blow-off and he went back and changed the entire life of that island. For instance, they had never had water supplies that were dependable. And with that money they built a reservoir to catch the rain that came at intervals and they set up a medical center. This $10,000 just changed the whole life of those people forever on that little island.

It's amazing what a radio show can do.

It really is.

Where did the idea come from for the House Party?

I was in San Francisco, flying up and back every week to do *People Are Funny,* 'cause I still was doing my shows in San Francisco.

Still doing those 20-some shows every week?

I cut 'em down to about four or five, but I like to live in San Francisco. So I stayed up there and I'd be doing a man-in-the-street show for a couple of hundred dollars on Market Street one night. The next night I'd be in Hollywood emceeing a coast-to-coast radio show. It seemed a little incongruous but I enjoyed both lives. So I started interviewing kids up in San Francisco as part of a show called *What's Doing, Ladies?* for Safeway Stores, and John Guedel and I had an idea. Why don't we sell a show called *Under 21,* five-a-week, daytime, where we take kids from three to 21 and [show] all the things they do, from accomplishments to little malaprops. So we cut a record and John took it back. Young and Rubicam liked it and submitted it to General Electric and they liked it but they said, "We want a five-a-week, half-hour show, but we only want kids for about eight or ten minutes. So we went to work, figured out a lot of other things to do, and used the kids as the only feature, five days a week and did things that I was doing in San Francisco, like looking in ladies' purses and, naturally, interviewing guest celebrities and authors and things like you're doing right now. GE bought it and that show stayed on the air for 25 years.

And that made a very easy transition to television.

Very easy. Much more so than the other.

Was it being simulcast at any time?

Yes, for three or four years, five years.

You must have had some pretty interesting experiences with the kids, because they really are unpredictable.

Yes. It led me into a whole new way of life, because I wrote the book *Kids Say The Darndest Things* out of my experiences. It was the number one bestseller for two years in a row, unheard of, in the nation. People remember the kids more than they remember the rest of the show. And a lot of people say to me you used to have that show where you interviewed kids. And I say that was only five minutes out of 30. How about the other 25? You know, *they* were good minutes, too!

But the idea of interviewing children was so unusual and was so difficult, very few people were able to do it. It was so startling and, in those early days of radio when censorship was quite intense, we couldn't use words like "pregnant." You couldn't say a woman was pregnant. That was a no-no. It was terrible! Now they not only say it but tell you how she got that way, in detail, in front of an audience and they'll applaud! How times have changed!

So, the kids would say things that the network would let go by, because they were said in innocence by a child that they would never let a writer write or a professional performer say. I'd say to a child, "What do your mother and dad do for fun?" and he'd say, "Search me, they always lock the door." Well, a CBS censor would faint at letting that pass on a show like *The Jack Benny Show* or *The Burns and Allen Show* but they could get by because what does a five-year-old kid know? They wouldn't let me repeat it as a story that was said because I know what he said. But he could say it.

And you, indeed, sometimes led them on a little bit.

Oh, yes. There's no doubt about it and I got criticized by people who said you shouldn't encourage children and I say, "Well, what do you want?" A kid says his dad's a painter or a plumber. That's not very funny. But if he says "My dad likes to play poker every Monday night in the basement with the minister," then we got something. But we never told them to say it and we never cued them to say it.

I had a very smart teacher who picked them up at school each morning at 9:00 in a limousine. The school chose the kids, you know. We had nothing to do with who the kids were and we went right down all the schools. We had a very difficult thing to get and that was the approval of the Board of Education, Los Angeles, for children to be taken out of school on a school day and taken to a commercial radio show. Now, you know, that takes a lot of approval. So we had to agree to go through all the schools. We had the black schools and the brown schools and we had the ghetto schools at a time when they never got any nod of recognition from anybody. That was a long time ago, before this whole matter of civil rights and equal rights and ethnic rights was even dreamed of. We went right down the line and those schools got television sets and radio sets and record players for their use, which were very valuable, and we also got kids who were great.

The teacher would be with them for about two and a half hours. They would tour CBS and so forth. And while she was with them, what she was really doing was interviewing them and they didn't know it. She'd bring up subjects and talk about things and if a kid said something that was very cute, she'd jot it down. Now, the chances of that kid saying the same thing to the same question was the shot I had. And quite often, they never said the same thing twice, because they weren't told to and they may not have really believed it or they may not have thought about it again.

I'll give you an example of a five- or six-year-old child who was riding along and the teacher said, "Well, let's play a little game. Who's the president of the United States?" And one of them says "Abraham Lincoln is the president of the United States right now." That's pretty funny. So she'd jot it down, make a little note of it. She'd give me the note. Meantime, in the bathroom, one of the other kids said "You're an idiot. Abraham Lincoln or George Washington isn't the president." And they'd say, "The real president is Lyndon Johnson" or Kennedy or Truman or whoever it really was. And so when I'd ask the kid the question, I'd get an answer that had been corrected. On the other hand, I got answers that were corrected wrong. They told him "Abraham Lincoln is not the president of the United States. It's George Washington," 'cause they didn't know either.

One time I had a note that a little boy had a pet turtle named Ozzie Nelson. I thought that was kind of cute, so I said to the boy "Do you have a pet?" and he said, "Yeah." I said "Well, what is it?" and he said "It's a dog." I said, "What's its name?" and he says "Rover" or something like that, dull. And I said, "Well, didn't you ever have any other kind of a pet?" And he said, "Oh, we used to have a turtle but my dad flushed that down the toilet." So you see, I got a better one! I also got disappointments where I had great answers from the children that I knew they'd said and I never could get it back. Never could get it back. That's the way it worked and so it was fun for me.

I got a lot of things, of course, that the teacher never heard of, because I had a way with children. The secret of my success with children was really quite simple. Number one: I'm a good communicator, anyway, with anybody. Number two: the children who are on the program had all seen the program. So they knew what was expected and that was, I was gonna talk to them. They weren't surprised, they weren't baffled and they also knew that they could do what other kids were doing. They'd just talk about things they knew about. They weren't going to be asked to juggle, sing, ride a unicycle or do something that was beyond their ability. So they're ready for it. They'd been brainwashed, so to speak, at least indoctrinated by just watching or listening to the show on the radio.

And then finally, in the third place, a most important thing occurred before we went on the air: I went in and talked to them for five minutes. In that talking to them I did something essential to the communication with children: I let the children see the child in me. In other words, I played games with the kids. I was not a big distant, grown-up figure. They recognized in me somebody of the same mental intelligence and level! At least the same emotional quotient. They weren't afraid of me. They knew I was gonna play games and they like to play games. I played games with them in the dressing rooms. So when I got out on the air, we were just going on.

Of course, the little ones didn't know what was going on. A four-year-old often would come up to me after the program was over and pull my sleeve and say, "Mr. Linkletter" and I'd say, "Yes" and he'd say, "When does the show start?" I'd say, "What did you think that was out there?" "Oh, that was the show." But, of course, those were the kind, the little three- and four-year-olds who are just, you know, floating free. They're just marvelous, like [one] little girl. I said to her, "What do you do?" and she said, "I help my mother in the house." I said, "Well, you're only three-and-a-half, four. What can you do around the house?" She says, "I help her with the breakfast." I said, "Come on, what do you do?" She says, "Well, I put the bread in the toaster. Of course I can't flush it." One of the little boys, I said to him, "Do you get an allowance?" and he says, "What's that?" I said, "Oh, I guess you don't know what that is. It's money you get for being a good boy." "Oh yeah," he says, "I guess I do." I said, "Well, what do you get?" He says, "I get a nickel every day I have a dry bed." I said to him, "Well, how much money have you made this summer?" and he said "Nothing."

Kids say the darndest things!

They were a delight. Just a delight. I had a little boy who had a Mickey Mouse wristwatch on. Somebody had given it to him for a birthday. I said, "Oh, you got a watch." He said, "Yes sir." I said, "What time does it say?" He said, "It doesn't say anything, you gotta look at it." Very direct. An older boy one time, I said to him, "What did your mother tell you when you came down here today?" "She just told me to be a normal boy" and I said, "Well, what is a normal boy?" He says, "I think it's 98.6." These kids, you know, come up with some surprising bits of flashes of information.

You often asked what somebody told them not to say.

Oh, yes. I had to do that protectively, because the parents were getting nervous and they were brainwashing the children. You see, we never told the children what to say, but it finally worked out that the parents did. They were telling them what *not* to say. And, of course, I double-crossed them very easily by asking them what they had been told not to say. And it came out letter perfect, because they had been rehearsed, you know. A little boy said, "My mother told me not to announce to the world she's pregnant." "Well," I said, "why not? That's a marvelous thing." He says, "She ain't yet." Or the little boy, I said, "What did your mother tell you not to say today?" He said, "Well, she told me I could say anything but don't get this shirt dirty, because it's brand new, it doesn't fit, and we're going to take it back when I get home."

Art Linkletter was born July 17, 1912 and was 64 at the time of our conversation.

Carlton E. Morse

Carlton E. Morse created* One Man's Family *and* I Love A Mystery, *two of the most outstanding radio series of all time. We met in his home in San Mateo County, California, on August 18, 1975. I asked if his home – with its beautiful view – was the highest point in the area.

 Yes, it's about 1500 feet. We're 17 miles from the ocean, and we're about 12 miles from San Francisco Bay. We're right in the middle of the peninsula on the ridge.

How far are we from Seacliff?

Well, that's in San Francisco, approximately 40 miles [from here].

So there really is a Seacliff area.

Oh, yes. As a matter of fact, the buses that pick up visitors and show them the city always had a *One Man's Family* house in Seacliff where they would say, "That's the Barbour house, and did you see, that was just Father Barbour going around the corner." They picked out, finally, one specific one that they used every time!

We were on that tour and I think they pointed that out to us. But we didn't see Father Barbour! One Man's Family, *of course, was probably the longest-running serial drama on radio. When was the first broadcast?*

In 1932, in April of 1932, and it ran about 27 1/2 years, ending in, I guess that would be 1959.

What were your credentials before you started writing One Man's Family? *You were a young man at the time.*

Well, the show started in '32. I was a young man of 31. I had been a newspaperman, both in Sacramento, on the old *Union* which Brett Harte and Mark Twain contributed to. Then I came down and was on the copy desk of the *San Francisco Chronicle* for three or four years. I was on three different papers in San Francisco. Then I went to Seattle – the *Seattle Times* – for, I guess it was two years. It was up there when we heard our first radio show. It wasn't a show; it was a boxing championship. I've forgotten who was fighting. We came back to San Francisco, and newspapers were folding awfully fast about that time. A friend of mine had a job over at NBC, and I went over and was taken on a week-by-week basis to see what I could do. I had written columns for papers, but had done nothing in a dramatic form at all. That was in – when was the crash? – in 1929.

October 29, 1929. Wasn't that Black Tuesday, the stock market crash?

That's pretty close. The week that I started with NBC came the crash. For the next couple of years they kept me on as a director and writer for radio. Nobody knew anything about writing for radio in those days. But I was learning. Then I did some adventure and mystery stories. Finally, I always wanted to do a family show. I was a very great admirer of "The Forsyte Saga" and so I wrote three episodes, half-hour episodes, and submitted them to the program department. Well, they thought I was crazy. Everything up to then had been "bang-bang" excitement and thrills and yelling and so forth. I didn't write that kind of thing for the family. I wrote the kind of family that I knew. I was the oldest child of a family of six children. The program department said, "I'll tell you what you do. You better resign and if anything comes along, why, we'll give it to you."

Don't call us. We'll call you!

Right. So I took it to Don E. Gilman, who was vice-president of the West Coast, National Broadcasting Company. After about three weeks he called me and said, "I never thought of a family show on the air, but I kind of like it. Maybe the audience will accept it and maybe they won't. Would you write it so that we could bring it to an end after six weeks if it didn't go?" Then we went on the air. I had been doing dramatic things for years. I did a show called *The House of Myths*. I did the tongue-in-cheek suggestion that everything that was done in the myths were a little bit on the erotic side. Everything was so very carefully edited, so I had to be very careful what I wrote. But, I got the point over. Then there were the mystery stories that I did. I came in '29 and the *Family* didn't start until '32. So, I had quite a long time to experiment. But I was learning – I was being paid to learn. That's how the career developed. With the financial crash, in those days nobody had any money to go the theatre or go out to dinner or anything, and the radio was a godsend.

It was built right into the Depression.

That's right, so we just grew in importance. All we had to do was stay on the elevator and we couldn't go any place but up.

You said you wrote six shows. This was called One Man's Family *at the time.*

That's right. I wrote three shows, and then at Mr. Gilman's suggestion, I made it six with the idea that we'd bring an end to the show if it wasn't satisfactory.

They didn't even give you 13 weeks!

No! And the show was never off from that time till the final ending of the show 27 1/2 years later.

I'm sure you hadn't developed the full family tree yet at this point.

No. I had Father and Mother Barbour, and Paul. It was close enough to the end of World War I that Paul had been a flyer in the World War. And then there was Hazel, second child. Her father was a very, very conservative man and very strict. She was her father's girl and was pretty prim, and as a result, didn't have many boyfriends. That was Hazel. Then Clifford and Claudia were twins. Clifford was a kind of a happy-go-lucky ne'er-do-well. He never did get very far. Claudia was the most independent and rebellious member of the family. Jack was just an adolescent boy at that time.

You set the personalities of these people right from the beginning.

That's right. You see, I had worked with these people – everyone except Mother Barbour – I had worked with the actors over and over and over again for two or three years. I knew what they did best. I knew how to write for them. I selected the characters that I wanted, the actors that I wanted and built the radio characters around those personalities. So it wasn't hard for me to tell which was Paul Barbour and which was Michael Raffetto. It was the same way with each of the others.

I must ask you about Father Barbour. He has the habit, I guess, of always going, "Mm hm. Uh. Mm hm." That kind of a thing.

Yes, yes.

Yes, yes! Oh, yes! Did you write that into the script? Every time he said that, was it on the printed page?

That's right. Mm hm. Yes. I'll show you in the first episode, when we go back upstairs. I have the original copy of it. I think that it demonstrates that I had full consciousness of what I was doing as far as the cast was concerned when I first started out to do that.

You were very positive about this One Man's Family *idea. Even though they wanted only six episodes, I believe that you felt it was going to run longer than that. Could you see going down the path of life years ahead that these things would develop?*

Oh, no. No. As a matter of fact, during the first 10 years of the show I didn't write ahead. I wrote from week to week. I was directing the shows. So I would write a show, we would go in and there would be some element in the show, or somebody would do an outstanding job, or I would catch something so that I would take that and build on it for the next episode. In other words, I wrote a show, they added something to it, I wrote on what they added. So we built together. It was that kind of a thing. It was something that was easy for me and easy for them because I was doing what they did best for them.

In the course of this first six weeks, at what point was it when someone said, "Don't stop. Keep going"?

After the second episode. We only started off with two stations: San Francisco and, I think, Los Angeles. After two episodes, three more stations asked if they could have it. By the end of the six weeks, we had the whole NBC Network on the West Coast, Mountain Time. And we had a sponsor. Snowdrift and Wesson Oil was our first sponsor, because their product was only in the mountain states on the West Coast at that time. I've forgotten the exact dates. Let's say a year or a year and a half after that, a cigarette company came to NBC with a new cigarette. I've even forgotten the name of the cigarette. Anyway, it was supposed to be waterproof so you could smoke it in the rain or in the shower. Well, at first they bought it for 13 weeks nationally. This was our first touch of national. All of their warehouses were cleaned out after the first episode.

It really sold cigarettes!

Yes, but after that nobody bought any more cigarettes. They were terrible cigarettes. More than that, the churches began to hit NBC with, "You can't do this to an American family" and "you're tying an American family into cigarettes." They just wouldn't have it. They wrote the cigarette company and said, "No, we wouldn't think of buying your cigarettes. You are ruining a family show." The cigarette company, after nine weeks, said, "We'd like to get out of this contract, because people won't accept it." That aroused national commercial interest immediately. Standard Brands snapped us up. I think one or two weeks passed before everything was set up, and they were with us for 15 years. We had the same sponsor for 15 years. Tender Leaf Tea was a little tea outfit up in

Massachusetts someplace that Standard Brands had bought, and we made it the number one tea in the nation inside of a couple of years. We went through the whole Standard Brands list of things in the 15 years.

It's really interesting that the public, who loved the radio show, wrote to the sponsor saying, "You don't belong as a sponsor of this" as opposed to them saying, "Oh, we're grateful for you to bring this to us."

But you see, they were just as loyal when they got Standard Brands. Everybody bought everything that Standard Brands put on the show. So it was a good, loyal audience.

You were on, in the beginning, for half an hour a week.

Until I went back to New York to put it on television, which was around '49 or '50. So it was a half-hour once a week all that time from let's say '32 to '50, 18 years. When I went back to New York to put it on television, we got a radio sponsor five times a week and I had to get some extra help, because I was back in New York rewriting the shows for television.

For the television series of One Man's Family, *did you pick up some of the previously written radio scripts and then adapt them to TV or did you write new things for television?*

I started the story from the beginning. I had the material, but except for the basic characters and plot, I had to change things. This was 18 years later, and already there were changes of all sorts in public thinking, in family thinking, as well as the media. Television hated words; they wanted action, they wanted pictures and I had never done anything like that before. So I had the double chore of learning a new way of entertaining people.

It must have been pretty exciting, though, to get into TV.

Well, it was and I enjoyed it tremendously. After we selected the cast in New York, because the radio cast was out here doing the five-a-week show, I had to have a director, and some production help. A lot of people had a part in the thing. To me, that was just the wonderful part of radio. I selected a cast. I wrote for it. I directed it. The final show was my conception of what the show should be. With television, you had a director in there who says, "I'm a person, too, and I've got some thinking about this thing." It's almost impossible to get exactly what you want, because somebody else wants something. This is the way I got out of television. After the first four or five years, I said, "First, I ought to be 20 instead of 49 or 50, and second, it isn't my work any longer." I was jealous of my work and I wanted to have it done my way. That was a little bit "dog in the manger," I guess, but, nevertheless if it was my work, I wanted it.

Getting back to radio for a while, did you write each and every episode totally?

I did, for the first 18 years.

Everything?

Everything. About the time I was getting ready to go east, Harlan Ware, who had written a number of very successful novels and had done some radio work in the East – in Chicago, I believe it was – came out to the Coast and was doing motion pictures. I got him started. He would do little excerpts on various characters until he felt that he had what I had been giving the public. Then he would write maybe a third of an episode. So when I went back east, he was thoroughly familiar with the show. This was five-a-week and that meant twice and a half more scripts than a half-hour once a week, so I put Mike Raffetto, who played Paul, and Harlan on the radio show while I was writing the TV show in New York. I'd fly back and forth every so often to be sure that everybody, everything was harmonious. I was ready to give up television. Then we brought the television show to the Coast and I had an entirely new set, because we were going to do it in a different format. They wanted it five times a week, for TV in the daytime.

Did it play five days a week in the daytime?

Yes, for about two-and-a-half years.

I don't remember the daytime One Man's Family *on television. I remember the prime show once a week. Their thinking was that it was a soap opera, wasn't it? It was never a soap opera.*

It never was. Just because a thing is 15 minutes, five times a week doesn't mean it's a soap opera. It was just that the critics, the people who talked about it in the papers and so forth, without even knowing what they were talking about, were calling it a soap opera.

Just because it was a more or less serious family show, as opposed to a situation comedy, they assumed it was a soap opera. But a soap opera sometimes doesn't have any relationship at all to real-life situations. Yet, One Man's Family *was absolutely cut from the cloth of real life.*

Well, thank you. I'm not the only one to say that, because that's what I felt all along. As a matter of fact, I was absolutely horrified by the fact that people couldn't distinguish between a dramatic family show and soap operas.

Now, you were 31 when you started this, and yet you were able to create an entire family from the mature father of the family, down to the younger children, and as you went along, the grandchildren and all that. Did you draw on any of your own life experiences?

It's basically what I absorbed from family life as a child myself. Actually, I felt that Paul, who was the idealistic one and very liberal, and Father Barbour, who was very conservative, represented two sides of my nature. I am very conservative and yet I am outraged by so many of the things that the conservative people do. So there was always a conflict in my soul. I was never able to have a business; I had no business instinct at all. As a matter of fact, when I was at the University of California, one summer I wanted to make a little money, so I got tied up with one of these book deals, you know, dictionaries and general information. My territory was to be up in southern Oregon, where I was raised as a boy. I knew a lot of people in that area and I knew the country. The only person I ever sold was a man who had once worked for my father on the ranch. When he lost his job on the ranch he had gone as a workman on the railroad fixing the tracks. Well, these books sold for about $50 or $60. I don't imagine he made more than that a month in those days. I sold this to him and got a $5 deposit. It just worried me to death, so the next day I went back and I said, "May I see your contract?" He showed it to me and I tore it up and handed him his $5 back and said, "You don't want this book." That can tell you my career as a businessman.

That reminds me of one of the members of the Barbour family.

Oh, that was Pinky, wasn't it? That was the grandson.

Pinky left school and he was all in love with this young lady and finally went up to the lumber camp to work! Those were very fine programs and they were so real. As we listen to them, even today, 25 years later, the philosophy and the feelings, the morality of it all, is still very valuable. It means a lot today, as it did then. Yet you were writing on a very contemporary scene. You seldom had a flashback. I don't remember any flashbacks.

No. The only flashbacks would come when one of the children was ill or in trouble or something. [Father Barbour] used to take them on his knee and tell them stories of his childhood. But, no real flashbacks at all.

Had Father Barbour been retired from his brokerage firm at the time of the inception of the show?

In the beginning? No, oh no. In fact, it was because he had hoped that Paul and Clifford would come into the brokerage house. Neither would. Clifford wasn't capable and Paul would have nothing to do with it. He thought our entrance into the First World War was not for the best reasons. He would have nothing to do with the business. So when Father Barbour got up into his middle-60s, I guess, he sold the business out and retired.

How did you manage to find and keep actors in a series for 18 years or longer? It's amazing that J. Anthony Smythe, who was Father Barbour, stayed with the show and didn't do much else.

Yes. Most of them did the same thing. Well, I paid them about twice as much as the ordinary actor was getting that day. We were in this together. I didn't feel that I was a boss, and I didn't boss anybody. I listened when anybody had anything to say. What the heck, it was an easy thing! The money was very good until we got up into the Second World War. Then it was nothing tremendous. A typical example: When Page Gilman [who played Jack Barbour] was drafted and went to Korea, we paid him all the time he was in the army.

You did? One Man's Family *really was your family, wasn't it? The family of actors and actresses putting the show together.*

Yes, that's right.

From time to time there would be a tragedy in the Family. *Someone would die or they would leave the* Family *situation. I'm sure there is no hard and fast rule on this, but in some cases was it prompted by an actor's decision to leave the situation?*

Yes. For instance, the original Claudia, Kathleen Wilson, married a publisher in New York. So we replaced her eventually. Mother Barbour [Minetta Ellen] was such a dominating part of the show. She must have been about 80 when she had to retire because she just couldn't get down to the studio sometimes and I replaced her. Clifford [Barton Yarborough], when he died, we didn't replace him. We sent him out to someplace else. In most cases, I didn't want to replace. For instance, Walter Paterson, who played Nicky, Claudia's husband, committed suicide. We didn't make anything of it, but it was Saturday night that he did it and the show was on Sunday. He was heavy in the script, so I had about three hours to rewrite. It wasn't possible to get somebody to do it so fast. I sent him to the Second World War, because he was an Englishman and I sent him back to join his old troops in England. I just wrote him out until three years later I brought both Claudia and Nicky back. We had very good people playing those parts [and] so it went off fine.

Did you ever create a character within or outside the Family *that you decided you didn't like any more?*

I learned this very quickly when I was doing my first mystery stories, adventure stories, up here in San Francisco. I would cast one and if one of the players was really bad or didn't sell a part, he would be the first one to go. When we started killing members off, we got rid of them awfully fast!

Note: *Mr. Morse and I took a break in our conversation to visit our wives, who* *were chatting in the Morse family living room. After a short while, we returned to Mr. Morse's den, its bookshelves filled with bound copies of* **One Man's Family** *and* **I Love A Mystery** *scripts and memorabilia. As our conversation was about to continue, he picked up a scrapbook filled with newspaper clippings and began reading:*

"On December 9, 1939, Harold Leopold, 31, switched on his radio in Colorado Canyon City, State Prison, Death Row and heard the final chapter of 'Hollywood Charity', the current *I Love A Mystery* serial. Two-and-a-half hours later, according to the *Denver Post* story, he was led to the gas chamber, saying, 'It was great. I got the final solution to the story just in time. *I Love A Mystery* is my favorite radio program.' Leopold died for the murder of a Denver restaurant proprietor."

People really turned on to your radio efforts.

They really did. I'm awfully glad that I got in first on these things, because it's terrible competition these days. I'm just as glad to be out of it.

You had done so much with One Man's Family, *when did you turn to writing the adventure and the mystery of* I Love A Mystery?

Well, in 1939, we had been on seven years with the *Family*. I suddenly began to feel that this was too much. I needed something besides the *Family*. It wasn't that I wanted to give the *Family* up, but I wanted to be free for a few hours with something else. An advertising agency suggested that they would like to see what I could do in the way of a mystery. They said, "Write two or three shows which you'd like to do and give us an outline." So I chose three characters: Jack, Doc and Reggie. I gave several titles; among them was *I Love A Mystery,* which the agency selected. They didn't even read the scripts. They just said, "Okay, we've set up a date with NBC. It will be five times a week."

Just on the basis of the titles you submitted and your credentials as a writer?

Well, of course, I'd been writing for them, for Standard Brands, for five or six years.

Were you employed by NBC or by the agency up to that point?

Up to that point and for quite a long time afterwards, I was on the NBC staff. Through sponsorship I began to make so much more money than as a staff writer that I was released from the staff and depended on sponsors for money after that.

It's traditional in radio that sponsors have more money than radio stations!

That's right.

They bought I Love A Mystery *and put you on right off the bat!*

I think *I Love A Mystery* was a wonderful title for a show. It would almost sell a show itself, and it did in this case.

My original thinking was there would be no drinking [and] they wouldn't carry guns. I had thought that they would solve situations for either individuals or a city, and that they would have no headquarters. They would go where the trouble was. But, I kind of got away from that as I got into it. You had to have more of a basis around which activity [could take place]. So, they finally settled down to the A-1 Detective Agency [but] they did travel a lot. What I tried to do was to give a variety of color, of places and situations. That may sound funny for radio.

Not at all.

Believe me, the listener's imagination is much more wonderful than any picture you can put on television. I was glad to get out of television, because faces get awful tiresome. The same background gets awful tiresome. But if you can imagine the thing, a face never gets tiresome. We proved that with the *Family* 27 years. If anybody could stand any show for 27 years, that was what was in themselves, not what I gave them, but they developed it in themselves.

You and the listener were participants together in One Man's Family *and in* I Love A Mystery *as well. Equal participation was very important.*

That's right. Several times I've had a request and gone down to local schools down here and played some old *I Love A Mystery* shows for them. Most of them didn't know anything about radio because there was nothing on to attract their attention, really. When they go in and turn on the television set [they] see everything. I would always start out by saying, "Now, you've got two wonderful ears. You can hear things and you've got a wonderful imagination up here. So I suggest, while you're listening to this, close your eyes. Just let your ears and your imagination take over and see if you don't get a very interesting picture. In most cases, I got an immediate response. People who weren't used to radio got all excited and interested in the thing. I think television is the worst thing that's happened to this country as far as children are concerned. This was good, this idea of making yourself work with the show. It gave you a feeling of being a part of it.

That's why radio could still be very big.

Sure. It's simply that the networks don't want radio to take away any of the [audience]; and they could do it so much cheaper, you know.

Let's get back to the great days of radio and I Love A Mystery. *You selected, as your three members of the A-1 Detective Agency, Jack, Doc and Reggie, people who had been very familiar to you because I think each one of them had roles at that time on* One Man's Family.

Yes. Mike Raffetto, Barton Yarborough, and Walter Paterson. Perhaps, on my part, I was being a little bit lazy instead of going out and getting new [actors]. But, what the heck, if you've got the best voices, why not use them?

They were people you worked with, so you had an immediate rapport.

Not only that, but financially, it was added to the hold that I had [on them].

We were talking about One Man's Family *before and we didn't even talk about the books and chapters that you had set up. Were you writing Chapter One, Book One right from the top?*

Yes. I had the feeling, in reading a book, if you'd had a book this long and it wasn't broken up, it was good reading but it would be an awful long time before you got to the end. But if you had, say, 13 episodes to a book, and the book came to a sort of climax, at least enough of a climax so that you felt the story had been told. It's like building a house: so many windows here and so many doors there, and that all makes sense. When the house is complete, there are 13 windows.

That, of course, is one of the things that really set One Man's Family *apart from the soap operas, because the soaps never ended. They just went on and on. The listener was not aware of how many chapters there were going to be in your book, because it varied from book to book, but at least by saying "Chapter One of Book 27" it implied that this story that we're hearing now was going to come to a conclusion.*

That's right. And also, it gave background to things that had gone on, whether you'd heard it or not, things that had gone on with these people before.

That was very unique. I don't think anyone ever used that chapter-and-book situation in any other radio or television show or motion picture. But I Love A Mystery *had "The Temple of the Vampires" and "The Thing That Cries in the Night" among so many others. This was really exciting radio. That came on late at night, didn't it?*

Well, I don't know. Did you hear the original Hollywood version?

I'm more familiar with the later version from New York.

Well, I don't know what the timing was on that, because I was back and forth from New York and doing television. So I didn't follow that as closely.

The first series, from '39 to '44, was on at one time or another on NBC and CBS.

Our second time was with Mutual.

What about that? Now, here you had a successful series, I Love A Mystery. *It ran for four or five years from '39 to '44. Then it was off the air for maybe three or four years. It came back again. Basically the same stories.*

Yeah. They all were the same stories.

Why did you do it again? Why did you do it a second time?

Money.

That's a good answer! Did they come to you and say, "We'd like you to do this again"?

Yes. They said, "We'll give you a thousand a week and pay the cast for a rerun." It was very good for them.

Apparently, some things had to be updated.

What I did was, on NBC, for a while, we did half-hour shows, quite a few of them. I broke all those down into 15 minutes, so everything was 15 minutes for them.

For Mutual, the second time?

Yes.

Tony Randall was in that, and Russell Thorson, who was part of the One Man's Family *scene, and Jim Boles. Was Jim in the* One Man's Family *cast?*

He was in the television [cast] back in New York.

You used Mercedes McCambridge a lot then.

Oh, very much, yes, both out here in Hollywood and in New York.

She was always the weeper, the screamer, the terrorized young lady.

She was an amazing girl. She was one of the most diversified actresses. She didn't sound always like Mercedes McCambridge, believe me.

The Carlton E. Morse style of writing mystery shows is legendary in the history of radio, especially as it relates to your use of descriptive material in the script for the actors. You used to write all kinds of special information, I guess, for the actor to read in order to help him deliver his lines. What kind of a setting was that?

You had to know where the actor was so that his action fitted into his background. He had to carry the scenery load along with his characterization. It had to be in the form of his character that he was doing this. For instance, I think of a wonderful scene in the "The Fear That Crept Like a Cat." They were on a small boat and it was wrecked up in Puget Sound. Here they were in the Sound trying to keep afloat. I let Doc [tell] his comedy about swimming around in the nude. He got onto the story about when he and his little girl cousin, Winnie Mae, used to go swimming in the hog pond in Texas, and wear gunny sack bathing suits. Pure comedy, and yet he set all the water scene that was necessary. It was so well on the public's mind that he carried on the conversation about getting out and who had run him down without having to keep referring to [his] swimming.

It's amazing. I think the director and the writer merged together. You'd done all the directing and in your writing, you're giving direction telling how to see that.

Another fine one was "The Temple of Vampires." The priests in the temple swung across two or three hundred feet from ledge to ledge. Doc was on one ledge on one side of the temple on a rope, and Jack was on another rope on the other ledge. Without knowing that the other was coming, they swung together and the rope twisted up. Here they were, 50 feet from the ground, 75 feet to where the ropes were tied. They were just hanging there. They had to climb up these ropes. Puffing and so forth, to the point where Barton Yarborough almost fainted. It was at a rehearsal and we had to stop and let him get his breath.

Something like that could never have been done on television. That's the beauty of the imagination being involved. Here, the actors obviously got caught up in this thing. I'm sure the actors looked at anything that they did for you as much more than just a job. Like the Family, *these people really took on the characters.*

Those old days, you had time not only to be thoroughly rehearsed, but you had time to be sociable. It was kind of fun to come down to the studio. It was like going to the club and playing golf or someplace else. These are things that very few people in their business life can do. The making of good money and a happy relationship is out of this world. You can't buy that.

You made some good friends with the radio audience over the years. They really enjoyed your material. You did other things besides One Man's Family *and* I Love A Mystery. *You had a series with Barry Fitzgerald for a while.*

Yes, *His Honor, the Barber.* That, unfortunately, only lasted about nine months, because the Irish were – I don't know to this day what he was or where he was with the situation in Ireland – but I know that in Boston the Irish came down and threw rocks at the radio station.

Really?

It scared the hell out of the sponsor!

You wrote a series for Mercedes McCambridge, didn't you?

Yes, called *Family Skeleton.*

What was that about? Was it a mystery?

It was in a hometown setting in the Northwest someplace. It was kind of a spy story. There was a big airplane factory near the place. Supposedly the Russians were either trying to get information or blew up the factory or something like that! Mercedes was a small-town teacher. Her father had been a district attorney at one time. He was kind of a person of importance. A stranger came into town and [the teacher] fell in love with him. Suddenly, he had to get out of town and, knowing the background of this thing, was he a spy or was he something else? He took her along, eloped with her, and that was the beginning of her trouble. They went to an airplane, finally, and he was taken aboard and went off toward Russia. So you didn't know whether he had just used her as an instrument for getting out. It was a long, involved story.

Most of the things you did were long and involved, but they were done in such a way that the listener could clearly catch on. You did I Love Adventure, *too, didn't you?*

Yes. I also did a syndicated series called *Adventures by Morse.* That was 52 half-hour shows.

That was a story about Captain Friday.

Yes. Then *I Love Adventure.* I did 13 of them for ABC, using Jack, Doc and Reggie, after the *I Love A Mystery* show.

After the second round of it.

Yes.

Did you have another version of a kind of a family story that was set on the North Shore in Chicago, up in the Wilmette, Winnetka area? Woman in My House.

Yeah, that was pure tragedy as far as I was concerned. I think that was while I was still doing the television shows. An agency came to me and said, "Couldn't we do *One Man's Family* from the beginning with different names and a different locale? And I said, "Why not?" I said, "It's going to mean that I'm going to have to get another writer and director to help me." Between the writer and director, and I was so busy in New York, they didn't follow the *One Man's Family* story, although the show went on for seven years.

Woman in My House *went on for seven years?*

Yeah, and paid good money, and I just hated every – I couldn't bear to listen to it.

I have never heard one of those shows.

Well, you've missed nothing!

People who didn't grow up with One Man's Family *or with* I Love A Mystery *missed something good. I want to thank you for all the good, imaginative radio you've provided millions of listeners.*

Well, thank you very much.

Carlton E. Morse was born June 4, 1901 and was 74 at the time of our conversation. He died May 24, 1993 at the age of 91.

Russell
Thorson
and
Jim
Boles

*Russell Thorson and Jim Boles
each worked extensively in radio
and co-starred on the* I Love A
Mystery *series. We got together on August 9, 1976 at Jim Boles' home in
Sherman Oaks, California. I noted that Carlton E. Morse had chosen Jim to
play the character of Doc Long on the popular series.*

 JIM: Yes, in the late Forties.

Were you very much involved in radio at that time?

JIM: Yes, I was quite involved in radio. I was getting acquainted with television.

Were you working with Carlton E. Morse on the One Man's Family *radio show at
that time?*

JIM: No, *One Man's Family* radio show was never done from New York. It was
always out here. He went back there and put *I Love A Mystery* on radio and then
One Man's Family on television from New York.

And you were on both of the shows, then?

JIM: Yes, Russ and I both were.

Russ, you were Jack Packard in the I Love A Mystery *series and, on the television
version of* One Man's Family –

RUSS: – I played Paul Barbour.

You were also Paul on the radio version, but not simultaneously.

RUSS: No. Well, in a way, yes, because after about three-and-a-half or four years in New York, we came back to Hollywood and I went into the radio version of *One Man's Family*. I was back here about six months and Carlton called me and said we're going to do *One Man's Family* as a television show, a daytime regular soap opera thing. We did that. I played Paul on that. We did that for about 75 weeks and it was a killing job, because we had to be at rehearsal, I think, at 5:00 in the morning, in New York. [It was] broadcast on the air here at 9:30, I think.

The One Man's Family *program was a daytime television series?*

RUSS: Yeah, yeah, on NBC. Originally it was a prime time radio show, out here for years.

Russ, where did your show business career begin?

RUSS: Well, I started out like so many kids do, in high school and college. I took a year off from college to go to a stock company down in Texas. That lasted for about a year and I came back and finished college [at] University of Montana. I went back to the University of Iowa for a master's degree. It was the height of the Depression and I couldn't get a job anywhere, so I came back to Montana. A friend of mine called me from Ogden, Utah, and said, " I think there's a spot here on the radio station for you." I'd done some radio work before, so I went down to Ogden, got a job there and then started working in a little theater.

I saved up a little money and in 1937 I said, "I've had it. I'm going to try New York." So I did and I was very lucky to run into an old college friend of mine from Iowa, Don MacLaughlin. Don and I were great friends in college at the University of Iowa – worked a lot together – and Don had a chance to come out to San Francisco to do a show for General Foods. It was a transcribed half-hour deal with Jay Jostyn as the star.

JIM: Oh, yes, knew him well.

RUSS: And so Don said why don't we try to put you in this thing in my place, which he did. And this kept on for a while and I picked up a few jobs. Then came the *Tom Mix* thing and I went to Chicago.

Because the Tom Mix *show originated from Chicago. How'd you get the job as Tom Mix? You were Tom Mix!*

RUSS: You won't believe this. My wife wanted to get into radio. There was a station that had a soap opera thing called *Daughter-in-Law* directed by Tony Leader. My wife wanted me to work with her, so I did. I wasn't working this one particular day. Guy by the name of Clarence Menser – he's from Montana – he's coming to New York to audition for a new character, Tom Mix. I heard this from somebody over at CBS, Marge Morrow, casting director. I'll call her. So at NBC, they're auditioning. Three o'clock this afternoon. So I went up, walked in one of the big audience studios. It's jammed. Two hundred people in there. Finally got through about 7:00 that night. We each had a few little speeches to read. He said, "I want to see eight of you tomorrow." I was one of the eight. So the eight of us went the next day and auditioned. He said, "I want four of you back here tomorrow to make a recording." So I came back with the three other guys. Mr. Menser said, "Good-bye, you'll hear from us." That was the last I heard of it for about three weeks.

I was working on a show called *My True Story*, up at NBC, and we had to do two shows, two broadcasts. It was between shows and I was sitting out in the lobby talking to some of the other guys out there and a page boy called me over to the desk. I had told my wife I was going to bring home a pint of gin so we could have a drink after the show. I said hello and she said, "Russ, make that a quart of Scotch! You're going to Chicago to do *Tom Mix*." So I was off to Chicago.

And I always thought Tom Mix was a teetotaler! Ralston Purina, you know.

RUSS: When the Ralston people – and they were wonderful people – came up to Chicago they always threw a nice dinner party for members of the cast.

How long did you do Tom Mix?

RUSS: Until it was cancelled. I think it was in 1942, I believe. I'm not certain about that.

It was cancelled?

RUSS: Yeah, when the war came along, you know. Practically everything in Chicago went. *Tom Mix* [later] went to the Mutual Network.

JIM: Did it go to Detroit?

RUSS: No, it stayed right in Chicago. Curley Bradley, one of the Ranch Boys who sang and also played a part on the thing, came out here, too. And then, suddenly, he disappeared and I found out that he was doing *Tom Mix* [in Chicago] when it came back on the air [in 1944].

I wonder why they wouldn't have called you back?

RUSS: Oh, I wouldn't have gone back. I was too old.

It started again back in Chicago, at WGN Mutual. So in the original series, you did the Tom Mix *shows live, five days a week. Were there repeats?*

RUSS: Yeah, you'd have to do repeats. They didn't have the taping facilities they have now, so we did *Mix* at 4:45 and 5:45. I did *Kitty Keene* at 12:30 and another one at 1:30 and was on at 8:30 and 9:30 in the morning, so I had six shows a day there, five days a week.

You were kept pretty busy.

RUSS: And there was a Saturday night show, I think it was called *Public Hero Number 1.* John Hodiak, who later made quite a name for himself in pictures, was the star of that thing.

Russ, you were one of the busiest guys in Chicago at that time. Jim, where did it all begin for you, show business-wise?

JIM: Well, I was living out here in California. I did a play in junior high school and got the bug. And then, before I went to college, I did a little radio. I went to college and there was something at the Pasadena Playhouse and before I was out of college I was doing radio, for not very much money. And then I worked a year in radio out here after I finished college. I went to UCLA and Los Angeles City College, and after a year of doing stage plays and radio, I decided to go to New York. So I went through the struggles that all young actors do. I did a play with Ingrid Bergman. I did *Anna Christie* by Eugene O'Neill and other plays in and around New York. I got a start in radio doing the various soaps, and *March of Time.* That was an interesting show, because you'd play all the famous characters, on radio.

How did a stage actor in New York get a job on radio? Was it that easy to walk into a radio station and try to get a job?

JIM: Well, I was a stage and radio actor from the beginning.

RUSS: Excuse me, Jim. I think you probably will agree with me. In those days, it was run entirely by the advertising agencies. You went to the agency for jobs, to the advertising agency.

Most of the agencies produced the programs for the clients.

RUSS: Yes, for the clients.

JIM: And I'd do movies from time to time, such as you did in New York.

What was the first big radio job of yours, Jim?

JIM: I suppose it was a Saturday show, where I played Walter Huston's grandson. I was quite young at the time and it was just quite a pleasure. I used to do

Calling All Cars and other shows out here. I'm thinking back to the beginning. After working in radio a year out here, I decided to go to New York. And I did all those darn shows.

You were in everything, weren't you?

JIM: Well, I was. I wish I had a list here.

You were in a program called Land of the Lost. *Did that come from here or New York?*

JIM: That came from there. That was a cute show. My wife and I both did that show. It was set underwater and that was a fun show, it was one of those Saturday morning things. It was quite fun and took a lot of imagination and a lot of voice sensitivity.

Did you do many varied voices in your career?

JIM: Yes, I did, I did in my earlier years, and I did many dialects. I am a Southerner, I come from Texas, and I did all of those. I did New England [voices] for years. I was on *The Fred Allen Show* for a year. We were with Parker Fennelly and a lot of it rubbed off, you know. And I enjoyed doing it, and I used to do lots of British and German.

When your careers met, was it for the first time with the I Love A Mystery *series?*

RUSS: Yes.

JIM: Yes, that was the first time.

Actually, that was the second time around for I Love A Mystery*, wasn't it?*

RUSS: That's right.

JIM: That's right. Carlton just updated his scripts. As a matter of fact, my wife and I did quite a bit of writing to update them. [We] had to change a lot of the dialogue to bring [it] into the present.

Jack, Doc and Reggie of the A-1 Detective Agency solving the mystery of "The Thing That Cries in the Night."

RUSS: Ah, yes!

JIM: I remember that one!

Mercedes McCambridge was on most of those shows, too, wasn't she?

JIM: She was on for a long time. Then she won an Academy Award and came to Hollywood and my wife, Athena Lord, sort of took over what she had done before.

Tony Randall played Reggie. Jack – that was you, Russ – was the brains of the outfit. He knew what to do and how to do it. Doc – that was you, Jim – would ask for the explanation of how this happened and then Jack would tell you and you'd say, something like, "honest to Grandma," and Reggie would say, "I say," and that was mostly what he did.

JIM: I think Reggie was the muscle man of the group. When someone was too big for Jack or Doc, they'd have Reggie take care of him.

Would you consider your time in that particular series just a job or did you think you were doing something special?

JIM: It was fun time, it was fun time.

RUSS: We had great fun on that show. *One Man's Family,* any television show, is work, hard work, and live television in those days didn't have cue cards or idiot sheets for you. You knew your lines or you forgot 'em, and that's all.

Or you were in big trouble. You worked, Russ, with One Man's Family *on radio and you were the eldest son of the Barbour family. How long did you do that?*

RUSS: Well, let's see. On television, I was not Paul Barbour when we went to New York. I'd been doing a character called Lusk, a German who helped Claudia get out of a concentration camp. It's kind of a strange story. I had gone back to Wisconsin to see my mother, who had been quite ill, and I came back on the train. My wife met me at the station and she said that Carlton Morse wanted me to call him immediately. I said, "Fine, I'll call him Saturday morning." I knew Carlton was up at about 5:30 every morning, to write. About 9:00 I called him and he said, "You have a nice trip?" I said yes. He said, "Well, don't unpack your bag." I said, "What do you mean, 'don't unpack my bag'?" He said, "You're going back to New York next Thursday." I said, "What?" He said, "Well, Mike Raffetto doesn't want to go and so," he said, "you're going to do Paul." That's the first I knew I was going to play Paul on *One Man's Family.* So we rented the house out, boarded the train, and went.

And how long did that last then?

RUSS: Well, we were supposed to go for 13 weeks, and we all went from here, from Hollywood. We went back and we rehearsed for about a week and then we video taped some of the episodes and showed them to the NBC executives and they said, "Oh, no, no way. You've got to start from the beginning." So Carlton called me and said, "The whole thing is off except for you. I'm sending everybody else back to Hollywood, but they want you to stay to continue doing Paul." So we started holding auditions: Bert Lytell, Marjorie Gateson, Lillian Shaff and Jim and Tony Randall as we started right from the beginning, the start of the original *One Man's Family* on radio in San Francisco, and that's the way it worked.

So the television series just started all over and it lasted for a good long time on television.

RUSS: Four years, I think.

JIM: Four years, yeah.

RUSS: And the *I Love A Mystery* thing was a complete shocker to me, because we used to rehearse, in the early days at NBC, *One Man's Family* in the morning. Carlton and I would usually go down to the restaurant, called the DownUnder, in the basement of the building, and have lunch. We were having lunch one day and he was paged to the telephone. He came back about five minutes later and said, "You want another job?" and I said, "What kind of job is this?" He said, "How would you like to do Jack Packard on *I Love A Mystery*?" He had set the deal on the telephone at lunch time. Then they started casting for *I Love A Mystery.*

Jim, how'd you get that role? Do you recall?

JIM: Yes. I think [someone] recommended me, I went for a quick reading and went home. I said I should be doing that role because for years people had told me I sounded like Barton Yarborough. I'd never met him and so I called and said I want to read again. Carlton said, "All right." And so I went over again and he said, "Do it!" And so that's how I got Doc.

RUSS: We had a great cast on that show, didn't we?

JIM: Oh, we had a marvelous cast!

RUSS: Luis Van Rooten and Bob Dryden did most of the character stuff. They could do voices, all kinds of voices, couldn't they?

JIM: Terrific, yeah.

You did it out of Mutual's New York studios?

JIM: Yes, out of Mutual.

Was that done on disc or tape?

JIM: No, I don't think it was tape then.

RUSS: I think it was probably disc.

JIM: It was probably disc, but it was done live, though.

RUSS: Yes, but they recorded it for distribution to other stations.

From that particular point, Jim, where did you go?

JIM: Well, after I was on *I Love A Mystery* a while, Carlton said, "Would you like to be on *One Man's Family*?" And I said, "Sure." So he wrote me a character that lasted a while, kind of a heavy, and then he wrote me something in the vein of Doc Long, a Marine sergeant who was courting Eva Marie Saint with a Texas accent. He named the character after Barton Yarborough, who had played Doc originally. I was Marine Sergeant Joe Yarborough for a long time. Tony Randall was a sailor and I was a Marine and we were both courting Eva Marie Saint, who was already married to somebody else!

Both of your careers were tied to Carlton E. Morse. What kind of man was he to work for? Was he a hard taskmaster or was he easy-going?

RUSS: He was the nicest person. Example: when we went back to New York, and my wife will swear to this, we were sitting in our bedroom on the train – which was the [Super] Chief back then – she suddenly turned to me and said, "What kind of salary are you getting for this job?" And I didn't know. We had never talked money. I didn't know till the first paycheck came in what Carlton was paying me. And I was amazed that I got as much money as I did, frankly.

Carlton and I had become very, very close friends during the years. I'd never had a contract with him – well, I did on *I Love A Mystery* – I never talked money. He was a wonderful man to work with. He had some very interesting methods working with actors. Some directors, they'll go at you, and at you, and at you to give a particular reading they want on a line. Carlton will do it three times and then quit. It was his theory, his belief, firm belief, if you couldn't do it right after the third time he directed you with it, you were never going to get it, so he'd just let it go. He was a very warm man.

JIM: Oh, yeah, very nice to work for. I never heard him say an unkind word about a single person on any of his shows. Extremely loyal to us all.

He had a good group of people, and he used them in all of his many enterprises.

RUSS: Oh, my, yes.

JIM: And he cast good people, and so well. I guess you don't have to direct 'em so much if you do.

I asked him, once, how he had so many top-notch people working for him for such a long time and he said, "I paid 'em well."

RUSS: And he treated them well.

JIM: I remember when we were talking contract when I first did the show and I was doing something on another show, you know, a running thing. I said, "Well, Carlton, couldn't you pay a little more than that?" And he said, "Well, if I paid it to you, I'd have to pay it to Russ and pay it to Tony." And he said, "All right!" I don't think Russ or Tony ever knew I got 'em a raise!

RUSS: I'm grateful to you, Jim!

Does Tony know that, I wonder?

JIM: I told Tony once.

After One Man's Family *and* I Love A Mystery, *the two of you went your separate ways, didn't you?*

JIM: Yeah, Russ came back to California and I stayed in New York.

RUSS: Until...

JIM: Thirteen years ago.

What were you occupied with, Jim, in all that time?

JIM: Well, radio was dying off and so I was doing mostly television and stage plays and movies from time to time.

You worked with Phil Silvers on the Bilko *series.*

JIM: Yes, yes, I did that. I didn't do it a lot; I did it on occasion.

Well, you were rather busy in television as a character actor.

JIM: Yes, I did Abraham Lincoln a number of times. I did Robert E. Lee. I did all kinds of characters.

And you got involved in motion pictures?

JIM: I did. It isn't too easy in New York, 'cause they don't do too much. I went down to Puerto Rico in 1950 and did *The Man With My Face*, which was an interesting character, and I did *The Pusher* in New York, and a few others, but I did most of my pictures after I came out here.

And some of those?

JIM: Oh, gosh.

He's looking at a magnificent wall in his home that has portrait after portrait, photo after photo of some of the great characterizations.

JIM: Go to Russ for a minute.

Russ, you came out shortly after the end of One Man's Family *and you were quite busy, too, in television, weren't you?*

RUSS: Well, yes, and in pictures. It's been good. When radio faded out I somehow managed to break into television. I had done two pictures here before I went back, so I knew a few people and I had the pleasure of working on one picture that got an Academy Award, *I Want to Live*. Susan Hayward got an Academy Award for that. Robert Wise directed it. Then I did a series with Robert Taylor called *The Detectives* for several years. It's just been one thing after another. My agent calls me and says do you want to do this, and I say yes or no, depending what it is.

Radio had, more or less, a rather short life.

RUSS: Well, it was a wonderful and exciting life to me. I thought a great deal of it. When I went to Chicago there was something like 41 dramatic radio shows coming out of Chicago. Forty-one a week! Separate shows and when we left there in 1942 to come out here, there were about five or six left. The bottom just fell out of it. And I miss it very much. I enjoyed the radio very much.

You were very much involved with radio to the very end.

RUSS: Right up to the end, yeah. I think I did the last network radio show, dramatic radio show, called *Johnny Dollar*. Bob Bailey, an ex-Chicagoan, played Johnny Dollar and I think that was the curtain.

The curtain may have fallen but the memories are still here. Lots of people really do remember the great radio shows.

RUSS: Oh, yes.

The most important part of it was the fact that it was the theatre of the imagination, because the listener could participate.

RUSS: He certainly could. I still hear *I Love A Mystery* once in a while on an FM station in Pasadena. I suppose it's pirating, but they play quite a few of the *I Love A Mystery* series with Jim and I and Tony.

JIM: Yes, I heard about it. In fact, those *I Love A Mystery* fans still call me.

RUSS: Oh, I get letters from guys in Chicago. There is a man back there who has a firm that manufactures or distributes or leases heavy industrial equipment – fork lifts and that sort of thing – and I can count on a three- or four-page letter from him every single year. He remembers incidents that I have completely forgotten.

There are lots of fans who recall those shows. Now I see that Jim has returned with a stack of memories in front of him.

JIM: I was blank before, so I went in and picked the magazine up that came out in April. There's an article on me and it lists pictures, pictures, pictures that I've done. It's ridiculous that I have to go find a book!

You have a copy of Films in Review, *April of '76.*

JIM: Yes, and it's a lovely article and they say lovely things about me, but I'll just read some titles: *The Tattooed Stranger* in 1951. *The Man With My Face*, 1957. *Naked in the Sun,* 1960. That's the one I did down in Florida. *The Pusher,* '62. *The Most Wanted Man in the World*, '64. That's one I did in French; I had to speak French. *Fate is the Hunter. He Rides Tall,* '65. *Fluffy,* was the one I did with Tony Randall. *The Greatest Story Ever Told*, which was an interesting story of the Bible. *John Goldfarb, Please Come Home. The Trouble With Angels.* I enjoyed that one with Rosalind Russell. *A Big Hand for the Little Lady.* That was a lovely picture, I thought. *The Ghost and Mr. Chicken. Reluctant Astronaut,* I did with Don Knotts. *Water Hole #3. The Karate Killer*, which was an adaptation of a TV thing where I played Joan Crawford's husband. *With Six You Get Egg Roll*, with Doris Day. *Shakiest Gun in the West, P. J., Angel in My Pocket. The Love God*, another Don Knotts. *WUSA* with Paul Newman. Did it down in Puerto Rico and they cut me out of it. *When the Line Goes Through*, I did in '71. That's when I played a man 130 years old. And *Skin Game.* I enjoyed that very much and my wife played a nice part in that. And *Le Mans. Dr. Death, Seeker of Souls.* That one I did, my wife did and my son and my daughter.

It shows how you have made a great transition and how many facets of your talent have been explored over the years, from the stage to radio to television, to film. I know Russ has a parallel career in many of those same areas, too.

RUSS: Pretty much the same, yeah. An awful lot of radio actors and stage actors had to make the transition into film and TV work. If you were going to stay in the business, you had to.

There are probably more radio actors who have been able to adapt to TV and the movies than there were motion picture actors able to adapt to radio.

RUSS: Well, I think it's because as a radio actor you had to be fairly versatile.

JIM: You had to be quick.

RUSS: You had to be quick. You had to run. You came in and picked up a script and you read it through for timing and then, *boom!* You had a dress rehearsal and then, *boom!* You did the show. There was no fooling around. You had your job to do and you did it.

JIM: Sometimes, in motion pictures, one day you have a few lines that you do, and you work on 'em and then they rehearse 'em and then, if something's wrong, you do them over. But in radio, you have pages to do and maybe you have one little rehearsal and, *bingo*, you've got to be on, so you have to be quick and alert.

You two fellows provided radio with some of the best that there was, and I'm happy to say thank you very much for giving us that pleasure.

RUSS: Well, you're very welcome. I've enjoyed it, haven't you, Jim?

JIM: I've enjoyed it very much.

Russell Thorson was born October 14, 1906 and was 69 at the time of our conversation. He died July 6, 1982 at the age of 75.

Jim Boles was born February 28, 1914 and was 62 at the time of our conversation. He died May 26, 1977 at the age of 63.

Tony
Randall

Tony Randall was an actor on radio before his career began on stage, screen and television. We met on September 16, 1970 at the Ambassador East Hotel when he was in Chicago to promote his new television series **The Odd Couple.** *I asked him if* **The Odd Couple** *was his first TV series since the* **Mr. Peepers** *show.*

 That's right. I played Wes on that and for two or three years after it went off the air, people would say, "Hi, Wes" on the street, you know, but then it perished. It faded and I never hear it anymore.

It was live television, wasn't it?

All the time, yes.

From 1952 to 1955. Did you ever do One Man's Family?

Yes, yes! Not on radio, but I was on the TV series. That was my first series. I was on that for about a year, a year-and-a-half. That was live, too, in the early days: 1949, 1950.

Was the TV series written by Carlton E. Morse?

He wrote some of it. They'd gone back to episode one in the radio series, all of which he had written, and he farmed out some of the writing [for the TV series].

Well, now, we've moved from the Odd Couple *to* Mr. Peepers *to* One Man's Family.

Yes, we're retrogressing.

We're going to bridge the sound gap and go back to the Golden Age of Radio, if you don't mind. Everyone who is a radio fan will remember you as Reggie York on I Love A Mystery. *You were in the reincarnation of that series.*

I was the second time around, yes. They put the entire series on, from the first to the last episode, twice.

The original series was on from 1939 to 1944, and then you came on in '49, right, till about '52?

I guess that's about right. I really don't remember the dates. But this was a Carlton E. Morse epic also. Jack, on this revival of the radio series, was Russ Thorson.

How did you get the role of Reggie York in the revival?

I think I auditioned for it. I don't remember any more about it than that.

Didn't you audition for the role of Doc?

I may have. That didn't matter. You come in and audition for every role. That happened frequently in auditions, and the director would probably have some idea in mind already of what he wanted. That's always true of auditions. Actors should never feel badly when they don't get a role, don't feel they've auditioned badly. The director already knows what he wants and he keeps auditioning people till someone comes in that coincides with this. Oh, I think "prejudice" is the best word.

So he has a preconceived notion of what he'd like and he hopes one of the actors auditioning will fit into the role.

Yes.

What else did you do on radio?

Oh, my. I made my living in radio as an actor on the soaps and on the nighttime shows. The nighttime paid well, you see. Soaps paid about $33, $34 for a 15-minute episode. If you did enough of them, you'd be making a good living. And some people did 40 or 50 a week. But the nightime shows paid $110, $115, $130 for a half-hour, and the hour shows paid considerably more.

Did you do most of this from New York?

All of it. I was never one of the Chicago radio actors.

And you hadn't done much radio in California.

I'd never been in California, except on visits. I was a New York actor, strictly. Although I had been a radio announcer for a year in Worcester, Massachusetts in '41and '42, I think it was.

You must have been very, very young at the time you were doing radio.

Yes. I was too young to be drafted, I remember that, 'cause the war was on then and you weren't drafted until you were 21.

Which programs were you on? What soap operas did you do?

Goodness, gracious! I did *When a Girl Marries, Portia Faces Life, Perry Mason* – that was a very popular soap – all of them! *Lorenzo Jones.* I was on [in] the small parts. [I'd] come in and out, sometimes run a week or two, sometimes longer. I was on *Light of the World.* Remember that one? One I was on, year-in and year-out, two or three times, once or twice a week, for years, was *My True Story.* That was a full, complete soap opera, a half-hour long, every day. Different story every day.

That was a tear-jerker, wasn't it?

Yes, every day a tear-jerker, and unbelievable writing. And that took place in studio 6B, I remember very well, at NBC, which is now where Johnny Carson broadcasts from. I remember I was on a number of things written by a woman named Irna Phillips.

She was based in Chicago and wrote a lot of soap operas.

Yes, yes, and everyone took her very seriously. If you were in an Irna Phillips script, that was supposed to be good. And if you changed a word of it, Miss Phillips was listening and didn't like that. And [the material] was really, really beneath contempt.

I've heard that you've said that you really didn't think much of the writing on radio.

Didn't think much of radio, no. All the old radio fans who hear me talk about it occasionally – I'm frequently asked about it and I have a good memory and remember it all – think that I'm a fan of it, and I despised it. I used to pray that I'd get out of it.

And you did.

And I did, yes.

You mentioned the nighttime programs that you did. I've checked a lot of reference books on radio and I can only attach you to I Love A Mystery.

Well, that was a contract job and I was on it for years. But the other things, you just came and did once. You were just an actor. I was on *Mr. District Attorney* many, many, many times, but if you look up *Mr. District Attorney* you only find Len Doyle as Harrington, Jay Jostyn as Mr. District Attorney, and Vicki Vola as Miss Miller. I did a pretty good imitation of Jay Jostyn. The announcer was Fred Uttal.

Let's hear your Jay Jostyn.

Well, I should tell your audience that it is very early in the morning here at the Ambassador East and I'm not in voice yet. Once when Chaliapin was asked to sing in the morning, he said, "Sing? In morning? I can't even spit!"
I remember the announcer saying, "Mr. District Attorney! Champion of the people, defender of truth, guardian of our fundamental rights to life, liberty, and the pursuit of happiness" and the music would come in. Peter Van Steeden's orchestra: dum dum da-dum, dum, dum da dum. Then, on an echo chamber, Jay Jostyn would say, "And it shall be my duty as District Attorney not only to prosecute all persons accused of crimes within this county, but to defend with equal vigor the rights and privileges of all its citizens."

Terrific! Can you remember the sponsor of that show?

Sure! Ipana, for the smile of health, and Sal Hepatica, for the smile of beauty. Vice-versa! And if you were on the show often enough, you'd get cases of the stuff sent to your home. And that was produced by a wonderful man, Ed Byron. He was a really good radio director. That show was fun to work.

What did you think of the scripts on Mr. District Attorney?

Well, they were melodrama and they were good. They were only cops-and-robbers melodrama, but for that they were good. But the soap operas pretended to delve into the human heart and all that crap, and that's all it was.

What's your opinion of the writing on I Love A Mystery?

Well, those were mystery yarns. They were only supposed to be cliff-hangers. They were very good for what they were, adventure stories. I remember "Temple of the Vampires" had a marvelous premise. I remember one episode that people still talk to me about. I thought Carlton E. Morse really used extraordinary imagination in that to build suspense. We were in a great temple, like Angkor

Wat, in the middle of the night and it was pitch-black and we were swinging by great ropes, back and forth, pendulum-style, and afraid of bumping into each other in the dark. Now, that's a good situation.

He was very precise about his sound effects, too, wasn't he?

Yes. He was a master of sound effects.

What other evening programs did you do?

FBI in Peace and War. L-A-V-A, Lava soap. So many I can't possibly remember.

Did you usually play a heavy?

Anything. It didn't matter. It didn't matter. You'd play anything, and you generally played two roles; you'd double. And your ability to double in radio had a lot to do with your ability to get jobs. This was abused and it eventually got to the point where only those who could double got jobs. See, the director and producers were saving money. Instead of having two actors, they'd have one, and eventually they'd have only three actors in the whole studio playing 20 roles.

It put a lot of people out of work.

Yes, and the quality was bad, because very few people can double really well. Luis Van Rooten was a great doubler. Everett Sloane was one of the great radio actors. Gary Merrill, Richard Widmark, they weren't good doublers; they always sounded exactly like themselves. I was a pretty fair doubler. So eventually, AFRA – now AFTRA – American Federation of Radio Artists, made a ruling that there could be no more than two actors doubling on any given show. They could only play two roles, instead of three actors playing five roles each, making a cast of 15. The quality of the shows immediately went up, although they were really doing it to protect, to give jobs to more actors.

There was an actor, Phil Kramer – he's still around – famous for having a [whiny, New York-type] voice and he could only be cast for roles like that. So a director said to him, "Can you double?" He said, "Double? Of course I can double. I can talk way up here or way down here..." So I asked him once if that story was true and he said, "No, that's a story they tell about me. I said, 'I can talk way up here or way down here.' " [But his voice didn't change at all.] Lovely Phil Kramer. Nice man.

Did you ever do any voices that caught on anywhere?

No, no, except my voice for Reggie, which I've forgotten. At that time Charlie McCarthy was still on the air and Ray Noble was the orchestra leader, the

Englishman who wrote "Goodnight, Sweetheart," and I sort of imitated Ray Noble, who had a slight Cockney in his voice. But the writing wasn't good British dialect. It was full of lines, words, that Carlton E. Morse thought were British, like "Righto" and "I say." Every line began with, "I say, Doc... suppose we climb up this old water tower and then have a look-see"....which, when I think back, was kind of a ridiculous style. Radio is full of lines describing what you were doing: "Here, let me open this door for you." "I'll turn on the light with this switch on the wall right here." *Click.* You know, so the audience would know what you're doing.

Well, you know, the Lone Ranger often talked to Silver: "Hi-yo Silver, away! We're going to head off the Cavendish gang at the ranch and then we're going to meet Tonto at the cave."

He'd recapitulate the story, yes. Of course, kid shows was another classification. I never really got into kid shows. *The Lone Ranger* was a kid show. *I Love A Mystery* was sort of a kid show. But the heyday of that took place in Chicago, although Chicago actors were a different group. When it moved to New York, many of them moved to New York, too. But there was one show that was good. Of all of radio, millions of radio shows, except for Fred Allen and Jack Benny, a few like that, there was one show that was genuinely good – good writing and good acting – and only one, and that was *Vic and Sade*. *Vic and Sade* was genuinely good and those scripts I would put up against the best American humor of James Thurber or Ring Lardner. And the acting was extraordinary. One of the actors is a pretty good friend of mine. He's at Paramount producing a show now and I see him every day, 'cause we're doing the *Odd Couple* and he's writing and producing *Love, American Style*. And that's Billy Idelson, who was Rush on *Vic and Sade.*

What about Easy Aces? *You remember that program?*

Easy Aces was very, very good, indeed. Very funny. It capitalized on the performances of Goodman Ace and his wife, Jane Ace. It was clever, very clever.

Another clever show out of Radio's Golden Age was The Henry Morgan Show.

Yes, I was on that! The original show, *Here's Morgan,* was something else again. Henry Morgan just talked for 15 minutes every day. He was the first to kid sponsors and be irreverent about anything. That was a big deal then. He then moved into the big time with a big nighttime, half-hour comedy show and that was my first job getting out of the Army. I auditioned for Henry Morgan and he used me and I'm eternally grateful to him. It broke the drought. I'd had quite a stretch when I got out of the Army before I found a job.

Did you do a number of different roles on that show?

Comedy parts, yeah, comedy sketches, all sorts of things.

What was your last radio job?

I have no idea. It petered out. As television came in, radio petered out and the first year or so of *Mr. Peepers,* I would get conflicts from the director to be able to make *My True Story* in the mornings and then those things died, they just were no more. And if they were, they'd lost their sponsors and so the pay was very small. It wasn't worthwhile to do them.

Today you are still a regular on the Opera Quiz *program.*

Oh yes, yes, that's right. I'm a regular on a radio show! That's true. I hadn't thought of it that way, but it's true, 'cause we do that live and in front of an audience. I sort of think of it as an appearance.

But you are regularly on the program.

I'm an irregular regular. I do it three, four, five times a season.

So from The Odd Couple *to* Mr. Peepers *to* One Man's Family, I Love A Mystery, My True Story, *to the* Opera Quiz, *you've come full cycle on the radio. Thank you very much for chatting with us this morning.*

It's a pleasure, Chuck.

We will be watching for The Odd Couple *every Thursday night beginning September 24th and we won't forget to remember Tony Randall as Reggie York on* I Love A Mystery, *too.*

It's better forgotten, but thanks, anyway.

Tony Randall was born February 26, 1920 and was 50 at the time of our conversation.

Mercedes McCambridge

Mercedes McCambridge starred in hundreds of radio dramas in a career that spanned broadcasting's golden days. We met on October 29, 1976, when she was in the Chicago area appearing at the Drury Lane Theatre in suburban Evergreen Park, Illinois. I commented that she was a local product, a Chicago gal.

 I was born in Joliet, but I grew up here and all of my schooling was here, through college. It was the first place I earned an honest dollar and it's home.

You went to Mundelein College.

Yes, indeed. I was on scholarship for drama and when I was a sophomore I was in a play and some people from NBC saw it and came backstage. As a result of that I signed a five-year contract with NBC and that was the beginning.

Were you a staff actress?

I was an NBC actress. They had contract actresses and actors in those days. Chicago was the hub of all of radio drama and soap opera. And the great comedies all came out of here, too. *Amos 'n' Andy, Fibber McGee and Molly* and a great many others. *Vic and Sade* was my favorite. But all of the soap operas and *Lights Out, First Nighter*... so many were here.

Can you recall your first radio job? Your first role on a show?

I can't really. Some people say it was a poetry reading on *The Chicago Symphonic Hour* with the Mundelein First Speaking Choir, which was signed to a year's contract with NBC. And other people tell me it was on a show called

Pretty Kitty Kelly. I think it was on *Guiding Light,* but I don't know. Those were the dim, dark ages, you know!

You were on Abie's Irish Rose.

Oh, yes, but that was out of New York, that was later. I played Rosemary on that. That was in New York, after my contract here had expired. So that was when I was an old-timer, five years later. I signed a contract when I was 17, a sophomore in school, so I had to continue school until I graduated, and then that left about two years on the contract and then I went in to conquer New York. Everybody thinks that New York is conquerable, but it proves to be a very formidable foe or friend, depending.

You terrorized a great many radio listeners over the years in your career as a lady who would scream at the drop of a hat or whimper or frighten the listener. Why did it seem that you always got involved in that kind of radio role?

I didn't. That's a gross misrepresentation! I was *Big Sister*, too.

Ruth Wayne?

You're darn right! I played all of the good girls, too. But people don't remember the good things. It's interesting for me now when, in almost every city, somebody will come up to me and say, "Oh, I remember *I Love A Mystery.* And the show that they remember most on *I Love A Mystery* was the sequence we did about bats in South America in a gigantic cave. And these people in places like Atlanta, St. Louis and Denver will stand on a street corner and they will depict the bats. Their arms will go up and they'll get a wild look in their eyes and they will tell me all about those giant bats in the cave. I don't have the heart to say, "Listen, it was four actors standing around a microphone on Sunset Boulevard!" That's all it was, but these are the things people remember.

That was "Temple of Vampires" and that was –

– You see, you remember it, too! Carlton Morse was one of my mentors. I've really been extremely fortunate with Orson Welles and Carlton Morse and Arch Oboler and Hi Brown, who did *Inner Sanctum* and did indeed do *Big Sister.* Radio is still the best of all. Of all branches [of show business] radio is the best. It's the most imaginative and the most participatory. It's the most involving and I prefer it to all the others.

As an actress who has worked on the stage and on the screen and in radio, you have to act visibly before the camera or before the audience in the theater, but when you're on radio, for the most part you've probably worked without an audience in the studio.

Yes, yes.

And there you stood with your script. Was it easier for you to do that, to emote on radio?

No, I don't think so. On stage there are a great many things to consider. In films and in television there are a great many things to consider. But radio has its own particular discipline, its own particular set of rules and principles. And I think they are as rigorous as any of the others. There is only one sense that you can use in order to communicate and you have to call up all kinds of things in your own bag of tricks or experience in order to make it felt.

You used your radio background to provide the voice – or sound – of the Demon in the film The Exorcist.

For me, the film is a 100 per cent radio performance because you never see me. All you do is hear me and yet, through the vocal apparatus, I made people throw up and pass out and faint and all that silly stuff. It was interesting to pull it off in a film, because it was really radio, but I wondered how I could convey through sound an impression of the Demon breathing. In the book, Bill Blatty describes very colorfully the horror of the sound that the two Exorcists feel when they are outside the closed door of the room. They are still aware of the breathing going on inside, of the Demon inside the little girl.

Well, how are you going to make that sound? I finally came up with something that worked and it's what's on the soundtrack. When I was little I had bronchitis – I've had it all my life and I wheezed and do wheeze when I get an attack of it – so really what you hear with the Demon, when the Demon breathes, is bronchitis! Well, that wouldn't mean anything in front of a camera or out there on that stage, but in radio you can do so many things, so many, many things, if you risk the amount of imagination you have and trust the amount of imagination of the listener.

Were you able to create the pictures that you were requested to create on radio with a minimum of direction from a man behind the glass? Could you develop much of this yourself?

Well, there were great directors in radio and there were a lot of mediocre ones and some absolutely useless ones. That's true in any branch of our profession. I worked with the greatest ones and sometimes with the worst ones, but a director who has a keen ear is a very rare bird and any actor who doesn't adhere to his director is a little silly. He's the boss, after all, and you're there to do his bidding. Go along with what the man is hearing in the control room. He is hearing it; you are only projecting it. And maybe what you think is effective loses all of its effectiveness in the distance between the microphone and the control room. So you listen to the boss and you do what he wants you to do.

Were you a part of The Mercury Theatre on the Air?

At the very end. I worked with Orson on a lot of radio programs and I'm devoted to him. His child is my godchild and I think Orson is probably one of the three or four great influences in my life.

You said you worked with Arch Oboler on the Lights Out *series. That was almost a regular job for you, wasn't it?*

Oh, yes, yes! Many of these things were. *Inner Sanctum* was. Hi Brown laughs at the story that I used to depend on *Inner Sanctum* in New York to pay my rent. One day I called my exchange for my call on *Inner Sanctum* and the lady of the exchange said, "You didn't get a call." I was ready to fire the exchange for their inadequacies, but she said, "The calls are out but there's no call for you." So I called Hi Brown and I said, "What is this about no call this week?" and he said, "No, I'm sorry, there aren't any women." And I said, "That's no excuse. I've got to pay my rent! Where's the call?" And he said, "Can you play an elevator man?" "Sure, you bet!" And I did and paid my rent. Yes, you would depend on these things and sometimes you'd get so confused with the shows on your schedule that it would run terribly close. You'd get elevators waiting for you. Buzz [Burgess] Meredith used to hire an ambulance to get from NBC to CBS in New York. It was two blocks, but if you got stuck on Fifth Avenue, you'd be dead!

You'd have shows back-to-back!

Oh, yes, many, many times.

But there was something about the radio group. Nobody had to get his nose fixed and nobody had to worry about weight and there wasn't the terrible competition about who was more attractive. A man who was not what you'd call "Clark Gable" – Everett Sloane – was the most romantic actor on radio. In a truly classic sense, he was absolutely the most appealing, masculine, macho, handsome, beguiling person. Well, that couldn't happen in any of the visual branches of the media.

That was the magic of radio.

You bet! It's the best. It truly is the best.

You mentioned Himan Brown. You worked with him on The CBS Radio Mystery Theatre.

Hi is a genius and we're all very indebted to him and we're terribly loyal to him and he is to us. But we go in to do *The Mystery Theatre,* for example, at 9:00 in the morning. For the first 20 minutes or so we sit around the table and congratulate each other on how we don't look a day older and isn't it marvelous!

"How come all the rest of the world is so rotten when we're so wonderful?" At about 9:20, Hi says "That's it now with the visiting, let's go to work" and he starts the stopwatch. We read the script cold, never having seen it. The sound man is at the end of the table making his notes. We get up on our feet after that when Hi's made whatever cuts are necessary. We do the whole thing. We're out at 11:15, having done an hour show in no more than two hours. That's fantastic!

That's almost the way it was in the heyday of radio, when you were doing live shows.

It seems to me that *Big Sister,* for example, was on at 1:00 – 1:00 to 1:15 – and I think we were called at 11:30. That was a 15-minute show. *Inner Sanctum,* I think, was on at 7:30 or 8:00 and we were called at 2:30. So you had a few hours then, but now since everything is accelerated, we do an hour show in two hours. That's wild and I must say in defense of all the people connected with it, it goes without saying that the people are very good at what they do or they couldn't pull it off.

I've read a quote by Hi Brown saying that he uses the pros on The Mystery Theatre *because he doesn't have to fiddle around with amateurs. He knows that he can get the job done in an economical amount of time and that, of course, is part of the whole thing. But you people do a great job with it.*

Well, I think most of us would do anything for him. I would. He's a great, great guy. See, that's what I mean: the loyalties that exist in radio. I've spoken about Orson and Hi. I feel that way about Carlton Morse. I'd do anything for Carlton Morse, anything in the world.

You worked an awful lot for Carlton E. Morse. You were on both One Man's Family *and* I Love A Mystery.

I would do *I Love A Mystery* for a while in California and then I'd get this itch about conquering New York again, so I'd go back and try that conquering bit for a little while. And then I wouldn't conquer it, and then I'd call Carlton and say, "Well, here I come again," and he'd put me back on the *Mystery.* They were very good to me. They indulged me in all of my whims.

I think they recognized your good talent, too. And we could listen to you and not be aware that you were an actress in front of a microphone. You were swinging on a rope in the "Temple of the Vampires"!

Well, we were swinging back and forth in the studio! A great deal of physical activity was going on! But terrible things would happen on the *Mystery.* Honestly, Bart Yarborough, who played Doc, was a delightful imp, but maddening sometimes. And sometimes, right in the middle of a very dramatic speech, he would come up and set fire to my script! He would just light the bottom of the page and walk away and leave me there! I'm trying to emote and I'm trying to get the flame to go out in my bare hand and he's over in the corner laughing! A lot of terrible things happened to us in the studios, but they were funny.

Did Carlton Morse buy that? Did he go along with the joke or wasn't he around then?

Oh, sure! Carlton was in the control room laughing! He loved it, just loved it! We had fun, that was the point! And I remember a marvelous thing on the Rudy Vallee *Sealtest Hour*. In 1941 on Christmas Eve, we did the "Christmas Carol" and John Barrymore and Lionel Barrymore in his wheelchair were on it and I played Tiny Tim, because it was a radio show and it didn't matter. I played the little boy. The only thing is that I was very, very pregnant. We finished the show at about 8:30 and everybody said goodnight and Merry Christmas and everybody went home for their Christmas Eve celebration.

I went home and immediately went to the hospital and my son was born four hours after I was off the air! The next morning I called everybody connected with the show and said, "My son and I would like to wish you a Merry Christmas!" They all reacted in the way I wanted them to and said, "What do you mean? You just left us – we were just on the air with you eight hours ago." I said, "Just the same, my son and I want to wish you a Merry Christmas!" When I called John Barrymore's house he was asleep and his Japanese houseboy took the message. That afternoon a wire came to the Cedars of Lebanon Hospital to me and it said, "Congratulations to you and the other wise man. Imagine his surprise when he found that the star he came to see was you. –John Barrymore."

And somehow, that's a very typical radio story, that a woman, very large with child, imminent with child, indeed, could be playing Tiny Tim with John and Lionel Barrymore and the next morning deliver her son and then have such a lovely thing happen to her that afternoon from one of the members of the cast. I don't mean that there aren't marvelous people in films and in the theatre, but – and I guess I am prejudicial because radio was my beginning – but I have great regard, great love and enormous gratitude to radio.

Radio – and the radio audience – have great regard, great love and enormous gratitude to you, too.

It's fun. God bless radio.

Mercedes McCambridge was born March 17, 1918 and was 58 at the time of our conversation.

Bill
Baldwin

Bill Baldwin was a network radio announcer and war correspondent. We met in the club room of the Pacific Pioneer Broadcasters in Hollywood, California, on August 9, 1976. After congratulating him on being elected that day to another term as president of the organization, I asked him where his long radio career began.

Well, I was born in Pueblo, raised in Denver, Colorado. [I] could never get a job in Denver! I auditioned and they said, "You'll never make an announcer," and sometimes I think they're right. So I went to work for Walkathon – that's before your time – being an emcee. We had four emcees a day over a 24-hour period in Walkathon.* The chief master of ceremonies was a fellow named Red Skelton. When they finally closed us up after a couple of years – they got smart to us all over the country – we were making money you can't believe! I was out of work, but [for] the Walkathon, every night, we did a radio broadcast of what was going on and how. [It was] sort of a special events-news type of thing, but it was play-by-play, really. Or foot-by-foot! I got training then, [but] had no idea of going into radio. The orchestra leader – his name was Harry Collins out of Grand Island, Nebraska – and I used to sing with the band as well as announce. We did everything. He called and said, "We're going to open with the band in Casper, Wyoming. Would you like to come out and sing with us?" Well, I had no money, no job, so I said, "Sure."

I arrived in Casper, Wyoming, and we were on radio there. You couldn't get it five miles out of town, but it was radio. One night the announcer didn't show up so, being the vocalist, I did the broadcast. Now, for a week prior to this time, a gentleman had come up [to the bandstand] every night, and said, "Do you play

---

* The Walkathon, or Dance Marathon, was a Depression-era contest to see which of some 50 or 100 couples had the stamina to drag themselves around a dance floor the longest before collapsing. The last couple standing won a cash prize.

the 'Nebraska Fight Song'?" He'd been at the bar. Of course, the band being from Grand Island, we played it and every time we played the "Nebraska Fight Song," he sent a round of drinks for the band! Consequently, every 20 minutes we played the "Nebraska Fight Song"! Well, this night that the announcer didn't show up, I did the broadcast. The same guy came up and asked, "Who did the broadcast, the announcing?" Harry said, "Bill Baldwin." He said, "Have him in my room tomorrow morning at 11:00." So I went up. He remembered everything that had taken place. He picked up the telephone and called Harry Burke of WOW in Omaha, and he said, "I found your new announcer." I got on the phone and talked to [Burke] and that's how I got really into radio. To be the announcer on a band remote in Casper, Wyoming, to go to WOW in Omaha! That was in 1936. They didn't take a chance, though. They farmed me out for about five months to KSSC, "The Voice of the Western Slopes, Grand Junction, Colorado." They [did not have a] news wire. I read *Christian Science Monitor* newspapers that arrived every day and that was the news. Then I went to Omaha and from there to the networks, and that was the beginning.

You found yourself in Chicago at one period of time.

Oh, yes. I went directly from WOW to WGN in Chicago when Quin Ryan was there, and Myrtle Stahl, and I became the king of the band remotes. At night I would do all the band remotes starting at 6:00 and finish up at 1:00 in the morning. Every other half-hour I had a show.

Were you doing that from a studio or from the site?

No, from the site. That's why, every half-hour or hour, we'd start out with dinner music at the Blackstone, and then go to the Palmer House and then to the Blackhawk, to the Drake, back to the Palmer House, and sign off at the Blackhawk at night with the Midnight Flyers. This was five days, six days a week.

So this was the kind of programming WGN was presenting at that time.

Well, at night they were known as the "Band Network," Mutual. They were the Mutual [affilliate] out of part of the Central area, and they were known as the "Band Network" all over the country. They made a great name for themselves. During the day – this was B.U., Before Unions – you made around a fast $50, $55 a week and all you could steal! I would be doing shows for Marshall Field or somebody else on the ball game with Bob Elson, and they'd send over a carton of cigarettes and a bottle of booze. That was instead of salary! Then came the unions. During the day we had the soap operas just like NBC and WBBM, and the variety shows and, of course, the great WGN Orchestra, a concert orchestra. Henry Weber and Marion Claire and all of the great and wonderful people.

The Chicago Theatre of the Air.

Yes! I used to broadcast on the weekends from Grant Park with the Chicago Symphony Orchestra.

I'd like to jump back to that point when you were moving from ballroom to ballroom. Did that create a problem? Did you ever get caught with the bridge being up or anything like that?

No, not really, because the only one I had outside of the bridge development situation there was the Drake Hotel. No, I never did get trapped that way. The only time I remember the bridge being up was being at one of the theaters one afternoon for a matinee and John Barrymore was doing his great thing, and one of the bridges was up and, you know, the whistles sound when the bridge is up. It just kept whistling and whistling and whistling. Finally, Mr. Barrymore walked down right to the lights and said, "would somebody go out and shut off that damnned whistle?" And then he went back into doing the act. [I have] heard of people getting caught [by open bridges].

You could walk from WGN to WBBM to WMAQ and they were all over the place!

Oh yes, that was the free-lance performer. We were staff announcers at that time, which is almost a thing of the past now. It's gone. The real true staff announcer.

As a staff announcer you got a single salary for a week's work, right?

That was it.

And no matter what they asked you to do, you had to do it.

That's right. All the commercials, all the breaks from morning till night. You could sign off at 1:00 at night and be back on the air at 6:00 in the morning. And they could work you. That wasn't just WGN, that was everywhere.

They all did that, yes. From Chicago, where did you go, Bill?

I went, for a short time, to Shreveport, Louisiana, and that was only because I developed an ulcer in Chicago, and there was a nice sanitarium-type hospital down there. WGN had a due bill.* I went down there and went to work at KWKH, the old W. K. Henderson station. Then back to Omaha. I went to KOIL in Omaha. "KOIL, Barnsol Oil. Be square with your motor." It's amazing how you can remember those things!

I got a little tired of sitting in Omaha again and the Roller Derby came through. Now, a lot of people think the Roller Derby came with television, but the Roller Derby was 1938, and I went with the Roller Derby from there to Denver to

---

* A trade arrangement between a radio station and a client.

Hollywood. That's my first trip into Hollywood, to work, to do anything like that. I went from here to San Francisco. I arrived in San Francisco in December of '38. The Roller Derby left. In the meantime, on all these stations and things, I'd developed a news thing and, before disc jockeys, a record show. I always tried to do the morning show because by 1:00 or 2:00 you could go play golf or do something. I created somewhat of a name in that field of morning shows and doing news. I stayed through 1939. Then back to Omaha. We stayed there. I married my wife in 1940, my wife Eunice. She was with one of the stations in Omaha-Lincoln.

I was wondering why you kept going back to Omaha. Now I know!

I could always get a job there. It was good to have and I could always come back to KOIL. I don't know where else I would have gone, really. But I never got back to Chicago or east. I never worked out of New York except later when I was doing network shows with Edgar Bergen and a few of those. [When] my wife and I married [we] left, went to Salt Lake City, stayed there a year, was picked up on the air there, and sent to Hollywood to KFWB here.

The war hit December 7th and here came the news again. The Blue Network then, which is now ABC, said, "We need a news director in San Francisco." So I went and they moved us lock, stock, and barrel. From that time, I had no idea that they were grooming me to be a war correspondent. I went overseas for the Blue Network in 1943, '44. Came home in '45. There was nothing more dead in the world after the war than a war correspondent, for radio especially. So, I went free-lancing in San Francisco and stayed there until 1949. Then came along a picture called *Champion*. Stanley Kramer said, "I would like you to come down and play the fight announcer." So I did. That was July of '49. We moved down here and have been here ever since.

Let's move back to the middle Forties, when you were a war correspondent. What were the duties of a network war correspondent at that time?

Unlike today, the Vietnamese War, the Korean Conflict, etc., at that time we had four networks: the Blue Network, NBC, CBS, and Mutual. Each of the four networks had four war correspondents. Now, imagine this. Sixteen broadcasters – four for each network – covered the entire World War II. Now, we had stringers that would help out at times, but each of us had an engineer. So eight men would cover an entire World War II for the Blue Network, for NBC, [for CBS, for Mutual]. Each [network had] eight men.

My assignment was the Pacific Theatre of Operations. I worked out of Hawaii and traveled from there. Clete Roberts, who is considered one of the finest, and is still here in Los Angeles, was assigned to General MacArthur. He is an expert on the exploits of General MacArthur. Martin – I'll think of the name in a moment – was assigned to the CBI Theatre with General Chenault and the others in the China-Burma Theatre. The great George Hicks was assigned to the European

Theatre of Operations with General Eisenhower. The four of us covered the entire war for the Blue Network. As I said, we had the stringers. Today, you have hundred-man bureaus in each city, so to speak. For instance, out here in Sacramento alone, the capital of the state of California, each television station has a minimum of 40 broadcasters: newscasters on that station, working newspeople. So that's how it has improved.

Of course, at that time, we were held to strict secrecy. We did not have satellites. When I went out and covered the first fast carrier strike against Japanese-held waters, which was after the Mariana Turkey Shoot, we did not have short wave. We could not tell even the ships we were on to send the tapes back because of security of where we were. So, we did not have to come into your living room immediately on these operations. In fact, it was better that you didn't because of security reasons. I was gone four weeks on that one trip alone, and no one knew where we were because Admiral Nimitz and Admiral Halsey did not reveal where we were at any time during that four weeks. But when we came back – *POP!* – you know you'd have to get on the air and go from there.

How did the word get from the Pacific, where you were, to the radio listener here? You took an engineer with you. You mentioned the word "tape." Were you using tape then?

Well, it was not really tape. What it was, if you'll remember, we had the old 16-inch transcriptions. It had to sit flat, and the needle would come down and emboss the material on aluminum. Well, when the war hit, you couldn't get aluminum. Therefore, those discs were made of glass. But, besides the fact that the head would knock all over the place if you fired a three-inch gun or the ship moved, and it would move. So the Navy got together with a company called Ampro. They developed a 35-millimeter, 50-foot endless belt of film. That 50-foot, endless belt would pass over a needle that would lock into place, that would emboss, and that needle would move. That was the first time you could ever edit, because you could count lines and move with that needle embossing. You could play it back, and play it back, and play it back, which you couldn't do on the 16-inch transcription. That's what we called "tape" at the time. It was 35-millimeter embossed film. Then they would take that and transfer it to the 16-inch transcription.

I had a boss and he lived in New Jersey. His name was Johnny Johnstone. He had been, prior to that, with Walter Winchell. Johnny was the news director of the Blue Network. He's the one who hired us. He had the smarts. At that time you couldn't get good booze, you know, good drinking material. But there was some to be had, and he would send it out to Red Sanders, who was my engineer. We covered the world. He would send it out in a wooden box marked "radio tubes" or "radio equipment" here. You open it up and here it's good sipping whiskey. We wouldn't drink it, but what we would do when we were on the way out to a story, would [be to] drop it off at the different censors or the air bases for the doctors or something like that. No one could ever figure out how come

Baldwin's Blue Network tapes always got back to Honolulu first. They just never stopped them. They would go right through. The censors wouldn't go through them or anything else. On this particular one, I knew we had an exclusive.

When this operation took place, it was in October of 1944. It was the first task area test for the Japanese-held waters. We'd never been there before. When our fleet was stretched out – it was the Third Fleet – it was 37 miles long and 17 miles wide, and a ship every 2,000 yards. So you can imagine how many we had. The Japanese were very good at counterintelligence. So, from Honolulu even, they dispatched one of us from each of the four networks. Foster from NBC, Tim Lemert from CBS here, and I forget who the Mutual man was at this time. But they dispatched the four of us on separate days in separate directions to not let the Japanese know that we were heading out for a big, major story, because they never assigned broadcast correspondents unless it was a major story. Throughout mine, I went to the Johnson Island, to Saipan, got a ship there. They flew us out of there. Oh, man, it was something! They had 16 torpedo warheads in the thing. If we'd ever hit, that's all she wrote, you know? We flew to a place called Ulysses. You couldn't find it on a map. I looked down and there was the entire Third Fleet sitting right there. We landed and went aboard, first time in real big combat. Four weeks later, we finished the operation. We'd been through two typhoons. We'd been all over the Pacific. Admiral Halsey did it again, and I had a story.

As we pulled out, and were refueling at sea, with a carrier on each side doing 30 knots with an oiler giving us gasoline and oil and aviation fuel, a war correspondent had just come out from Hawaii. He came aboard and said, "Bill, you've got an exclusive." I said, "You're kidding. The other three..." He said, "No, they got caught in Australia in a typhoon and were not able to get out. You have the only broadcast story." Well, that's once in a lifetime.

I asked permission to send a visual message to Admiral Halsey, and told him of what I had just found out. Could he expedite my getting back to Honolulu? We're 75 to 100 miles off the Japanese-held land. It came back and he said yes, and they transferred me by breeches buoy. That's an interesting thing if you've never been transferred from ship to ship on a line. I had 29 hours of tape boxes under my arm. They did it at midnight with no lights. They handed me a big, long white pole and I said, "What's that?" They said, "Hold on to it. If we drop you, turn it up. It's got a light. We can find you." So we had no lights, under complete secrecy. They transferred me to a destroyer then to another carrier, to Admiral Halsey, who gave me my papers. He's smart, too. He gave me a pad of 25 copies of his order making me an "officer courier" so that no one could touch me or stop me. I was under orders of the Admiral of the Third Fleet to report to the Admiral of the Pacific Fleet, Admiral Nimitz, in Hawaii. Censors couldn't touch me. Oh, and they died! They didn't know where we were for four weeks. I finally wound up on a Jeep Carrier. They flew me off to a place called Babble Swamp, which was under fire, put me on a plane and got me back to Hawaii and 72 hours from the time I left the fleet, I was on the air.

Admiral Halsey had held radio silence until I got there. My material was cleared, written and everything else so we could broadcast and I was the pool.

The first five minutes had to be pool operations for all four networks to accept, then I could go on my own. They radioed Admiral Halsey when I had arrived. He went on the air 30 seconds before me and said, "This is Admiral William F. Halsey. I have raised all six ships sunk by Radio Tokyo, and am retreating toward the enemy." I'll never forget it as long as I live. Then he said, "And now, here's Bill Baldwin." I had to wait 30 seconds for the switch and went on the air. That was it. I still have tapes of it. It is one of the great thrills from my life.

It is one of the most exciting war stories I've ever heard!

Oh, yeah! He got me back and got it on the air. Then I waited a minute after the five, and said my network, the Blue Network. All of the sounds – no one had ever recorded them before – they had never had the opportunity, of [actually] being under fire, and our guns firing, and what goes on! It's like a football field when you look down from that carrier and see what's going on. It was a thrill.

Did you broadcast that from Hawaii?

Oh, yes. It went to San Francisco by short wave. No satellite, no nothing. At one point it went out and they would come back and give you a four-zero, a zero to four-zero, for acceptance on the short wave. Whether it was receiving a good quality or whatever. One night, I had sent them a 15-minute show that I'd worked on for about three weeks. This was long after that. I'll show you what can happen on short wave. I sent it to them and I didn't hear back, the report. So I got on the thing again and I said, "Would you please give us the markup of the script, of what it was?" They said, "What broadcast?" They said it hadn't even hit the lines there, so I entertained millions of fish somewhere between Hawaii and San Francisco! But that was just one portion of a lot of work. I later went out with a submarine war patrol. It was very exciting but it was not as exciting as the first one you're in.

You were in danger much of the time.

Oh, sure. The casualty rate of war correspondents is the greatest of all the services, and was at that time. Because you're noncombatant. No side arms, no knives, no nothing like that in case of war. You are given a rank; if you're in the Army or the Marine Corps, you're a major. If you're in the Navy, you're a lieutenant commander. That is in case of capture and prisoner of war, so that you have the rights and privileges of an officer. That's part of the Geneva Conference.

Otherwise, if you are a civilian, you could be a spy.

Oh, sure. Many people say, "Did you ever meet Ernie Pyle?" I met Pyle only once. I was with him for about two hours in Honolulu, and I felt he had been my friend for 10 years. Great man. I met great and wonderful people. In Chicago, for instance, we had three Smiths out in the Pacific and you would say, "Where's Pack Rat?" And you knew who they were talking about; or where's "Horrible" or "Wonderful"? Well, those were the three Smiths. "Wonderful" was Eugene W. Smith, *Time-Life* photographer. I asked him what W was and he said "Wonderful," so he got that name. "Pack Rat" was Harold Smith of the *Chicago Tribune*. He would run a mine field to pick up something to send back to the colonel to have for a bond rally, so they could raffle them off to sell war bonds at that time. And "Horrible" Smith was a wonderful man who was a newsreel photographer for Pathe News, and he'd just walk around and say, "Oh, it's horrible, just horrible." So that's how he got his name.

You found yourself in Hollywood then, you said, about 19 –

– 49, the second time. Moved back and have been here ever since.

What was your first job here then?

It was either move to Hollywood from San Francisco or stay in San Francisco. I wanted to better myself. However, I was working very hard in San Francisco. The first television show I ever did was the first show ever on KPIX, the station there. Money wasn't that big up there at all. You know, you worked yourself to death for the money you could get. So I decided to make the move, and talked with my wife. She said, "Well, we'll make the move without a job." But I kept two shows on Sunday in San Francisco, and I would commute.

I fell into my first real job here as an announcer at the Paladium [Ballroom] going back to the band network days of doing that, while working and looking for another job. On a plane running from San Francisco to Los Angeles on one of those Sundays, I met a gentleman named Paul Lewis sitting next to me on the plane. I said, "What do you do?" He said, "I'm with the D'arcy Advertising Agency." I said, "What do you do?" He said, "Well, we handle the Coca-Cola account." I said "What're you going to Hollywood for?" He said, "To find another announcer for *The Edgar Bergen Show*."

Well, you know, two and two make four. I said, "I'm an announcer and I'm going back to Hollywood." He said, "We've auditioned 26 announcers already, and they won't do what we want. We don't want them to *sell* Coca-Cola. We want them to just *suggest* Coca-Cola after the show is over." So I said, "Well, look, can I get in on the audition?" He said, "We're going to audition actors." I said, "I'm an actor." (I'd just finished *Champion*.) So he said, "All right." And by golly, he called me. I walked in and I really knew this fine actor, Theodore Von Ells, had won the show, because when he came out of the control room he had a smile that wide. So they called me in and I looked in the booth and there must have been 20 people in that booth listening to that audition. I think at WGN they had the best idea. When you were auditioning, they had a big curtain that went down over that glass and you could see nobody and they couldn't see you. They'd [hear] you work. But here there were 20 people. But they were handling the thing and it was the "benediction."

At that time, Coca-Cola had only 15 seconds on the opening of the show and 15 seconds on the close. That was their commercial on Sunday afternoon with Edgar Bergen. And [with] Mario Lanza, which I did later. It was: "And remember, whoever you are, whatever you do, wherever you may be, when you think of refreshment, think of Coca-Cola. Buy Coke, for ice cold Coca-Cola is everywhere." I read it, put the thing down and walked out. They said, "You wouldn't mind reading it again?" you know, half-miffed at me. I said, "No." I read it, and the door opened. Edgar Bergen walked out and said "Welcome to the club" and that was it. Seven years with Edgar! Then we went into television for a little bit. Now Edgar is Chairman of the Board of the Pacific Pioneer Broadcasters, and I'm the President of PPB.

You got on the radio with Edgar Bergen after he had completed his long association with Chase and Sanborn.

Yes. Everybody said, "We associate you with..." So Edgar went off the air for one whole year. [He] wasn't on the air at all. That's when he left Chase and Sanborn and went with the Coca-Cola Company. We were with Coca-Cola and then we went with a cosmetics outfit too, later. But yes, that was after Ken Carpenter, who is the Vice-President of Pacific Pioneer Broadcasters, was an announcer with Edgar for all those years. Not many people remember, but I was the announcer the longest time with Edgar. Don Ameche was an announcer for a while, and Bill Goodwin.

Was Bill Goodwin with Edgar Bergen?

Oh, he was. Early. Yes, Bill was early with Charlie.

Were you working exclusively for Bergen on that or were you free-lancing?

No, I was free-lancing but signed to the Bergen show. I could not do any other product that associated itself with Coca-Cola. Even today, not as much. But then it was very important. I was asked to audition for the *Burns and Allen* television show. I went over and I auditioned for it, and had it. I went to Coca-Cola, I don't know why, and I just said, "Look, I've been asked to do *The Burns and Allen Show* for Carnation," and they said, "Oh?" I said, "Is that all right with you?" They said, "It's fine with us, but if you do that show, you can't do Coca-Cola. You can't do *Bergen* or *Mario Lanza*." I had them both, and I was doing all of their spots at that time, too, and their early television commercials. I said, "Why?" They said, "Look, if you drink a glass of milk, and they pitch orange juice, or you eat ice cream, you won't drink a Coca-Cola." When you stop and think about it, it makes sense. So, I didn't get it and Von Zell got it and he's a millionaire!

What else did you do, Bill, on radio and television into the Fifties?

Radiowise, as I said, *The Mario Lanza Show*, which was a great education. He was a wonderful man. He was wonderful to me. It's a shame what happened to his life because he was such a talent. *The Jack Kirkwood Show* was [another], and that's an education, too.

Kirkwood was really a zany kind of a guy, wasn't he?

Oh, yes, with him and his wife and daughter [were] George Wright, the great organist [and] two sound effects technicians. And they drove the director, J. C. Lewis, up a wall every day. Kirkwood would walk in, say "The hell with him! We won't rehearse. We'll go over and have coffee."

Was this the half-hour Kirkwood *or the 15-minute show?*

No, this was the half-hour *Kirkwood*. He had done the 15 minutes for Oxydol or something on CBS. This was on Mutual, and it was live five-days-a-week radio, and fun, and four years! I played straights to him, and played parts and everything else. He found out I could not do an Irish accent worth anything. Every other show he would throw in the Irish policeman. Just to say, "See, that's all he can do is announce." He was a great and wonderful man.

And from there, let's see, to other radio shows. Now television started to sneak in. That's when we were doing the billboards on shows. Then I went, in 1956, with Robert Cummings and was with Bob for six years on the show when he was a photographer.

Paul Henning, God bless him, was the writer and producer of those shows. Paul did for me what very few performers got the right to do and that was use your own name. So, I was always the announcer, Bill Baldwin, on the show. When *The Beverly Hillbillies* came along, which he did, I played Bill Baldwin of KBH, the "Voice of Beverly Hills. Drive carefully, protect our millionaires." That was nine years of a great and wonderful time. On all of those shows, we had different sponsors. On *Beverly Hillbillies,* for instance, the first five years were for Winston. The same with *The Bob Cummings Show.* So, they just stayed right with that announcer, like Hal Simms had certain shows, Ken Roberts had certain shows, Ken Carpenter had certain shows. You stayed with those sponsors and were identified with them. Or an agency that had multi-products, but now, I don't think you can find, outside of *The Bell Telephone Hour,* a show that is sponsored by a product. Maybe a special one, but never across-the-board. I don't think you will find an across-the-board show sponsored by a [single] sponsor. It's multi-sponsored.

It gets too expensive. That's what has changed the face of broadcasting, I believe. In the so called "old days" they used to complain that the control of the program was in the lap of the sponsor –

– and the agency, yes.

– and that wasn't good and they looked forward to the day when the networks would have the control. That's today.

And some of the major production companies have control. ABC has their shows that they do. NBC has theirs. CBS is aligned with so-and-so. It's a rat race today. For the performer, I can say this, with my other hat on now, as a former national president of AFTRA, the American Federation of Television and Radio Artists, where the union was born, by the way, in Chicago. The Chicago union was underneath the street between WBBM and WGN. We used to meet down there in that little restaurant behind the furnace. That's where the union started down there. That's become a great union we're very highly proud of. But the union came along and thank God, because you used to make a commercial for $4.11, and it could play 16 weeks all over the country, unlimited. Now, they're protecting our people. They have not priced themselves out of the industry. We try to work with the organizations and with the people. So, it's one of those things. Some unions have white hats. Let me put it that way. The Screen Actors Guild has a white hat.

You're a good guy with a white hat. You've talked a lot about your great contribution to broadcasting and it's been very interesting. We appreciate your time to share these moments.

Well, thank you. It's great to be here and to be with you and to be able to share them. I lecture at universities across the country and I keep telling these people, "Go find a little coffee pot [station]. Don't go to the big city first, go find a little station, go learn your craft, go learn your trade. Sell your product, learn the agency and always remember that a microphone is human because when they turn it on and invite you in, they've invited you into their homes. And when they turn it off, they've slammed the door, if they don't like you on that program. That microphone is pretty human.

Bill Baldwin was born in 1913 and was 63 at the time of our conversation. He died November 17, 1982 at the age of 69.

Harriet Nelson

Harriet Nelson co-starred on radio and then television with her husband and children on **The Adventures of Ozzie and Harriet.** *We met on August 28, 1989 in her Pacific Ocean-front home in Laguna Beach, California. I told her that her fans and friends in the Chicago area sent their love. She said that she had played Chicago many times since she was a young girl of 16.*

 Singing was kind of a sideline. In vaudeville, in the old days, you had to do everything. You had to sing, you had to dance, you had to do sketch comedy. You did all those things and you just took it for granted.

My mother and dad were in the business. As a matter of fact, my dad worked out of Chicago. Chicago was the center for dramatic stock, and he was a director-actor, so I've been kind of a Chicagoan almost since I was born.

I started working with my parents when I was six weeks old. My mother was a leading lady in stock. She carried me on and I played my first speaking part when I was three. So in stock I began as an actress. Then I went into New York and I joined the Castle Ballet. Then I met up with Ken Murray, through friends, who was looking for a straight woman. He took me on and we were in the first year of the RKO unit that was ever on tour. It's a long story. You don't want all of that.

We love the stories. We know what you accomplished over the years, but we don't know much about the beginning. It's fascinating to know about those early vaudeville days. How long were you with Ken Murray?

A whole year. Then I went to Danny Duncan's act – that was sketch comedy in vaudeville. You'd pick a play which was successful, condense it, and you were on for 20 minutes with it. I did the whole tour again and wound up again back in Chicago.

Were you Harriet Hilliard at that time?

Yes. My father was Roy E. Hilliard. Then I went into New York with my mother. You were based in New York if you were with RKO, which was the big circuit. From there I went into a very large nightclub called the Hollywood Restaurant in New York City. I was the mistress of ceremonies there. I was pretty young to be a mistress of ceremonies, but I was.

I met Ozzie at that time. It was his idea to have a girl with a band. I was the first girl with a band. It was his idea. He wanted to do musical comedy duets at the bandstand. He said the boys would have something to look at as well as the girls!

How long had Ozzie had his band when you joined it?

Well, he was still in school. He had a degree in law and was still going to law school when he had his band. I think it was the first band at the Glen Island Casino in New York, where a lot of bands started. I just had the engagement for the summer. If it didn't work out and he didn't have a job in the fall, I was going to go back to Hollywood. But that was the end of that. At the end of the summer we had fallen in love. We had a very long run – 45 years, as a matter of fact.

It was wonderful that you could work together all those years.

And it just kept growing and growing and we went into radio. We were on radio first with Joe Penner and after that with Red Skelton. I played the mother of the Mean Little Kid! Then I did Daisy June with Clem Kadiddlehopper and I did Deadeye and Calamity June! [Red is] such a brilliant comic. I've often said, when his timing was so right, I used get chills down my back. It was like listening to a great symphony. Such a talent!

Where did you get the idea to start The Adventures of Ozzie and Harriet?

Red was taken into the service. We were going to go on with another comedian doing the same thing we did with the band. Ozzie used to work with Red, too, on straights. Then, when he was taken into the service, we were going to go on with another musical group. One day Don Quinn [the writer on *Fibber McGee and Molly*] was talking to me and Ozzie at the Brown Derby and he said, "Oz, why don't you write your own show?" It never occurred to us before and so Ozzie wrote the first show all by himself and we got a studio at CBS and did the audition show. That was scary. You don't know whether you're going to be top gun or not. When that first laugh comes rolling in... ahh, it's heaven! You think, "We've got it made! They're going to laugh at us!"

Had Ozzie done much writing before?

I think Ozzie's written his whole life. But we didn't know if he could write a whole show. We didn't know if we could get laughs, because we had never done that kind of comedy before.

John Guedel, who was very active in radio, took the [audition] platters and flew them to New York and a week later we were signed with International Sterling Silver. They were our sponsors for five years. I don't think we ever had a sponsor that was less than five years.

When your show began, you and Ozzie played a husband and wife bandleader and band singer.

That's right, it started differently. He wrote the first show like a day off in the life of a bandleader and his vocalist wife. It was a wild comedy. Jack Douglas was one of the writers, and J. P. Medwick. But it didn't make any sense. It wasn't a sensible kind of thing. It was just wild comedy. Then it eventually grew. Before we'd done, I would say, five or six shows, it started to get more "legit." Audiences tell you what they want you to do. We got that feeling from them and it just evolved. We didn't ever start to do anything but a half-hour comedy show, and pretty soon it started to get more legitimate.

We had two bunches of kids who were able to read on sight. They were right at the age where their voices were changing, so we had gone through three sets of boys and we were sitting at the dinner table one night and Bing Crosby was going to do a guest shot on our show. We never had guests, so this was a special thing. The boys, my boys, used to play tennis with Lindsay, Bing's son, and they said, "Why can't we do the show if Bing's sons do it?" We didn't know [why], but they said they wanted to do the show. In those days you'd do a preview, then cut, then do the proper show.

A preview before a studio audience? Like a dress rehearsal?

Exactly. It was like a dress rehearsal, so we could overwrite the show and then bring it down to time by cutting, because the more you cut the better it is.

Well, we told the boys they could do the preview, but not the show. There wasn't enough experience there. We weren't about to put our careers in the hands of a couple of kids who had never been on before. Well, they did the preview for the audience. The first time that either one of them spoke up, the laughs came from the back of the studio! And I thought, "Oh, they've tasted blood! This is it!" So, they did the show with us. It was very successful. People loved them right away.

Had the boys expressed any interest in doing this before that time?

Once in a while, when we were looking for another set of kids, but we would always say, "You're too young, you can't read." They didn't have to read. Ricky would do the sketch and then have it memorized.

How old were David and Ricky when they came on the show?

Ricky was eight and David was 11. Of course, David could read, but Rick couldn't read that fast to do a radio show. It didn't seem to matter. He was too little to reach the microphone, so we had a table set up at center stage and he'd sit in a chair with a script in front of him. He had a knack for learning fast. As a matter of fact, there were many times that he'd almost given me a heart attack. He couldn't see his feet and so long as he couldn't see them, he didn't see why the audience could. So he'd kick off his shoes first thing. He'd be sitting there looking at the ceiling and doing everything this side of whistling and he'd have a line coming on and I'd think he's not going to make it. But he did! He'd give me a heart attack! I got used to it after a while. As long as we'd come up to his cue, he'd look down like he was reading and say the line. But we lived through all of that.

Rick always had the snapper and would always get the big laugh. And I tell you, David griped about it one time. I said, "Listen, everybody needs a straight man. A comic can't get a laugh without a straight man. You're a straight man and I'm a straight woman. Both of 'em need us to get along." That soothed his ruffled feathers.

Did the boys really enjoy doing this work?

Yes, they did. Then, as time went on, we always worked around them, like when we went into film for TV. They went to public school all the time that they did it. We'd work around them. We'd save what they had to do till Saturday. Then they got into sports. Rick got into tennis and David got into football, and we worked around that, too. So they led a perfectly normal life. They seldom worked outside of the family. We were 14 years on television. We had the same crew and we worked in the same studio from the time we started. It was like home, being at the studio, because we had our bungalow over there. Everything was set up in advance. It was a long and happy career.

Which studio did you use to produce the TV show?

General Services, in Hollywood, about 10 minutes from our house. We drove down the hill about 12 blocks and we were at work.

Then you really didn't live at 1847 Rogers Road?

No!

Did you have any trouble moving from radio to television?

No problem at all, because I had been in pictures. I did my first picture, *Follow the Fleet,* in 1935 with Rogers and Astaire. Ozzie had been in several pictures with the band. So it was a very easy thing for us to do, the move from radio to TV. Of course, you didn't have the leeway in television that you did in radio, so that took some doing.

You were more confined on TV?

Yes, and it wasn't a breeze, because we began our own company. So we had to, in a hurry – one big hurry – learn about making pictures and we'd never made pictures before. We'd been in them, but we'd never made them! So, there was one year and a half that was rather frantic!

It was astute of you to decide to make your TV shows yourself rather than have someone else produce the programs.

Ozzie was always head honcho. He determined everything.

It's amazing, Ozzie Nelson always came across on the radio and the TV shows as a very easy-going, relaxed kind of person. Over the years they kidded him because he didn't have a job or visible means of income.

Number one question!

But in reality, Ozzie the businessman was a sharp taskmaster and knew what he was doing.

Yes, he was a graduate in law. In New Jersey you had to be a clerk for a year in a law office before you could hang out your shingle, but by that time he was doing too well with the band and he couldn't afford to do that.

He never actually practiced law?

Only as far as we were concerned. But he was a good enough attorney to know that you don't work in your own behalf that way. So we had the same outside attorney for 35 years. He and Ozzie had a wonderful relationship.

In the beginning, when Ozzie was writing the radio shows, he had some other writers. A brother?

That's right, Don. Donald, his younger brother, was going to school at Southern California. He used to write scripts and turn them in, too. Part of everybody's script was used. Ozzie would edit the whole thing and write one master script from it. They would have a meeting once a week trying to decide what to do. Then each writer would write a script, turn it in to Ozzie. He would get them together, taking parts of everybody's script, edit the whole thing and put it together. That's how he worked.

Did you have any input into the scriptwriting process?

No, I did not. That wasn't my cup of tea. Can't sit still too long! Ozzie had everything to do with the business, totally. Of course, he would ask my opinion. There isn't a husband in the world that doesn't ask his wife her opinion, and I would tell him. I was a pretty good editor. But I took care of the house and the boys and I had everything to do with that. He figured I knew more about that and I did. We had a wonderful working relationship, besides the other relationship.

At what point did Ozzie give up the band?

It sort of phased out when we started *Ozzie and Harriet,* about the first few years after we got into more "legit" comedy. For a while we would do both. Where there was a break in the script, there would be a band number. We would either sing together or one or the other would. It just gradually phased itself out.

And eventually the whole half-hour was the "legit" comedy. There were some marvelous warm laughs and entertainment on those radio shows. I assume you had a good time doing all those things.

Yes, we did. I think it was successful because we had such a good time with it. We never got tired of it. I got a little tired at the end of 14 years on TV. Ozzie never lost interest in it, because he did it all. He directed, he produced, he laid the music. He was the head cutter. He also had more variety to do than I. I sort of stood in the same spot in the same set and said the same thing, more or less.

You washed the dishes and said, "What time are you coming home, Ozzie?"

[Laughs] That's right!

So many people grew up with David and Ricky and with Ozzie and Harriet. How did you respond to that, being in the spotlight as your family grew up? How did it affect your life together?

I don't think that it affected us, but I think we affected a lot of other people through the mail and all that I receive, even now. I am so thrilled and flattered – especially for Ozzie – that this could happen. He hasn't been here for a very long time and he's still playing on the Disney Channel. I have little people come up to me when I'm in stores. It's such a thrill for me, because little five- and six-year-olds look up and say, "I watch you on television." Do you know how wonderful that is? Not to have done the show for so many years.

Did Ozzie's Girls *begin after David and Ricky left the original series?*

Yes, but David produced *Ozzie's Girls* because Ozzie was ill and wasn't really well enough to do it. David understood his father, saw that Ozzie was getting a little worn out, a little pained. David would just close shop and say that's all for today. He had learned under Ozzie's tutelage, because he grew up in the studio. So he knew every department and knew the way Ozzie worked. He had directed several of our shows, too, before he quit. He was sort of broken-in that way. Ozzie would give him the shows that had to do with young people in our cast.

Why did the Ozzie and Harriet *TV series end?*

Both Ozzie and I had the feeling that we had come to the end. We were worn out and the show was being worn out. We just had a feeling about it and, sure enough – at the end of the season – it was no surprise to us. It was a sad thing, the closing, because we had all been together for so long.

Your fans were with you, too, for a very long time. First in radio, then on television. We embraced your family and shared the joys and sadness that you had through the years.

Thank you. I know they're still friendly. I get such mail from people. Now I get mail from the younger people who grew up with the show, who now have children and tell me about them. So it goes on and on. We didn't intend to represent the American family when we started, we really didn't. We just started out to be a half-hour comedy show, but our audience decided what we would be.

What was the best time for you?

Well, I loved radio best and I'll tell you why. You could have a life of your own in radio. It was the best of all worlds. It was big time. You did it live. Then you had the thrill of working in front of an audience and having one crack at it. You didn't dare make a mistake, so you were absolutely on your best. It only happened once a week, so you could live like a human being the rest of the week. You could go to the movies, you could have people in for dinner. When we went to television, it was 24 hours a day, seven days a week. So I had more personal time when we were in radio, and yet had the best of it all. I still get such a kick out of those radio shows.

Harriet Nelson was born July 18, 1909 and was 80 at the time of our conversation. She died October 2, 1994 at the age of 85.

David
Nelson

David Nelson grew up before our ears and eyes on radio and television as the older son on **The Adventures of Ozzie and Harriet.** *We met on August 29, 1989 in his office at Casablanca Productions on Sunset Boulevard in Hollywood, California, where he produces commercials and industrial films. I asked about his* **Ozzie and Harriet** *career.*

 My first appearance, which was kind of interesting, was with my father's orchestra. I got away from somebody and walked out on stage while they were performing in Chicago at the Palmer House. I was backstage. I came along with the luggage and Rick wasn't around yet. Actually, when Rick was a year old he stayed with Grandma Hilliard, my mother's mother, in New Jersey. I continued to go on the road with my parents. I always blame my father for the fact that I couldn't get up and wake up for school in the morning. They kept me up till two or three in the morning, because those were their hours. Of course, they slept till 11 a.m.! My father was always on band hours.

He gave up the band some time into the radio series, didn't he?

He kind of eased out of the band. The first trumpet player and arranger was Billy May. As they got into the *Ozzie and Harriet* show, Billy really took over the band and it became more of a studio band than it was a touring band, up until the time they left Red Skelton. Red went into the Army, as it happened. They started to do the *Ozzie and Harriet* show, but during that time my father still had the orchestra.

In your dad's heyday as a bandleader, before he started playing for Skelton and his own show, how popular was his band?

Well, he won the *Times-Mirror* Poll Award. I think he was still going to Rutgers University and had just started the band. Then he got a radio show and he was on the air for a furniture company. This was 1928, 1929. But there was a popularity contest and I guess it was conducted by the *New York Times-Mirror*. He won that; I still have the plaque. He was very popular with the young people, because he was an athlete, played football and did all those things while going to Rutgers. He had, probably, the youngest band around the New York and New Jersey area.

He did a very smart thing, I think. Rudy Vallee was very hot and Dad saw that most of the gals would stop dancing and stand in front of the band shell when Rudy would sing. So he devised a method of hiring a female vocalist to be up on the bandstand with him, so that the guys would have something to watch as well as the girls. But he was very much like Rudy Vallee in his interpretation, because Rudy was from Yale, and he promoted that and of course Dad promoted Rutgers.

Then my next appearance was really on the Art Linkletter show, *House Party,* and that was the first for my brother and myself.

"Kids Say the Darndest Things."

Yes. He asked my brother – he asked all the kids this – "What do you want to be when you grow up?" Rick said he'd like to be either a "Club Scout" or a "Lone Stranger." He asked me and I said – at that time my father had gone to law school – so I said, "Well, I'm going to go to law school and become an attorney and then I'm going on the radio."

And that happened when I was 11! Bing Crosby was a guest on the show. Child actors had been playing David and Ricky's parts for the first three years into the work.

Tommy Bernard and –

– Henry Blair. Tommy played David and Henry played Rick. And I believe that Joel Gray played Rick for maybe six to seven months. When they first started the show there was a guy about 40 years old playing Rick. He had a hoarse voice and Father'd say, "Gee, we gotta get the kid's tonsils out!" It was pretty broad in those days!

Did you want to be on the radio?

I think we did. If somebody had said, "Okay, you can go on now, but you're going to have to spend 14 years doing this every week, day in and day out," we might have had second thoughts. But at the time it was something our parents did and we thought would be fun. Plus, the fact that the first show we did, Bing Crosby was on and he brought his son Lindsay to play himself. So we said, since we knew Lindsay Crosby and played tennis with him, couldn't we be on the show, too?

At that time, Rick couldn't read. So the first two years on the show, Rick memorized all the radio scripts. They didn't have a microphone short enough for him, so they sat him down at a table and had, like, a gooseneck mike that came over him. But he refused to go in front of the studio audience – about 250 people – without a script, even though he couldn't read. He would watch us out of the corner of his eye, and when we turned the page, he'd slide a page over. He said he felt the audience would think he was dumb, so he had a script.

Did he memorize all the lines or just the cue lines?

The cue line and his line. I don't know how he did it, to be honest with you.

But you, of course, were standing at the microphone with script in hand.

Yes, I was just reading it off.

Can you describe what the radio studio setup was? Where you stood, and your folks, and where Rick's table was.

We had an audience of about 250 people. There was a center audience, then two aisles, and then seats on the aisle. It was really like a small motion picture theater. The stage itself was maybe about four-and-a-half feet above, at kind of head-height to the audience. If you were in the audience looking at the stage, the sound man and his equipment were all to the right. They had big glass shields that surrounded him, so that he wouldn't lean over into the mike. The two main mikes were center stage. Rick has his table right behind the two center mikes and a chair, and behind that was the band. The band was set up on tiers. To the left of that was the control room with the director and the sound engineer. Above that was what they called a sponsor's booth, and that's where Rick and I went most of the time during the first two years when we'd go down and watch the show. We'd go up into the sponsor's booth and watch.

Before you were on the show, did you go to the studio every week?

Yes, we did quite often go down to the studio with them. They had a preview and then an air performance.

When you were on the show, how much rehearsal did you have before you actually got to the preview or the actual broadcast?

I think we just really read the script over a few times, but then Dad would always try lines out with us at home. He would even try the lines out with us at home, lines for Tommy and Henry. They were good friends, too, so we could go down to the studio to see them.

Did you have a good time when you were doing this?

Yes, I had a wonderful time and it was great! There was the band and we knew all the guys in the band.

Were you nervous on your first Ozzie and Harriet *show?*

You know, I can't remember back that far, but I'm sure I was. We wanted to do a good job, too.

Had your folks said to you, if this works, okay, but if not, we're going back to the other kids?

I don't think they made any particular commitment. It was only after we had done it that they started thinking about it. I think my father thought real serious about it because Rick got so many laughs. He was this little skinny kid who just stood right up and spoke out. Funny!

On both radio and TV, you were the more serious of the two boys and Rick was a little more of the cutup, a little more spontaneous.

You have to understand that my parents came from vaudeville and the stage and that my mother played with George Burns and Gracie Allen, while she was still dancing. She was out on the road with Ken Murray. She had specialty acts that she did, but she worked with and was straight for Bert Lahr. So she knew stand-up comedy, vaudeville, burlesque humor. That's where radio came from, at least according to what I've been told. I'm old enough to remember *Blackouts* with Ken Murray. There was a straight man and a comedian. Abbott and Costello, Martin and Lewis – there was a straight man and a comedian. I was told – I was sold the line – that I was the straight man, Harriet was the straight man and Ozzie and Rick were the comedians. A comedian was no better than a straight man who gives him the lines and he does the joke.

It certainly worked. The Adventures of Ozzie and Harriet *was among the best of shows.*

You have to give my dad credit for all of that, I think, because he was a man with six hats. He did everything. He wrote it, he produced it, he directed it. If he was mechanically capable, he probably would have shot it [for TV], too!

He loved doing it all, didn't he?

It was like a third child in our family, the show itself. There was David, Ricky and the show. We all sort of felt that way, it was a little bit bigger than all of us. My father signed one of the first, if not the first, 10-year agreements with a major network. I know Lucy did a year later, but it was a play-or-pay situation for 10 years. So he knew we were going to be there for 10 years. So his thinking, in terms of how the show would progress, was really from year-to-year and growing with the Nelsons, if you will.

People would say, "To what do you attribute the success of *The Ozzie and Harriet Show*?" I'd say, "It's really my father. He has a finger on the pulse of Middle America." My dad would say, "That's not true at all! If you're out there guessing what an audience is going to like, you're in trouble. You have to listen to yourself." I think that holds true today and I still remember that. If it's a question of making a decision of whether you direct somebody in one direction or another, do what you think is right. Don't do what you think somebody else will appreciate or what you guess that the audience would think is funny. It has to be funny to you first. There are an awful lot of people who have made livings in the business by stealing other people's material and changing it a little bit, because they knew it worked. In my father's case, he was really honest and just did what he thought was funny.

About your mother...

I don't think she's gotten her due for all the films and all the work she's done outside of *Ozzie and Harriet,* because she had a whole successful career before that even started.

She was a fine singer and a very appealing film actress.

She was a good dancer, too. A lot of people don't know that my grandmother was also a hoofer. She had an act with her sister and she married my grandfather, who was a director with Morts Brothers Night Company in the Midwest. So our family goes back another generation in show business. He ran the amateur vaudeville house in New Jersey. My grandmother played this wonderful kind of honky-tonk piano.

You and Rick grew up on the shows, and you got married on the show.

Well, we had a strange phenomenon, because by the time we went off, we actually had three shows in one. We had what my father nicknamed the "Pozzie," which was the older group, the women's club and Joe Randolph and Clara. Then I was an attorney and was married and had my life. Rick was married to Kris and somehow they were still going to school and Rick was singing. So there was the fraternity and school in one, my involvement with clients in another, and then we would all come back together. There were actually three shows at once.

When we went off the air, it was really ABC who made the decision. Rick and I were ready, but my father never was.

In fact, he continued, then, with Ozzie's Girls, *didn't he?*

I produced that with Al Simon and Filmways. We did 24 shows until my father got sick. I started directing on *The Ozzie and Harriet Show*, through the good graces of my father. As I mentioned, the show was a third child in our family, so for him to lend me his third child for a week was – I have to give him credit, because I wasn't that old. I was 20 years old.

Did he really let you do it or was he a shadow standing behind you?

My dad went to Bobby Marino, who was our cameraman at that time. Bobby tells this story, but Dad didn't tell me. Dad asked Bobby, "Do you think he's capable of doing it?" Bobby said, "Absolutely! There's no doubt in my mind. We're all here so there's nothing that David can do that's going to be wrong. But there's one condition." My father said, "What's that?" Bobby said, "That you don't come on the sound stage!"

We shot the show and my father lived up to his agreement. He did not come on the sound stage. He came in and saw the dailies every day, and worked on another script. But Bobby came over to me on about the third day into the show and said, "Come here, I want you to see something." We walked over to the stage door, and he opened it a little bit and there was my father, pacing back and forth in the alleyway on Stage 5 at General Service Studio!

It's hard to give up a third child!

I think that the only person, other than himself, that he would have allowed to direct it was me. He did all of them except for the first year, where we had a director for the first two shows. My father had no experience directing up until that time. But by the time they had done the second or third show, he felt qualified enough to direct.

He had an important hand in the writing of all these shows and he knew the characters.

Absolutely. As far as the crew was concerned, he also went out and hired the best people that he could possibly hire.

Did your family produce the radio and TV series? Did you own it?

Yes, we did. And the contractual agreement as well, with ABC. It was the only deal that I know, that was a 10-year deal where the network was putting up the money, giving us the money and father had full artistic control and ownership of the thing.

He knew what he wanted and he knew what would work.

That's the advantage of going to law school. He never practiced law, but he was always guilty of practicing without a license! He graduated from law school, but never took the bar, because his band was so successful. One of his professors said to him, "You're crazy. You should open a small law firm in Jersey." Dad said, fortunately, he never had to do that.

After the [TV] show went off the air in '67, late '66, my father edited 200 of the 435 shows for syndication. They had to be shortened in time for syndication, so he took that opportunity to update a lot of the shows. He was mainly interested in music, so he changed the music in the majority of the shows he edited.

You mean the bridge music, the background music?

Yes, he just felt that they were too old-fashioned. And to this day I still like to go back and look at the original films that have the old music in it, because it's almost like looking, for me anyway, looking at a Rolls Royce where they changed the fenders!

It's interesting to me that, although we did two years in color – the last two years – my father felt the show was funnier in black and white. Since he had done 12 years in black and white, we had black and white prints made from the color negatives! So the whole series of 200 are all in black and white. My mother said, too, that she felt the comedy was funnier in black and white.

David Nelson was born October 24, 1936 and was 52 at the time of our conversation.

Alan Reed

Alan Reed was the owner of a familiar, yet versatile, voice that brightened many a comedy and dramatic show on radio. We met on February 17, 1975 in his large, rambling ranch-type home, tucked away in a beautiful residential corner of Hollywood, California. I asked him when he first used that voice to make a living.

 Well, this is my 53rd year in the entertainment business. By using the voice, I suppose you mean radio. I started before that. I started when I was 14 as an extra with the French *Opéra Comique,* who came over here. I had to learn some lines in French and help carry a king around on a sedan chair. I got $1 a performance and an agent got 10 per cent of that.

When did you first get involved with radio?

It was 1926. I had been working at a summer place called Copaque. It's still in existence in New York State. It was an adult camp. From this place emerged a great many, many people. Moss Hart, for instance. Jacques Wolfe, who wrote "Shortnin' Bread" in the glory days. Mischa Auer, George Tobias, myself, a great many people were on the staff of this place. A guest came up the summer when I was 19, and talked about working for the Judson Radio Program Corporation. He told me that they were doing all of the radio programs for the networks. This was a newly formed subsidiary of the Judson Concert Bureau, which is the largest booking company of concert attractions. He told me [to come] up to his office in New York. He was a kid [and it] turned out he was an office boy up there, but he was learning the business. His name was Herb Polesie, who later on had *Twenty Questions.* Later on we did a program together called *Henry and George* for Henry George Cigars. He introduced me to the secretary of Charlie Skank, who was the producer [of] *True Detective Mysteries*, *My True Story, Physical Culture*, all [based on] the Bernarr McFadden magazines. They had an exclusive on the stories in them.

He introduced me to [Skank's] secretary, who took a look at my youthful face and said, "He has only one part open this week, and that's of a head mobster and I'm afraid you're too young for that. All the rest of the parts are cast." It was around lunchtime and I waited for her to go out to lunch, and I saw her go out to lunch, and I went into Herb's office and got the phone, and asked for Charlie Skank, who was in the other office. He got on the phone and I said, "Hello, Skank, uh…" He said, "Who is this?" I said, "Never mind who this is. I'm just gonna tell you somethin'. I'm comin' into your office in a couple of minutes. You're gonna give me a job, or you're goin' for a ride. You understand?" He said, "What the hell! Who is – come in here!" So, I went in there and got the job! That was the beginning of radio. I had done one thing before that. I'd been with a group in the Village called The New Playwrights Theatre. We, as a semi-professional group, met in competition with a supposedly amateur group of radio actors that WOR had. We each presented a play. It was a phony set-up publicity contest, but that was the first time. This was the first time I got paid.

Well, it's a good time to remember, then.

Yes! Well, from then on, Charlie and I became very good friends. I worked all of the shows and got a good, firm, early footing in the radio business. Because very shortly, the radio business emerged to the place where knowledge and quickness were very important to the director. He didn't have time to stop and teach a guy how to read a line, or what to do, because you're always fighting a time thing. So I was in at the beginning and got the experience, and by the time radio started to get really big, I was there and working like mad.

You were quite versatile and able to do all different kinds of voices. That was invaluable before the union days, when you could double and triple and all that.

Yes, true, true, true. I'm one of the founders of the union. I don't know if you knew that. There were three of us: George Heller and John Brown and myself, and belonged to the Forum in Equity. We sat down and we started talking of the need for a union. By this time, there were a lot of people working, but in radio, from the beginning to the end, there was like a hierarchy. Maybe 90 per cent of the work was done by 10 per cent of the people. Of that 10 per cent of the people, maybe 10 per cent of them were always going. It was due to the early stock [companies] and friendships that were formed, and knowledge of the business. Everybody threw his hand in those days in many varying things. For instance, I was on one of the phones at CBS where I was working mostly then, when Orson Welles had his "War of the Worlds" thing, and everybody was at a phone answering calls. It was frantic! It was frightening.

People really were taken in by that.

Oh, it was so believable, they were frightened, really frightened. People were calling.

What did Welles think about that?

At the time, he didn't think about it, but it certainly caused a lot of new directions in the radio business. They had to be informed, if there was even a remote possibility of anybody getting frightened, that this was a radio broadcast. It was not real. It was a strange, strange time in radio in those days.

Did you work most of the time in New York in those early days?

Yes, I worked in New York until 1943. Then out here ever since. Half my life there, half here. A lot of strange things happened in the early days. The soap operas were like a factory [with stories] that were being turned out. The same writers would be engaged [to] write two shows at once, so that you would find plots that you were playing on one show, were also running with different names on another show. Now, I did *Big Sister* and *Myrt and Marge* back to back. One was on from 10:00 to 10:15, and the other was on 10:15 to 10:30. I would just walk across the studio, you know, into the other room. I played heavies for two years straight on both of these. One, [heavy] was called Asa Griffin and the other [heavy] was called something like Zefferini or something…a hard-nosed gangster. Asa Griffin was seemingly a kindly old man who was a horror! He burned down orphanages for personal gain. He did all kinds of things. And the same bloody plots were occurring back and forth all the time!

In those early days, they tried to get the sponsor's name involved in these things. Like Myrt and Marge *were Myrtle Spear and Marjorie Minter, sponsored by Wrigley's Spearmint gum.*

Myrt and Marge! I mentioned before that Herb Polesie and I did *Henry and George.* We were plugging the Henry George Cigars. We played characters called Henry and George, and we had an orchestra, and a male singer and a female singer on the show. We were like the traveling bellhops. Later on, Major Bowes went to cities and told about the city. We had the same thing. Never left the studio, of course. We told all about what was happening in Detroit, Minneapolis, Chicago and all around. There'd be one-minute blackouts, then there'd be a musical number, and it was for Henry George Cigars.

And you were on a program called Harv and Esther.

Right. And it was the same company. I'll tell you, there is a very interesting tale connected with that. *Harv and Esther* was for Harvester Cigars. The Consolidated Cigar Company was the owner of both the previous *Henry and George* and *Harv and Esther.* They were related to the Paleys. The Paleys made the La Palina Cigars. Now, there was some connection, and I don't remember what it was now, between Consolidated Cigar Company and Paley, who founded the CBS Network. But, I had been doing *Henry and George* for three years. I got $50 a show the first year, and $100 a show the second year, and $150 the third year. This was a lot of dough for me. This was time when you were kids, and that money meant a lot more than today.

I went to a party one night, and a little man came up to me. He said, "I'd like to introduce myself. My name is Lichtenstein," he said. "You're a young fella. I'm surprised we're paying you so much money." I said, "Well, I appreciate what you're paying me, but 'so much money'? It's not that much." He said, "A boy your age? You're making $750 a week." I said, "What?" and I told him what I was getting. Judson Radio Program Corporation had been billing him for my services at $250, $500, and $750. I was getting $50, and $100 and $150. Well, this kind man got on the phone the next day to Judson, and raised Holy Cain with them. He said, "If you ever want to do business with me again, you will adjust that for that nice young man that I met last night." I got a check for $12,500. And it was fantastic!

Oh!! When was this, about what year?

Ninteen thirty. Not many taxes then, either.

Oh, boy!

Incidentally, in the beginning, when I started, what turned into CBS Network was originally station WABC in New York. They rented two hours of time from WOR and used their own call letters, WABC, while their station was being readied. Very few people know that. That's part of the history of the business. Paley had come up with his father's cigar money, and they owned a radio station down there, WCAU [Philadelphia]. They decided that they were going to see if they couldn't build another network, which they did. A pretty good one.

I want to tell you something that happened in 1931 and '32. Columbia, or CBS, was experimenting with television in their building at 485 Madison Avenue. On the 23rd floor they had a tiny studio, and in those days, television was done with something that looked very much like a make-up mirror. Just a string of strong lights in back of which was the camera. Well, Stoopnagle and Budd and myself were waiting to go up and ad-lib. They asked everybody working at CBS to come up and do a stint. There were then 54 sets in New York. They were all closed channel, you know, in advertising agencies and in a few [wealthy] homes.

Anyway, we're waiting to go on, and on the [television] receiver in the lobby, in this very small space, a girl was singing, a beautiful girl. She came out just as we were ready to go on, and I followed her. I said, "Can you wait downstairs? I want to talk to you." I wanted to make a date with her. She was gorgeous! So, Stoopnagle and Budd and I went in and we ad-libbed our way through [our routine]. We went downstairs, with the result that I asked the girl out for dinner. When we went across to a drugstore, which was on the street, we had dinner at the counter. I took her home, and that night I met her mother, who happened to be visiting New York. (They were from Washington.) Six months later we were married, and we've been married ever since. That was probably the first television romance. We now have our 43rd anniversary, and we have three children, boys, they've all married and we have 10 grandchildren.

You were the voice of Falstaff Openshaw on The Fred Allen Show *for years and years.*

Before Fred Allen there were many things. I did straight for a lot of the comedians. I worked for David Freedman, who had a comedy factory. He had Fanny Brice, Eddie Cantor, Block and Sully, Burns and Allen. Every comedy act that was in New York, David Freedman supplied the material for. Again, the same jokes in different dialects! Jokes all around the place. I did the voice of Rubinoff on the Eddie Cantor show. Rubinoff never wanted to talk. He was frightened. Once he went to Pittsburgh. His home, union local was there and they were giving a big benefit. They invited Rubinoff and his violin – a radio benefit, you know – for the musicians. Eddie bet him $100 that he wouldn't open his mouth, that he would just play his violin, because he was afraid to talk. He was a little embarrassed about his accent, but he shouldn't have been. He got on the air, was introduced by the master of ceremonies, "Rubinoff and his Violin," and he talked. All he said was, "Eddie Camphor owe me 100 dollar."

Well, when you were his voice on the Cantor show, did you do it with a Russian accent?

Oh, sure. Just as I sounded just now. "Eddie Camphor, vhat's da matter vit you?" We had Rubinoff's wife. We had Rubinoff's everybody on the show. We played all kinds of things. I found a Russian accent once. I was driving in a cab in New York, and the cab driver turned around. I told him where I wanted to go. He said, "I will inform you, sir, that you have the honor of being driven by a genuine Russian baron." So I said, "Keep driving." We drove around Central Park and I picked this thing up, but he was quite a character. Dialects have always been a kind of specialty of mine.

When you were in radio you were using the name Teddy Bergman.

Which was my name. It was my father's name. I'll tell you how the name change came about. That happened in 1939. I changed it because by that time I was the busiest what we called, in those days, *stooge* in radio. I worked all of the comedy programs. Every time I wanted to get to do a dramatic program, which I was proficient at, because I had some theatre before radio, the guys would say, "Ah, all you funny fellows, you want to act." I did want to act, and I couldn't get to first base. So, I decided, the dickens with this, I'm going to become a whole

Bam Bam in which each of the Flintstones have segments and the kids have segments. But they're repeated and repeated and repeated. My residuals ran out long ago, but what's great about it is the commercials. I have between eight and 16 commercials going every year for Flintstone products. They keep running them and playing them.

Well, that's good. You were working with Mel Blanc on that show.

Mel and I worked together very closely.

You worked a number of years ago in radio with Mel on his show.

I was on Mel's show. Yes. He had his own show and I had my own show, and others – Hans Conried once had his own show. It is impossible for a good character man to come up with a central pleasing character that can carry a show. We've had to come to the realization that we belong in a certain spot. We are character men. We can play character leads, as we do in *The Flintstones.* But, in the old radio days, I had – you mentioned it – the *Harvester* show. I was the guy and I had top writers. But I never made it. Of course, I had tough opposition. I was on opposite *Rudy Vallee and his Toppers.* It was at his height.

As a main character, a good solid supporting character in so many shows, you literally stole the show week after week.

In a lot of shows.

You were Pasquale in Life with Luigi.

Life with Luigi. That's a-right. You got-a memory! I loved that show. I like that more than any show I've ever done. That and with Fred [Allen]. Fred was an experience all in itself. Falstaff became a household word during the wartime period. On the strength of Falstaff, I did an awful lot of work in hospitals and canteens and things like that.

Didn't Falstaff open with a poem of some kind?

Yes, he'd knock on the door, and the door would open, and he'd say, "Blow the bugle. Toot the trumpet. It is Falstaff. Where shall I dump it?" And Fred would say, "Do you have a poem for us tonight?" He'd say, "Oh, indubitably. I might go so far as to say, in-double-dubitably. Have you heard, 'Make for the Roundhouse, Nellie. The Brakeman Can't Corner You There'? or, 'She was a girl just down from Vancouver. He was a sailor bent on maneuver'?"

Now wait a minute!

And then we would end up with a poem, about eight lines that would have relevance to the topic of the day in the Alley. It was a thing many people grew up with, as they've grown up with *Flintstones*.

Just about a month ago, along with a bunch of other radio people, we went up to Cal Arts University, which is the Disney-sponsored art school, full college upstate here, a little ways up. There were 21- and 22-year olds. We addressed the Humanities class who were studying radio at the time of the Thirties. We did *Cisco Kid*. There were a lot of people who had worked in the original and who have since become personalities. First, we did *Cisco Kid* and I did Pancho, which was the thing that Mel did for awhile. He replaced Harry Lang, who did it originally. "Hey, Cisco. What's the matter, Cisco?"

Later on, the master of ceremonies introduced each of us as what we're doing today, and when the guy mentioned *Flintstone*, it was amazing. It was like I was adopted by these people because they had grown up with it. They were just the right age in 1960, 15 years ago. They were seven years old, eight years old, six years old and they listened all through the years. Boy, the questions we were besieged with! It was an exciting experience.

You were on Abie's Irish Rose. *And there again, you almost stole the show. You were Solomon Levy, the father of Abie, right?*

Yes, Abie's father. That was one reason I couldn't come out here with Fanny Brice. Along about that time, I was the original Daddy to Fanny Brice's Baby Snooks.

Before Hanley Stafford.

Oh, we were in New York before Hanley even thought of doing it. We did it for about eight months. Then Fanny decided she had to come to the Coast and wanted me to come along with her. I couldn't. We had done, for two years before that, *Famous Lovers in History* in Yiddish dialect. We did Antony and Cleopatra, and Isabella and Columbus, imaginary things, which she wrote up and it was very funny. Fanny was very near-sighted, and she had her script done in very large type on special paper with a special machine. Each page was on a cardboard, so that her script was this thick and she had a big podium. We knocked the podium down, and the script went all over the floor one show. I grabbed my mike and we're sorting out and ad-libbing. We did the whole program from the floor, with the audience sitting out there. That was a highlight. Fanny was a wonderful woman.

Abie's Irish Rose was fun. Menasha Skulnik was great on it. Everybody was great on it. Incidentally, Rosie was Mercedes McCambridge. She won an Academy Award. She was so great in *All the King's Men*. She came from Chicago and this was her first show in New York and she played Rose. It was a very cute show.

You were on The Shadow *for a while, weren't you?*

Yes, I played Shrevie, the cab driver, mostly, for a lot of years. There's an interesting tale about *The Shadow*. In the old days, getting personnel experienced in radio, which was a new medium, was rather difficult. So people would have to learn it from scratch. *The Shadow* was one of the early shows. Not the earliest, Ruthrauff and Ryan was an agency that had come from a small office and one account – the Rinso account. It expanded into a huge organization. They had an awful lot of soap operas on and *The Shadow* was one of their shows. A fellow was put in charge, made supervisor of all daytime programs. He came up to Knight and Jordan. Knight and Jordan were the independent producers for Ruthrauff and Ryan of *The Shadow*. They both wrote and directed it, and hired and cast it. This guy came up to his office – Lamont Cranston was, of course, the Shadow. This great brain – I don't think he lasted much longer after this – came up and seriously sat down in their office and he said, "Now, I've been doing a lot of thinking, and I think that after this much time, you should develop a scene between Lamont Cranston and the Shadow. It would be very interesting." He had no idea what it was all about. He was in on the cuff, you know. There were a lot of people like that who had a brother-in-law or somebody and they just knew nothing.

Incidentally, in those days, there was no tape. There was just big, 16-inch records with 15 minutes on a side in those days. *Joe Palooka* was a 15-minute program, three times a week. If a mistake was made anywhere in the show, we had to start all over from the beginning. There was no snipping off a little bit and saying, "All right, pick it up from there." Frank Readick, who was the Shadow, incidentally, most of the time that I played it, played Knobby Walsh to my Joe Palooka. He had a tag line on the show, and he said, "Why, Joe will hit him with everything but the water bucket." That was the tag of the show. We get to the end of the show. We'd done pick-ups. We'd stopped two or three times, and we were exhausted. Now it was maybe the fifth time we had gone over it. Finally, we get to the tag line and he said, "Joe is gonna hit him with everything but the gloves." And we were dead. We were dead!

And away you go, all over again!

Oh, yeah. It was bad.

Did you, on any of these broadcasts, have to do repeat shows for the West Coast?

On any of them? On *all* of them from New York. It's the chief reason I moved out here. I had a growing family, three little children. We lived in Riverdale in New York. I never got to see my family or have a meal with them more than once a month. The kids would be asleep. I'd get home late. By the time I'd get up, they'd be off to school. I had to get down early for the next morning because it was a long haul. I'd go from 9:00, 10:00 in the morning. My first show would be 10:00, sometimes earlier. I did one show that was on the air at 7:30. *Peggy Windsor's Letters,* we dramatized. There was an experience I had with that. We would rehearse that in the afternoon, and then come in at 7:30 in the morning. It was on NBC, and we'd do it. We would play all kinds of parts, background voices and everything. In the afternoon, they asked another fellow and myself if we'd play a couple of kids hollering good-bye [in high-pitched, kids' voices], "Good-bye, Daddy. Good-bye, Daddy." Well, we got in in the morning, and in the early morning voice, when I heard the thing it came out "Good-bye, Daddy" [in a low-pitched sleepless-night voice]. It was sickening. It was awful.

You were on My Friend Irma *for a while, weren't you, for a long while?*

Yes, I played her boss, Mr. Clyde. It was a fine experience. That and *Luigi* were on at the same time. As I said, *Luigi* was my favorite show.

He was, himself, a very lovable guy and you, as Pasquale, were always trying to marry off your daughter on the show, Rosa.

Yes, [Pasquale] was a villain with not too black a heart. But what I liked about the show was the sincerity of it. We approached it as if we were those people. In the orchestra – and this stands out in my mind as one of the rare life experiences – one of the orchestra men in our group was Italian and his father had never been out of Worcester, Mass., from the time he came over here. He had opened an Italian restaurant eventually in Worcester, Mass., and was there for lo all these years. *Life with Luigi* was a must. Serving stopped when the program went on. The big radio went on. Everybody had to listen to *Life with Luigi*. We kept getting reports and the son would read letters to us. Finally, he brought his father out to see the show. He was sitting in the first row. The man couldn't believe that he was seeing this. Tears were rolling down his eyes. I had all I could do to get through that program without breaking down because I realized what it had meant. If it meant that to him, I had realized that we had really succeeded in legitimacy, in believability. Both [J. Carrol] Naish and I were honored guests of the Italian American Society. It was an enjoyable experience.

The end of it was not enjoyable. The end of it – and this is to give you an idea of the times – the girl who played Rosa [Jody Gilbert] was called up before the Un-American Activities Committee. Instead of admitting that she had made a mistake, she raised hell and threw things around the place, and the sponsor took advantage of [the] moral turpitude clause and canceled the program. It cost me a quarter of a million dollars in both radio and television shows that we had going. We were just breaking into television. But, the aftermath of that, six months after it went off, the way times were and rumors got around, I went into a butcher shop that I frequented rather well. As the butcher was wrapping up my stuff he said, "Is it true that both you and Naish were canceled on the *Luigi* show because you're communists?" This is the way the thing happened. It was a frightening, frightening time.

Indeed. You said you were on the TV version of Luigi. *Did you make a fairly easy transition from radio to television?*

Well, yes, and I had done some TV before that, but it wasn't the kind of transition that I wanted. I'll tell you why. I had spent most of my time in radio doing an average of 35 programs a week. The money was very good, and with money you acquire responsibilities. Coming into television, you can only do one, at most two programs a week. I hadn't built enough of a name to be the star of a show where the money would be comparable. So, I decided that I'd better have something else going because I had a big home and family to support. Schools and things like that. I started a business in specialty advertising. This was 20 years ago. My son is running the business today. It was quite successful and my younger son has made it even more so. I've retired.

From that business, but not from show biz?

Well, the only thing I do is *Flintstone* or *Flintstone*-connected things now, and that is commercials. I do have a major activity now that I'm very excited about. I'm on the Board of Directors and Finance Chairman of a group called Theatre Forty. We're sponsored by the city of Beverly Hills. Beverly Hills is the only high school in the country that has, in residence, our own theater, which they built for us.

You've made an important contribution to the entertainment scene over the years.

I played in every phase of it. Pictures, legitimate theatre, radio, television, nightclubs, vaudeville, every phase of it.

Alan Reed was born August 20, 1907 and was 67 at the time of our conversation. He died June 14, 1977 at the age of 69.

Bret Morrison

Bret Morrison starred on radio as **The Shadow** *and as* **Mr. First Nighter.** *We met on December 13, 1973 at his home in the Hollywood Hills. He did a lot of radio work in Chicago and I speculated that he certainly must have been a member of the now-famous "Bridge Is Up Club."*

Yes, yes! That's the club that all the Chicago actors get together on Wednesday afternoons for luncheon and discuss the old days and our friends and exchange information about various people in the business and what they're doing and one thing or another.

It's called the "Bridge Is Up Club" because you share one thing in common with each other: You all got stuck somewhere along the line when the bridge was up in Chicago!

Yes. In order to get from the Merchandise Mart to either the Wrigley Building or the Tribune Tower, where the Mutual Network was, we had to cross the Michigan Avenue bridge. So, if it was open at an inopportune time, we were apt to be late. As you know, in radio everything had to be down to the second and there's some very strange and amusing excuses, but that was always a very good excuse to use if you were unavoidably detained. One actor – I don't know who it was – came in and said, "I'm terribly sorry I'm late today, but just everything went wrong. The bridge died and my landlady was up!"

Did you, indeed, ever get caught by the bridge?

Oh, yes, yes!

You were on The First Nighter Program. *Did you ever get on-the-air credit as*

Bret Morrison, the First Nighter?

I don't remember whether we had air credit at that time or not. I did *First Nighter* from 1937 until World War II and I don't think our union at that time had a mandatory clause that we would be given air credit.

Did that come about because of the union? The air credit?

I think it came about a little bit later, like in the late Forties, shortly after the war when a lot of the actors sort of complained about the fact that they were doing important roles on shows and were getting no identification. Some of the advertising agencies were using this as a wedge, also, to threaten the actors so that if they made demands for an increase in salary, the agency said, "Well, we can just fire you and get somebody else, and after a few days nobody's going to know the difference anyway." So we sort of asked, you know, that this be included in new contract negotiations and it finally was.

You were the genial "First Nighter," the host.

Mr. First Nighter, yes. I was always ushered to my favorite seat. I was on the aisle, down in front, I guess it was.

This, of course, was in Chicago. You were quite busy as an actor in Chicago in the late Thirties and early Forties.

Yes. Chicago was really, I think, probably more active even than New York, and certainly more active than the West Coast in those days, being centrally located and being so near so many of the major sponsors. General Mills and others, being located pretty much in that area, felt they had a little more control of their shows from Chicago rather than New York. After the war, however, things just sort of shifted, and then they came out to New York and Hollywood.

You were on all of the big shows in Chicago.

I started in radio in Chicago way back in 1929 when I was still in high school.

Where did you go to high school?

Nicholas Senn. We have a lot of alumni from there that have done some great things in theatre and pictures. Burr Tillstrom from *Kukla, Fran and Ollie* was just after me. Jerry Lester was in my class, the dramatics class. Hugh Marlowe, who has done a great deal in films, and oh, gosh, there were just loads of them, it seemed, that came from that particular era.

You had an interest in drama and the arts in high school?

Yes, that really started me. I didn't really go out for it until I was in my junior year at Senn, and then I saw a performance of *Beau Brummel* and I thought this would be kind of fun. I was majoring in art and history of architecture and painting, and so they were sort of allied arts to me. I've always been interested in theatre, so I decided I'd try out for it and I broke a precedent. You had to have two semesters of preparatory work before you could become a "Player," which naturally meant that it would be one year of what they call "B" and "A" dramatics before you became a "Player." Well, inasmuch as I was in my first semester of my junior year, that meant that I would only have one semester in "Players" to do anything. So I found I had enough English credits that I could skip the "B" dramatics and go right into "A", which I did.

That same year they were doing a play at Senn called *Happy Go Lucky* or *Tillie of Bloomsbury* and it seemed that we used to give two performances and we'd have a different cast at each performance, because the casts were usually large enough to give everybody a chance to play. But there were always more women than men, as a rule, and you had to meet certain scholastic standards in order to be able to qualify for the "Players." For some reason or other, they only had one lead to play both nights. So, for protection they called on the "A" dramatics class to understudy and finally, about a week or so before the actual performance, our director said, "I'm going to announce something that's unprecedented in the history of our dramatics class, but I think he's earned it. Bret Morrison is going to play the lead on Friday night." So that gave me my extra semester as a "Player" and then I took an extra semester's post-graduate course so that I'd have an additional chance to play.

You mentioned that you first got involved in radio in 1929.

Right. That was at WCFL, the Voice of Labor, in Chicago. I had my own poetry hour there. And then later, as a result, we formed a little theater group with a nucleus of players that we had at Senn, under the same director. We used to do one-act plays on the air. Then, eventually, I did some publicity work for Universal Pictures and we did across-the-board, five half-hours a week and did the complete version of *Dracula*, which they had just filmed, and on the basis of this I came out to the West Coast to work in a picture called *The Road Back*, which was the sequel to *All Quiet on the Western Front*. That was in the early Thirties, 1931 or '32 I believe it was, and I was here until about 1937. I got into radio out here on the West Coast and I did *Hollywood Hotel, Lux Radio Theatre* and a lot of the big shows and a lot of other shows that came up. We had mostly half-hour shows out here. We didn't have the big-time soap operas on the West Coast at all.

Was it tough to get an acting job on the major shows on radio out here, back in those days?

Well, it was, of course. This was the height of the Depression and the average price for a radio show in those days was $5 and some paid as little as $3. Some of the recordings we did, some of the series paid $3 for a 15-minute recording.

Did that include your rehearsal time?

Oh, yes, that was the whole business! *Hollywood Hotel* and *The Lux Radio Theatre,* when they started, paid the most. They paid $50, but you had to rehearse all week for that. I mean, you were at their disposal for the entire week. But, as I said, this was the height of the Depression and $50 a week was a lot of money in those days.

I was out here in California – this was 1937 – and I was visiting some friends, sort of bemoaning the fact that things were not too good in radio. I was making a living, I was getting by, but I felt sort of stifled. My family was still back in Chicago and I was sort of anxious to go back. My friends mentioned the fact that they knew someone who was in town from Chicago, looking for some other type of talent, writing talent, actually. But they said, "Why don't you call and find out what the situation is in Chicago?" So I called this man and I asked him what the leading-man situation was and he said, "Well, there's always room for one more, if they're any good." He said, "I'll tell you what I'll do. I've got to catch a plane back to Chicago late tomorrow afternoon, but if you want to meet me at –" There was a recording company out here called Freeman-Lang, where we did a lot of our shows for radio in those days, and he said, "If you want to come out and cut an audition record, I'll take it back. I can't promise anything," he said, "but at least I'll see what can be done." So I went down with him, and his wife very graciously read with me on the script and I sat down at the piano because I discovered they were going to do a musical. He picked up the record and off he went and I thought, well, you know, I won't hear anything more about that. Then I got a wire saying, "I can't really guarantee you anything, but the chances are very good, if you want to come out on speculation, that you can get something on this show."

I decided to take the jump and I pulled up stakes here and went back to Chicago, into the agency for my interview on the show. They seemed to be very impressed with the audition that I had done and the fact that I could do both the singing and acting. It made it that much better. They were originally going to split it up and have someone do the acting and somebody else do the singing. So they asked me how much I wanted for the show. We didn't have strip shows, as we call them here, in those days – five days a week. They were mostly half-hour shows, costume-drama things, "Peter the Great," "Catherine the Great," things of that kind. All I was thinking in my mind at this time was $50 'cause that was the highest price that you could get out here for a show. So I said, "Well, if you pay for all the arrangements, everything else –" "Oh, yes, we'll take care of that." I said "Well, $50 a show." And he said, "Well, that's $250 a week." And I just gulped and I said, "Yes, it is." And he said, "Well, I guess that's satisfactory." I nearly dropped dead, because I didn't expect that. In those days – 1937 – $250 a week was considerable!

Have you ever thought what you might have asked for that? You know, $3 for this show and $5 for that one and the top was Lux, *and this was not* Lux, *so what might you have asked? Ten dollars for the show?*

I don't know, I really don't know. I had just one figure in mind and I figured that $50 – in those days – if I could average $50 *a week,* I could get by. And this is all I was looking for. We've come a long way since then.

What was that show?

It was called *Love Song* and it died an early death, because it was a very bad show, actually. It developed into a burlesque sort of thing. And finally they did away with the dramatic show idea and it resolved itself into Vincent Pelletier and myself. I sang and Vinnie read poetry. And we were on for quite a while with that format.

You were rather versatile, because you had announcing jobs as well as acting jobs.

Yes, I specialized in dialects, too. I'll tell you, a lot of the actors in the early days had to be versatile. In order to make enough money to make a living even at the height of the Depression, when a few dollars went a long way, you had to be versatile. If certain areas sort of petered out, you had to be able to step into something else and do it. You couldn't be a specialist, really, because there was no room for specialization. You had to be as versatile and flexible as you possibly could if you wanted to work steadily – which, fortunately, I always have.

You were on a lot of the soap operas from Chicago.

Oh, yes, yes. And then in New York. I don't think there's one on the air that I haven't played in at sometime or another.

Did you have the lead in any of them, any of the soaps? I know you were on Woman in White *and* Guiding Light.

And *Big Sister, Helen Trent, Ma Perkins, Stella Dallas.*

You had an important role in The Light of the World.

Yes, I was the announcer on *The Light of the World,* or rather the narrator.

You were the one who came on and said –

"The Light ... of the World!"

You mentioned New York. How did you get to New York from Chicago?

I was in Special Services during the war and they were utilizing my talents as far as the theatre and radio was concerned and they approached me and said, "We have been screening people and your name keeps constantly coming up. You seem to be the only one who is familiar with all of these various phases of theatre and show business which we require for this specific job that we have in mind," which was the "WAC Caravan." It was the recruiting of WACs throughout the New England states primarily and then, also, I went up to Canada and organized the same thing up there.

My job was to produce and direct a 15-minute radio show every day with all Army personnel, including myself, and then be stage manager and emcee a three-hour stage show every night, to be familiar with any kind of a light board, or to improvise as far as settings and lighting and so forth was concerned, depending upon where we were playing and what we had to do. This was very interesting work. I enjoyed it tremendously. There were 125 people in our company and we were all stationed in Boston for Service Command. Anyway, when I completed my work with them, I went to New York from Boston and I'd no sooner arrived in New York when – I was just working steadily that first year I was here, 1944 – I got *The Shadow.*

I was called down to audition for something. I was doing another broadcast and they were losing the studio at 2:00 and I was called in. I didn't get off the air until a quarter of two. I said, "Well, I'm not sure that I can make it, but I'll sure try my best." I got there about three minutes to two. They said, "Well, we're losing the studio at 2:00," but they handed me this thing and said, "Just read this. It's the opening and closing of this thing." And that was it. I looked at it and it was the opening and closing of *The Shadow.*

And you didn't know the audition was for The Shadow?

No, I didn't know what it was for. So I just read it as I'd always remembered hearing it, you know, because we used to follow *The Shadow* – us *First Nighters.* And so I always heard the closing signature. So that was that. I read it and forgot about it. We were constantly doing auditions and some we get and some we don't. About a week or so later, I got a call that said, "Oh, you're it." And so I did it from then until it went off the air. I did *The Shadow,* I guess, longer than anyone.

From 1944 until the end?

Until it went off the air, in the middle Fifties.

And there were brand new shows being presented every Sunday. Sunday afternoon with The Shadow.

"Five o'Clock Shadow" I was called!

Did you have to take a trip to the Orient to learn how to cloud men's minds?

No, I managed to do that without having to go to the Orient! I did the opening and closing signature, the "Who knows... "

Do you think that –

Oh, yeah! It won't sound the same, because I worked on a special microphone which gave it a filtered effect, but I'll do it for you: "Who knows... what evil lurks... in the hearts of men? The Shadow knows [sinister *Shadow* laugh]!

And at the end there was –

"The weed of crime bears bitter fruit. Crime does not pay. The Shadow knows." It's sort of a mixed metaphor, I guess.

And it was a great, great radio show! You had the longest run as an actor playing The Shadow. Who preceded you?

Bill Johnstone. And Orson Welles, before that. Originally, well, there was a Robert Hardy Andrews who was before Orson Welles. This went on in the very early Thirties – I'm not sure. He was just like Raymond on *Inner Sanctum*. He was merely a host. And then the story had nothing to do with the Shadow until Orson Welles stepped in and then he became a central character in the story itself. Bill Johnstone followed him and then, as I say, in 1944 I followed Bill Johnstone.

What was the reason for the switch?

I don't know. I never had any idea. I didn't know what the reason was.

When you were playing Lamont Cranston, The Shadow, who was your lovely friend and companion, Margo Lane?

Well, I had four. Marjorie Anderson was the first, Grace Matthews and Lesley Woods, and then Gertrude Warner was the last one. I think Gertrude did it longer than anyone else. Agnes Moorehead did it with Orson Welles.

Did you enjoy doing The Shadow?

Yes, I did, I did. When I first did it, you know, we were "live." We used to work from the Longacre Theatre in New York. I don't believe radio shows should be watched, but the audiences seemed to enjoy it. But it's such a small percentage of the listeners that it doesn't, I guess, destroy the illusion.

Some of the radio shows, such as First Nighter, *for a good example, had the actors "dress" for the performance.*

Oh, yes. We always did ours live before an audience, yes. And we dressed. We even took it on vaudeville. We had a vaudeville turn with *First Nighter.* I don't think there's anything I haven't done!

What about television?

I did television in the early days, you know, when television was live. I did *General Hospital.*

Did you do anything on the screen?

Oh, yes, yes. I did some pictures way back in the Thirties, some things back then. I was in *Cavalcade*, that's the Noel Coward thing, and the remake of *Tess of the Storm Country* with Janet Gaynor and *Hell Below* with Clark Gable, and a few others.

There were a couple of Shadow *movies. Were you in those ?*

No, no. That was before. I think they only did two pictures on that. *The Shadow*, they've never been able to do anything with it on television. I know the reason why. Because they wouldn't accept the fact that it's sort of an adult fairy tale. It was fantasy and it should have been treated like *Topper* was done, with special effects and on film. And the few times that they tried to do something with it, they've always tried to rationalize it, you know, and make it believable and it just never came off.

Wouldn't you say, too, that The Shadow *is really radio material, because the listener had to add his imagination?*

It is, right, right.

It's been a treat to talk to the man who was the Shadow and the First Nighter and the voice of so many great characters on radio.

It's nice to see someone from the old home town, and I hope radio comes back and the time will come when every radio set will be a color set.

Bret Morrison was born May 5, 1912 and was 61 at the time of our conversation. He died September 25, 1978 at the age of 66.

Ken Roberts

Ken Roberts owns one of the most famous voices in radio. He started as an announcer in the late 1920s. We met on October 24, 1998 at the Friends of Old Time Radio convention in Newark, New Jersey. I asked him when his broadcast career actually began.

Actually, I'd forgotten that it was in the late Twenties. I started when I was still in high school, I guess, in the mid-Twenties. I had a friend who was writing a program for WOR called *The Story Behind the Song*, and he called me and asked me if I would like to be on the program one evening. And I said, naturally, I would. And that was my first exposure to the microphone, somewhere about 1926 or 1927, I suppose.

Your first professional radio job?

My first professional radio job was at WMCA in New York. I had always wanted to be an actor. I had no intention of being in radio or announcing or anything of that sort, but getting jobs in the theatre was rather difficult in those years as it still is, but there was a depression at the time and the theatre felt the Depression like most business did, except maybe even more so. But there was a need to make a living and I just went up to WMCA and asked for a job if they had an opening. They said, "We have a temporary job open." I was lucky enough to do it and I got wonderful experience there. But it didn't last very long and I didn't have too much time to give them, because I did have a summer job waiting for me as an actor in a stock company. So I left WMCA, after just a couple of months, and went to work in the stock company, acting.

Did they feel that your voice had a radio quality at that time?

Yes, I think they did. Actually, WMCA was responsible for my name. My name was not Kenneth Roberts when I started. My name was Kenneth Truman. The man who hired me was the chief announcer. His name was A. L. Alexander and he enjoyed some sort of fame for a while. He had something called *The Court of Human Opinion*, or something of that sort, that he conducted on the air.* But he looked at me and said, "You have a very nice voice and I'd like to hire you, but you'll have to change your name." I said, "What's wrong with Kenneth Truman?" He said, "People won't understand it over the microphone. It's too explosive. *Truman, Truman, Truman.* It doesn't have a sonorous sound." I said, "Well, Mr. Alexander, the job is important to me, more important than the name. Why don't you give me a name?" He thought for a moment and said "Well, how about Clyde Roberts?" I said, "Well, the Roberts sounds all right, but you can keep the Clyde!" That's how I became Kenneth Roberts. It was at WMCA in New York.

You were baptized under fire right off the bat with a new name.

That's how it happened.

So you went on the stage then.

Yes. I was in this little stock company up in Connecticut. That just lasted a couple of months and then I needed a job again. I spent my days on what we call rounds: knocking on doors of agents and casting directors and producers, and all to no avail. There was no work, so one day I said, "This can't go on; I've got to get a job somewhere. What about this thing called radio? I had a little exposure. Why don't I try that a little more seriously?" Now, this was all to myself, of course! I said, "I can't look for work at NBC or CBS," which were just starting to get very important. "I don't have enough experience in this. I'd better start at a small station."

In New York, at that time, there were a number of small stations, mainly in Brooklyn. Brooklyn had four radio stations of their own, each on the air for about four hours a day. They shared the wavelength. That was the custom in those days, one wavelength for four radio stations. I said, "I'll go out to Brooklyn and I'll visit each of those stations and see if I can get a job. I'll devote a day to that instead of a day to walking around Broadway." So out to Brooklyn I went, by subway. The first station I visited was WLTH, the "Voice of Brooklyn." They were in the *Brooklyn Daily Eagle* building, which was a Brooklyn newspaper of some note at that time, and that made it sound very important to me. So I walked into the station, which turned out to be two rooms. One room was the reception room, where all the business of the station was conducted, and the other room was the studio. And I walked in. There was one person sitting at a desk and I approached him. I said, "How do you do, Sir. I was wondering if I could get an audition for a job as a radio announcer?" And he looked at me and said, "How

---

* A. L. Alexander conducted the *Goodwill Court*.

old are you?" and I told him. He said, "What is your experience?" I said, "Well, I worked at WMCA for three weeks." He said, "I see. Well, it so happens that my announcer left this morning and I need somebody. You've got the job." And that's how it started.

Not even an audition.

No audition, no nothing. He hired me and he gave me a wonderful salary for that time. I just couldn't believe it. And after three months, he gave me a $5 raise. And that was delightful! After another three months, during all of which time I did everything at this station, another raise! I was the only announcer and I was the only person on the air. I did the news, I did music programs, I played the piano, I read poetry, and I swept up the studio in my spare time. I answered the phone when we got off the air. I even sold time over the telephone, acted as a salesman. So I had a lot of experience and I learned how a radio station operates. I therefore felt I was ready for the big time, and so I went to CBS. I decided to try CBS first. I liked their attitude on the air. I liked the kind of programs they were doing. I preferred their sound to that of NBC's. I don't know why, but it appealed to me more than NBC did. So I went to CBS and arranged for an audition, which they were giving in those days. I did my audition and I was hired that day! On CBS! And that was the start of my real career.

And your first assignment, then, for CBS?

Well, as a staff announcer my first assignment was to sign on the station at 7:30 in the morning. That was the first thing, I remember, that I had to do. I would get up at six or so, so I could get there on time to put the station on the air. News had not started as yet, news was not on the air. Most of the programs were music or drama.

This was the local CBS station, WABC, at that time?

This was the key station. At that time it was WABC, correct. Those call letters later went to another station. But CBS was originally WABC, and some years later it was changed to WCBS. That was in New York, of course. It was already a part of the Columbia Broadcasting System, because the Columbia Broadcasting System predated WABC. Mr. Paley was given a gift by his father when he graduated from the University of Pennsylvania. His father asked him what he wanted most. He said "Well, I'd like to get into this new broadcasting business." His father was a very wealthy man and he bought the Columbia Broadcasting System for him.

The Columbia Broadcasting System, in those years, was a program-supplying entity. They supplied programs to WOR as well as WABC and other stations throughout the country. Eventually, CBS bought its own radio stations and in New York it bought WABC, which was the Atlantic Broadcasting Corporation.

From there on they bought WBBM in Chicago, as you know, and they bought WCCO in Minneapolis. That's how it grew and by the time I got there, which was in 1931, they had already been in existence four years, I think, after they started in 1927. I was part of that whole growing-up scene.

Many of the CBS network programs originated from New York.

Yes. We were already at 485 Madison Avenue with five studios, I believe, and they were constantly busy. Pretty soon soap operas came to be very, very popular and all of the work, I must tell you, for announcers was done by staff men. There was no such thing as a free-lance announcer; everything was staff. I had not been there very long when CBS landed its first big, big show and that was for Chesterfield cigarettes. Lucky Strike was already on the air, but they were on NBC, so that the landing of the Chesterfield account was very important to CBS.

To announce it, they held auditions to see who would get the program, and the only people who auditioned were the staff announcers. I was fortunate enough to win the audition and get the program, which was a big feather in my cap, considering that I was a newcomer. I'd only been there a few months and here I competed against people like Andre Baruch and David Ross and Frank Knight and Louis Dean and Harry Von Zell, who were all on staff with me at that time, and I managed to win this program. It was important because the more programs you did to the satisfaction of sponsors, the more certain was your job at CBS. You got no money for doing these programs, you got no extra fees, nothing of that kind, you just received your salary from CBS. But you wouldn't have been on staff very long if you didn't have your share of commercials, so it was very important to get that.

What was that Chesterfield program?

It was six nights a week, 15 minutes a night. I think it went on at 9:00 every night with Andre Kostelanetz and his orchestra, and there were three singers, each of whom did two nights a week. Jane Froman was one of them. I believe Bing Crosby did two nights and Arthur Tracy, the Street Singer. Then they varied after that. Others were added. I think Lily Pons came on it for a while. Oh! I did the Morton Downey program, too. That was for Camel cigarettes. *The Camel Quarter-Hour*, with Morton Downey. The orchestra was Jacques Renard, who came from Chicago, I believe.

Was this at the same time you were doing the Chesterfield program?

Oh, no, you couldn't do two cigarettes. Chesterfield was the first, then I went on after that to [the other].

Remember that I said you didn't get a fee? You might find this interesting. I received a call one afternoon to visit with the vice-president of CBS, a man by the name of Klauber, Ed Klauber, who really ran the company. He said, "Mr. Roberts,

I have something to discuss with you. Chesterfield is very happy with your work and they would like to give you a fee for doing their program. However, I would like you know that while we can't stop you from taking the fee, we would not smile happily upon it, since it is not our policy to allow our staff announcers to take fees. We would like you to continue working for us instead of for Chesterfield, so if you take this fee, that would be the end of your relationship with CBS. However, we understand and are happy that you are doing such a good job for Chesterfield, and so if you don't take the fee you would continue to work for us and Chesterfield and we will give you an increase in salary." There was no question in my mind what decision I would make, so I said, "I'll be happy to stay with CBS." So I got a $15 increase.

That's wonderful! And you certainly got a nice pat on the back.

Chesterfield was prepared to pay me $200.

Oh, boy! May I ask what your CBS salary was at that time?

Yes. I was making $55 a week.

But you didn't know how long the Chesterfield relationship would last.

That's right. Working with CBS became a permanent job, and when Chesterfield went off the air, I stayed with CBS. There came a time when Chesterfield decided to change announcers and I did lose the job, but my increase continued. More than that, CBS, a wonderful company, took into note that it might be uncomfortable for me to be relieved of my job from Chesterfield and they took me aside and they said, "Now look, you don't want to be here when the change is made. Why don't you go on a little vacation. We'll pay for it." And they sent me to Atlantic City for two weeks, at their expense, while this change was made.

They most certainly had a wonderful regard for you.

It was very considerate. It was very considerate.

When you came back then you had –

I had a marvelous career after that. I did two or three soap operas a day. I did *Joyce Jordan, Girl Intern; Life Can Be Beautiful; This is Nora Drake.* Oh, I did so many of them. I did *Easy Aces*, which also had come from Chicago.

Did you work, early on in your career with CBS, with Fred Allen?

Yes. I was on the Fred Allen show when it first started, the very first Fred

Allen show, which was on for a product that no longer exists called Linit. The program was called *The Linit Bath Club* [*Revue*] and it starred Fred Allen and Portland Hoffa and Charlie Cantor and John Brown, a fellow by the name of Jack Smart, and Minerva Pious – Minnie Pious – who was a wonderful comic actress.

Some of those people stayed with Fred through his radio career.

Yes, they did. I did not, because CBS had another rule, which was that you were exclusive to them. If you worked for CBS you couldn't go to NBC or anywhere else. You had to stay with CBS. [So] I was left behind at CBS.

Did you work with Phil Spitalny?

Yes, I worked with Phil Spitalny and his all-girl orchestra. That was also, I think, for Linit.

This is still in the 1930s?

Yes, yes.

And was it at this time when you first became associated with The Shadow?

I became associated with *The Shadow* when it was still sponsored by a magazine. It was sponsored by Street and Smith [Detective Story] magazine, and at that time the Shadow was the narrator of the program, not a character in the show. He would introduce the program and it became very, very popular, as you know, with this strange voice telling the audience that "crime does not pay" and "the weed of crime bears bitter fruit" and so on. It was very popular.

Sadly enough, after about two or three years of this program, it went off the air. Street and Smith decided they didn't want to do radio anymore for whatever reason. But there was such a clamor from the public for this program to return that it was picked up by a product called Blue Coal. But in doing so they changed the format of the program. Instead of the Shadow being just the narrator, he became the star of the program, known only to his friends and to his girlfriend in particular, as Lamont Cranston, a wealthy man-about-town who had been to the Orient and learned the secret there of how to make himself invisible. To play the Shadow they were able to get the services of a young actor who was just making a great sensation, a man by the name of Orson Welles. So Orson was the first Lamont Cranston known as the Shadow. And I was lucky enough to be the announcer. I had been the announcer on the original series and so I continued working for Blue Coal and selling Blue Coal while introducing *The Shadow*.

We heard The Shadow *in the Chicago area on the Mutual Network station.*

That's right. The reason I was able to do that even though I was on staff at

CBS is that *The Shadow,* which you heard on Mutual, was a recorded program, so when I appeared on *The Shadow,* I wasn't really working for Mutual, I was still working for CBS, but working for one of their clients on a recording. And the recording was made on a Wednesday or Thursday afternoon, or some such, and then it was played on WOR and the Mutual Network on Sundays. But I was never on Mutual or WOR. I was on the recording which was made, oddly enough, at the RCA studios. The whole thing was very complicated, but I was within the law and within the rules of my contract in that I was not appearing on another station.

You stayed as the announcer on The Shadow *for a good many years in the Forties.*

Oh, yes, I was on *The Shadow,* I think, for six or seven years, and the reason I left was that I had developed my own program called *Quick as a Flash,* an audience participation program that was very much in the style, if you please, of *Information, Please.* I not only helped develop it, I owned part of it and I was also the host. Because of that, not because it was going to be sold to Helbros Watches and they bought time on WOR, it interfered with my contract with CBS. So at that time I took a leave of absence from CBS.

They knew what you were going to do?

Yes, and I would have to leave staff in order to do it, but it was worthwhile. It was worth it to me because it was a step up in my career. Instead of being just an announcer, or just a voice, I was now, in my view, a personality, if you will, in my own right, with my own program. I was a so-called "leading personality," rather than a supporting announcer, so it was worth it to me to do *Quick as a Flash.* Did you ever hear of it?

I remember listening to the program, faithfully on Sunday afternoon, before or after The Shadow.

Immediately before.

You had taken a leave of absence from CBS to move on to Quick as a Flash. *How long did that run?*

I was on it for three years. The program continued but I left it in about 1950, I guess, or 1951, something like that.

Did you then return to CBS?

Yes, I did. I went back to CBS and stayed with them another two or three years. And then I got very, very busy. I received a lot of offers to do shows on other networks, which I wanted to do, and the only way I could do them was by leaving CBS, and they said to me, "Well, we'll give you another leave of absence, but only for three years. If you can't come back after three years, we'll have to just sever our relationship." That was a fair deal and I took the leave and never went back.

It's really amazing that a company would be willing to do that. Today it would be totally unheard of.

That's right. Well, the announcers were very, very important to the companies at that time. Not just CBS. NBC was very loyal to its announcers as well, because they had a wonderful staff, too, as you know: Milton Cross, Kelvin Keech and George Ansbro. And the announcers were very important, because the announcers actually were the ambassadors, or representatives, of the company. Who was NBC? NBC was a company, but George Ansbro was a personality, a person that the audience could identify with. And so the announcers became very important to the broadcasting companies and that, perhaps, is why they were loyal to them, or maybe because they were decent people. I don't know, one or the other.

You appeared on a great many nationally broadcast programs over all the networks at various times and became identified with some of those programs as the announcer on that show. You were on Crime Doctor *and* Grand Central Station *and* It Pays to Be Ignorant *for some time.*

You see, a lot of these programs became my programs, if I can use that expression, because I became the Philip Morris announcer. As the Philip Morris announcer I did all of their programs. They sponsored *Crime Doctor* and they sponsored *It Pays to Be Ignorant*. They sponsored the *Philip Morris Playhouse*. They sponsored a musical program on NBC, so being their exclusive announcer, I did all of their shows and they had shows on all networks, as you remarked. I also did *Take It or Leave It,* which was on CBS for a while and then it moved to NBC and when it did I moved with it, so I had a connection with the advertising agency, which was the Beal Company. They were fond of my work and I had almost an exclusive arrangement with them that I would do only their programs [and] all their programs. I wasn't the only announcer who had that kind of arrangement. There were many advertising agencies by that time who used their own, so-called, stable of announcers.

You would work not only for the Philip Morris-sponsored programs, but other programs produced by that agency.

Exactly right. They represented Procter and Gamble, they represented Eversharp, and so I did all those shows, you see. That was the way that worked.

How important to the production of the program was your role as an announcer?

Well, I think the announcer was very important to the sponsor. You had to be able to deliver the copy in a satisfactory manner to the sponsor. As a matter of fact, early on, before I went with the Beal Agency, I was on for a laxative [company]. I would have to go out to the office of the president of this company every week and read the copy for him to make sure that I was reading it properly and to his satisfaction. And he would have the, what shall I call it, not the gall, but he would have the nerve to tell me how to read the copy. And I took it, because I wanted the job. I was receiving a fee at that time from him, and he was my boss, and I would listen to him. He went so far as to have a microphone installed in his office and a loud-speaker in the next room. I would be in one room with the microphone and he would be in the other, listening on the loud-speaker to how I read the copy that I was going to read on the air that night. So that was the importance of the announcer to a program. I think you had to please the sponsor first, and the audience second.

But if you didn't please the audience, the sponsor would not be getting the results.

Well, they didn't think that. I mean, if I managed to please both, that was great. But I had to please the sponsor first.

Even though you may have had to read it his way, I'm sure you couldn't always understand why he wanted it that way.

Well, I must tell you this. I laugh when I think about it now! This visiting of the sponsor's office became onerous after a while and I really was very upset about the whole thing. I'm laughing about it now, but at the time I was younger and I was angry at the whole situation. I eventually said to him one day, I said, "Look, Sir..." He made some remark about he didn't like the way I had done the commercial that night. I said, "Sir, I don't understand it. I left your office [yesterday] and you liked the way I read the commercial. Now you tell me the next day that you didn't like it but I tell you that I read it exactly last night as I read it in your office." He said, "Yes, I know, Kenneth. I'm very upset. I like the way you do it, I really do, but when I get home my mother says 'You know that announcer didn't say that word properly.'" Well, that made it even worse for me. I knew him well enough by that time, even though he was the sponsor, to call him by his first name. I said, "Look, Sidney, I've done everything you wanted in this job. I've wept with the audience, I've begged them to buy the product, I've ordered them to buy the product. I've cajoled with them, I've screamed at them. I've done everything you wanted, but I can't go on like this." I used an expletive of some kind and I said, "I can't do the job any more." And I walked out. Well, all I know is that the next day he called me and said, "Kenneth, you do the commercial your way."

You can only take so much.

Yeah.

It reminds me of a scene in the Woody Allen movie Radio Days *where there's a sponsor and his wife in the booth auditioning a commercial for a laxative. The talent is singing the commercial and the sponsor likes it. "That was very good, very good." But the wife says, "I don't like it at all," and so the sponsor says, "Neither do I! Get rid of them!"*

That's exactly what happened! Maybe I told Woody the story! It's quite possible. I was in *Radio Days,* you know.

Yes, I know you were.

Yes, in the very last scene, up on the roof of the building on New Year's Eve. It was fun. Wasn't that a lovely movie?

A great movie for any radio fan.

Charming. Really delightful.

When you were doing all these radio shows there was one you did, for a while, with Milton Berle.

Yes. I think that was also one of the Philip Morris programs. I think Philip Morris was the sponsor of that.

Your radio career was tied into Chesterfield and Camels and now Philip Morris.

Philip Morris, yes. But never at the same time.

Fred Allen, Milton Berle... did you work with any other major comedians?

Yes, there was one who was very popular at the time; Al Pearce, for the Ford Motor Company. Al Pearce came from California, I believe, and there he had had a very successful little 15-minute program. CBS liked his work very much and they decided to develop him as a big-time star. I don't know if he ever became one, but he had a wonderful show, a full-hour program for the Ford Motor Company. Tizzie Lish was with him, I remember, as one of the so-called stooges on the show. And Elmer Blurt was another character. It's all coming back. This is a marvelous moment for me! Thank you so much! I would have forgotten all this, but it's all coming back now.

Elmer Blurt was the character played by Al Pearce – the reluctant salesman, "Nobody home, I hope, I hope, I hope."

"I hope, I hope, I hope." That's right! Well, Al was very, very sweet. He became a good friend of mine. I had fun doing that show, because we traveled a lot with it. We used to go to different cities every week, as a promotion for the Ford Motor Company, I suppose.

You were mostly centered in New York.

Oh, yes.

Had you, at any time, been on the West Coast?

No. I used to visit out there, but I never worked out there. Maybe with Al Pearce we went out for a week or something, but New York was my home. My favorite show in New York, I must say, at that time through those years, was *Easy Aces.* I thought that was just the brightest, most amusing show of them all, and I was fortunate enough to get to know Goody Ace rather well 'cause, as I say, I announced his program for a while. And he was a delightful, witty gentleman. He was just marvelous, and I also have such fond memories of him because he decided to use me as an actor on his show and for many years I played his adopted son, Cokie.

Cokie?

Yes, Cokie was their adopted son, and he was not too bright a young man, and he spoke rather haltingly. "Hello... everybody... how... are... you... today?" and "Yeah... yeah." He was that kind of person, which was completely different from my own persona. And I had a great time playing that part. I used to do that three nights a week. He was on the air three nights a week at that time on NBC. I was still on CBS. I had met him at CBS and when the show moved over to NBC I could go there as an actor, but I wasn't Kenneth Roberts. I was Cokie, you see?

You didn't get any credit on the air then?

No, no credit. That's why I'm telling you all this! I want people to know I was Cokie!

We'll put it up in lights! In some cases an announcer would be more to a broadcast than the announcer. People like Harlow Wilcox and Don Wilson and Harry Von Zell were integrated into the program content. About the only program that I'm aware of in which you had a greater role than the announcer might have been It Pays to Be Ignorant.

Exactly right. I also had something to do on Milton Berle's program. Milton would use me once in a while as his straight man. I would do more than just the commercials but, you're right, there were not that many in New York. Oh, well, I did the Steve Allen program for a while on television and I used to have lines with Steve, but that's about all.

Aside from working with Easy Aces *as an actor, did you have many opportunities to act on other programs?*

Yes. I used to do some acting. I was on *The March of Time.* They impersonated famous people in the news, and I was their "Alfred Lunt." Alfred Lunt was an important actor of the time on the Broadway stage. Every time there was a news item concerning Alfred Lunt, Kenneth Roberts played that part, so I was on *The March of Time.* What else was I on? Once in a while I would do a small part on *The Shadow.* I was there anyway as the announcer, so I would play a cab driver or a policeman or something of that sort, somebody who had maybe two or three lines in the story. I never had a big, important role as an actor, except I used to be on *Columbia Workshop* in the early days of its history.

Did you do any of the You Are There *programs?*

I was a correspondent on *You Are There.* There were three newscasters who were used: John Daly, Don Hollenbeck and myself. We were the correspondents on *You Are There.* As a matter of fact, I am very proud of that. I'm glad you mentioned it, very glad you asked. One of the best shows I ever did! I'm so happy to have been a part of it.

You have had a marvelous radio career. You contributed an awful lot to the enjoyment of millions of listeners over a great many years. I know you were compensated properly for it, I know you had a wonderful time doing it, but we had a great time listening to you. For all the work you did, I want to represent lots of people out there in Radioland who say, "Thank you so much!"

Well, I want to thank you. This has really been very enjoyable. I'm glad you caught me and brought me to this microphone. I wish you all the luck in the world with your show, because the more successful your show is, the better it is for people like me.

Ken Roberts was born February 12, 1910 and was 88 at the time of our conversation.

Agnes Moorehead

Agnes Moorehead was known as "the first lady of radio drama" and over a 20-year career on the air she appeared on a great many programs. We met on July 17, 1971 when she was in Chicago to promote the "new concept of mini-theaters" for United General Theatres. I asked her about the Mercury Theatre.

 I was one of the founders of the Mercury group – Joe Cotten, Orson Welles and I *founded* the Mercury Theatre.

How long was the Mercury Theatre on Broadway?

Well, we started in 1934-35 and 'round about 1937-38, Orson left Broadway and came out to the Coast. *Citizen Kane,* of course, was done in 1938.

You were in the film Citizen Kane *and so was Joseph Cotten, for that matter. But just before you went to Hollywood, you were on* The Mercury Theatre on the Air. *Were you – inevitably I must ask – were you involved in the "War of the Worlds" broadcast?*

Yes, in the background. We were all screaming – the women. You see, he used all of the people that he had – a nucleus of Mercury Players – he always used them. We were sort of a stock company and we'd play leads or we'd play anything that he wanted us to play. You had to be rather versatile to be in with the group that Orson used. And you had to be rather versatile to be in a radio show that I did for eight years, *The March of Time.*

You played Eleanor Roosevelt on that series.

I was the only one that was allowed to.

What is the story behind that? How did they select you?

Well, before I had permission, she negated all of the people who were impersonating her, because they were lampooning her. She had a strange kind of voice quality and they would, you know, lampoon her voice. And she got rather tired of it and said no one was supposed to do this. She was in the news so much that the people who were at the head of *March of Time* wrote to her and asked her if it would be possible to use her on *The March of Time*. She said, "Well, I'll have to interview the young lady who is going to do me and I also want a record of how she sounds." So I made a record and I was interviewed by Mrs. Roosevelt and she approved of me and she said, "This is the woman. She's the only woman that I will allow to impersonate me."

How many times did you impersonate her?

Oh, many times. Constantly. She was in the news a great deal at that time.

And this was broadcast from New York?

Yes, in the Thirties.

You must have been really busy, because at the same time you were playing on The Shadow *with Orson Welles.*

I averaged, I would say, five shows a day. And many times it was seven or eight.

Soap operas?

Everything.

Adventure programs?

Everything. From the beginning of the day to the end, because at that time, you must remember, there was a repeat of shows. You'd go on one time for the East Coast and then another time for the West Coast.

When you went to Hollywood with Orson Welles and Joseph Cotten for Citizen Kane, *you appeared in a number of Orson Welles productions.*

I was with him for 17 years.

It must have been an interesting partnership.

Terribly exciting, and a great privilege to be with him.

How did you manage to keep up a very active radio career in Hollywood, while at the same time getting involved in so many films?

Well, I was the only one allowed to do this. I went under contract with Metro Goldwyn Mayer and they didn't want any of their people to go on radio. They wanted to have control of anything that one would do outside – recordings or radio. I was on radio when I went under contract. They said that actors didn't have the knowledge or the taste or the judgment to be on the right kinds of shows. And I said, "Ohhh? Well–" and then I named all the shows that I was on and said, "I don't quite agree with you." I guess my argument was so strong that they said, "All right, we'll allow you to go to do radio right along with your contract." So that was the reason that I did so much radio.

How did you manage to fit it all in?

Well, it depended. It sometimes was Saturday, sometimes Sunday, sometimes late at night.

Your broadcasts, you mean.

My broadcasting, yes. And, of course, you must remember that after you finished a picture, you sometimes had layoffs of weeks that you didn't do a picture. There wasn't a picture available. You were still under contract, you know, but you were free to do pretty much what you wanted to do.

Has there ever been a time in your career that you have been out of work, not of your own choosing?

Oh, yes, plenty, plenty. I starved when I was first in the theatre. That was very difficult, very difficult. And I remember out in Hollywood, as far as that's concerned, I believe there was one time that I didn't work for 11 months.

Can you recall your first radio role?

Yes. It was over KMOX and KSD in St. Louis, Missouri, and I was called "The Girl Baritone."

"The Girl Baritone"?

Yes! That was before you! But that was the first radio and that was at the time when they had those crystal sets.

Did you ever do any radio work in Chicago?

Yes, but not anything that I had to stay here to do, a particular series. I was just guesting. I played a great many radio shows that I can't remember. As a matter of fact, when I would do radio, you know, and do so many shows per day, I couldn't tell you what I played in the morning.

The role, of course, that you and so many of your fans all over the world remember is Margo Lane on The Shadow.

Yes. Well, I was the first one. That was when Orson was in *The Shadow* and they wanted a girl to come in and play his girlfriend or his good Girl Friday or something of that sort, and they asked him who he wanted and he said, "Agnes Moorehead."

How long did you play on The Shadow?

Oh, I can't remember how long. It was quite a while. As long as Orson played it, yes. And I think it was longer, too, because [after he left] they brought someone else in.*

What about "Sorry, Wrong Number"? How did they decide that Agnes Moorehead was the right person to play an invalid?

I don't think they decided at all. The script was written for *me* by Lucille Fletcher. And it was presented to me and I started to read it. And it was so nerve-racking that I thought, "No one will listen to this" because it just unnerves you as you go along with the story. Bill Spier was the director and he asked me what I thought of it and I said, "Well, it's a howling story. It'd be kind of fun to do because, you know, it's a *tour de force.*" *So* we went on the air with it. And the first time we went on the air, they got so excited at the very end that they didn't do the right ending. The men were so excited that it kind of frustrated the actors and the sound. There were a great many people who had been listening in and they called in and said, "What is the end of it? Tell us the end of it!" So, in about five weeks, I would say, I repeated it. Then, it was almost a command performance. I did it 18 times on the air. Then I made a recording of it for Decca and then I did it on my one-woman show. I did about 17 minutes of it on my one-woman show and I did that for quite a while.

I want to thank you for doing it. It was terrific and everyone who has ever heard it thinks it was magnificent and great.

They use it, you see, as a sort of study for craft in colleges and universities. The craft in that type of writing and the craft of the acting, which is kind of interesting.

And then they made a movie out of it, too.

---

* She played opposite Welles in 1937-38 and opposite Bill Johnstone in 1938-39.

Yes, but I didn't do that.

Barbara Stanwyck.

Yes. But it wasn't like the [radio] show. It wasn't, because it wasn't a *tour de force.* You see, the whole thing is all the woman and you should never break it for all those other things, 'cause when you break it, then you break the suspense and the whole thing is to keep it on the woman, and she hears all these voices coming in. But [the movie] wasn't made that way at all.

It was a great suspenseful story and, of course, it was on the radio series Suspense.

I played on *Suspense* many, many times. There were some marvelous shows in there.

You were Homer Brown's mother on The Aldrich Family *and –*

– I was the aunt, Aunt Harriet, too, for a while.

You worked with Jackie Kelk a couple of times, didn't you ?

One of the first things that I ever did after *Mystery House*, which was the first series I ever did, was a thing called *The Gumps.* I played Min Gump and the boy, Chester, was played by Jackie Kelk.

As radio was changing to television in the late 1940s, you were on just about every anthology series that was on in those early days, but you were a regular only in the Bewitched *series.*

[*Bewitched*] was the only [television] series I have done. I've done guest shots in various series, but [other than *Bewitched*] I've never done a series that I had a definite character to do all through.

Was it easy for you to make the transition from radio to TV?

I never thought anything about it. There's lots of times that you can't make the adjustment from the stage to pictures or from pictures to the stage. The only thing that I feel is the fact of the medium being either small or large. But as far as emotional values are concerned, there's no difference at all. Playing isn't any different and so I never even thought about it.

Would you say that "Sorry, Wrong Number" was your most exciting radio performance?

No, no. I've done loads of exciting radio performances. That just happens to be a memorable one. I have done many of them. Many of the ones on *Cavalcade of America*, many of the ones on *March of Time*. So many were exciting. Every night, as far as *March of Time* was concerned, was exciting.

That was a good challenge for you?

A wonderful one. I had to do all kinds of characters and the fact that you were impersonating a great many people in the news and had to be accurate about them was kind of an exciting thing to do.

I don't know of a role that isn't challenging. It doesn't make any difference what it is – on stage, screen, radio, television, anything – it doesn't make any difference. I think they are all challenging, everyone of them. If it isn't a challenge, why do it?

You spent about 20 years working in what is now called the Golden Age of Radio. We'll always be grateful to you for providing so many memorable performances on the air.

I'm glad they asked me to be on radio. I'm very grateful to radio.

Agnes Moorehead was born December 6, 1906 and was 64 at the time of our conversation. She died April 30, 1974 at the age of 67.

Howard Koch

Howard Koch wrote the script for one of the most talked-about radio plays of all-time, "The War of the Worlds" for **The Mercury Theatre on the Air.** *On October 6, 1988, just a few weeks before the 50th anniversary of that classic broadcast, we spoke on the phone and I speculated that at the time he must not have had any idea that the world would still be talking about his script a half-century later.*

 Well, that's true. I hadn't the slightest suspicion that this would be any more than a play on the air, and I was very surprised when the panic happened.

Before you got to The Mercury Theatre*, what were you doing? How were you earning a living?*

I was writing plays that one or two got on Broadway, and one in Chicago, with John Huston playing the lead, and I was kind of, I would say, an amateur playwright learning my trade when [John] Houseman and Orson [Welles] asked me to do the writing for the radio plays on their *Mercury Theatre on the Air.*

How did they hear of you? How did they know of you?

They knew about the play in Chicago and I think John Houseman had read it.

Were you with them from the beginning of The Mercury Theatre on the Air *in July of 1938?*

Not from the very beginning. At first they had tried to produce, direct and write their own scripts, and they found it was too much. That's when they decided that they needed a writer on the program.

What would they do, typically? Would they bring a story to you and then ask you to take that story and adapt it for radio, or to start from scratch with a story of your own?

It would depend on the material that they wanted to use. Sometimes there was a lot of material there waiting, so that would be an adaptation. Other times, like in "War of the Worlds," they just had an idea in the H. G. Wells story, and Orson's instruction as to how he wanted it done. But that was more than an adaptation; that was practically an original story. So it varied from one week to another.

Some weeks, I suppose, you would knock out the script in just a couple of days and others you were right down to the wire.

Yes, it did vary in that way.

When you first got the word for the adaptation of the H. G. Wells story, what was your reaction to it?

That the way Orson wanted it done – news bulletin form, and contemporary and first person singular – that it couldn't be done. That would be an original play and it couldn't be done in the six days that I had. I tried to switch them to another story [by] a friend of mine, [but] no, Orson was adamant about it. He wanted *that* done. So I did it, and it just got done before they went on the air.

It was Orson's idea then to do this, in effect, as a breaking news story.

Yes.

So, basically, you just took the idea of the fact that there were Martians invading the earth?

Yes. I did it as though it were really happening at that moment.

Did you write the whole thing and then say, "Okay, here's the script" or did you send them an idea or a draft of what you were doing? How did it develop?

John Houseman, the co-producer, sort of commuted between my apartment at 72nd Street and the studio where Orson was preparing the production. He would bring pages down as I finished them and the last pages went down just before it went on the air.

Just before it went on the air? Are we talking hours?

Well, probably perhaps, oh, an hour or two.

An hour or two! Well, now, was Orson Welles and/or John Houseman the final authority on this? Were they the last ones to approve of this?

Yes. There wasn't any interference by the station, CBS station. They had pretty much a free hand in what they did.

I had heard that CBS had to have some approval of anything that went out over the air. Did they not know the treatment that was being given to this story?

I don't see how they could have known it because there wasn't time to get a completed script over to them, wherever their executive offices were, and get their reply. And anyway, how could [that] show not get on the air? There would be no show for that evening if they disapproved at the last moment.

So they didn't have any input on it then?

No. I think they had to trust the people who were doing the show.

And I assume that they did because they had turned a whole hour of the network over to Orson Welles and his company, and just rolled with it.

Yes.

Now, did you, at any time through the week prior to this, get to the studio itself? Were you at the studio at all?

No, not that week. I'd been down for talks at other times, and so on, but there wasn't really time. As I said, this was too much to do in the six days that I had that I couldn't possibly get to the studio. That was the help of John Houseman in that respect.

So you really didn't come face to face with Orson Welles in the production of this particular story.

No, no I didn't.

And Houseman was, I don't mean to diminish his role, but he was, in fact, the go-between between you and Orson in the studio at this time.

Yes and, of course, he was a little more than that in that he sometimes made suggestions and so on, for changes. In other words, he was acting somewhat as an editor. So he had a real part in it.

Did he mess around with much of the stuff that you put down on paper?

Once in a while. If you look at the script, you'd see what notes were made by Orson himself. That script, by the way, the original, is now considered such a unique record that it is going to be auctioned off by Sotheby's on the 14th of December. So it has assumed a character of its own.

Well, once again, you never dreamed that that would be the case as you were just trying to break the time barrier and get that script done.

No. I just valued my job and I wanted to do a good job, and be kept on the assignment.

How much, if I may ask, how much money were you making with the Mercury Theatre?

Well, you will laugh at this: $75 a week! When, of course, the broadcast changed from a station [sustaining] broadcast to Campbell's Soup commercial [sponsored], I was raised to $125.

That must have been an incredible raise for you at that time.

Well, you know, in those days, it wasn't so bad. And also, we must remember that it led to other things for all of us, Welles, Houseman and I, it led us to Hollywood and our work out there.

You wrote the screenplay for one of the most famous motion pictures of all time, Casablanca.

Yes, I co-wrote that with the Epstein brothers.

You have really left your mark on the entertainment world with your contributions. Those were just two of the things that you did. When you finished the "War of the Worlds" script, how did you feel about it? Did you think it was a passable script, a good script?

To tell you the truth, by that time I was kind of numb, but when it went on the air, I listened before I went to bed. I listened to the broadcast. It was 8:00 to 9:00, and I thought, "Well, it's a pretty exciting play." I mean, I did have that reaction when I heard it. But before that, I don't think I was able to judge it. I was just working too hard just to get it done.

And hoping that you had at least one day off before you got the next script from Houseman and Welles?

Yes.

But you were pleased with the treatment that they gave it on the air?

Oh, yes. I thought it was beautifully done and surprisingly dramatic.

While you were listening to it, did you have any idea that the broadcast of the dramatic program here would be misread by so many listeners?

Not the slightest idea until the next morning when I found out.

How did you learn about that?

Well, they tried to reach me at night because of the excitement at the studio, with the police coming in and confiscating scripts and so on, but I was too dead tired. I didn't hear the telephone ring. So the next morning, I was walking down 72nd Street on the way to Broadway to get a haircut. That was my one morning before I had to start on the next play. I heard sounds from passers-by like "war," "invasion" and I thought, "Maybe Hitler's made some move. Maybe we're at war!" I rushed into the barber shop and I said, "What's happened? Are we at war or something?" He laughed and held up the morning paper, I don't know which one. The *Times*, I guess, and it was a headline, "Martian Invasion Broadcast Panics Nation." Well, that was an odd moment in my life.

I would bet. You thought, "Oh, my gosh, they're going to take me away!"

Yes! Well, you know, it was touch and go for three days whether we were heroes or villains, whether we'd be taken off the air, and maybe even sued. But it all turned out quite the other way.

It was a tremendous broadcast, and it certainly showed the impact that radio can have on the public. You were on opposite perhaps the most popular radio program of the time, The Edgar Bergen and Charlie McCarthy Show, *and you really only had a small percentage of the listening audience, but yet what that broadcast accomplished, if that's the right word, was incredible.*

Well, you know, they say that what happened is a lot of people who started on the McCarthy program switched over to our program and, of course, they didn't hear the disclaimer. So they were more subject to panic than any of the others.

They didn't hear the introduction of the show.

No.

There really was no disclaimer as such saying, "This is only a radio play. It's not actually happening." They didn't say that. They just said, "Here's The

Mercury Theatre *and this is what we're doing tonight." Right?*

That's right.

In fact, the first intermission, and the only intermission in the hour, came about 40 minutes into the hour. So, by that time, I suppose, so many people were in a state of fright that they didn't even hear that.

That's true, because by that time, the rest of the play, the second act, the other 20 minutes, was really just an aftermath, a description of how the earth was after it happened. So that was not the part that would cause the panic.

The news bulletin sequence was all in the first 40 minutes, and then afterwards it reverted to almost traditional drama.

Yes, well, it came down to first person, singular, wandering over a devastated Earth, and telling what he saw. Orson did that beautifully, of course.

It was an amazing broadcast. When you went into that barber shop and you learned of this, what did you do next? Did you still sit down for the haircut or did you get over to CBS?

I think I had my hair cut! But I went down to the studio pretty fast after that to find out what was happening. That was still a time of suspense because we didn't know. I guess the turn came a day or two later with the Dorothy Thompson article in the paper in which she said we had done the country a favor. We had made the people and the authorities aware of what could happen in a real situation. So that sort of changed things around, and everything was okay from then on.

It did cool down, but I guess there were, as you mentioned earlier, threats of law-suits. But who would sue whom?

Well, I guess they would sue *The Mercury Theatre* and CBS, and all of us that are connected with it. If it got in a lawyer's hands, he'd probably make it as general as possible. But, none of the suits came to court, and, actually, no one was killed, fortunately. The few accidents, broken arm and so on – they didn't seem to follow through with any legal action.

No one was killed, meaning no one in the panic that followed the reaction to the program while it was being broadcast. People were really fearful that the Martians were coming into, not only Grovers Mill, New Jersey, but all around the country, because there were sightings in other areas as they were described on the program. What kind of reaction was there from the public at that time?

The Grovers Mill people, where I landed the first machine, were very upset because the people were storming in and tramping on their fields. You know, it's a farming community. That's an interesting change too, because now Grovers Mill has been on the map and they are celebrating the 50th anniversary [of the broadcast] with a big three-day fest of affairs. So it's changed completely.

How did you select Grovers Mill?

By accident. I was driving down on the west side of the river, and going through New Jersey, and I needed a map in order to plan the campaign between us and the Martians. The map they gave me was a New Jersey map. I spread it out on my desk when I got back to my apartment. I didn't know where to start the thing, but I had to start somewhere, so I closed my eyes, put my pencil down, and the point fell on Grovers Mill, not knowing that that little pencil point, what that fell on, would be someday a very famous place.

I suppose you felt it would be a nice name for a community rather than having the Martians land in New York City, or Philadelphia, or Chicago, or someplace like that.

Yes. It sounded very real and homey and American.

People who listen to it today, 50 years after the fact, cannot help but be impressed by the style, the technique, and the realism created there, even as you listen today, knowing that this is a radio show. But you also know that it caused quite a stir so long ago.

Yes. Well, they're doing, you know, a new broadcast of it this year. They're being very careful in the way they're doing it. This is also at my request, not to do it in a way that could create another possible panic. So that will be on the air just for people who missed it before. But it will not be done in any way to incite a panic.

Will that be your same script?

It will be my script with different actors and probably some changes in it. Jason Robards, Jr. is going to play the Orson part. I think that's going to be on October 30th.

That would be the actual 50th anniversary of the broadcast of your script. Do you feel that if a newsradio station today were to take its anchors, were to take all of its on-the-air personalities, and adapt the story much the way you did, only in contemporary terms, do you think the public would buy into that? Do you think the public would really believe that Martians were landing today?

Well, I suppose there might be a lot of incredulity about it because of the fact that everybody knows about the Martian broadcast and the panic. But, I would say, if someone did it today, in sort of new terms, that it would be very dangerous because of the state the world is in with the nuclear threat hanging over us, and the cold war. I have a theory about it that if the Martians came here – you know they're seeing a face on Mars now, and there's some thought that it was once inhabited, which they're studying – but if the Martians, or any other planet systems, were able to come to earth, I think they would be intelligent enough so that they would not come as warriors. I think, we read into aliens what is in our own minds. I think the invasion that is happening today is from inner space. I think we're invading the minds of people with threats of war, with the cold war, and all the jingoism that's going on... the politicians are playing on our fears in order to have a big defense budget and so on. They're invading us in a way the Martians never will.

I think you've got another script in your –

– Well, we're talking about a world war, with a subheadline, "Invasion from Inner Space." Some of us are talking about that now.

How long has it been since you've written for radio? Almost 50 years?

Well, I don't think I've written for radio particularly. I mean, radio has done some of my things which have been movies and like that, but I don't think I've written directly for radio since I left *Mercury* programming.

Did you enjoy your work in radio?

I enjoyed it immensely. I was working with very good people, and I would say that, with pretty good standards, pretty high standards. At the end of that four or five months that I was with them, I think, at that time I could call myself a professional. I don't think I could have up to then.

You did a wonderful job with that script and you contributed one of the most remarkable broadcasts in the history of radio, something that will live, indeed, forever. On behalf of all the folks out in Radioland, for your effort, I do want to say thank you very much.

Well, I want to thank you for your kind words.

Howard Koch was born December 2, 1902 and was 85 at the time of our conversation. He died August 17, 1995 at the age of 92.

Rudy Vallee

Rudy Vallee was a pioneer of radio broadcasting, headlining one of the top variety shows from the early days of radio. Towards the end of his professional career he was performing a one-man show and would be at Chicago's Arie Crown Theatre in October 1971. Prior to his arrival in the Windy City, on September 9, 1971, I phoned him at his Beverly Hills, California, home to talk about his life in show business. The "Vagabond Lover" spoke of his radio days.

 The Fleischmann Hour started in October 1929 and finished in October 1939. Ten years. It ran 52 weeks a year.

No vacation? No rest at all?

No. We didn't need any. It was only once a week. It was very easy.

Was your announcer Graham McNamee?

He was the first announcer. He was with us four or five years and then he died and then we had several other announcers. I did the announcing for the show, that is, the program of the songs and the guests when we first started, and then McNamee gave the commercials. He did not do the announcing of the show from the standpoint of telling about the songs or the artists who were going to be on the show. That was my job.

You were instrumental in giving radio breaks to a great many people.

I did not only great things for the program, but we did a great deal to introduce a lot of personalities for their first coast-to-coast radio broadcasts – Eddie Cantor and all the rest – but also I think I probably saved radio itself from going downhill almost into oblivion, because it was becoming so damn monotonous with the boring type of programs which they were offering [and] which were pretty bad.

The president of NBC said to me, "Mr. Vallee, you have demonstrated how powerful radio can be. We are deeply indebted to you. We feel that, in a way, you have saved the National Broadcasting Company."

That's quite a tribute! You said you were on the air once a week with radio. What were you doing the other days of the week? In the 1930s?

I was at the Brooklyn Paramount, doing four, five, six shows a day – five or six on weekends, and four shows on the normal days of the week. That's including Sunday for a year and a half steadily for the New York or the Brooklyn Paramount Theatres. And also playing what is now the Copacabana, which became the Villa Vallee, from 12:00 to 3:00 in the morning.

You started doing some things on film then, didn't you?

Yes. I made a very bad picture in 1929 at RKO called *Vagabond Lover,* a picture that was so bad that it almost finished my career.

Why do you say that?

It was just a badly written story, a very bad story, and the director was Marshall Neilan, who had directed some very fine pictures before that, but had never directed anything with a band in it, anything in the nature of a musical. His mother died about halfway through the picture and he went off on a binge and didn't show up for two or three weeks and an assistant took over and the assistant didn't know his rear end from his elbow and it was just a very bad picture.

How did you get the tag, the Vagabond Lover?

I ran across this song when I heard it played in Indianapolis in the summer of 1927 when the Yale Collegians played the Circle Theatre. On a Saturday night we went to a room at the top of a hotel there and listened to Charlie Davis and his Indiana Band, his Hoosier band. It was a marvelous orchestra, all young college boys, and they played beautifully. And one of their boys sang this song and I found out later that it was more or less considered a song from one of the universities in Indiana. It turned out later it was written by a lawyer from Chicago. It became quite famous through our radio and our recordings.

I want to know how many recordings Rudy Vallee sold.

My records never sold well. My singing never meant very much. It wasn't my singing that was the main portion of our success in 1929. It was the way the band played as I asked them to play, what we played, the way I talked about the songs, the odd name and the picturization of what I must look like physically, although I did sing fairly simply and pleasantly, with a very thin voice, somewhat nasal. It was not really comparable to the recording quality that Crosby had. When I heard Crosby's first recordings, I knew that he was going to kick me so far out of the picture that it wasn't even funny. Which, of course, he did, because his records sold in the millions whereas mine very rarely sold.

After you more or less closed The Fleischmann Hour, *you moved right into* The Sealtest Hour *on radio.*

Not much later, 1940.

And didn't you do that program with John Barrymore?

It didn't start with Barrymore. It started with a format that was written by Paul Henning, who [later] created *The Beverly Hillbillies, Green Acres* and *Petticoat Junction.* Henning, at that time, conceived the idea of taking historical figures such as Christopher Columbus, Captain John Smith, etc. and, in 27 minutes, doing a little operetta with two or three songs to be sung by me or the King's Men, a group of four male singers, and using Mary Boland as Queen Isabella and for me to portray Christopher Columbus.

The show started off with a rating of 17, which is a fairly good rating, in March of 1940 and went down to a summer rating of four. We went east in summer so that I could go to my lodge in Maine. They threw "Slapsie Maxie" Rosenbloom [who was a regular on the show] out the window, threw Vick Knight, who was directing, out the window, they kept Paul Henning and then said to me, "Will you pick from a list of six or seven directors a man you think can pull this show out of this abyss?"

I picked Ed Gardner, who later on became Archie of *Duffy's Tavern,* because I had worked with Gardner on my *Fleischmann Hour* when he substituted for several weeks in 1935-36. And I knew that although he was a very difficult person, he was a very gifted and a very talented person in writing and in direction. He took the show from a low of four – and it was his idea, not mine, to use Barrymore – to a rating of 25. He was really a blessing. He was a tremendous shot in the arm and made this show truly great.

We had writers for $250 a week that you couldn't buy today for $5,000 or $10,000 a script. We had not only Ed Gardner supervising all the writers, because he was essentially a writer more than he was a director. Under him he got Abe Burrows for $350 a week and he was still only getting $250 a week [himself]. We had [Norman] Panama and [Melvin] Frank, $250 each; we had Jess Oppenheimer, who created *I Love Lucy,* at $250 a week; Charles Isaacs, who used to do the Skelton show, for $250 a week; Keith Fowler and... we had some of the greatest writers that ever wrote for radio.

That's amazing. That must have been one of the key reasons why that show was so great. Do you have any of those scripts yet?

Every one of those scripts. And I have all the acetate discs of them!

You were in the Coast Guard during World War II.

I was in the Navy, in World War I, at the age of 15. They discovered I had lied about my age and they sent me back to school, for which I am very grateful. And then in 1942, I enlisted in the Coast Guard as a Chief Petty Officer Bandmaster with an orchestra of 18 men that I had built to 47. One of the finest musical orchestras out on the Coast, and I came out of the war as a Lieutenant Senior Grade. All my experience in the Coast Guard was as a bandmaster.

What did you do on radio after the war?

I was on the Drene program for Procter and Gamble. Two years with them, the most money I ever made in radio. We were on at a rather bad time, at 10:00 in the East and we got a rating of no more than 11. They were paying me $13,500 and $14,500, out of which I paid the other guests and the band. We were supposed to get $1,000 per [rating] point and an 11 rating didn't justify their expense. They offered me the third year if I would let Carlton Alsop direct it [and if I would] stay on for $5,000. And I said, "Gentlemen, you can have it," because I had no respect for Carlton Alsop, who took the show over with Don Ameche, who replaced me. The show never got above where it was with me. I think it stayed about 11 [in the ratings] and they dropped it at the end of the third year.

Rudy Vallee was born July 18, 1901 and was 70 at the time of our conversation. He died July 3, 1986 at the age of 84.

Ezra Stone

Ezra Stone created the role of Henry Aldrich on the Broadway stage and on radio. My wife and I met him on August 28, 1975 in his Hollywood Hills home above Grauman's Chinese Theatre. He invited us to join him on his patio, poolside, where we had an unobstructed view of the area. He took pleasure in pointing out to us the homes of his celebrity neighbors! Turning to his broadcast career, I suggested that he probably sold as much Jell-O as Jack Benny did in his time on radio.

 I take quick exception to that commercial statement, Chuck. I wish we could have been as successful and sold as much Jell-O as Jack, but we didn't have his vast audience, nor did we have the longevity that Jack had, but we did very well by Jell-O Puddings!

You did all right, I would say. Where did you first enter show business?

Philadelphia. At the age of seven.

And what were you doing?

Radio and the legitimate theatre. [Children's] roles in plays. Touring productions that would come through Philadelphia and wouldn't tour children because of the labor laws, [but] would pick up local kids as they picked up local stagehands. But mostly radio back in the late Twenties. *The Children's Hour* in Philadelphia. Quite a few folks that you know in show business and the entertainment business came out of that show: Kitty Kallen, Eddie Fisher. It helped create that whole area of acceptance for performers, performing children, who obviously grow up and some continue to be performers. Philadelphia, especially the south side of Philadelphia, has made considerable contributions, especially in the musical field.

Was it a long trip for you, then, from Philadelphia to New York?

Professionally, my work in New York started as part of the touring company of a children's theatre company called the National Junior Theatre. And that company played up and down the East Coast from Washington up to Boston, on Saturday mornings, doing standard and not-so-standard children's theatre. That's what brought me to New York first, professionally, and Broadway, as a matter of fact. I played Jim Hawkins in *Treasure Island* at the Alvin Theatre on West 52nd Street, back in my early teens.

Was show business your idea, or your mother's idea, your father's thought?

My folks are not of the theatre, but they always have been devotees of the theatre and of music, opera, concerts. No, it actually came as a result of a bad debt! An old actor-friend of the family in Philadelphia was having hard times and had borrowed some money from my father. My father didn't want him to feel obliged to pay it back and he very cavalierly said one afternoon, I believe, "I'll take it out in trade. Teach my son how to speak."

I had developed a lisp, which I still have. I have great difficulty and approach very carefully any word with more than one "L" in it. Mr. Maurice Sloan was his name, a very colorful actor and director of the drama group at the "Y" that I used to attend. He gave me elocution lessons. (In those days they were called elocution lessons.) It really turned out to be more of a situation where I was his audience of one. For hours he would read and recite the standard works for me and occasionally get me up to do the same.

You were in Clifford Goldsmith's play What A Life *that started the Aldrich thing.*

Very much so. Yes, I created the role of Henry Aldrich. It was down-to-the-wire, two days before rehearsals started, as to who would get the part, Eddie Bracken or me. And the rose fell on my side of the court. Actually, it worked out beautifully for both of us. I never could have had Eddie Bracken's career. He certainly could have had mine and more, as he did, but I'm very happy that I got my share.

How long did What A Life *play on Broadway?*

Over 800 performances. About three seasons. And about half of that we ran co-operatively. Mr. [George] Abbott gave the rights to the play to the cast and I was instrumental in organizing the cast into a co-operative and we ran at that pace doing lots of in-school promotion. The radio show was just catching on and it seemed to be a good bet to continue the run of the play. Yet it never could gross enough to make it profitable for Mr. Abbott.

But as a co-operative, we could all declare our salaries at minimum, which is what we did until we built a nest egg. And, any week that the "take" did not exceed what would have been our normal contracted salaries with Mr. Abbott, we automatically went on minimum for the following week. It worked quite well. As a matter of fact, when Betty Field, who was my first leading lady – first and only – when Betty left the company of *What A Life* to come out here to California to do *Of Mice and Men*, her share of our nest egg at that time, I recall very vividly, was a stupendous sum of $700!

This was in the late Thirties, wasn't it?

It was 1938.

Was this an unusual thing? This co-operative?

I've never heard of it since. It may have happened before.

Why did Mr. Abbott decide to do that? Because he wasn't making any money with the show?

Right. And it would have been unprofitable for him to try. He just couldn't. He would have had to shut the doors and close the company down. No. Mr. Abbott is, and always has been, a tremendous enthusiast for youth in the theatre and always seemed to reach out and use and cast young people as opposed to established stars. Some people cynically say because he didn't have to pay them as much. But having been on Mr. Abbott's staff, I kind of, over the years in hindsight, realized it was much more than that. He had a fine appreciation of young talent and received an inward joy from helping. And here he saw a company of young people who were ready to pick up a production and promote it and bear the risk of it, within their limited means. It meant, too, that certain members of his staff would be on salary to the production, minimum salaried, so to speak. It gave him at that time, that summer of '39, three productions running on Broadway during the World's Fair in New York and it all came together quite well for him.

Was this common knowledge that it was that kind of a production, a co-operative? Did everyone up and down Broadway know that, or did they care, or was it supposed to be a secret?

No secret at all! It was the basis of our publicity thrust. It was the basis of our entreaty to Mr. Lee Shubert to give us reduced rent [on his theater]. It was the basis for getting bank loans and all kinds of things.

Did members of the cast actually try to negotiate those bank loans, and a better rate at the theater, and all that sort of thing, or was it still being handled by Mr. Abbott?

No. I undertook, for the company, the responsibility of leadership in that direction. I was playing the lead. I was very interested at the time in the production phases of my craft. I was on Mr. Abbott's production staff – a junior member – and I just was that cocky a kid. I wouldn't have the guts to do it now.

I think you might be wrong on that. How old were you at that time? Were you a teenager?

I was a teenager. I'm a terrible mathematician. It's all in the books if you want to figure it out. I don't hide anything.

As a teenager taking on this responsibility, it must have been a fantastic training ground for you and gave you a great experience.

It was. It was indeed.

The first appearance of The Aldrich Family, *as they were called on radio, was with Rudy Vallee. How did that come about?*

Mr. Vallee, at the time, had a show policy. Whether it was his or his producers, I'll never know. I tend to think it was Rudy's because he is that kind of a gentleman and showman. He had a policy on his old variety show of doing scenes or numbers from current hits on Broadway, and giving both the production and the artist a tremendous personal and full presentation with great dignity.

You just weren't an anonymous individual on *The Rudy Vallee Show,* even though you might be, in fact, an anonymous individual. And so came our turn. *What A Life* got its turn on *The Fleischmann Yeast Hour* to do a scene from the play, with all the wonderful build-up that Rudy, as a master of ceremonies and a devotee of the theatre, would provide for the production and the artists involved. I'll tell you it was quite a kick I'll never forget, to hear the billboard of that show: Graham McNamee running down that list of stars for *The Rudy Vallee Hour* that night and ending up with "Ezra Stone." That was, in fact, the first time my name went in lights, not literally, but figuratively.

There seemed to be a superb reaction to that one scene. It was an eight-minute scene from the play. And the J. Walter Thompson people, who were the agency producing the show at that time, asked Clifford Goldsmith if he would write a special sketch for a subsequent *Rudy Vallee Hour.* He did, very hesitantly. He felt that he had written all he knew about that boy in the three-act play.

We actually did three appearances on the Vallee program through that summer period, and then the bidding started between Standard Brands and General Foods. That is between J. Walter Thompson and Young and Rubicam [who represented Kate Smith]. Kate Smith won and we were on her show as a regular eight-minute spot, along with Abbott and Costello, for 39 weeks. We were still an eight-minute spot for the first 42 times at bat on a variety show. And our first half-hour came as a summer replacement for Jack Benny, also [on the air] for Young and Rubicam, General Foods. I remember Jack flew me out. I was vacationing with a high school buddy of mine, and he flew me out here to Hollywood on very short notice to guest on his last program of the winter season and give me a kind of pitch and welcome to his time slot for the summer replacement. I remember sitting at the table down here at Sunset and Vine for the first rehearsal of *The Jack Benny Show*. What a high moment that was in my life, having been a fan until his dying day and forever, a devoted fan, and I'm happy to say, a friend of Jack's. Watching him handle that show and construct with his genius of elegance and wit, [then] turning it over to me. I remember his one line, "But be sure you give it back, come fall!" Came fall, of course, Mr. Benny got his time back and we were very fortunate to start on our own time, and that went on for 15 years!

That was a great run on radio! When you first moved into your own slot, what night were you on then?

Most of our 15 years, we were on Thursday nights. There was a short period, when I don't know, we were on Tuesdays. We were primarily on NBC, although there were a few years when we were on CBS. As I recall, they were the years before I went into the service and when I came back, but I'm not really sure.

Was the play What A Life *pretty much like the radio show?*

The radio show sprung from the characters. In the play you only met Henry [and] his mother. [There was] much talk about his father, however, off-stage. He was a very powerful off-stage presence in the motivation of the play. You met one girlfriend and that role was created by Betty Field. You did not meet the sister. Betty Field was the first "Mary," the first actress to play my sister on radio. You met one sidekick, who in the play was called "Dizzy" and, in fact, Henry's first sidekick in *The Aldrich Family* [on radio] was "Dizzy," and was Eddie Bracken until Eddie came out to California. Then we thrashed around trying other actors, giving them different names as sidekicks until the heavens smiled down upon us and Jackie Kelk appeared and then forever on was "Homer."

You were Henry Aldrich through the entire run of The Aldrich Family *on radio with the exception of the time you were in the service, is that right?*

Almost. I was in the service for a year before Pearl Harbor and my day off was granted to me by Commanding General, Second Corps Area, which was in New York, and I was stationed at Camp Upton as the morale officer there. So Thursday was my day off. I worked weekends and I continued my radio show with my entire income going to Army Emergency Relief, which helped supply non-appropriated funds, which we very much needed back in that era. Soldier shows and Special Services were unheard of.

We were a morale branch and all the activities were voluntary. Those of us in the entertainment industry felt that morale – if it was necessary for fighting troops and as necessary or almost as necessary as food and clothing – should have the recognition from the War Department in the form of table of organization, ratings and budget. Until that time came about, and it wasn't far off, but within a year or so, Special Services companies were being formed. There was a training school at Ft. Belvoir and so *The Aldrich Family,* in a very small way, helped contribute to that incentive and to the birth of *This Is The Army,* which I assembled and staged at Camp Upton. Then it toured the United States and then the world – all theatres of operation – for over four years.

Did you have anything to do with the film This Is The Army?

I was in the film and was so-called "technical consultant" on the film. We made that here at Warners and immediately after that film I was transferred to the Air Force at March Field, here in Riverside.

How did you find yourself in the service BEFORE the war broke out? I understand a lot of people would volunteer immediately after Pearl Harbor, but here is a successful actor on radio who –

– You never heard of that fishbowl and that magic number "158"?

You actually were drafted?

Oh, sure.

So, you were a reluctant –

I wasn't reluctant, but I wasn't rushing the process!

How did This Is The Army *develop?*

I think it was a convergence, a timeliness of the needs and intents of several people and several groups of people. By the time *This Is The Army* was under way in a firm planning process, I had been transferred to Special Services office for Second Corps Area on Governor's Island and later moved to 90 Church Street in New York. We had 30 posts, camps and stations in our command in four states in the East.

We had systematically screened the wealth of talent coming through the reception centers in our Corps area, mainly Fort Dix and Camp Upton, and had selectively placed people at each post, camp and station so that we had the nucleus of a production unit at each place: musicians, producer, writer, director type of talents. And, having this wealth of talent within our command, we could very easily order some commanding general to put together a show, as we did for Mayor LaGuardia, who wanted a show from all the services in his area to thank the people of New York who had provided USO services for the military. It was a thing the mayor wanted, and we put together a gala for him in less than two weeks at the Metropolitan Opera.

Mr. Irving Berlin, at the same time, was thinking, "Now is the time for there to be a revival of a soldier show I did in World War I," namely *Yip, Yip, Yaphank,* in which "Oh, How I Hate to Get Up in the Morning" was introduced. At the same time, Army Emergency Relief had just got its official status at the War Department as the relief agency for the Army, and it wanted a blast of some kind of patriotic, military entertainment that would bring its organization and the Army Emergency Relief needs, which were considerable and mounting, to the general public for support. So all these factors came together. Mr. Berlin came to Upton to the commanding officer of the post, and asked if he could do a revival of *Yip, Yip, Yaphank* for the Army, and then I was brought down to the general and it went forward.

You stayed then, with this military entertainment unit, more or less, for the duration?

For the duration and much beyond. [Now] with Sarah, my wife, we do workshops. We're leaving tomorrow for Fort Sill, Oklahoma. The following weekend we'll be in Fort Lewis in Seattle and then we're back in Washington, D.C. for a worldwide conference of recreational officers, again to beat the drum and spread the faith on the value of the entertainer in the military. The Army has a marvelous program. We've toured West Germany doing our workshops, Honolulu, we're down in the Canal Zone, Fort Lee, Fort Polk, we're still very much a part of the Army.

What else have you been involved in, after the end of The Aldrich Family *on radio?*

Well, I've been involved, very pleasantly, Chuck, with ladies and gentlemen like yourself and very young people who somehow have become radio buffs and do us the very great honor and great pleasure of being remembered.

Ezra Stone was born December 2, 1917 and was 57 at the time of our conversation. He died March 3, 1994 at the age of 76.

Index

Warnow, Mark 95
Waterman, Willard 47, 48, **51–63**,
  66, 67, 74, 75
Waters, Ethel 68
Wayside Theatre 123
WBBM 54, 55, 122, 318, 319,
  327, 365
WCAU 345
WCCO 365
WCFL 54, 112, 116, 356
We, the People 82
Webb, Jack 263, 265, 266
Weber, Henry 318
Weeks, Anson 213
Weems, Ted 15, 49
Weist, Dwight 257
Welles, Orson 108, 167, 312, 314,
  315, 343, 344, 360, 367, 374,
  375, 377, 380, 381, 382, 383,
  385
Wells, H. G. 381
WENR 2, 3, 4, 5, 6
Werblin, Sonny 213
Wesson Oil 69, 280
West, Brooks 45, 46
West, Mae 135, 136, 145
West, Paul 58
WGN 53, 54, 55, 100, 123, 134,
  294, 318, 319, 324, 327
WHA 51
What's Doing, Ladies? 272
When a Girl Marries 306
Whistler 253
White, Andy 58
White, Bob 116, 134
White, George 29
Whiteman, Paul 154, 222
Who's Dancing Tonight 268
WIBA 51
WIBO 2
Widmark, Richard 308
Wilcox, Harlow 23, 372
Wildroot Cream Oil 240
Wilkerson, Marty 236
Williams, Bert 213

Willson, Meredith 156
Wilson, Don 155, 176, **177–193**,
  197, 199, 372
Winchell, Walter 321
WIND 54
Winslowe, Paula 204
Witch's Tale 204
WJR 65
WLTH 363
WLW 257, 258
WMAQ 5, 54, 319
WMCA 362, 363, 364
Wolff, Johnny 6
Woman in My House 290, 291
Woman in White 126, 358
Woods, Lesley 360
WOR 343, 345, 362, 364, 368
Words Without Music 163, 164, 165,
  167, 168, 169
WOW 318
WQXR 162
Wright, Ben 264
Wright, George 326
Wrigley's gum 344
WTAM 65
WXYZ 65
Wynn, Ed 82, 143

Y

Yarborough, Barton 284, 287, 289,
  298, 299, 315
You Are There 373
Young and Rubicam 82, 86, 234,
  235, 272, 395
Youngman, Henny 32
Your Hit Parade 37

Z

Zero Hour 129, 244

NOSTALGIA
DIGEST
PRESS